For Sidney J. Levy

Marketing mage,
   symbolist seer,
heroic hermenaut,
   spirit of our place,
Your shifting of
   our boundary stones
has made our field
   work deeper
than we know.
   This solstice gift
is yours.

ACKNOWLEDGMENTS

We are grateful to our visionary Dean, Donald Jacobs, and to our encouraging publisher contacts, Larry Alexander at Wiley, and to Henning Gutmann and Rob Kaplan.

D.I.

CONTENTS

Foreword
Looking Backward and Forward   ix
  Sidney J. Levy

Preface
Reflections on Marketing   xiii
  Philip Kotler

Introduction   xvii
  Dawn Iacobucci

Section I
STRATEGY: THINKING ABOUT
THE CUSTOMER AND MARKETPLACE   1

Chapter 1
Segmentation and Targeting   3
  Brian Sternthal and Alice M. Tybout

Chapter 2
Brand Positioning   31
  Alice M. Tybout and Brian Sternthal

Chapter 3
Brand Design   58
  Bobby J. Calder and Steven J. Reagan

Chapter 4
Creating and Managing Brands   74
  Alice M. Tybout and Gregory S. Carpenter

Chapter 5
Market-Driving Strategies: Toward a New Concept of
  Competitive Advantage   103
  Gregory S. Carpenter, Rashi Glazer, and Kent Nakamoto

Chapter 6
Managing New Product Development for
  Strategic Competitive Advantage   130
  Dipak Jain

Section II
INTELLIGENCE: LEARNING ABOUT THE CUSTOMER AND MARKETPLACE   149

Chapter 7
Understanding Consumers   151
  Bobby J. Calder

Chapter 8
Qualitative Inquiry in Marketing and Consumer Research   165
  John F. Sherry Jr. and Robert V. Kozinets

Chapter 9
Quantitative Marketing Research   195
  Dawn Iacobucci

Section III
IMPLEMENTATION: MANAGING THE MARKETPLACE   213

Chapter 10
Advertising Strategy   215
  Brian Sternthal

Chapter 11
Market Channel Design and Management   247
  Anne T. Coughlan and Louis W. Stern

Chapter 12
Pricing Strategies and Tactics   270
  Lakshman Krishnamurthi

Chapter 13
Valuing, Analyzing, and Managing the Marketing Function
  Using Customer Equity Principles   302
  Robert C. Blattberg and Jacquelyn S. Thomas

Chapter 14
Services Marketing and Customer Service   320
Dawn Iacobucci

Chapter 15
Managing Market Offerings in Business Markets   330
James C. Anderson, Gregory S. Carpenter, and James A. Narus

Chapter 16
The Successful Selling Organization   366
Andris A. Zoltners, Prabhakant K. Sinha, and Greg A. Zoltners

Chapter 17
Marketing in the Age of Information Democracy   386
Mohanbir Sawhney and Philip Kotler

About the Contributors   409

Index   419

FOREWORD
LOOKING BACKWARD AND FORWARD

SIDNEY J. LEVY

$\mathbf{I}$ have the unique perspective on the Marketing Department of the Kellogg School that comes from being a member of its faculty for 36 years. As Professor Emeritus, I can look back on the coming together over the years of a wonderful group of people whom I have enjoyed as co-workers, colleagues, and friends. Some relatively few have come and regretfully left, but the department has had the amazing stability of a large core group that attests to its superior environment, an ethos that inspires vitality, encourages individual development, and rewards outstanding contributions. If the department had a motto, I would say it is Achievement and Aspiration.

As Robert Bartels points out in discussing the beginning of marketing thought, the Midwest provided the most pronounced influence on the early development of this field, and the Marketing Department at Northwestern University was a major contributor to these efforts. As early as 1903, Walter Dill Scott, director of the psychological laboratory and later president of the University, wrote *The Theory of Advertising,* one of the earliest applications of psychology to this area of business. In 1922, Fred E. Clark wrote *Principles of Marketing* which established him as a pioneer in the fundamental literature of marketing. Professor Clark was one of the founders of the National Association of Teachers of Marketing and was elected the first president of the American Marketing Association. His reputation extended far beyond academic circles into business and government, and his last assignment was as staff economist to the U.S. Senate Subcommittee on Trade Policies.

Several other faculty members gained national recognition before 1950: Delbert J. Duncan and Ira D. Anderson in retailing, Lyndon O. Brown in marketing research, Lloyd D. Herrold in advertising, and James R. Hawkinson in sales management. They worked toward the derivation of principles, of useful generalizations in their respective fields, going beyond the all too common descriptive treatments of marketing that characterized the early years.

Our strength in the area of channels of distribution started in the early 1950s with work by Richard M. Clewett. He was a pioneer in the study of marketing channels through his books, essays, and painstaking attention to students who wrote dissertations under his direction. Among these students were Louis P. Bucklin, who developed a theory of channel structure rooted in economic theory; Louis W. Stern, who based his theory in both economic and behavioral theory and applied it to designing and managing channels of distribution; Stanley F. Stasch, who put channels into a systems analysis context; and Frederick D. Sturdivant, who developed new concepts and raised questions concerning channel effectiveness and efficiency from the social point of view.

Later in the decade, the thrust turned to the role of marketing in the firm and how to manage marketing effectively. The "marketing" concept became a touchstone generally and the focus of the department's case efforts. Harper W. Boyd, Richard M. Clewett, and Ralph L. Westfall developed and published the widely used texts, *Cases in Marketing Strategy* and *Cases in Marketing Management.* Westfall and Boyd, later with Stasch, also brought new insights to marketing research in *Marketing Research: Text and Cases,* which is still widely used.

Dissatisfied with existing tools and concepts, marketing scholars increasingly looked to other disciplines for help. The behavioral and social sciences as well as management science were exploited, and faculty with a variety of academic backgrounds were added to the staff. Among them were Stuart Henderson Britt, Sidney J. Levy, Philip Kotler, and Gerald Zaltman. Britt was a major leader in the field of consumer behavior and long-term editor of the *Journal of Marketing.* Levy's work on brand imagery, symbolism, and qualitative research stirred new directions in the behavioral area. "Broadening the Concept of Marketing" by Levy and Kotler has had a remarkable impact on the role of marketing in the past 30 years. Kotler's premier texts and writings on the nature of marketing established him as the world's foremost professor of marketing. Kotler and Zaltman innovated in the area of social marketing.

From the mid-1960s to the 1980s, with Dick Clewett as chairman and Sidney Levy the coordinator of the doctorate program, the department grew in a steady and increasingly visible fashion. Bright new doctorates from nonmarketing but related areas who expressed interest in applying their knowledge and experience to marketing problems, were given preferences. Thus, between 1970 and 1976, the department was able to attract Bobby Calder,

Alice Tybout, and Andris Zoltners. Louis W. Stern joined the faculty after holding business, government, and academic positions elsewhere. Brian Sternthal, who had worked with Stern at Ohio State University, also joined the faculty about the same time.

Stern focused on interorganizational behavior while Calder, Sternthal, and Tybout, who had done extensive graduate study in psychology in addition to work in marketing, began to develop a sustained body of research in the field of information processing, with special relevance to consumer behavior. The work of Andris Zoltners contributed to the analysis of marketing systems, especially in the application to sales force management.

In the 1980s, the faculty continued to grow in size and diversity with the addition of Anne Coughlan with a background in economics; James Anderson, specializing in the study of business marketing relationships and structural equations; and the ethnographic interests of anthropologist John Sherry. The department had great good fortune in continuing to grow with the addition of Lakshman Krishnamurthi, the current chairman, widely known for his work in management science; Dawn Iacobucci, who added to her stature in the field of networking with innovative thinking in the area of services marketing; Greg Carpenter, an authority on branding; Robert Blattberg, the leading thinker in database marketing; innovative researchers Mohanbir Sawhney and Sachin Gupta. Dipak Jain, a remarkable statistician and teacher, also serves as Associate Dean of the Kellogg School. More recently, Christie Nordhielm, Angela Lee, Robert Kozinets, Anand Bodapati, and Alex Chernev have brought their lively intellects and diverse research interests to thinking about consumer behavior.

The faculty has contributed substantially to the field of marketing in research, ideas about the nature of marketing, and training students. The marketing doctoral students from Kellogg have won more American Marketing Association awards for first and honorable mentions in its dissertation competition than any other school. Faculty interest in developing and teaching executive programs at the James L. Allen Center has contributed greatly to balancing theory and practice.

This volume is an indication of the way the Kellogg marketing department looks eagerly to the future, as the importance of marketing in the modern world steadily grows. The diversity of the chapters and the stimulating content in the many different areas discussed are the outcome of a vibrant enterprise and will make absorbing reading for both scholars and practitioners of marketing.

PREFACE
REFLECTIONS ON MARKETING

PHILIP KOTLER

Conventional marketing thinking has served business practice well. Yet the passage from an Industrial Economy into an Information Economy is introducing new considerations that question the suitability of conventional marketing thinking in developing today's and tomorrow's marketing strategies. The advent of computers, the Internet, wireless communication, and other technologies are presenting new opportunities as well as discontinuities. The advent of global businesses is raising new questions about global branding and the desirable degree of localization of product and message. We are noticing a blurring today in the distinction between products and services, between buyers and sellers, between companies and their environments. The changes are such that today's companies despair of establishing a sustainable competitive advantage in their industry, and are no longer even sure of their industry's boundaries.

Conventional marketing thinking has emphasized the following:

- Organize by product units.
- Focus on profitable transactions.
- Judge performance primarily by financial results.
- Focus on satisfying shareholders.
- The marketing department does the marketing.
- Build brands primarily through advertising.
- Emphasize customer acquisition.
- Measure customer satisfaction.
- Over-promise to get the order.
- Make the firm the unit of analysis.

Today there is a new marketing paradigm emerging with the following elements:

- Organize by customer segments.
- Focus on customer lifetime value.

- Look at marketing metrics as well as financial ones.
- Focus on satisfying several stakeholder groups.
- Everyone in the company does marketing.
- Build brands through company behavior.
- Emphasize customer retention.
- Measure customer value and loyalty.
- Under-promise, over-deliver.
- Make the value chain the unit of analysis.

A whole set of other changes warrant questioning conventional marketing thinking:

- Hypercompetition is rampant.
- Power has been shifting from manufacturers to giant retailers.
- Power is now shifting to consumers.
- Consumers are more price and value sensitive and better informed.
- Brands are looking more alike and brand loyalty is declining.
- Mass advertising is losing some effectiveness.
- Direct marketing tools and public relations are becoming more effective.

The bottom line is that *markets* are changing faster than *marketing*. Today most company marketing strategies are obsolete!

The intense pace of change is throwing companies into a state of confusion as to proper strategy. To protect their profits, companies have primarily responded by cutting their costs. They are reengineering their processes and downsizing their workforces. Yet even when companies succeed in cutting their costs, they fail to grow their revenue. And the stock market is now putting more weight on revenue growth than profit growth.

With the World Wide Web, we are moving into a new marketing era. In this brave new world, technology-empowered customers target the marketers. The hunters are becoming the hunted.

Marketers need to fundamentally rethink the processes by which they identify, realize, communicate, deliver, and recapture customer value. They need to seed, feed, and weed relationships with their community of customers and their community of allies.

Marketers need to shift from a "customer-as-target" focus to viewing each customer as a relationship that must be cultivated; from fixed to adaptive product and service offerings; from planning to discovery; from interpretation to facilitation; from competition to collaboration; from substitutes to complements; and from value chains to business webs.

The New Economy is posing a whole set of new questions to our marketers. In the New Economy, what will be the future of retail stores vis-à-vis the growing competition from e-commerce? What will the advertising agency of the future look like? Will the sales force physically travel to customers or telecommute to customers? Will top brands still command their high price premiums in the face of growing price transparency over the Internet?

Marketers generally prefer to look at the positive side of the New Economy. We see companies amassing and mining rich customer databases, enabling them to target and customize their offerings and messages more accurately. Companies are using their Intranet platforms to enable their employees to learn more quickly from each other and to download information they need. And through their Extranets, companies are saving huge sums through effecting faster order transmission and improved supply chain management. Creating an Extranet enables a company to network with its suppliers and dealers in a "frictionless" ordering, distribution, and payment system.

Some companies have understood the opportunities spinning out daily from the New Information Economy. Dell, Charles Schwab, AOL, Amazon, and E★Bay are mastering e-commerce and attracting huge audiences. These companies are developing first-rate Communication, Content, Community, and Commerce. They are going beyond e-commerce into becoming true e-business firms that aim to conduct *all* of their business with customers, suppliers, and distributors electronically and efficiently. Companies can save megadollars by going paperless as Microsoft and Cisco have done.

The rapid emergence of e-tailing threatens to disintermediate major retailing sectors, particularly travel agencies, insurance agencies, stock brokerage firms, book/music/video stores, electronics and computer stores, car dealerships, and print newspapers. Here the question is whether "e-tailing will kill retailing" or whether "click and brick" will outperform pure e-tailing.

And yet the biggest use of e-commerce is not in buying cameras or books over the Internet, but in business-to-business relations and transactions. Forrester Research predicts that business-to-business (B2B) will be at least 10 times larger than business-to-consumer (B2C) e-commerce. Company purchasing costs will fall thanks to Internet auctions, exchanges, catalogs, barter, and shopping "bots." General Electric claims significant savings in purchasing its MRO items (maintenance, repair, and operating supplies) using its *Trading Process Network.*

We are witnessing the rapid emergence of vertical cybermarkets or e-hubs (such as plastics.com or steel.com) on the Internet. For example, thousands of buyers and sellers of plastics can compete in their prices and offerings on plastics.com.

I can predict with some confidence that the Internet will lead to lower purchasing costs for buyers. By the same token, it will mean lower prices and margins for sellers. Because every company sells goods and buys productive inputs, the question is whether their purchasing costs will fall faster than their selling prices. For firms with high material input costs, the purchasing savings might more than compensate for the lower selling prices.

If your company is not turning into an e-business now, it may not be in business later. The question is not whether to go into e-business, but rather how soon, and with what sequence of steps. The main thing is not to think of e-commerce and e-business as add-on activities but rather as providing a radical opportunity to transform your business. As GE's Jack Welch recently told his division heads, "Embrace the Internet. Bring me a plan how you are going to transform your business beyond adding an Internet site." The moral: Make and implement your Internet decisions before you need to; when you need to, it may be too late.

We are proud at the Kellogg Graduate School of Management to have embraced the New Economy in our degree programs and in our executive programs. Recognizing the importance of the Internet, we have created a new major in e-business for our students. Our faculty is chosen for their leadership and scholarship in advancing marketing science and practice in their respective areas of expertise. All of us believe in the primacy of the marketing concept as the chief driver of business success in the new economy.

INTRODUCTION

The Marketing Faculty of the Kellogg Graduate School of Management at Northwestern University has compiled a collection of chapters reflecting our varied interests and areas of expertise in marketing. Our department's strength and heritage has always been its intellectual diversity, represented in our academic training and continued scholastic pursuits of anthropology, computer science, economics, operations research, psychology, statistics, and consumer behavior and marketing. We firmly believe that these diverse perspectives contribute to an overall richer understanding of the many facets of consumer and market behavior.

Given these different vantages and the complexities of marketing, we purposely did not seek to write a book on marketing from only one point of view, with one overriding theme. We believe that in representing our different perspectives, readers will be able to garner much more and draw even more creative solutions to marketing issues than if we spoke with a single voice. Having said that, the reader should nevertheless detect commonalities across the chapters—there are only so many ways to say, "Think about, listen to, and try to understand your customers!"

We believe that marketing is the effort toward trying to understand customers, so as to deliver goods and services to satisfy their desires. By *customer,* we mean both people as end-users or consumers as well as firms as corporate clients. (Different chapters emphasize different customer constituencies and the context will make the intended meaning clear.) Similarly, when we speak of marketing phenomena, we believe most of the conceptual thinking is applicable to goods as well as services, except where specifically noted. Finally, while a number of examples throughout the chapters are international in flavor, here too, we believe that strategically or conceptually, marketing in one country does not differ greatly from marketing activities in another (one wishes to please one's Peruvian customers as much as customers in Singapore), although we certainly recognize that day-to-day tactics can differ greatly. With those philosophies stated, let us turn to the structure of this book so as to provide a roadmap for the reader.

Sidney Levy wrote the Foreword, "Looking Backward and Forward." Sidney is currently the Department Chair at the University of Arizona, but he had been our guiding light (as Department Chair) for many years. He was also co-founder, with Philip Kotler, of contemporary marketing as a discipline that affects all individuals and groups, commercial and non-commercial exchanges in any setting. Levy remarks on the historical development of marketing in general and the Northwestern Marketing Department in particular. His career's worth of writings have been collected and published recently (*Brands, Consumers, Symbols, and Research,* Sage Publications, 1999) and the book has already become a cherished volume in the field.

Philip Kotler introduces this book in "Reflections on Marketing." Kotler frames the philosophies of contemporary and future-oriented marketing. Who better to make such observations! Through his *Marketing Management* text (Prentice Hall, 2000) in numerous translations, Kotler has taught the world marketing.

Following this introduction, the first section of the book considers "Strategy: Thinking About the Customer and Marketplace." There are many elements to strategic, visionary thinking about customers. In "Segmentation and Targeting," Brian Sternthal and Alice M. Tybout urge the marketing manager to think strategically about how customers differ and how to select the customer bases to pursue. Those choices must be expressed in communications to customers (i.e., how a firm's market offering can benefit the user in a manner not met by competitors), issues addressed in "Brand Positioning" by Alice M. Tybout and Brian Sternthal.

In "Brand Design," Bobby J. Calder and Steven J. Reagan complement the issues of positioning by arguing for a purposive approach to brand management; one that goes beyond share projections or advertising to a consumer-centered creation and maintenance of a brand. In their chapter on "Branding," Alice M. Tybout and Gregory S. Carpenter illustrate that while much is being said these days about brand equity, loyalty, co-branding, and the like, these are not particularly new phenomena. These authors provide their perspective on these issues, and in so doing, offer a richer, more integrated structure for thinking about these effects for wider applicability.

"Market-Driving Strategies," by Gregory S. Carpenter, Rashi Glazer, and Kent Nakamoto discusses how consumers learn about brands and markets, and how, by the action it takes, a firm can teach consumers about its brand's unique advantage. They draw on their research on pioneering brands and discuss the nature of the advantages of being first, and what market followers can choose to do. Dipak Jain writes on "Managing New Product Development for Strategic Competitive Advantage," and walks the marketing manager through the key decisions in bringing new products to customers, discussing issues that should enhance the likelihood of their adoption and success.

In Section II, "Intelligence: Learning About the Customer and Marketplace," the focus is on obtaining useful information about customers' needs and desires so as to make sensible marketing management decisions. Bobby J. Calder writes on "Understanding Consumers," contrasting the marketing research mindset in which sophisticated methodology seems to be an end in itself, with a philosophy that the research should serve the marketing manager to explain the marketplace behaviors of customers. John Sherry and Robert Kozinets write in "Qualitative Inquiry in Marketing and Consumer Research" of the philosophy of marketing research to make meaning of consumers' words and actions. They describe a number of qualitative techniques (e.g., participant observation, interviews, and projective tasks), including their contemporary cyberspace counterpart methodologies. "Marketing Research" by Dawn Iacobucci focuses on quantitative tools, introducing networks as models of consumers' connections between a product and its attributes, and, separately, describing the analytical basis for "recommendation agents" on the Internet.

The marketplace action tools that may be manipulated by the marketing manager are often referred to as the 4Ps (product, promotion, place, price). That is, to successfully serve the markets that have been targeted, the marketer must deliver a good product, communicate messages to inform the customer about the product's strengths and to entice purchase, making the product available with relatively easy access, all at a price deemed worthy and valuable to the customer. Issues involving the product have been discussed in some detail in the first two sections, but indeed strategic thinking about the product will be of continued importance in this section to integrate the issues of promotion, place, and price—always so as to maximize customers' utilities. Thus, Section III, "Implementation: Managing the Marketplace," considers issues of advertising, channels of distribution, and pricing, value-added customer service, business-to-business marketing, and sales force management.

In the chapter on "Advertising Strategy," Brian Sternthal conceptually blends the concerns of the advertising and marketing manager with psychological theories about how people process those communications and use them to make decisions and judgments.

In "Market Channel Design and Management," Anne T. Coughlan and Louis W. Stern describe issues that arise in the flow of product from the creators to the users. They provide frameworks for the decisions of channel design to be made (e.g., to minimize conflict and facilitate coordination among the channel members).

"Pricing Strategies and Tactics" by Lakshman Krishnamurthi offers numerous rules for setting prices. He demonstrates how pricing cannot be a simple, ad hoc marketing decision; rather it is as integral a strategic question as any marketing element. In the chapter that follows, "Valuing, Analyzing, and Managing the Marketing Function Using Customer Equity Principles," Robert C. Blattberg and Jacquelyn Thomas tie the customer equity principles of acquisition, retention, and add-on selling to marketing strategy, segmentation, and targeting, and marketing mix variables.

"Services Marketing and Customer Service" by Dawn Iacobucci discusses the key distinguishing factors between goods and services and the additional challenges of marketing and managing services. In "Managing Market Offerings in Business Markets," James C. Anderson, Gregory S. Carpenter, and James A. Narus focus on businesses as customers, and the particular issue of offering flexibility and customization to address different customer needs. "The Successful Selling Organization," by Andris A. Zoltners, Prabhakant Sinha, and Greg A. Zoltners considers issues inherent to selling organizations, such as sales force productivity, the measurement of selling effectiveness, and organizational culture, all with an eye toward pleasing the customer.

Finally, we close with the chapter, "Marketing in the Age of Information Democracy" by Mohanbir Sawhney and Philip Kotler. This chapter is not intended to be a prediction so much as a prescription (i.e., not, what will marketing look like in the future, rather, what should marketing look like in the future).

We hope you enjoy these points of view and that they stimulate fruitful discussions in your own marketing efforts.

DAWN IACOBUCCI

STRATEGY: THINKING ABOUT THE CUSTOMER AND MARKETPLACE

CHAPTER 1

SEGMENTATION AND TARGETING

BRIAN STERNTHAL and ALICE M. TYBOUT

Segmentation and targeting are two key elements of marketing planning. Segmentation involves dividing the market of potential customers into homogeneous subgroups. These subgroups may be distinguished in terms of their behavior patterns, attitudes, demographic characteristics, psychographic profile, and the like. Marketing effort is focused on target(s) whose needs correspond to the firm's capabilities. The process of segmenting and targeting is illustrated by Americatel in the long distance phone service market.

During the past several years, long distance carriers have introduced "dial-around" services that offer consumers relatively low long distance rates. MCI introduced 10-10-321 and AT&T launched 10-10-315 under the Lucky Dog Phone name to offer consumers low flat rates on their long distance calls. A spate of small firms has also entered the market with low price, long distance service. As a result, there is substantial price volatility in the market.

Although the offerings by these major carriers provide attractive alternatives to customers who are calling long distance within the United States or to Europe, there has been little focus on those who do their long distance calling to other countries. For example, with more than 12 million persons in the United States, the Hispanic population is substantial. Many Hispanics have family in Mexico, Cuba, Puerto Rico, or South America. They make frequent calls of substantial duration to family and friends in their home country. Research indicates that these consumers want a carrier that offers low price but also a service that will sustain the price that they agree to initially.

Americatel entered the market with a 10-10-123 number targeting Hispanics. It was positioned as the 10-10 service to use when calling from the

United States to Latin countries because it was a fairly priced service that pledged not to change prices. Advertising was done exclusively on Hispanic television programming. Despite an advertising budget of $1.3 million, which is a small fraction of competitive dial-around ad spending, Americatel became a major player in the dial-around long distance category.

While it is relatively easy to identify examples of successful segmentation and targeting, many managers find undertaking these tasks for their own products daunting. One reason is that the list of potential bases for segmenting a market is seemingly endless and there is little guidance as to how to choose among them. Further, when the segmentation analysis is complete, many or even all of the subgroups may represent attractive targets, making it difficult to decide how to focus resources.

In this chapter, we address these issues by presenting a *strategic* approach to segmentation and targeting. The cornerstone of this strategy is the belief that usage patterns should provide the starting point for market segmentation. Other factors, such as demographics (age, gender, family size, income, education), geographic location, attitudes, lifestyle, and the benefits that consumers seek from products in the category, may be used to make the usage-based approach actionable and to enrich the positioning. Once segmentation is complete, a "path of least resistance" approach should be adopted whereby priority is given to targets that generate the greatest revenue with the least investment.

The presentation of our approach is structured around three distinct situations that a manager may face. We begin by considering the most common scenario, that of a brand that is currently competing in a category and, thus, has a customer base. Next, we explore how firms that lack an established customer base in a category may modify this basic strategy. Finally, we examine the situation in which both the firm and the brand are new to the market. However, before we turn to the details of how to segment and target, we briefly consider the question of whether segmentation is necessary at all.

WHY SEGMENT?

Market segmentation is the strategy of last resort. Brands would rather attract a large market than partition the market into homogeneous subgroups and target one or several of these subgroups. Yet segmentation is frequently used because a brand does not have the means to differentiate itself from the competition when targeting the mass market. Along these lines, consider the approach taken by Quaker Oats after it purchased Gatorade from

Stokely Van Camp. At the time, Gatorade distribution was confined to the southern part of the country. The question was whether segmentation would be needed to accommodate geographic differences in the levels of brand and category knowledge. Whereas Southerners were likely to have tried Gatorade, Northerners' knowledge of it was likely to be based on seeing the brand when television cameras panned the sidelines of professional football games.

A geographic segmentation strategy was devised to reflect the different levels of brand use. Two separate ads were developed for northern and southern states. In a test market, it was found that ads developed for the south not only were effective in that region, they were no less effective in the north than the one developed specifically for northern states. These outcomes suggested that segmented ads would produce about the same response as a national campaign using the ads developed for the south. Because the media cost of a national campaign is much lower than that of a series of regional campaigns, and because production costs would be lower with a single creative strategy, Quaker used a single campaign to cover the entire country instead of one based on geographic segmentation.

In many other circumstances, substantial differences in consumers' responses to a particular marketing strategy are likely, and segmentation is appropriate. The need for segmentation emerges when men have different motivations for purchasing than women, when children are motivated by different product characteristics than adults, and when small firms have different needs than large ones. In these cases, firms attempt to build brand equity by targeting one or a few segments. We begin our discussion of segmentation and targeting by describing usage-based segmentation and targeting.

SEGMENTATION AND TARGETING FOR AN ESTABLISHED BRAND IN A CATEGORY

The Usage-Based Approach

Brand Users. A starting point in selecting targets for established products and services involves the examination of current users. The logic for this focus can be explained in terms of current understanding about how people make decisions. In response to brand information, consumers access their own knowledge about a brand and relate it to new information presented by some marketing effort. This depiction suggests that current users should be the center of focus because their status as users makes them likely to activate favorable associations to the brand and thus be attractive candidates to repurchase the brand. Following this strategy, the goal is to increase brand consumption by prompting its greater use by current users. Retaining customers for an extended period is demonstrated to have a significant positive impact on profits. Specifically, studies reveal that increasing customer retention by as little as 5 percent, can result in a corresponding 100 percent increase in profits. For example, in the case of regional banks, a 20-year customer is worth 85 percent more in profits than a 10-year one. As years pass, older loyal customers will take out loans for cars, homes, and so on, without adding to new client development costs. In fact, due to the high cost of acquisition, the customers of many firms are profitable *only* when the relationship endures for more than a year.[1] When current customer retention is high and there is little opportunity to expand usage by these customers, a current user strategy may evolve to focus on attracting more people with the same profile as current users.

The efficiency of focusing on users makes them a prime targeting strategy for growth. The "Got Milk" advertising campaign attempted to increase milk consumption among current users of the product by reminding them of the discomfort associated with running out of milk. Arm & Hammer attempted to grow the use of its baking soda among current users by suggesting that it could be a deodorizer as well as a baking ingredient.

Level of use is often the basis for refining the segmentation strategy. For many brands, it is appropriate to focus on heavy users rather than on the broader category of all users, because heavy users of a brand often account for a disproportionate share of a brand's volume and thus are worthy of special focus. Major brands of beer typically find that 80 percent of their consumption is done by 20 percent of their users. Men 18 to 34 represent a disproportionate percentage of consumers who visit McDonald's on multiple occasions per week. Heavy users of Campbell's soup purchase over 300 cans per year, which suggests a consumption of close to one can per day!

Thus, the first obligation is to sustain current users and especially heavy users of a brand. When a brand is in erosion, the obligation is to halt the decline which typically involves focusing on current users. When other segments are considered for targeting, it is critical to assess the impact on current users. For example, Dewar's and other brands of scotch are faced with the need to develop strategies to attract new users between the ages of 25 to 34, because these individuals are likely to be the source of category growth. This goal might be achieved by suggesting that scotch be consumed with a soda or juice mixer as a way to address 25- to 34-year-olds' taste reservations. The viability of this strategy should be assessed not only in terms of its likelihood of attracting 25- to 34-year-olds, but also in terms of its impact on scotch drinkers over the age of 45, because these individuals represent the majority of current heavy users. Particularly when a brand is in erosion, it is important to make efforts to sustain current users of the brand and the category.

This is not to say that a firm should never abandon a brand's equity. However, there needs to be a compelling reason to do so. For many years, Miller Lite Beer aired a popular advertising campaign "Tastes great, less filling," featuring real beer-drinking personalities. When Miller Lite sales began to falter in the early 1990s because the brand's imagery was attracting moderate users who were older rather than the heavy beer drinking 21- to 24-year-old, Miller replaced the campaign with one that was directed at the point-of-entry target. Abandoning the current user was rationalized by the notion that focusing on heavy users of the category was essential to reversing Miller Lite's sales decline.

Competitors' Users.   When a product category has slow growth, targeting competitors' users may be a viable strategy. The success of this strategy depends on the firm's ability to convince consumers of the superiority of its brand in relation to the incumbent. For example, Pantene was able to expand its market share rapidly by providing visual demonstrations of the brand's superiority in leaving hair shiny. Consumers found "shiny" to be a compelling way to say "clean and manageable."

However, presenting a product that is perceived to be superior is often not sufficient to attract competitors' targets. An incumbent brand may be so strongly associated with a benefit that claims of superiority on this benefit by an attack brand results in greater growth of the incumbent particularly if a competitor counterattacks to halt share erosion. Such reactions are particularly likely when a core business is involved. For example, Burger King spent $100 million to promote the superiority of its new fries over those offered by McDonald's. This campaign involved advertising that reported more favorable consumer reactions to Burger King's fries than to McDonald's fries, as well as offering free samples of the product to consumers who went to Burger King. McDonald's responded with its own taste test, which not surprisingly favored its fries and they increased the amount spent on advertising their fries. The result was that while Burger King experienced an increase in the sales of its fries, its share of this business dropped in relation to McDonald's. Activating the notion of great tasting fries apparently prompted many consumers to consider their own knowledge about the topic, which for many people was the belief that

McDonald's makes better fries than Burger King. The heavy advertising for McDonald's fries reinforced this belief.

More generally, a strong competitive response can be expected when the attack is on a competitor's core business and target. Reebok was able to grow its business dramatically by constructing athletic shoes of garment leather that provided greater comfort than competitive athletic shoe brands. The primary target for these shoes was women, who were not being targeted by the competition. When this strategy was successful, Reebok attempted to attract the male athletic shoe market, a strategy that met with a strong reaction by Nike to defend its target as well as to attract Reebok users.

Category Nonusers.   When consumption by current brand users no longer represents a viable opportunity for growth because of saturation, or the opportunity to make inroads on competitors' targets is modest, it is appropriate to analyze the opportunity offered by attracting nonusers of the category. One segment of nonusers that warrants consideration is composed of those who are entering the category for the first time. The goal is to attract this point-of-entry target to your brand.

Point of entry.   "At 1:58 P.M. on Wednesday, May 5, in Houston's St. Luke's Episcopal Hospital, a consumer was born. Her name was Alyssa J. Nedell, and by the time she went home three days later, some of America's biggest marketers were pursuing her with samples, coupons, and assorted freebies. Procter and Gamble hoped its Pampers brand would win the battle for Alyssa's bottom. Johnson & Johnson offered up a tiny sample of its baby soap. Bristol-Myers Squibb Co. sent along some of its Enfamil baby formula."[2]

In many product categories, there are nonusers who are likely to enter the category coincident with some life stage or life event. The idea underlying a point-of-entry strategy is (1) to identify who will enter the category; (2) to determine when entry is likely; and (3) to direct their consumption to your brand. Point-of-entry is analogous to a first-mover strategy, but here the user is new to the category rather than the product being new to the market.

Producers of baby formula, disposable diapers, and other infant products have long used point-of-entry targeting to grow their franchises. Potential mothers are identified prior to giving birth and provided with product information. Pediatricians are detailed by producers to enhance the chances that they will recommend use of the firms' brands and category to prospective and current mothers. Free samples are given to mothers after giving birth in the hope that if consumers try the brand at point-of-entry, they are likely to be loyal users.

Point-of-entry targeting is a particularly attractive strategy when two circumstances exist. One factor is the level of brand penetration, which refers to the percent of category users that have used the brand during a specific time period (usually one year, though it varies with inter-purchase interval). For example, Tide has over 90 percent annual penetration, which means that of every 10 consumers who used detergent in a year, over 9 purchased Tide at least once during that period. When penetration is low, focusing on building the number of people who try the brand can develop a brand franchise.

Consider Netzero, which was a new entrant in the Internet access business in 1998. Netzero noted that while AOL, Compuserve, and other firms provide Internet access, none of these offerings was designed to address the concerns of first time users, who might balk at the subscription fees charged by many vendors for Internet access. In response, Netzero developed a business model that offers consumers free Internet access in return for having advertising appear on users' screen while they are online.

The second condition needed to make point of entry a viable strategy, is the presence of high brand loyalty, that is, an ability to retain the people that are attracted to the brand. This issue is the long-term challenge that Netzero will face. Such loyalty can be achieved by providing consumers with monetary incentives to sustain their brand use, as airlines do with their loyalty programs, or by providing a superior product on dimensions important to consumers.

Point-of-entry targeting typically involves a narrowing of the target to those users who are entering the market. When this target is deemed to be too narrow, point of entry can be deployed in conjunction with other targeting strategies such as maintaining current users. It can be used by category leaders or by followers.

For some products, there are multiple points of entry. For baby food, for example, point-of-entry targets might include families with new arrivals where the users are children and older adults for their own use. In such instances, it is usually appropriate to segment the market, as the motivations for consumption differ between the point-of-entry targets.

Category build. Another approach to attracting nonusers involves category build. Unlike point-of-entry targets, where consumers are likely to enter the category at some point, category build focuses on individuals who have no intention of using the category in which a brand holds membership. Targeted groups might be composed of people who do not use the category or ones who do use the category but not for the purpose the firm has in mind. The goal of a category build is to convince people to consider achieving some goal by using one category rather than another. Category build is an appropriate strategy when there is a lack of saturation of the category and the firm has a means it believes will be successful in directing the demand generated for the category to its brand.

A category may be unsaturated in a variety of circumstances, for example, when a category is new, as was the case with light beer in the 1970s, yogurt in the 1980s, and sports beverages in the 1990s. In these cases, diffusion of information about the category increased its consumption. But there might also be a lack of saturation in a mature category that has lost its consumer base. For example, in 1990, per capita coffee consumption was about 65 percent of the level it had enjoyed in 1960, largely because that generation of young people drank far less coffee than had preceding generations. Or, the lack of saturation might be attributable to consumers' failure to recognize the problem for which the category is a remedy. This situation arises frequently in the pharmaceutical arena where consumers are often unaware of their depression, low thyroid condition, and the like and thus do not prompt their physicians to prescribe the ethical products available to treat these conditions. Finally, sales of categories with seasonal skews such as barbecue sauce or chocolate morsels may be viewed as unsaturated contra-seasonally.

There are a variety of devices that are used to direct the demand generated by a category build to a firm's brand. Most frequently, the assumption is that brands will attract category sales in proportion to their share of market. Thus, it is typically market leaders that engage in category build. However, market share leadership is but one means of directing category demand to a specific brand. In the absence of market leadership, firms with strong sales forces might use advertising to build the category and their sales force to direct this demand to the firm's brand.

When following a category build targeting strategy, it is important to monitor competitors who reside at the edge of the market. Supernormal profits attendant to rapid category growth might attract these firms to the category. In this event, spending is appropriate to support both brand and category growth. Thus, Gatorade might devote dollars to telling people why they should drink a sports drink, but with Coke and Pepsi offering alternative brands of sports drink, it is also prudent to support a brand sell. When both a category build and a brand build are planned, separate strategies are generally needed to avoid consumer confusion.

A major impediment to introducing a category build strategy is the lack of certitude about whether demand in a category is saturated. Electric razors are purchased by about 30 percent of the population. Is this category saturated or not? Two-thirds of the estimated million people who suffer from depression use an antidepressant medication. Is this category saturated, or is there an opportunity to build the category? Assessing the level of saturation is an issue that benefits from empirical data through which the reasons for people's failure to use a category are illuminated. The prospects for a successful category build are far greater if research suggests that the category growth is constrained by a lack of category awareness than if the problem is a negative disposition toward the category. Consumers who have once used a category and no longer do so are typically poor prospects for a category build unless there is category news that has emerged since they used the product. Getting adults to drink milk or eat peanut butter has limited prospects for success, unless there is information about the products that is unknown to the target. In addition, as we discuss later, insight about the extent of saturation and the appropriateness of a category build may be obtained by an assessment of how the brand performs in relation to how the category performs.

There are occasions when a firm uses both a category build and point-of-entry to attract customers. Norelco is the leading brand with more than 50 percent market share in the $400 million electric razor category. Traditional users of electric razors are men 35 and over. While Norelco targets these users, they also support the building of electric razor usage. Doing so entails efforts to attract point-of-entry consumers by targeting first-time shavers, who are presumably making a decision about whether to use a blade or electric razor, as well as consumers over 50, who are experiencing less comfortable blade shaves because of drier skin that typically accompanies aging.

Competitor analysis. The analysis to this point has focused on consumers' use of the brand and the category in which the brand holds membership as a basis for targeting strategy. In developing a targeting strategy, consideration might be given to how consumers respond to competitive brands. This analysis is typically done by comparing the performance of the brand against a particular target in relation to the category's performance against the same target. We illustrate this analysis in the context of a geographic segmentation, though it also applies to other segmenting variables as well.

When a firm has distribution in multiple areas of the country, it can create a brand development index (BDI). The BDI is computed by dividing the per capita sales for the brand in a particular region by the per capita sales for the brand in the country as a whole and then multiplying the result by 100. A BDI that falls below 100 is considered to be low, whereas a BDI above 100 is viewed as high. For example, if Tide's per capita sales in Chicago are $250 per year, whereas in the country as a whole they are $125 per year, the BDI for Chicago is 200 (250/125 × 100). In this way, regions can be divided into low and high BDI areas. Thus, Chicago would be considered a market in which Tide's performance is relatively strong (high BDI). A similar analysis can be done at the category level to produce a category development index (CDI). The category analysis entails a consideration of the per capita sales of the category in a region in relation to the per capita sales of the category for the entire country. This computation allows the determination of high and low CDI areas.

The product of this analysis, the fourfold classification shown in Figure 1.1, is a useful basis for designing strategy. For areas where both the category and the brand exhibit high indices, the first course of action is typically to maintain demand. Market saturation may have set in and investment spending may not be warranted. However, it is possible that a brand with a high BDI can make inroads in a high CDI area if the brand's market share is relatively low. Alternatively, a point-of-entry strategy might be possible if penetration of the market is low and loyalty is high. Low CDI and high BDI suggests an opportunity to build the category. Caution is necessary here to ensure that (1) the market is not saturated and (2) market share leadership or some other means is available of directing the demand created for the category to the brand. In situations where there is high CDI but low BDI, there may be an opportunity to grow the brand.

Figure 1.1
Brand and Category Development

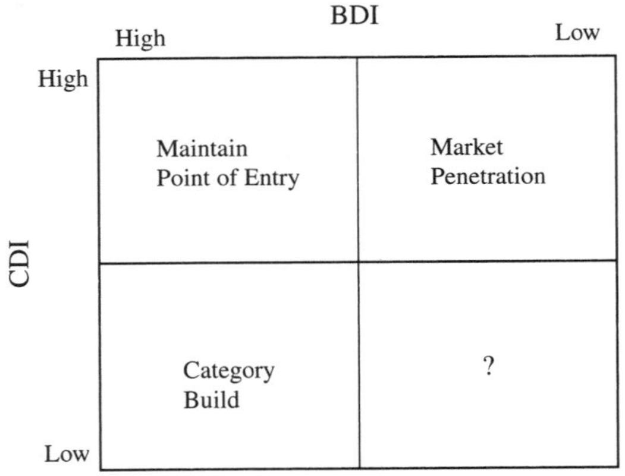

	BDI High	BDI Low
CDI High	Maintain Point of Entry	Market Penetration
CDI Low	Category Build	?

Here the market might be penetrated if a brand had a point of difference in relation to competitors on dimensions important to consumers. Finally, when both CDI and BDI are low, it may be possible to build the category, though here the judicious approach may be not to support the brand.

Summary.   The procedures we have discussed for usage-based segmentation and targeting are represented schematically in Figure 1.2. From top to bottom the targeting strategies represent a progression from ones involving low risk and modest return to ones that involve high risk and substantial return. For ongoing concerns, the starting point in targeting is the current user of the brand. Growth may be achieved by attempting to attract more use per customer or more customers like those who are currently using your brand. Next, it might be appropriate to consider a point of advantage in relation to competitors to attract users of the category who are not using

Figure 1.2
Usage Based Segmentation and Targeting

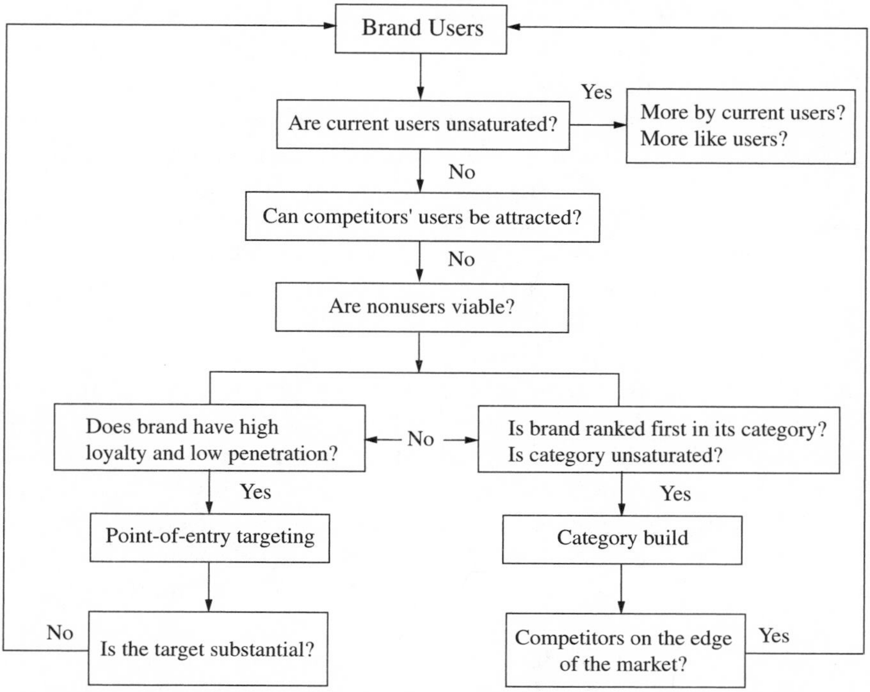

your brand. In attacking competitors, analysis is needed of the competitor's ability and motivation to retaliate.

Once current user opportunities are exhausted, focus centers on nonusers. This shift typically does not mean that marketing support for current users is abandoned. Often, a segmentation strategy is implemented whereby support is given to current users as well as to nonusers. A category-build strategy is attractive when the category is believed to be unsaturated and the firm is ranked first or the firm has some other means of directing the demand created to its brand. When there are competitors poised to enter the market, consideration should be given to supporting both a brand and category build in separate efforts. A point-of-entry strategy is appropriate when a firm experiences a high degree of brand loyalty and at the same time has modest category penetration (i.e., low brand trial by category users). When the potential yield of this strategy is limited, supporting current users as well as point-of-entry consumers warrants consideration.

Employing Correlates of Use in Segmentation

Brand and category usage are the primary bases for segmentation and targeting strategy. But to make strategy operational, it is helpful to identify factors that co-vary or correlate with usage. Demographic correlates of use identify who uses the category and various brands and guide the selection of where to distribute a product and where to advertise it. For consumer products that involve repeat purchase, such target identification is facilitated by the availability of survey data that describe consumption. Services such as Simmons Market Research Bureau conduct large-scale surveys to collect data that allow the strategist to estimate the extent of category, brand, and media use, classified primarily by consumer demographic data. This information is used to describe the demographic profile of consumers who are heavy, moderate, and light users of various categories, the consumer profile of those who use a firm's and competitors' brands as well as the profile of these groups' media consumption habits.

Some correlates of use offer insight about buyer motivation. For correlates such as users' age, social class, and gender, this insight emerges directly from knowledge of the brand's or category's profile on these factors. For other correlates, such as psychographic profiles depicting buyers' activities, interests, and opinions, custom items must be administered.

Age.   Age is perhaps the most frequently used variable in segmentation. Targets are usually described in terms of age categories that are used for the census so that projections can be made to the population. These categories include 20 to 24, 25 to 29, 30 to 34, and so on. While age is used because it is an indicator of product and brand usage, current understanding of how age affects consumers' responses is also of value in deciding whether or not segmentation is warranted.

As children's cognitive development progresses, their responses to advertising change. Children under the age of six have limited processing abilities. The absence of prior knowledge makes it difficult for them to elaborate on incoming information or to retrieve the information that they have previously processed. At the same time, the absence of existing knowledge makes memory fertile ground for rote learning and verbatim recall. Young children thus show an ability to play back product information word for word. In addition, young children acquire information that has a story grammar. Such information takes the form of problem or goal, a series of episodes and an outcome.[3]

Elderly adults represent another age segment. Older people comprise a substantial proportion of the population, including the most affluent people. With the attrition in their life space because of retirement, death of their spouses, and cohort members, older adults rely on mass media for information to a greater extent than do their younger counterparts. Yet, with the exception of products that are specifically of interest to the elderly, little marketing attention is devoted to attracting them. Indeed, most marketing plans only include people who are 49 years of age or younger.

Even when advertising features older people, the appeal often does not reflect an understanding of the elderly consumer. They are treated as if there is one elderly segment. This practice is not consistent with the data suggesting that the knowledge and lifestyles of those under 75 years of age are quite different from their older counterparts. The elderly people under 75 typically view themselves as being healthier and younger than younger people view them. The typical elderly's self-perception is that they are 10 to 15 years younger than their chronological age. One implication of this observation is that in developing advertising targeted to say a 70-year-old, it is more effective to show a 55-year-old rather than a 70-year-old person.

The conventional wisdom that elderly people's ability to recall information is diminished with age is not supported by evidence. The findings are that older people retain proficiency in previously learned tasks and suffer deficits primarily when the tasks are ones that require skills that have not been learned earlier in life. For example, today's elderly have a difficult time when television advertising employs quick cuts—rapid movement from one scene to another. In addition, limitations in learning that do occur generally do not start at age 65, but rather there is a diminution in learning ability that becomes somewhat more pronounced after 45.

Social Class.   The availability of demographic information, and particularly the educational attainment of the target, can be used to infer social class. This factor may be important to consider in segmenting because there is evidence that social classes differ in the types of marketing strategies to which they are likely to be responsive.

Affluent or upscale people value uniqueness and individuality. Information that emphasizes how a brand may reinforce one's feeling of individuality is particularly appealing to the affluent. Thus, they are more willing than other social class groups to try unknown brands. Middle-class people value neatness and organization. Showing convincingly that a product can help achieve these goals is typically well-received. Less affluent people value functionality and believe that luck is critical to success. They exhibit greater reliance on major brands than do other social classes, perhaps because they lack confidence in their ability to make appropriate brand choices.

Affluent or upscale people often engage in downscale consumption. They shop at Saks Fifth Avenue as well as Kmart. By contrast, downscale people typically confine their consumption to downscale products and services. This asymmetry in social class behavior may explain why little marketing effort is typically focused on downscale consumers: There is also a market for these products among more upscale individuals and so mass marketing is used for these products.

These observations do not imply that downscale people refrain from buying expensive products. Some downscale people have greater disposable income than do upscale consumers. This privilege-within-a-class occurs because more downscale people underspend for housing and lifestyle activities in relation to their more upscale counterparts. As a result, downscale consumers have the income to purchase big-ticket items. They often do so in categories that represent their aspirations. For example, they were among the first to purchase televisions and color televisions.

Notions of social class can be applied not only to consumers, but also to products. Products that are plentiful or used in large quantities and lack potency are considered more downscale than ones that are consumed in small quantities and are potent. In the context of beverages, for example, liqueurs and champagne are perceived to be more upscale, whereas beer is perceived to be downscale. Advertising needs to consider the social class of the user as well as the social class of the product category in developing persuasive messages.[4]

Gender.   There is substantial evidence that men and women differ in how they respond to persuasive messages. Women tend to be slower to make decisions, they exhibit greater uncertainty about their decisions, and they are more persuadable. These findings are thought to reflect differences in how men and women process information and make decisions. In part, these differences probably emerge because of socialization that is particular to each gender. In part, they are believed to be biological.

Women are encouraged to be communal, which involves a consideration of self and others in decision making. In contrast, men tend to be agentic, which entails a self-expressiveness and goal-directedness. Support for these characterizations comes from a wide variety of studies. In investigations of children's activities, it is observed that boys are frequently asked to go to the store or to undertake some other activity that requires them to be goal-directed. Girls are often given tasks that require them to coordinate with or navigate among the other members of the household, which enhances the development of their communal skills. Similarly, in studies of parent-child play, such as those involving the solution of puzzles, boys are left to complete a part of the puzzle by themselves, which enhances the development of their agency, whereas girls and parents solve the puzzle together, which enhances girls' communal skills. Instructions given to girls are often particular to the task (put the dogs with the dogs and the cats with the cats), whereas boys are given more general rules (put things together that share common features). General instructions are likely to be more useful than particular ones when attempting to achieve goals beyond the immediate context and thus promote agency. Finally, in assessments of adult speech, it is found that women are likely to exhibit community by expressing a concern for others as well as self. Males' responses tend to be more directed toward achieving their own goals. Whereas a woman might ask "Isn't it warm in here?" a man might say "Turn on the air conditioner!"

It appears that a communal focus prompts women to consider both self and others in making a decision. Applied to information processing tasks, community is manifest by females' tendency to be more detailed processors of disparate bits of information than are men. This difference is manifested in females' greater likelihood of processing message information that includes different types of product benefits. Males' agency often prompts them to focus on the information that they feel is critical to decision making. This approach may be manifested by their greater focus on a single benefit, and their greater reliance on prior knowledge and other heuristics (cognitive shortcuts) as a basis for judgment.

The observation of gender differences in information processing implies that the information to which men are likely to respond favorably differs from the type that will have a positive impact on women. For men, messages that focus on a single benefit are suggested. If multiple benefits are to be communicated, using separate communications is recommended. For women, the presentation of disparate types of benefits is appropriate.

It is important to note that these gender differences emerge in a limited set of circumstances. In many situations, these differences are swamped by contextual factors. Under time pressure, women are likely to invoke the same heuristics as those used by men, and when a decision is important, men typically exhibit the same use of disparate types of information as those used by women.[5]

As is the case for social class, brands often are perceived as either masculine or feminine. For example, Burger King is perceived to be more masculine than McDonald's and Nike is seen as more masculine than Reebok. These perceptions reflect the heritage of the brand. Burger King was initially positioned to appeal to the big appetites of men, whereas McDonald's was positioned as the all-family restaurant. Reebok was introduced as a woman's fitness shoe, whereas Nike was marketed as a man's running shoe.

Geography.   In the United States, consumer products firms with national distribution typically cover the country with national media such as national magazines and network television. They then use local media including segmented versions of magazines and spot (local) television to "heavy up" in areas where there is opportunity either because of market dominance or underperformance. Alternatively, some advertisers target one or several geographical regions where the opportunity is greatest for their brands. These efforts can be facilitated by the use of geodemographic services such as PRIZM. For example, Lexus might use PRIZM or a similar service to target those areas of the country (zip codes) that have a high incidence of people who earn $200 thousand or more per year.

While geographic segmentation is common in the United States, it seldom takes the form of different product offerings and price. Nor are different advertising strategies typically used in different geographic areas, with the exception of differences in the advertising weight. Even when the brand might be a leader in some markets and ranked a distant third in other regions, the same marketing strategy is used nationally. This approach seems to run afoul of the notion that market leaders and followers typically find different strategies to be effective. Whereas leaders generally position a brand against the main category benefit, followers adopt a niche position.

The reluctance to segment in response to different competitive positions in different areas of the country is justified by the fact that multiple strategies add considerably to the cost of marketing. For example, geographic segmentation implies the use of non-national media, which adds substantially to the cost of media. Indeed, the budget that would be required to cover the entire country with a network buy would cover only about half the country if the purchase were made on a market-by-market basis. There is also a concern that such localized strategies would undermine a national strategy, though it should be noted that the consideration of a geographic segmentation strategy emerges because disparities in markets have already emerged.

Segmentation by region is done as a matter of course when the geographic locales are different countries, perhaps because a media savings is often not available through blanket coverage of different locales as they would be within a country. There is a growing trend toward using a common strategy in different countries and developing executions that are local. For example, Pantene is positioned as the shampoo that makes your hair shiny, but uses nationals from the country in which advertising is aired to illustrate this benefit.

While there is validity to the argument that using different advertising strategies in different geographic regions of a country may be too expensive, it should be recognized that this is an empirical question. To answer it requires an assessment of the benefits of tailoring campaigns in relation to the added media, production, and other costs of following a geographic segmentation strategy. Test markets are typically needed to make a judgment about the cost-benefit of geographic segmentation. This testing involves yet another cost. Rather than incur these costs, a frequently used alternative approach to geographic segmentation via advertising involves varying the promotions by region. However, promotions are much less flexible than advertising in supporting different positioning strategies.

Psychographic Analysis. Our focus on demographic data is not intended to imply that it is the only way to make targeting strategy operational. It is also possible to perform this analysis using psychographic data. This approach focuses on lifestyle rather than demographic information as a basis for describing segments. For this purpose, questions about activities, interests, and opinions are asked. In some instances, psychographic measures are customized for the brand of interest. In other situations, data collected by commercial services are used.

Are psychographic measures of value? Generally, they cannot be used in lieu of demographic descriptors of the target because most psychographic measures are not linked to media consumption habits. Thus, it is usually not possible to link a target to the media it reads and watches. Further, the psychographic measures do not allow the identification of individuals that might be needed if further research is to be conducted. Some psychographic services address this problem by correlating the psychographic measures with demographic ones and then using the demographic profile to recruit research respondents. But this solution only serves to underscore the fact that psychographic measures are best viewed not as a replacement for demographic descriptors of the target but as a supplement that enriches the description of the target.

Thus, the primary analysis of segments and targets is typically performed using demographic data. Once a target is selected, its demographic character is supplemented by psychographic data to offer additional insight about consumers' dispositions and goals. This information is often useful in developing a brand's positioning and in the execution of creative strategy.

The recent marketing program for Altoids,[6] a white, thumbnail–size peppermint, illustrates the use of demographic and psychographic data in developing a brand's target. Altoids are sold in a red and white tin box that has the inscription "The original celebrated curiously strong peppermints." Until recently, Altoids was an obscure brand that had little penetration in the $237 million U.S. breath freshener market in which Breath Savers, Tic Tac, and Certs have 87 percent of the market. The exception was Seattle, where the brand built a devoted word-of-mouth following among Seattle's coffee and beer-drinking bar and club goers. Altoids is now a full–fledged phenomenon throughout the country.

In 1993, Kraft acquired Callard & Bowser, which owned the Altoids brand. The following year, Leo Burnett was hired to develop an advertising campaign with a budget of $1 million. A Burnett researcher who was sent to Seattle to do focus groups as a basis for developing the campaign learned that Altoids had a special status among young males. As a 29-year-old online graphic designer put it, "If someone's doing a mint, it's going to be an Altoid." And while drinking coffee, someone approached the researcher and "bummed" an Altoids, which put the product in the same class as cigarettes.

Altoids are particularly popular among single, urban, young males. These are men between the ages of 20 to 28 who are socially active but without a serious relationship. They are working and have money for the first time. They go clubbing and to the movies frequently. They smoke and they drink the strongest Starbucks. Their refrigerators more often than not are stocked with a six-pack of beer and a slice of pizza.

A target was developed on the basis of these insights. The target was men aged 20 to 28 who are working full-time. To this demographic description of the target, a psychographic description was added. These were counterculture young men who were self-focused and engaged in hedonic activities. This psychographic profile guided Burnett's development of the creative and media strategy. Burnett developed a series of distinctive posters that ran in bus shelters, telephone kiosks, subways, and alternative weeklies such as *The Reader*. For example, one execution showed a bodybuilder squeezing a tin of Altoids with the copy line "Nice Altoids."

In 1996, additional research was conducted to assess the meaning of the Altoids brand to its users. People were asked to write obituaries for different brands of breath mints. While all brands had the status of making the users feel secure and confident, Certs and Tic Tac users indicated that it would not be a particular hardship to switch to another brand. Altoids users said their brand was irreplaceable.

In another study, Burnett gave Altoids' users 10 magazines and asked them to develop a collage that represented their feelings about Altoids. An analysis of the respondents' collages suggested that there were three dimensions to their feelings about the brand. One was the notion of freshness, which was depicted by open space and water falls. A second dimension was British, which was depicted using pictures of Prince Charles and Princess Diana. The third dimension was sex appeal, represented by young male fantasies such as "hot" women dressed in red. For women, a romantic embrace represented sex appeal.

These investigations offered support for Altoids' brand positioning. They suggested that Altoids was associated with empowerment in social situations. The brand was also perceived as being old and traditional, perhaps because of the British heritage and the metal box in which it was packaged. With an advertising budget of about $7 million, Burnett developed a series of male and female empowered retro characters to sustain the brand's equity. For example, one was a 1950s' style female cigarette vendor who was holding Altoids and a whip. Alternative media were again used in a 1996 campaign, which reached A and B counties (metropolitan/urban areas) in about 50 percent of the United States. Seattle was excluded from the media plan because of a concern that the retro ads might alienate the original counterculture Altoids' users.

The results have been outstanding. Altoids has grown dramatically in the past several years. Sales in 1996 were over $23 million, giving Altoids a 10 percent share of the category. In 1997, a second Altoids flavor, Wintergreen, was introduced. Seventy percent of the consumers attracted to this brand were new Altoids' users. Two years later, a cinnamon flavor was added. By the end of 1999, Altoids had the same 25 percent share of market as Tic Tac, the other leading brand in the $320 million breath-freshener category.

Segmentation by Role in the Buying Center.   Segmentation can also be based on the role an individual plays in the buying center. Buying center roles include the influencer, decider, purchaser, and user. In business-to-business settings, these buying roles might be filled by engineers, VPs of marketing or finance, purchasing agents and operatives (users), respectively. In some consumer settings, the buying center might include parents as deciders and purchasing agents, and children as influencer and user.

Segmentation on the basis of the role played in the buying center is appropriate when different roles imply different concerns in evaluating alternative products. An example of buying center segmentation is found in the lighting industry. GE has dominated the lighting industry by focusing on the needs of corporate purchasers, who seek lower purchase prices and longer bulb life. GE's strong share position enables it to market traditional fluorescent bulbs for as little as 80 cents, a price their competitors cannot match. However, because these bulbs have a high content of toxic mercury, there is a hidden cost. Replacing a traditional fluorescent bulb costs $1 due to restrictions in collection and disposable and to legal coverage against damage in dumping sites. While purchasing agents are not sensitive to these replacement costs, corporate financial officers are. To take advantage of this situation, Philips developed Alto, a low mercury bulb that could be disposed of in the regular trash, and marketed it to corporate financial officers. Alto has gained favorable press coverage and political support due to its environment-friendly status. More importantly, it is a high margin product that has helped enable Philips to break GE's stronghold on the lighting business. Similar differences attributable to the role in the buying center arise for common household purchases. Mom, the purchaser, may be concerned about the nutritional value of the products whereas the child as the consumer may be focused more on the product's taste and brand image.

It is often productive for manufacturers to view both the distribution channel and ultimate consumers as buying centers. In developing advertising messages to consumers, efforts are also made to energize the channel. For example, manufacturers in bottling businesses such as soft drinks and beer recognize that bottlers are instrumental in determining brand sales. They use consumer advertising as one of the devices to motivate the bottlers. Franchise operations use vehicles such as the Superbowl to renew the motivation of their store operators as well as to prompt consumers to purchase their brand. By advertising to the channel as well as through the channel, the goal is to reinforce the same brand position to both resellers and ultimate consumers.

SEGMENTING AND TARGETING TO LEVERAGE COMPETENCIES IN A NEW MARKET

To this point, our focus has centered on situations in which a firm has an established customer base. However, in an effort to grow, a firm may also seek to leverage its competencies or resources by entering new markets. To address segmentation and targeting in this situation, it is necessary to begin by considering the different types of competencies that firms might develop. Successful firms are said to exhibit discipline in how they organize their competencies to create value.[7] Three approaches or disciplines each produce a different kind of customer value: operational excellence, product leadership, and customer intimacy.

Operational Excellence

Firms that are operationally excellent are not primarily product or service innovators, nor do they cultivate deep, one-to-one relationships with customers. Instead, they provide middle-of-the market products that can appeal to the mass of consumers in a category by offering the best price with the least inconvenience. Firms with this orientation have core business processes that sharpen distribution systems and provide no-hassle service; a structure that has a strong, central authority and a finite level of empowerment; management systems that maintain standard operating procedures; and, a culture that acts predictably and believes one size fits all. Southwest Airlines is a prime example of a firm that has risen to the top by its operational excellence. Southwest uses many means to minimize its costs and provide simple, yet adequate service to customers. They include using just one type of aircraft (which streamlines maintenance work and expedites gate turnaround time), not providing in-flight food service, and offering its low-cost service on only short-haul routes between secondary (i.e., cheaper) airports.

Product Leadership

Firms that adopt a product leadership orientation focus on developing new and better products, often making their own products obsolete. In so doing, they must address three challenges. One is to foster creativity, knowing how and where to look for it and how to recognize it. Another challenge is to get products to market expeditiously. And, product leadership implies being the first to present the latest technology or the best new service to the marketplace.

Product leadership companies have core business processes that nurture ideas, translate them into products, and market them skillfully. They have a structure that acts in an organic way; management systems that reward individuals' innovative capacity and new product success; and a culture that experiments and thinks "out-of-the-box."

Hewlett-Packard (HP) is a firm that pursues a product leadership discipline. When HP put its new ink jet printer on the market, it essentially eliminated demand for the world's best-selling computer printer, an old HP model. HP counts on its new products to generate 60 percent of orders, and, like all innovative leaders, HP responds swiftly to changes in the market. In an effort to not let its mammoth size affect its product-leadership stance, HP created 38 decentralized committees that rule on everything from product pricing to where new products should be launched. This freedom from headquarters enabled HP's printer business teams to dominate its competition in the color-ink jet printer category.

Customer Intimacy

A firm that selects customer intimacy as its primary means of delivering value is integrated into the minds and behavior of its customers. Instead of selling a product, a customer-intimate firm offers a solution to the buyer's problem and, thereby, forges a close relationship with the buyer.

In an industry that often has the appearance of a commodity to consumers, British Airways is striving to be customer-intimate. When they recognized that their first-class transatlantic flight passengers' primary objective was to sleep, British Airways adjusted its services to provide an interruption-free flight. Premier fliers are given the option of being served dinner on the ground in a first-class lounge prior to takeoff, and once on board pajamas are available, as well as real pillows and a duvet. Not ending its assistance once the plane arrives at the gate, British Airways offers breakfast, shower stalls, comfortable dressing rooms, and freshly pressed clothes to its highly valued customers.

The presence of three disciplines on which to compete does not imply that a firm should focus all its resources to excel in one. The conventional wisdom is that successful firms meet the industry standard in two disciplines and are superior to competitors in performing the third. Dell Computer, for instance, whose discipline is operational excellence, would not likely be a leader in the PC market if its computers were of poor quality or if it were out of touch with its customers.

Discipline-Based Segmentation and Targeting

When a firm has committed to a discipline it is reflected in its leadership style, structure, processes, and culture. Thus, firms cannot readily shift disciplines or adopt different disciplines for different markets. When entering an existing category in which the firm has not previously competed, the first goal is to segment in a way that identifies a potential target that will prefer the value that can be created by the firm's discipline over current market offerings.

Consider the case of BIC. When BIC entered the disposable shaving market in 1981, it was committed to operational excellence in marketing its disposable pens and disposable lighters. Operational excellence was based on efficient, high-volume manufacturing of molded plastic and broad distribution. These capabilities allowed BIC products to be marketed as good, basic products that were inexpensive and conveniently available. Entry into the disposable shaving market was attractive because it enabled leveraging both the firm's production capability and its distribution system.

The challenge in segmenting the shaving market was to do so in a manner that separated consumers who desired a low cost, conveniently available basic razor from those who would prefer an expensive, technologically advanced razor. One possibility was to employ gender as a surrogate for the different benefits that consumers might seek. There was evidence to suggest that women, who tend to be less involved in the shaving task than men, might be willing to tradeoff the latest technology in favor of greater convenience and lower price. Thus, the market could be segmented on gender, with women becoming the target for BIC's disposable razor. While such an approach would identify a target compatible with the benefits that BIC could deliver, it might be less than optimal from the standpoint of the operational excellence discipline. Although the absolute number of women shavers is similar to that of men (in the United States), women replace their razors much less frequently and, therefore, account for significantly lower volume sales than men. Further, an overt effort to cater to women might prompt those men, who would otherwise have found the convenience and low cost of BIC appealing, to view the product as inappropriate for the masculine shaving ritual. Thus, targeting women might limit potential sales and, thereby, reduce production and distribution efficiencies that are necessary to practice the discipline of operational excellence.

A superior approach, and one that BIC appears to have adopted, would be to segment based on age and associated lifestyle. A disposable product would seem to have the greater appeal for people who are active and have occasion to shave away from home (e.g., at the health club, in a hotel while traveling). Moreover, such individuals are likely to be younger, have less entrenched shaving habits than older shavers and, thereby, be good prospects to switch to BIC. Finally, BIC might attract even "couch potatoes," whose self-perception is that they are active, vital people. As a result, an age/lifestyle approach would potentially attract a larger segment of the market than one based on gender. In putting the discipline of operational excellence into practice, a bigger target is a better target for BIC.

In summary, for a new entrant with an established discipline base, the attractiveness of alternative ways to segment a market is determined by whether the approach identifies a target that will find the benefit created appealing and thereby will be willing to switch from competitive products. It is also influenced by whether the identified target meets other constraints imposed by the discipline. When the discipline of operational excellence is practiced, it is generally important that the target be sizable.

When the discipline of product leadership is practiced, different considerations emerge. In particular, a firm that pursues product leadership and is heavily invested in R&D, may create "new to the world" products. Such products by definition are not obvious members of any existing product category. Instead, they may combine the functionality associated with one or more types of products, but bear little physical resemblance to these products.

Consider the market for personal digital assistants (PDAs). The first PDA was Apple's Newton, launched in the market in 1993. Newton and other devices that followed it combined features commonly associated with appointment books or secretaries, notebooks, computers, faxes, and pagers. In this situation, segmentation is done on a relatively abstract level. It entails a consideration of the needs and goals associated with consumption across categories, rather than focusing on usage patterns within a single product category. The objective is to segment on the goals served across products and to target consumers whose goal is better served by the new product than by existing ones. Methods such as substitution-in-use, in which consumers indicate how sets of products relate to specific usage contexts (e.g., What beverages might you drink after exercising on a hot summer day? Possible answer: Bottled water, Gatorade, Snapple), may be helpful in identifying existing across product category competition and thereby uncovering underlying needs.[8]

Initially, the targeted segment for a new-to-the-world product may be modest in size. However, it must prompt the perception among consumers of a cutting-edge technology that is worthy of a premium price. Moreover, if the long-term objective is widespread product adoption, it is also desirable that targeted consumers serve as opinion leaders to accelerate product diffusion.

Finally, when the discipline of customer intimacy is practiced, the motivation to enter a new market is likely to stem from unmet needs of the firm's current customer base. This is because the focus on customers' needs may reveal an opportunity to expand the relationship into products that are new for the firm. As a result, the initial segmentation and targeting task is, to a large degree, already accomplished. However, there may be opportunities to grow the current customer base by using the new product or service to attract new customers whose needs resemble those of current customers.

SEGMENTING AND TARGETING WHEN LAUNCHING A NEW COMPANY

When a new company is created, there is neither a customer base nor an established discipline to leverage. While this freedom from any constraints may be attractive, it also creates challenges in tackling segmentation and targeting issues. One approach in this situation is to start with an examination of consumer motivations and goals in using a product category as a basis for identifying gaps in marketplace offerings. This consumer insight is the basis for developing a product or service that addresses unmet goals.

Starbucks illustrates this approach. When Starbucks was conceived, coffee manufacturers were focusing on the rational benefits of their brands such as the superior taste attributable to a particular growing process as a way of competing in a declining market. In contrast, Starbucks created a coffee-based experience in which the range of preparations and atmosphere of the stores encouraged customers to view having a cup of Starbucks as a way of indulging themselves. In essence, Starbucks targeted people seeking an indulgence experience rather than simply coffee consumption.

Anita Roddick, the founder of Body Shop, followed a similar strategy but with a different emphasis. Observing that cosmetics were purchased primarily on the basis of emotional beauty promises, she launched her company with a more rational approach. Women were encouraged to choose Body Shop products over competitive brands on the basis of the natural origin of the ingredients, the absence of animal testing, as well as the company's commitment to invest in developing economies and to conduct business in an environmentally friendly manner. Body Shop's line of products are targeted at people who embrace a particular set of values rather than ones who are merely striving to make themselves more attractive.

These new companies tackled the problem of how to segment, target and position by beginning with competition-based positioning, which is discussed in our next chapter. They created their identity by focusing on motivations for product use that had been neglected by competitors and then built business models that could support the desired positioning. The intended positioning then guided the segmentation and targeting effort.[9]

TARGETING DYNAMICS

Our analysis of segmentation and targeting suggests that there are a variety of alternative approaches to growing and sustaining the market. In this section we examine the segmentation and targeting strategies that are likely to be most effective as the market evolves.

We have argued that, for established firms in a product category, focus is initially on current customers because marketing to this target is most cost-effective if saturation has not occurred. At some point, firms discover that targeting current customers limits brand growth. Detroit automotive manufacturers have been particularly vulnerable to this problem with their luxury brands. Cadillac owners have a favorable disposition toward their cars and would be likely to repurchase if they were to repurchase a car. However, because the average age of a Cadillac owner is about 63, current users do not represent an attractive long-term target. Moreover, the image of Cadillac as the luxury car for a previous generation reduces the likelihood that the next generation of 65-year-olds will aspire to drive a Cadillac. A similar problem prompted Oldsmobile to target younger customers with the advertising slogan "It's not your father's Oldsmobile!" However, the effectiveness of this approach was limited both by the profile of people seen driving Oldsmobiles and the conventional styling of the car.

What is an appropriate strategy when faced with this situation? Should the firm focus on its loyal but declining customer base or should it shift its attention to higher growth segments? The answer depends on both the reason for stagnant or declining growth and the relationship between current customers and higher growth segments of the population. Consider the case of Entemann's baked goods, which observed that its current customer base liked its product but was consuming less because of middle-aged "spread." They encouraged customers to pay greater attention to the calories they consumed. Entemann's choices were to expand its customer base to include younger, less weight-conscious customers for its current products, or to develop new, lower calorie products for its aging current customer base. The company chose to serve the needs of its current customer base with a low-fat line extension. In the process, they found that this line of products also attracted new, younger customers who were concerned with health and fitness. Apparently the new line of products served an unmet goal and thus stimulated a category build as well as sustained current user consumption.

In many situations, success with one segment undermines a product's appeal to another potentially attractive segment. Cadillac's success with older consumers limits its potential to attract younger buyers. Had BIC launched its disposable razor as a women's razor it would have been unlikely to attract men. This sort of bifurcation in market segments is most likely when the product category is closely tied to one's self-image and the brand choice is visible to others.

A good example is the situation that Black & Decker faced in the portable power tool market in the 1990s. During the previous decade, Black & Decker had significantly increased its presence in consumers' kitchens with its line of small appliances such as coffee makers, mixers, toasters, and so on. It also had achieved a strong position in the basement as the tool of choice for the occasional home project. However, Black & Decker's success within the home coincided with a dramatic decline in its acceptance by professionals and tradesmen, who relied on their tools for their livelihood. Tradesmen did not want to be seen using the same tools as their customers. Only when Black & Decker launched a separate line of power tools under the DeWalt brand name was it able to regain a leadership position with the professional/tradesmen segment. Thus, when segments have different, conflicting goals, developing a separate brand for each segment may be an appropriate strategy.

CONCLUSIONS

This chapter presents a usage-based approach to segmentation and targeting. We prefer this approach to alternative approaches for two reasons. First, the segments that are identified through this approach require distinct marketing *strategies,* not simply different marketing tactics. When current customers are targeted, the goal is to retain these customers and, if possible, expand their usage. When competitors' customers are targeted, the goal is to offer a proposition that is sufficiently attractive to overcome switching costs. And, when nonusers are targeted, the reasons for abstaining from category consumption must be addressed. Second, the usage-based approach focuses attention on the costs and potential return associated with pursuing alternative targets. Current customers are easiest to reach and are most profitable to focus on in the short run. Attracting nonusers can be costly, but may be important to sustaining the brand over the long run.

While we believe these are compelling reasons to adopt the usage-based approach to segmentation and targeting, the ultimate test of any such approach is whether it leads to a compelling positioning strategy. We address this issue in the next chapter.

Notes

1. "Managing for Quality," *Business Week* (1991), Special Issue (October 25).

2. David Leonhardt and Kathleen Kerwin, "Hey Kid, Buy This," *Business Week* (June 30, 1997), pp. 62–66.

3. Deborah Roedder John, "Consumer Socialization of Children: A Retrospective Look at Twenty-Five Years of Research," *Journal of Consumer Research,* vol. 26 (December 3, 1999), pp. 183–213.

4. For further analysis of social class, see Sidney J. Levy, *Marketplace Behavior: Its Meaning for Management* (New York: AMACOM, American Management Association 1978).

5. Joan Meyers-Levy, "Gender Differences in Information Processing," in *Cognitive and Affective Responses to Advertising,* eds. Patricia Cafferata and Alice M. Tybout (Lexington, MA: Lexington Books, 1989), pp. 219–260.

6. Thanks to Gary Singer, Leo Burnett Company for the description of the Altoids history and strategy.

7. Michael Treacy and Fred Wiersema, *The Discipline of Market Leaders* (Reading, MA: Addison-Wesley, 1995).

8. George S. Day, Allan D. Shocker, and Rajendra K. Srivastava, "Customer-Oriented Approaches to Identifying Product-Markets," *Journal of Marketing,* vol. 43 (fall 1979), pp. 8–19.

9. W. Chan Kim and Renee Mauborgne, "Creating New Market Space," *Harvard Business Review,* vol. 77 (January/February 1999), pp. 82–93.

CHAPTER 2

BRAND POSITIONING

ALICE M. TYBOUT and BRIAN STERNTHAL

A variety of handheld electronic devices were introduced during the 1990s to help consumers manage information more efficiently. Apple marketed Newton, a notepad and organizer with the distinctive feature of handwriting recognition that made it possible to store handwritten notes digitally. Newton's sales were disappointing, an outcome attributed to the poor performance of the character recognition function rather than to the lack of a market opportunity.

Newton's limited success did not deter other firms from launching similar products. Motorola introduced the Envoy, which offered features including an agenda/calendar, an address book, spreadsheet capability, and Internet access. Envoy was unique in that fax and e-mail could be sent via the built-in modem without a wire-line connection. Like Newton, Envoy's sales were sufficiently disappointing that the product was withdrawn from the market.

As Envoy was exiting the market, U.S. Robotics launched Palm Pilot, a hand-sized digital personal organizer that was significantly less expensive than either Newton or Envoy. Palm Pilot sold more than one million units in its first year and a half on the market, making it the most rapidly adopted computer product in history.

Why did Palm Pilot meet with greater success than either Newton or Envoy? We contend that a key determinant was how these brands were positioned. Successful positioning involves affiliating a brand with some category that consumers can readily grasp and differentiating the brand from other products in the same category (competition-based positioning). For sustained success, it is also useful to link a brand to consumers' goals (goal-based positioning). In this chapter, we describe competition-based and

---

This chapter incorporates material that was initially presented by Alice Tybout and Brian Sternthal in the *Financial Times* (September 1998).

goal-based positioning and demonstrate how these approaches can be integrated. We also discuss challenges that arise in developing and sustaining a strong brand position. And we suggest how a positioning strategy might be represented in a planning document that we refer to as a *positioning statement*. The chapter concludes with an analysis of how information technology is likely to influence segmentation, targeting, and positioning.

COMPETITION-BASED POSITIONING

Current understanding of how people represent information in memory provides a starting point for developing a competition-based positioning strategy. One way information about a brand is stored in memory is in terms of natural categories. Thus, information about Bud Light is represented in memory as an instance of the subcategory light beer. In turn, light beer is an instance of the category beer, which is an instance of the superordinate category alcoholic beverage. As we show schematically in Figure 2.1, the objects Bud Light, light beer, and alcoholic beverage are nodes in memory that are related to each other hierarchically by associative bonds. The bonds imply that the object lower in the hierarchy (Bud) is an instance of the object that is higher in the hierarchy (light beer).

The depiction of four levels of the hierarchy is arbitrary. In some cases, more levels of the hierarchy might be worth assessing. For example, we could add a fifth level to the hierarchy under Bud Light that indicated

Figure 2.1
Hierarchical Organization of Natural Categories

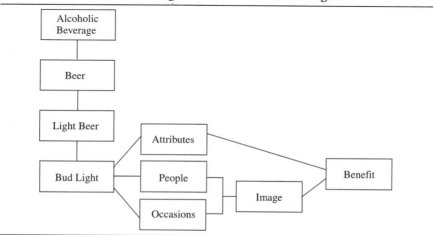

whether the brand form was bottle or draft. For most analytic purposes in consumer behavior, however, only two levels of the hierarchy, the brand and the category in which it has membership or its frame of reference (Bud and light beer) will suffice.

At each level in the hierarchy, an object might have three types of associations: attributes, people, and occasions. Attributes are physical characteristics of a product such as its color, size, and flavor. People and occasions together are regarded as image. Most positions involve some combination of attributes and image, though for some categories the positioning is predominantly attribute-based (computers), whereas for other categories, it is predominantly image-based (fragrances).

Consumers typically do not make decisions on the basis of attributes or image alone. Rather they use attributes and image to infer some benefit. A benefit is an abstract concept such as convenience, pleasure, or fun. The rationale for a benefit is the fact that it has some attributes or that certain people use it on particular occasions. In the Bud Light example, the taste benefit might be supported by specifying the brand's choice of hops, or by showing young adults enjoying it after work.

In some instances, the benefit is supported by an irrelevant attribute as a means of persuasion. For example, Natural Silk Shampoo claims that it puts silk in every bottle. This attribute is irrelevant to the silkiness of hair. Similarly, claiming that a coffee has superior taste because it is mountain grown is irrelevant because most coffee is mountain grown. Irrelevant attributes are persuasive because they suggest that there is a reason to believe the implied benefit (i.e., silky hair, better tasting coffee) in a situation where consumers are unlikely to scrutinize the veracity of the claim.[1]

A debate sometimes arises about whether a product feature is an attribute or a benefit. For example, taste might be considered an attribute that affects the benefit enjoyment. Or taste might be viewed as a benefit, where its attributes are the amount of sweetener and the amount of carbonation. From a strategic perspective, the important task is to assess the antecedents and consequences of a feature and to decide whether the antecedent, feature, or consequence (or some combination of these characteristics) should be highlighted. It matters less whether the feature is termed an attribute or a benefit.

Category Membership

A starting point in establishing a brand position is to identify its category membership. Membership indicates the products with which a brand competes. It informs the consumer about the goals that might be achieved by a product. For highly established products and services, category membership is not a focal issue. Consumers know that Coca-Cola is a leading brand of soft drink and that Kellogg's Corn Flakes is a leading brand of cereal. Category membership for leading business-to-business brands is also obvious to the purchaser. However, there are many situations where it is important to inform consumers of a brand's category membership. Perhaps the most obvious situation is the introduction of new products, where the category membership is not apparent. When personal digital assistants were introduced, a decision had to be made about whether it was a computer accessory or a replacement for an appointment book.

In some instances consumers know a brand's category membership, but are not convinced that the brand is a good member of the category. In such cases, alerting consumers to a brand's category membership is warranted. For example, consumers may be aware that Dell produces computers. But they may not be certain whether Dell computers are in a class with IBM and Compaq. In this instance, it might be useful to reinforce category membership.

There are a variety of ways to convey a brand's category membership. Benefits are frequently used to announce category membership to ensure consumers that a brand will deliver on the fundamental reason for using a category. Thus, industrial motors might claim to have power and analgesics might announce their efficacy. These benefits are not presented in a manner that imply brand superiority, but merely that the brands possess these properties. The benefits that imply category membership are common to most, if not all brands, and thus can be thought of as *points of parity*.

Attributes and image can be used to provide rationales that give consumers reason to believe that a brand has the benefit that implies membership in a category. A cake mix might attain membership in the cake category by claiming the benefit of great taste and support this benefit claim by possessing high quality ingredients (attributes) or by showing users delighting in its consumption (image).

Attributes and image might also be used in their own right to claim membership. An electronic device might be positioned as a computer by emphasizing that it has memory, a monitor, a keyboard, and can be used for electronic mail. Alternatively, describing the people who use the electronic device and the relevant occasions of use informs the consumer about the brands against which the product is intended to compete. In beer advertising, varying the age of the drinker and the place in which consumption occurs influences whether the brand is viewed as competing in the super-premium, premium, or price category. When image is used to create membership, a brand attribute is often used to create a point-of-difference.

Thus, 7UP is positioned as a soft drink by its occasions of use: with meals, with friends, at sporting and other events. It is distinguished from other soft drinks by the fact that it is colorless in appearance and it has a tart taste, both of which imply the benefit superior thirst-quenching.

Exemplars are also used to specify a brand's category membership. Subaru advertising compared the brand to Volvo, not because they compete for the same customers, but because this approach represents an efficient way to say that Subaru is a member of the "safe car" category. Similarly, Wheaties introduced a presweetened cereal by telling consumers that if they liked Frosted Flakes, they should try Wheaties Honey Gold. The idea was not to compete with Frosted Flakes, but to tell consumers in an efficient way that Wheaties Honey Gold is a member of the adult presweet cereal category. When Tommy Hilfiger was an unknown designer, advertising announced his membership as a great American designer by associating him with Geoffrey Beene, Stanley Blacker, Calvin Klein, and Perry Ellis, who were recognized members of that category.

The preferred approach to positioning is to inform consumers of a brand's membership before stating its point-of-difference in relation to other category members. Presumably, consumers need to know what a product is and what goal it might help attain prior to assessing whether it dominates the brands against which it competes. For new products, separate marketing programs are generally needed to inform consumers of membership and to educate them about a brand's point-of-difference. For brands with limited resources, doing so implies the development of a marketing strategy that establishes category membership prior to one that states a point-of-difference. Brands with greater resources can develop concurrent marketing programs where one features membership and the other the point-of-difference. Efforts to inform consumers of membership and point-of-difference in the same campaign are often not effective because there is insufficient development of either claim when both are addressed at once.

Sometimes brands are affiliated with categories in which they do not hold membership rather than one in which they do. This approach is a viable way to highlight a brand's point-of-difference from competitors, providing that consumers know the brand's actual membership. For example, DiGiorno pizza is a frozen product with a fresh-baked crust that rises when the pizza is heated. DiGiorno positioned the brand as a member of the delivered pizza category rather than the frozen category. For example, an ad for DiGiorno showed a party scene in which people were eating pizza and asking the host which pizza delivery service he used. He keeps repeating, "Its not delivery, its *DiGiorno!*" By associating with a category in which it did not hold membership, delivered pizza, DiGiorno was able to highlight that it was different from other members of its category, frozen pizza. The difference was taste.

While it is important to establish a brand's category membership, it is usually not sufficient for effective brand positioning. At best this may help grow the category. If many firms engage in category build, the effect may be consumer confusion. In an effort to draw a significant share of consumers' Christmas spending, a spate of dot.coms ran advertising emphasizing their category membership. For example, Fogdog, Sportsline, and other online sporting good firms promoted that they had a vast array of sporting goods. In many cases, these ads appear to have had little impact as the vast majority of online sales went to either established e-tailers, such as Amazon.com and eToys, or to familiar bricks and mortar brands such as Toys "R" Us, that had evolved to "bricks and clicks." Thus, a sound positioning strategy requires the specification not only of the category in which a brand holds membership, but also how a brand dominates other members of its category. Developing compelling points of difference is thus critical to effective brand positioning.

Points-of-Difference

A starting point in developing a point-of-difference is to identify accepted consumer beliefs. What are consumers' beliefs about the category that might be used to promote a benefit? For example, the (false) belief that honey is nutritionally superior to sugar led General Mills to produce Honey Nut Cheerios. When a brand cannot dominate competitors on a factor that reflects an accepted consumer belief, an effort is made to teach consumers beliefs that imply the brand's benefit. It generally is more expensive to teach consumers new beliefs than to adapt the appeal to an accepted belief. Illustrative of such market driving strategy is the campaign by Listerine that convinced consumers that its bad taste was what made it effective. Perhaps consumers were willing to believe that bad taste implied efficacy because of the accepted consumer belief that medicinal products taste bad.

The strongest positions are ones in which a brand has a clear point-of-difference on a benefit that prompts category use. Large brands are generally positioned using these benefits. Thus, advertising for Tide detergent stresses superior cleaning power and Microsoft claims the most advanced software. Category leaders often follow this strategy even when they do not have superiority in relation to competition. They use their superior advertising budgets to outshout competition and thus claim the benefit that motivates category consumption for themselves.

Smaller brands typically attempt to establish a niche as their point-of-difference. This niche is achieved by using the primary category benefit to establish category membership and by selecting some benefit other than the focal one for the category to establish brand dominance. IBM presents its cutting-edge technology as its point-of-difference, whereas WinBook positions its brand as a technologically advanced product at a low price. For many years, Jif was positioned as the best-tasting peanut butter, whereas Skippy was positioned as the great-tasting brand with the greatest nutritional value.

In developing a brand position, it is important to limit the number of benefits that are made focal. Processing a benefit often requires substantial cognitive resources. Unless the product is of great interest to consumers, they are unlikely to devote the resources to process many brand benefits. Even when one benefit is presented to represent a brand's point-of-difference, it is often the case that multiple benefits are considered in order to understand the brand's membership and point-of-difference. When multiple benefits are presented, caution is needed to limit the likelihood that one benefit undermines another. For example, it might be difficult to position a brand as inexpensive and at the same time assert that it is of the highest quality. Similarly, customers might not find it credible if a brand were to claim that it is both nutritional and good-tasting, or powerful and safe. When these situations arise, it might be judicious to focus on only one benefit.

In selecting a benefit, an assessment is needed about whether the benefit motivates consumption or whether the benefit is *normative*. Normative benefits are ones that customers say are important because of societal standards rather than because these benefits actually influence their behavior. For example, people frequently claim safety is an important factor in their selection of cars and that nutrition is an important factor in their selection of food products. Inspection of their consumption choices, however, often reveals that these benefits are not important determinants of the brands selected. Apparently, consumers rate safety and nutrition highly because it would be inappropriate in their roles as parents, homemakers, or responsible adults to do otherwise. It is important to note that when nutrition, safety, and the like are normative features, they are not important determinants of brand choice. Similarly, in business-to-business selling situations, purchasing agents may rate price as the critical determinant of their supplier selection and report that they are uninfluenced by factors such as their relationship with the sales representative. However, an examination of the suppliers actually selected often undermines the credibility of this claim.

While a main focus in competition-based positioning is to situate the firm's brand, in so doing an effort is often made to affect the performance of other category members. Brand positioning might serve to make competitors' attractive brands seem deficient. This goal may be achieved by introducing a new benefit to the category. Starbucks' positioning of coffee as a destination rather than a product made other coffees seem ordinary and unexciting. Alternatively, introducing a comprehensive position might make less complete offerings seem deficient. The introduction of Lever 2000 as the deodorizing bar soap that was good for your skin made other bar soaps that performed only one of these functions seem alike and incomplete.

In other instances, brand positioning might be undertaken to muddle the reason for consumers to purchase a category and thus undermine consumers' interest in the category. Crystal Pepsi was introduced to compete with Coca-Cola's Sprite. Crystal Pepsi was a clear soft drink that contained substantial calories. To protect Sprite, Coke responded with the introduction of Tab Clear, which it positioned as a dietetic clear soft drink. This introduction confused consumers about whether the clear category was dietetic or not. This problem was exacerbated by the fact that Crystal Pepsi's packaging and color implied light and thus prompted the idea of dietetic among consumers. The result was that neither Crystal Pepsi nor Tab Clear generated substantial demand and both brands were withdrawn from the market, allowing Sprite to sustain its market position.

Summary

Competition-based positioning can be represented by the positioning triangle in Figure 2.2. The triangle provides a visual representation of the two key facets of positioning: membership and point-of-difference. Membership in the category is developed by highlighting benefits that are points of parity with other brands in the category, or by relating the brand to a category exemplar. Providing a rationale for believing a benefit gives consumers a reason to trust a membership claim. This rationale typically takes the form of some physical characteristic. Once a brand has achieved membership in the category, its advantage over other category members is presented in terms of a benefit(s) that represent a point-of-difference. Again, a rationale might be provided to enhance the likelihood that consumers will believe the brand's point-of-difference.

To illustrate, Visa and American Express have established membership in the charge card category. Visa's point-of-difference is that it is the most

Figure 2.2
Competition-Based Positioning Triangle

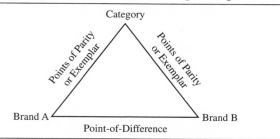

widely available card, which underscores the category's main benefit of convenience. American Express, on the other hand, has built the equity of its brand by highlighting the prestige associated with the use of its card. Having established these points-of-difference, Visa and American Express now compete by attempting to blunt each other's advantage. Along these lines, Visa offers a platinum card to compete and enhance the prestige of its brand, and American Express has substantially increased the number of vendors that accept American Express cards to reduce Visa's advantage on this dimension.

GOAL-BASED POSITIONING

Competition-based positioning focuses strategy on one's position in relation to that of the competition. The effort is to dominate competition on benefits important to consumers. While this approach provides a sound way to build an initial position, once the target attains a basic understanding how the brand relates to alternatives in the same category, brand growth may be achieved by deepening the meanings associated with the brand position. This entails demonstrating more explicitly how the brand relates to consumers' goals and requires insight about what motivates consumers to use a brand. The brand is then positioned such that its essence implies goal attainment. The process by which this can be achieved is termed *laddering up,* and the product of laddering up is *brand essence.*

Brand Essence

Laddering up is based on the notion that in developing a product point-of-difference, two types of characteristics are considered: one is attributes and image, and the other is benefits. These characteristics are related to each other in a specific manner. Attributes and image are concrete factors that can be used to infer a benefit, which is abstract. In turn, a benefit can be used to infer even more abstract benefits. By analogy, these inferences are like rungs of a ladder that become more abstract and general as you ascend the rungs. Thus, an initial campaign might emphasize some attribute of the product. A second generation might move up a rung on the ladder by stressing the benefit implied by the attribute. Typically this is a functional benefit. Subsequent generations address inferences implied by the functional benefit as a means of moving up the ladder until a point is reached where the benefit defines the essence of the brand. Brand essence is related to some consumer goal. We refer to this approach as laddering, and when the progression is from attribute to benefit to more abstract benefit, we refer to the process as laddering up. This process is shown schematically in Figure 2.3.

A US West cellular advertising campaign illustrates a laddering up approach. The focus of the initial advertising spot was on unique product attributes that made the service reliable (functional benefit). In a second generation, advertising examined the implication of having reliable service, which is that there would be less concern about being tied to the office to await important calls (functional benefit). Following this approach, the next generation of advertising might focus on the implication of having the freedom of movement afforded by a cellular phone (emotional benefit). In effect, laddering up involves repeatedly asking what the implication of an attribute or benefit is for the consumer. Laddering from attribute to

Figure 2.3
Laddering

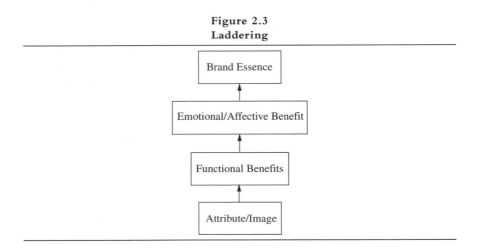

benefit to more abstract benefit provides a basis for informing consumers of a brand's essence.

Brand essence uses the insight that consumers classify disparate product categories together because they share a benefit that is related to their goals. For example, advertising for McDonald's depicts a blind date, in which a man named Larry calls on his date. He immediately attempts to manage her expectations by clarifying who he is and who he is *not*. He indicates that he is not a doctor, lawyer, banker, or CPA, rather he is a clerk in a record store. He states that they will not be dining at a place that calls itself a bistro, casa, or maison, nor will they attend a play, the opera, the symphony, or the ballet. Instead, he proposes driving in his plain old ordinary car to McDonald's and a movie. These assertions suggest that McDonald's is a down-to-earth place and the bedrock of the community. This brand essence is attractive when the consumers' goal is enjoying an unpretentious meal. This brand essence scenario is diagrammed schematically in Figure 2.4.

The association of a brand to various objects often results in the anthropomorphizing of the brand. Thus, brands often have a gender, age, and social class, as well as personality characteristics. Because Burger King originally featured large sandwiches such as the Whopper and had sit-down facilities inside the restaurant, these objects became associated with the brand and implied a masculine image. McDonald's is for kids and the family and thus is viewed as more feminine than Burger King. Apple Computer is young and IBM is mature. Alpo is downscale and Science Diet is upscale. Cartier watches have an upscale association, whereas Timex is more downscale. Levi's dropped its line of coveralls in an effort to elevate the social class of their brand. Marlboro cigarettes are seen as honest, genuine, spirited, dependable, romantic, and tough. A recent study suggests that there

Figure 2.4
McDonald's Brand Essence

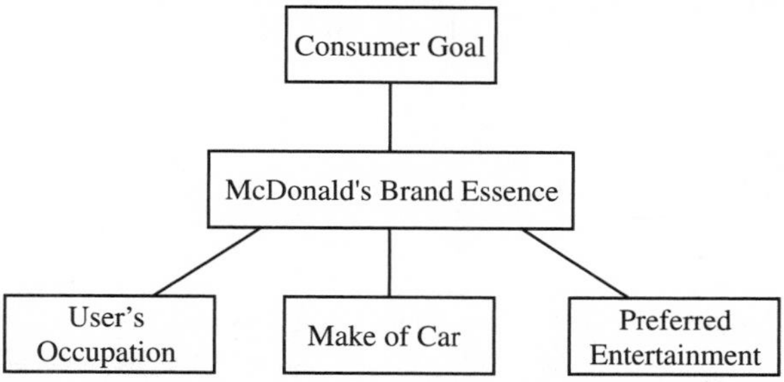

are at least five personality dimensions that can be related to a brand: sincerity, excitement, competence, sophistication, and ruggedness.[2] The elaboration of demographic characteristics of a brand as well as its attributes of character implies its essence.

A more general version of this schematic can be represented so as to make explicit the differences between competition and goal-based positioning. The diagram in Figure 2.5 depicts two concepts in consumers' memory. One concept represents information about a brand and inferences about its essence. Another concept represents consumers' goals. As Figure 2.5 suggests, consumers' perception of the relationship between a brand and other objects is one of complementarity. These points of complementarity converge to imply the brand's essence. Brand essence has points of commonality with consumers' goals that allow the consumer to infer the goal that might be achieved by using the brand from the brand's essence.

Category Essence

A focus on consumers' goals as the basis for positioning can be undertaken at a category level as well as a brand level. Like brand essence, category essence can be achieved by relating the brand to other objects that imply the essence of the category that is associated with the achievement of some goal. However, any device that makes salient the connection between the category and some goal can be used to deliver category essence. To illustrate the notion of category essence, consider the following statement describing the essence of beer for 18- to 34-year-old men and how it might be used to develop advertising:

> These individuals may feel threatened by the complexities and conflicts of everyday life. They are confused and perhaps depressed about how to

Figure 2.5
Goal-Based Positioning Triangle

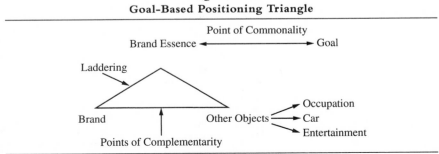

achieve harmony between their desire to discharge their primal passions and the constraints imposed by society. They desire intimate relations without the attendant commitment. They are searching for the opportunity to give expression to their talents without being encumbered by the demands imposed by formal organizations. Beer allows these individuals to indulge themselves and perhaps to make less salient the conflict between their aspirations and the limitations imposed on their behavior by society.

Category essence uses insight about how a category fits with consumers' goals as a brand's point-of-difference. The assumption is that if consumers perceive a brand to be positioned in a manner that is sensitive to their problems, that brand is viewed as a solution to their problems. There are a substantial number of campaigns that offer testimony to the effectiveness of this strategy. Ramada showed the problems travelers encounter at comparable hotels and implored consumers with the slogan: "Next time Ramada." No rationale for why Ramada would be superior in handling these problems was given beyond the suggestion that if Ramada understood the problem, it was the solution. Similarly, Lee jeans showed the difficulties women encountered in trying to get into jeans. Consumers were urged to buy Lee jeans to remedy this problem, though no rationale for this choice was provided.

Category essence may be a viable way for a brand to compete when it does not have a product point-of-difference. However, a focus on category essence is a strategy of last resort. If a brand had a strong point of differentiation that was important to consumers, a competition-based approach would be used. Further, as more categories have become commodities, the use of category essence has increased. The result is that advertising has developed a sameness that depicts consumers' attitudes rather than brand features as the brand news, and the impact of the advertising is compromised. In this situation, it is more productive to use consumer insight as a basis for developing brands that address consumers' goals than it is to use the insight as a basis for advertising that merely signals recognition of consumers' aspirations.

While it is appropriate to focus on laddering up in the context of a discussion about goal-based positioning, some mention of laddering down is also warranted. Laddering down involves giving credence to the assertion that a brand delivers some benefit. Laddering down often occurs in the context of a laddering up campaign as a means of reinforcing the foundation on which brand essence is built. More generally, laddering down is used to provide a reason for consumers to believe a benefit in the context of competition-based positioning. For example, laddering down is in evidence when Lexus provides support for the contention that it is of the highest quality by showing the tightness of the car's metal joints, or when

Reebok uses its pump attribute to give credence to its claims of superiority in its shoes' comfort.

Summary

All positioning efforts take consumer goals into consideration. Even when announcing a brand's category membership, a connection to some goal is implied. What distinguishes goal-based positioning is the depth of understanding sought about consumers' goals in using the brand. The implications of a brand's attributes and benefits are used to infer a brand's essence. In advertising, brand essence is often expressed in terms of a brand's relation to other objects that share a benefit related to consumers' goals. Goal-based positioning can also be developed at the category level, a strategy that is usually pursued when a brand is at parity with competitive offerings. In following this strategy, insights about consumers' goals in using the category serve as a brand's point-of-difference.

INTEGRATING COMPETITION-BASED AND GOAL-BASED POSITIONING: THE VALUE EQUATION

The discussion of competition-based and goal-based positioning makes evident that these approaches differ primarily in their focus. Both pertain to how a brand's benefits relate to a consumer's goals. They differ in the extent to which the focus is on competition versus consumer goals. The integration of these approaches is manifest in the conception and development of brand value.

As a starting point in illustrating this issue, we assess the notion of brand value as it existed in the 1980s:

$$\text{Brand value} = \frac{\text{Product/Service quality}}{\text{Price}}$$

This definition is intended to be conceptual rather than mathematical. Quality is evaluated in terms of average performance as well as in terms of variance about that average. A Toyota Camry is viewed as being of high quality because it receives favorable scores for styling, comfort, and engine performance, and because the car is perceived to deviate very little in its performance on these dimensions. The dominant way to provide value in the 1980s was to offer superior quality at a competitive price.

When the substantial economic downturn occurred in 1987, consumers' notion of value began to change. While product or service quality remained an important consideration in determining value, psychic quality received increased attention. Psychic quality refers to the feelings or emotions and other abstract benefits related to using the product or service, which we have discussed in terms of brand essence. Faced with tighter economic circumstances, consumers sought comfort and self-expression in the brands they chose.

At the same time, the price charged for goods and services became a more important factor in the determination of value. Indeed, by the early 1990s, for some consumers price was the single most important consideration. Value involved providing the same quality at a lower price. Private-label brands emerged as leaders in many categories because of their reasonable quality and significantly lower price in relation to the leading brands. The response by leading brands has been to reduce the price disparity with private labels and thereby enhance the value of their offerings.

While it is well known that the price of the product or service is a cost, it has only recently been realized that the time exerted in a purchase transaction and product use are also important costs. In the United States, there has been a contraction of leisure time and an expansion of work time. Between 1980 and 1990, the average American increased his or her work hours from 40 to 48 which significantly compromised leisure time. With downsizing in the 1990s, the average worker added approximately 45 minutes per day or one additional month per year of work time. The consequence is that many people now experience time famine (i.e., lack of time to accomplish the tasks they feel need to be managed), and time has become an increasingly important factor in customers' assessments of value. Even for those who have not experienced a reduction in leisure time, the fragmentation of leisure time has led to the perception of time famine.

The predominant strategy used to cope with time famine is multitasking. Multitasking typically involves engaging in some obligatory activity and at the same time accomplishing an unrelated goal. People make phone calls while driving in their cars, they eat while driving, they exercise while walking to work, and the like. There has also been an adjustment in the choices that are made. The population of dogs in this country has leveled off at about 58 million, while the population of cats has increased to over 70 million. These trends can be explained by noting that the care of cats requires less time than the care of dogs. The purchase of nutritional pet foods such as Science Diet has grown dramatically, in part reflecting consumers' efforts to reduce the incidence of a pet's digestive distress that might require time-consuming visits to the veterinarian. Consumption of bagels and other portable breakfast foods has grown dramatically during the 1990s, whereas the sales of less portable ready-to-eat cereals lost more than 15 percent of its dollar sales during this time period. The sale of push lawn mowers has increased dramatically since 1995. These devices enable the user to exercise while accomplishing the grass-cutting chore. The value equation that reflects these considerations can be represented as:

$$Value = \frac{Product/Service\ quality + Psychic\ quality}{Price + Time}$$

The value equation offers a means of linking a brand's position to the marketing mix. Consider for example, Goodyear's strategy in marketing tires during the mid-1990s. Goodyear is the largest producer of tires in the United States with over 13 percent share of market. However, because sales and share were stagnant for several years, research was conducted to aid in developing business-building ideas. These data indicated that tread life was the most important product feature in purchasing tires, followed by wet traction, snow traction, and dry traction.

While a tire that offered an advance in tread life would be highly attractive to customers, there had not been a major innovation on this attribute since the steel-belted tire was developed in the 1960s. Michelin supported its brand with advertising that focused on safety. The typical advertisement showed a baby sitting inside a Michelin tire, which symbolized the child's protection from the hazards of the road.

Research also indicated a dramatic change in consumers' tire purchase behavior. Whereas the decision to purchase a replacement tire typically was made over a period of about a month during the 1960s, in the mid-1990s, over 50 percent of consumers made a tire purchase within two days of recognizing the need. Almost all consumers made the tire purchase decision within a week of problem recognition.

Goodyear's response to these observations was to develop a new strategy. In part, this was reflected in the introduction of a new tire called the Aquatread. It had a deep groove around the middle of the tire's circumference to throw off water from under the tire, and thus increase traction in wet weather. This feature gave Goodyear a perceived quality advantage. In addition, Goodyear launched three new products. While these were not as innovative as the Aquatread, they fostered consumers' belief that Goodyear is a technological leader in the tire category. Aquatread is a premium-priced tire, which is consistent with the positioning of the brand as the state-of-the-art in the category. Perhaps most important, the cost of time was reduced by increasing the number of outlets where Aquatread and other Goodyear tires could be purchased. Goodyear's 2300 captive outlets were bolstered by the addition of Sears and discounters, a channel strategy that increased outlets by 35 percent.

The response was impressive. One year after launch, earnings had increased by 25 percent, the stock price tripled in three years, and consumers' intent to buy Goodyear increased dramatically while the intent to buy Michelin dropped.

CHALLENGES TO EFFECTIVE POSITIONING

Even when the principles of positioning are understood, there are a variety of impediments to their successful implementation. At times, effective positioning is undermined by the poor selection of focal benefits. In other instances, advertising is compromised by the failure to sustain a brand's position.

When entering a category where there are established brands, the challenge is to find a viable basis for differentiation. A frequent occurrence is that the point-of-difference selected is one on which a brand dominates its competition and not one that is important to consumers. Along these lines, several analgesic brands including Aleve have found limited demand for the claim that their brand was long-lasting or that infrequent dosing was required. Most consumers have fast relief and not long-lasting relief as a priority. Indeed, long-lasting may imply slow acting—just the opposite of what is desired.

A variant of this problem emerges when a benefit on which a firm dominates is important to some consumers, but not to the ones who are responsible for brand choice. For example, several regular cereals in the past 20 years have tried to position themselves as good tasting and nutritional children's cereals. Halfsies, for example, was a good-tasting cereal that had half the sugar of other presweet cereals. This positioning appealed to the adult purchasers who is concerned with her children's nutrition and also wants to minimize parent-child conflict. However, Halfsies' position did not appeal strongly to children, who are typically the ones responsible for the selection of a cereal brand. Halfsies may have tasted better than regular cereals, but it was not perceived as better tasting than the presweets that children were being asked to give up.

One approach to addressing the concern that any single benefit may be unimportant to some segment of consumers is to claim multiple benefits. In so doing, the hope is that brand will offer something for everyone. This approach to differentiation may also emerge as a means of compromise when strategists cannot agree on the benefit to promote. Such positioning by committee or any other multiple benefit approach is often fraught with problems. One benefit claim might undermine another; for example, consumers are skeptical of products that claim high quality *and* low price. Further, claiming a variety of benefits can confound consumers' efforts to define what the product is.

Once a position is developed, most of the activity is directed toward sustaining it. For many years, Coca-Cola has been positioned as the soft drink that provides superior taste. While this position has not changed, advertising has continually sought to sustain the superior taste benefit in a modern way. Sustaining a benefit over time often serves as a barrier to competitive entry.

The competition between Eveready and Duracell in the alkaline battery category illustrates the virtues of sustaining a brand position. In 1974, Duracell became the first company to advertise alkaline batteries on television. These batteries cost about twice as much as the then more popular zinc carbon batteries, but lasted six times longer. Duracell developed advertising illustrating how its brand outlasted alternative batteries in a variety of different products. In what is perhaps the most memorable execution, a room full of mechanical pink bunnies were shown beating on snare drums. At the end of the ad, only the bunny that was powered by Duracell was still in motion. This campaign aired until 1984.

In October 1989, Eveready launched a campaign that also touted longevity by showing a pink mechanical bunny breaking into contrived and phony commercials. This campaign was supported by heavy advertising. Eveready spent about $22 million in the last quarter of 1989, which was double the expenditure for the last quarter of 1988 and far more than Duracell's $15 million fourth quarter 1989 advertising expenditure.

The initial response surprised Eveready. It showed that Duracell had increased its share from 39 percent to over 40 percent share of market, whereas Eveready dropped a share point to 36. The problem was thought to be a lack of connection between the advertising and point of purchase. To remedy this problem, Eveready referred to its bunny advertising in its retail displays and sustained the campaign. Nevertheless, the Duracell share of the alkaline battery business continued to grow while Eveready's share did not. By 1998, A.C. Nielsen estimated that Duracell had 48 percent share of the alkaline battery market and Eveready had about 36 percent.

While sustaining advertising serves as a barrier to competitive entry, it also reduces the strategic alternatives available to a brand. For example, Procter & Gamble (P&G) introduced Dash detergent to attract consumers who used front-loading washing machines. Dash was the low sudser that was required for such machines. Over many years of advertising, Dash, in this manner, made this position impenetrable by other brands. In fact, Dash was so closely associated with front-loading machines, that when this type of machine went out of fashion, so did Dash. This outcome occurred despite the fact that Dash was among P&G's most effective detergents, and despite significant efforts to reposition the brand.

Firms sometimes undermine the ability to develop a sustained position by how they promote the brand when it is launched. Rather than attempting to establish the brand's position as a foundation for future advertising, the goal of introductory advertising is seen as creating awareness. The belief is that once consumers are aware of the brand, the position may be developed. While awareness is important, advertisers should not settle for this goal in introducing a brand. It is far more efficient to establish brand awareness and the brand position at the outset of a campaign. While Taco Bell's campaign featuring a talking Chihuahua as a spokesperson garnered huge awareness, it failed to enhance Taco Bell's market position. Similarly Nissan's use of an Asian gentleman in their advertising prompted great awareness of the brand but sales declined. And it is typical for dot-coms to launch their online businesses with advertising that does nothing more than deliver brand name awareness.

A superior approach is to communicate the brand's position when launching the brand. Consider the advertising campaign for Apple that was originally developed by the Chiat/Day advertising agency. The firm spent $1 million to air an ad once on the 1984 Superbowl. This spot, used to introduce Macintosh, not only created brand awareness, it also established the brand position as the user-friendly computer for independent-minded users. This position was sustained over the next decade by advertising that illustrated what user-friendly meant to independent-minded clerical workers, mid-level managers, upper-level management, and small businesspeople. Despite this sustained position, with the emergence of the Windows platform as the industry standard, Apple's brand share eroded dramatically. By the mid-1990s, Apple's share was just over 2 percent of the personal computer market, a decline of over 10 percent from its peak share.

While sustaining a consistent position was not sufficient to ensure Apple's success, it did serve as a basis for relaunching the brand. In the late 1990s, the reintroduction of Apple's heritage as a user-friendly brand for independent-minded people was the basis for the successful introduction of iMac and the G3 computer. The iMac appealed to people who were purchasing their first computer and were interested in easy access to the Web. The G3 appealed to the large number of Apple owners who had not purchased a computer in over three years in the hope that Apple would again produce a competitive model. By relying on the brand's heritage, Apple was able to turnaround the brand quickly, increasing its share of market to over 4.5 percent by the beginning of 2000.

Even when positions have been sustained for some time, firms sometimes unwittingly abandon their position in response to some minor change in consumer preferences, or in an effort to generate incremental volume for a brand. For example, when General Mills' successfully launched Honey Nut Cheerios to address parental concerns about the sugar in children's ready-to-eat cereals, several brands responded by dropping their association to sugar. Sugar Crisp became Golden Crisp and dropped the brand icon, a Sugar Bear. In effect, the brand walked away from its equity and sales plummeted. A diet bar brand that consumers used primarily as a lunch substitute attempted to add incremental volume by promoting its use as a snack. This position appeared to undermine the main usage occasion by leaving consumers wondering about whether one wafer was too much for a snack when the firm was recommending two wafers as a meal.

Summary

Our analysis of positioning is summarized schematically in Figure 2.6. Establishing category membership is the first priority. This goal can be achieved by presenting a benefit and the attendant attributes or image to support the benefit. Alternatively, attributes or benefits alone might be used to introduce a brand's position. In some cases, an exemplar might be used to establish membership. If consumers know a brand's category membership, focus centers on establishing a point-of-difference. A starting point along these lines involves finding a product point-of-difference that is important to consumers and distinguishes the brand from alternative offerings. Leaders should consider the benefit that motivates category consumption and outshout competition on this benefit. Followers use the category-defining benefit to establish membership in the category and focus on some niche benefit where they have a barrier to competitive entry. Over time, consideration should be given to laddering irrespective of whether the firm is

Figure 2.6
Positioning Summary

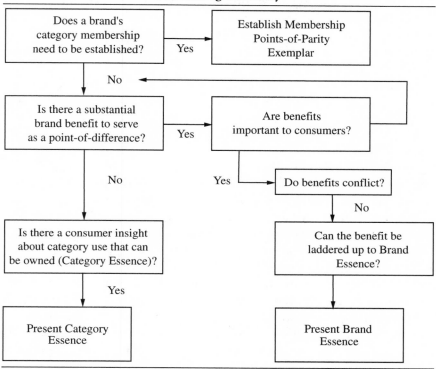

a leader or a follower. If no product differences that are important to consumers are available, the viability of using a superior understanding of the consumer might be considered to establish a point-of-difference. Here, category and brand essence may be of value in establishing a position that resonates with consumers because they perceive that the firm understands what they experience with regard to the category and can satisfy their goals. In the absence of a product or consumer point-of-difference, it is worthwhile to examine some other opportunity.

WRITING A TARGETING AND POSITIONING STATEMENT

After a firm has made the targeting and positioning decisions for a product, it is useful to summarize these decisions in a positioning statement. This statement is an internal document that may be shared with the sales force, the advertising agency and, more generally, with those for whom it is important to understand who the target is and what prompts them to choose the company's brand. A positioning statement is *not* ad copy. Rather it is a general summary of the key aspects of the marketing strategy and, as such, it serves as the foundation for decisions about all elements of the marketing mix.

While the specific format used for a positioning statement may vary, in one way or another, each of the following four questions should be addressed:

1. *Who should be targeted for brand use?* It is important to understand who the target customer is. This answer requires describing target customers in terms of their current usage patterns, demographic characteristics, and general goals. Insight into the target's goals is especially important because purchase decisions are rarely motivated by a desire for a product per se. Rather, there is a belief that having the brand will facilitate achieving some more fundamental goal that the target has.

2. *When should the brand be considered (i.e., what goal does the brand allow the target to achieve)?* Answering this question entails defining the immediate competition for the brand. This is often done by invoking membership in a particular product category, as described in our discussion of competition-based positioning. Thus, Mountain Dew might assert that it should be considered whenever the target wants a soft drink, or when a rejuvenating beverage is desired. Such an approach is particularly appropriate when launching a new product because it links the new product to ones that are already familiar and thereby facilitates understanding. In part, the failure of Motorola's Envoy seems attributable in part to the lack of a clearly defined competitive set. By contrast, Palm Pilot, a product that performs many of the same functions as Envoy, achieved considerable success by claiming membership in the electronic organizer category.

While it is common to define the competitive set, that is, the products with which a brand competes by reference to an established product category, this is not the only viable approach. When a brand moves from competition-based positioning to goal-based positioning, the competitive set may span several product categories and be defined by usage occasions or users. Thus, a non-alcoholic wine might define its competitive set in terms of products that are consumed when both sociability and clear thinking are requisite. As such, competition might include bottled water and soft drinks, as well as other non-alcoholic wines. Similarly, Waterman pens might be positioned as heirlooms that can be passed on to the next generation, thereby competing with antique furniture and jewelry.

3. *Why should the brand be chosen over other alternatives in the competitive set?* A brand must offer a compelling reason for choosing it over the other options that might be considered. Moreover, the firm must find a way to make the claimed point-of-difference believable. The simplest approach is to point to a unique product attribute. Thus, Mountain Dew might contend that it is more energizing than other soft drinks and support this claim by noting that it has a higher level of caffeine. Palm Pilot might assert that it is more convenient than other electronic organizers because it offers one-button synchronization with the user's desktop computer.

When the point-of-difference is more abstract or image based, support for the claim may reside in more general associations to the company that have been developed over time. Thus, Chanel No. 5 perfume may claim to be the quintessential elegant, French perfume and support this claim by noting the long association between Chanel and haute couturier.

It is best to claim a single point-of-difference, though this point-of-difference may be an abstraction based on multiple features of the product. For example, BIC might claim that its disposable razors offer greater convenience than other disposable razors. The brand's broad distribution, in-store placement near checkout counters, low price, and narrow product line might be used to support this claim.

It is also desirable that the point-of-difference be specific and meaningful. Claims such as that the brand is the highest quality or best value are vague. What defines high quality or value for one target may mean only moderate quality or value to another. Quality or value should be defined in terms that are meaningful to the target. Along similar lines, using a brand's sales leadership in a category as a point-of-difference is a weak position that can be strengthened by informing consumers about why a brand dominates category sales.

When a brand's benefits are at parity with those of the competition, the point-of-difference might be the depth of insight into consumers' goals in using the product. Consumers often make the inference that if a brand presents information that reflects an intimate understanding of consumers' goals in consuming the product, it must also offer a superior way to achieve those goals.

4. *How will choosing the brand help the target accomplish his or her goal(s)?* The final element of a positioning statement links the brand's point-of-difference to the target's goal(s). The energy (caffeine) in Mountain Dew soft drinks may be argued to enable sleep-deprived students to remain alert in class and thereby obtain a higher grades than they would have been able to earn otherwise. The convenient availability of BIC disposable razors may free busy people to focus their attention on more important matters than shopping for a razor.

The following targeting and positioning statements have been developed using the notions we have described:

- *Mountain Dew:* To young, active soft-drink consumers who have little time for sleep, Mountain Dew is the soft drink that gives you more energy than any other brand because it has the highest level of caffeine. With Mountain Dew, you can stay alert and keep going even when you haven't been able to get a good night's sleep.
- *BIC Disposable Razor:* To men and women who lead active lives that sometimes result in shaving away from home, the BIC disposable razor offers you greater convenience than other razors because it is inexpensive and widely available. With the BIC disposable razor, you can focus on the things you want to do and not on keeping track of your razor.
- *Palm Pilot:* To busy professionals who need to stay organized, Palm Pilot is an electronic organizer that lets you carry your address book, schedule, and notepad in your pocket. It is superior to other organizers because only Palm Pilot allows you to backup your files and synchronize with your PC at the touch of a button. This feature saves time and ensures the availability of a back-up copy of important information.

Judging the adequacy of a positioning statement is necessarily a subjective exercise. However, common problems can be avoided if your positioning statement passes the following simple tests:

1. If you substitute a competitor's brand for yours, does the statement make equally good sense? If so, you should reconsider the competitive set or the point-of-difference claimed.
2. Does reading the statement provide a clear understanding of who should buy the brand, when they are likely to buy it, and what would motivate purchase? If not, the aspect of the statement that is vague should be reworked and made more specific.
3. Is it clear why the target should consider the brand to be a compelling idea? If not, work to develop the linkage between the brand's point-of-difference and the target's goals.

THE EFFECTS OF INFORMATION TECHNOLOGY ON SEGMENTATION, TARGETING, AND POSITIONING

The rapid advances in information technology that are currently being experienced have an important impact on positioning. One effect of technology (along with changes in the political climate in key countries such as the former Soviet Union and China) has been to facilitate global operations. The effect is that the world, quite simply, has become smaller. Anxious to capitalize on the efficiencies and power than may result from operating on a global scale, many firms are striving to build global brands.

What does the goal of building a global brand imply for segmentation, targeting, and positioning? According to P&G, a global brand is, by definition, a brand that has a single position worldwide. Further, a single positioning implies a target that is not defined by national borders. Coke is a global brand. It is targeted at people around the world who seek refreshment and reward with the positioning that Coke is the best tasting and most satisfying soft drink.

While information technology may afford global communications and distribution, global brands can only succeed if the consumers' tastes and the benefits that they seek are relatively homogeneous around the world. In many product categories, this is not the case. The flavor of coffee that is appealing to the French may be too strong for an American and too weak for a Turk.

The challenge thus becomes one of anticipating whether the many differences between consumers across markets necessitate different positioning of the brand by markets (or perhaps different brands altogether), or whether these differences merely require that a single positioning be implemented in a manner that accommodates the local distribution system and media. Products that are linked to universal goals or life transitions would seem to be potential candidates for global branding. Thus, Coke can be linked to the universal need for refreshment and reward. Prestige brands Chanel, Hermes, and Louis Vuitton enable consumers to signal their fine taste and wealth to others irrespective of their nationality. By contrast, tastes and benefits sought for other products may depend on experiences or market conditions that are unique to a particular culture or geographic locale. For example, the taste for certain foods and seasoning may be tied to childhood experiences that are culturally or ethnically based. Similarly, the benefits sought in laundry detergent may be determined by the size of the washer, whether it is a top- or front-loaded washer, the hardness of the local water, and the frequency of washing and, thus, how dirty the clothes typically are, and so on. These conditions may be very different in Tokyo versus Des Moines, Iowa.

As it stands, there are a small but growing number of global brands. For example, about a dozen of P&G's more than 200 brands are presently considered global. Brands such as Pringles, Pantene, and Always are global in the sense that they share a common brand position. However, even these global brands employ local execution. Along these lines, the flavors of Pringles that are marketed vary by country, as does the model shown in Pantene ads.

While global branding rests on what consumers have in common, information technology also enables firms to pay more attention to what makes consumers different from one another. Focusing on such variation serves as the basis for positioning a brand as being highly intimate with consumers. Companies such as Amazon.com use customers' purchase histories to make suggestions about additional books that they might enjoy. The system is based on detecting patterns in the purchase histories of other customers who have bought some of the same books as the target customer. Such automatic response systems are simply usage-based segmentation systems that capitalize on the firm's database (which is constantly being updated) to create more customized communications than traditional mass media.

A more extreme form of customization is true one-to-one marketing and the attendant intimacy positioning. As the name implies, one-to-one marketing fosters a consumer intimacy position by changing what the firm does in response to customer input and customers' past behavior. An example is Levi's custom jeans. Women visit a Levi's store and try on one of a number of pairs of jeans to identify which have the closest fit. Detailed measurements are taken to adjust the fit and these are entered into a computer program. This information is then used to make a pair of jeans that are customized to the woman's body. After the initial visit to the store, additional jeans can be ordered by phone.

A consumer intimacy position can involve approaches other than adapting the product to customer needs. It also may involve individualized communications and distribution. The defining feature of one-to-one marketing is an ongoing, responsive relationship with customers at an individual level.[3]

One-to-one marketing and a consumer intimacy position will not be optimal for all products or all consumers. It is most likely to be valued by consumers and thus profitable for the firm when the tastes are highly idiosyncratic. Further, it depends on consumers' willingness to participate in an exchange of information with the firm so that appropriate customization can occur. It is most likely to succeed when the consumer is highly involved with the product category for either economic or emotional reasons. Thus, fashion-minded women may desire a customized response when they are buying jeans or a swimsuit, but not when choosing socks or household staples.

In summary, there appear to be two seemingly opposing effects of information technology on positioning. On the one hand, the ability to reach customers worldwide and the economic advantages of scale encourage firms to focus on how people are similar and to build global brands. On the other hand, firms may use information technology to gain a competitive advantage by capturing and analyzing individual-level data and then creating highly customized offerings. In reality, these effects of technology co-exist by affecting different levels of decision making within the firm. Global brand building is a high-level strategic initiative that is undertaken by senior management. Customization most commonly affects tactics or implementation of a more general (if not global) strategy. Thus, customization of media and distribution occurs for global brands and brands that are positioned as highly intimate to create a brand image of personalized attention that is recognized by all customers. The difference is a matter of emphasis.

Notes

1. Gregory S. Carpenter, Rashi Glazer, and Kent Nakamoto, "Meaningful Brands from Meaningless Differentiation: The Dependence on Irrelevant Attributes," *Journal of Marketing Research,* vol. 31 (August 1994), pp. 339–350.

2. Jennifer L. Aaker, "Dimensions of Brand Personality," *Journal of Marketing Research,* vol. 34 (August 1997), pp. 347–356.

3. For a more detailed discussion, see Don Peppers, Martha Rogers, and Bob Dorf, "Is Your Company Ready for One-to-One Marketing?" *Harvard Business Review,* vol. 77 (January/February 1999), pp. 151–160.

CHAPTER 3

BRAND DESIGN

BOBBY J. CALDER and STEVEN J. REAGAN

Companies *sell* products; companies *market* brands. The distinction is commonly made, but what does it mean? To examine the difference, let's assume we are selling something, say, hamburgers. We could take the position that our product is hamburgers and that a hamburger is a hamburger. This position is certainly *selling* hamburgers.

If we are ambitious, our hamburgers do not have to be the same as just any hamburger. We can seek to offer a particular version of the hamburger, a better hamburger—one with a special sauce, for instance. Alternatively, and this amounts to the same thing, we can offer an ordinary hamburger but include other things to make it better, an extended offer (free french fries, delivery, or access to the Web while you eat). But we would still be *selling* the hamburgers, albeit a particular version or an extended offer.

What does it mean to *market* a brand of hamburgers? First of all, it does not mean selling a particular version of the product. A hamburger with a special sauce or an extended offer is not necessarily a brand. We have to go beyond selling the product, no matter how superior the product is in and of itself.

To *market,* we have to go beyond the product. We must transcend whatever the product is as a physical or objective entity. We must create and convey the meaning of the product.

Suppose we did have hamburgers with a special sauce. For us to have a brand, however, we must address the meaning of our hamburger. "Meaning" can sound strange in the case of something ordinary (hamburgers), but on reflection it is not. What if a hamburger has a special sauce—what is anyone to make of this? What does it mean? People are always concerned with what things mean.

Enter marketing.

As marketing managers, we must tell people what to make of our hamburgers, we must make them meaningful. To wit: Our hamburgers were created by Dave, the founder of the company. He invented a special sauce by experimenting in his kitchen. Because of the sauce, our company is successful. Naturally the sauce is a family secret: You can only get it on our hamburgers.

Dave's burgers are more than a particular kind of hamburger with their special sauce. They have become a brand with a meaning attached to them. These burgers are something someone might value more by virtue of comprehending this meaning. Now: A hamburger is a hamburger is a hamburger.

Meaning is more than description or wordsmithing, although words are a way of expressing meaning. Nor is meaning to be confused with fabrication or exaggeration, though this can be involved (our secret sauce may or may not be hype). Meaning is the idea of the thing. Whatever the product *is,* meaning is how it is to be understood from the consumer's perspective. Does it matter if we offer Coke versus Pepsi with our hamburgers? It does because the two have very different meanings. Coke is tradition; it is classic refreshment. Pepsi is the future; it is the taste of youth and possibility. Whatever words we use to express the difference, we are not describing what Coke or Pepsi is so much as what they stand for.

What something is versus what it means may strike some as a distinction without much of a difference. But the difference can be profound. If you need proof, think of things that are the same but which have very different meanings. Gestures are like this. A finger to the side of the head means a rueful "my mistake" in some cultures. In others it means, "you're stupid" and is a grave insult. The gesture is the same, but the difference in meaning is profound. Foods are like this too. People eat things with delight that others find disgusting. Grasshoppers might not do well in the United States as condiments at Taco Bell. In Mexico, things are different (they're great, by the way). Though the difference may be sharper in these examples, the distinction between a thing and its meaning is an important difference for products.

Meaning is the stuff of brands.

MARKETERS AND BRANDS

Knowledgeable marketers share a sense that brands are all about meaning. Unfortunately, most discussions of branding in business books and the press tend to oversimplify. The core issue of meaning is often obfuscated by catchy terms that imply that there is some magic, and even a proprietary secret at stake. Thus over the years we have been given a panoply of buzzwords for talking about branding that probably do as much harm as good. According to various accounts, branding entails a unique selling proposition, a big idea, an image, a benefit, a promise, or positioning. More recently, we've seen the terms: brand essence, brand equity, and brand personality. Such discussions often obscure the fact that branding is the complex business of making a product meaningful.

Once we know what it is to market a brand, the obvious question is how do you approach branding as a matter of business practice? That issue is the focus of this chapter. It is an issue that has received almost no systematic attention in the literature. We believe, however, that it is becoming imperative for companies to give their approach to branding more active consideration.

We should hasten to clarify what we mean by "approach to branding." We do not mean the organizational structure of the marketing function or the business processes involved in marketing. The issue we address is more fundamental. What paradigm (or theory or framework or, for that matter, what logic) should guide how a company puts branding into practice? The one thing about paradigms is that if you are engaged in any practice you have one, even if you think you don't. Branding is no exception. There are in fact two paradigms that now guide (at least imply) the practice of branding in many companies. One we call "Branding by Marketing Planning," the other "Branding by Advertising." We will describe each of these paradigms. Our purpose is to discuss these two existing paradigms as background to proposing a third approach that we call "Brand Design."

BRANDING BY MARKETING PLANNING

Branding can be approached as part of the strategic planning process. Usually this occurs in the context of the annual marketing plan.

Marketing plans vary widely. Most are heavy with sales projections and budgeted expenses for marketing activities. But even the most operationally oriented plan must give some sense of strategic initiative. The typical plan thus begins with a review of the market situation including consumer trends and research, and competitive intelligence. Whether a big part of the plan or not, there is an effort to develop a strategy based on this information that gives direction to the marketing activities and gives credibility to the sales projections.

The strategy takes the form of "increase distribution in channel X" or "take share from competitor Y." Some companies have learned that such statements of strategy are not enough. Strategy statements have to make it clear why consumers/customers will respond. To leap from "take share from competitor Y" to spend more for "advertising that targets current buyers of Y" begs the question of why these consumers will switch and, more important, limits strategic direction.

What is missing from these statements of strategy? A sense of what it will *mean* to buyers of Y to switch. In other words, strategy must specify why the existing meaning of the brand or, more likely, why changes in the meaning of the brand will produce the desired response. The link from intent to brand to action provides a much more complete strategic direction.

Perhaps the most common way of making the strategy more complete is to include a *positioning statement* in the plan (see Chapter 2). This is a short description of the meaning of the brand or the revised meaning of the brand. Formats for writing the positioning statement vary. A common one is to define the brand in a single sentence written for (but not to) targeted consumers:

To *(target)* our Brand is *(concept)* that *(point-of-difference)*.

The concept is the main idea of the brand that makes it meaningful. The point-of-difference is how this idea differs from and is more credible than related (competitor) ideas. Alternative formats might be stated in terms of meaningful benefits or frames of reference that are supported (versus competitors) by reasons to believe (reasons why).

To illustrate, let's return to hamburgers. Our plan is to attack a competitor who has a broad customer base by focusing on young males. Our research shows that young males prefer large, oversized hamburgers. Our product line will feature big hamburgers. But we also need to develop branding in our marketing plan. What will it mean to our consumers to leave the competitor and switch to us? We could, of course, just *sell* the big hamburgers. The better plan, however, is to *market* a brand that helps us attract the customers. Our marketing plan might look like Figure 3.1.

Branding by Marketing Planning makes a lot of sense. It allows the planning process to give real strategic direction to marketing activities. We want to consider here, however, the implications for relying on the annual planning context to formulate brand meaning.

Note that the positioning statement and related formats necessarily lead to a description of brand meaning that is very abstract. Brand meaning may be clear at this abstract level but it is not concrete enough. There is only the general idea of the brand. It is not that we want the idea to be completely concrete (this poses its own problem as we will see in the next section). But it would be better if the idea were what Bill Backer has referred to as an

Figure 3.1
Branding That Is Developed from the Marketing Plan

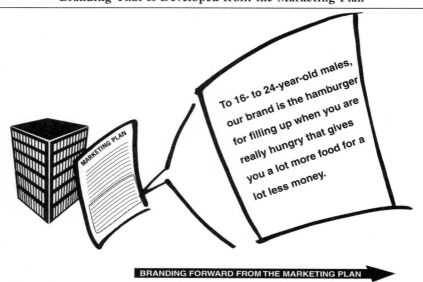

executable idea.[1] An executable idea is one that is readily turned into concrete manifestations, without being locked up in particular executions. Branding by Marketing Planning typically lacks this executability and though clear, it is still abstract and overly encompassing.

We have a clear sense of the meaning of our brand from the positioning statement in Figure 3.1. But there are many ways to go if you try to pin down the meaning a little more. Does "really hungry" mean hunger pangs or being in a certain mood? Or does it relate more to a social situation, guys going out?

With this approach, the wordsmithing of a brand's positioning is notoriously challenging. At such an abstract level, it is difficult to know what words to choose and the choice often seems arbitrary. There are pressures to be as general and inclusive as possible to attract the maximum number of consumers. Unfortunately, doing so can have a watering-down effect. Phrases such as "when you are really hungry" are likely to become "really hungry or in a hurry."

Along the same lines, it is also easy to lapse into management speak with words like "quality" and "reliable" creeping in without any clear meaning ("a high quality hamburger for when you are really hungry").

Beyond this, even the best descriptions of brand meaning under this approach have the limitation that they are buried in the marketing plan. Once the plan is done, it is apt to sit. Many of the people who may need to know about the meaning of the brand may never even see the marketing plan.

BRANDING BY ADVERTISING

Branding can also be approached in more of a functional, as opposed to a strategic, way. Usually this approach means that branding is addressed in the creation of advertising, which in turn often means that the advertising agency takes a leading role. In many ways, this approach to branding is the flip side of the Branding by Marketing Planning approach.

Advertising creatives must be concerned with the meaning of the brand. It is possible to create an ad that simply presents the product, gives a few basic facts about it, and maybe a picture. But any creative person would know that this is not the absence of any branding. Meaning is being conveyed through such minimalist style. Advertising is the attachment of meaning to the product and is thus necessarily linked to branding.

The issue is whether the creation of the advertising is used to define the meaning of the brand. Does the branding come out of the advertising? Or is the branding guiding the advertising (as in the Branding by Marketing Planning approach)?

Return to our product line of big hamburgers. An ad agency might well conclude that the campaign has to show that our burger can fill up any young man. A creative idea would be to show football players—huge linemen—eating the burgers; something like Figure 3.2. A number of players known for their size could be used to generate interest. The expressions on the players' faces would show that they are serious about getting filled up. The meaning is obvious: If our hamburgers satisfy them, they will satisfy you, too.

The agency might well prepare a communication plan and a copy platform in creating the campaign. Chances are, however, that the creative tack (the football players) taken in the actual advertising will influence the brand meaning. That is, in this scenario, the description of brand meaning will be predicated on advertising's creative direction rather than vice versa.

In addition, many agencies like to describe brand meaning so that it is closely linked to advertising execution. For instance, many agencies see brand meaning as a *promise* to the consumer. An ad for a wireless phone promises it "has the rate plan that is perfect for your calling needs." Advertising lends itself to promising and therefore it is natural to view brand

Figure 3.2
Branding That Is Developed Backward from Advertising

BRANDING BACKWARD FROM ADVERTISING

meaning as the promise. However, you can see with the wireless phone example that while this might work as an executional device for ads, it is rather hollow and empty when it comes to the brand. The ad promises the right plan for me, but what is the meaning of the brand (the wireless phone) that makes the promise credible.

The Branding by Advertising approach is not limited to ad agencies. Its biggest practitioners are found in companies where managers believe that they should not think about the meaning of their brands until they see advertising creative. There have, indeed, been very high-level executives known to repeat as a mantra: "How can I know what my brand is until I get some advertising that works? Then I'll know."

What are the implications for relying on the Branding by Advertising approach? The critical thing is that the advertising must be good. Advertising failure means brand failure. On the other hand, great advertising can produce a meaningful brand.

If the lightning of great advertising does not strike, however, there are real limitations inherent in the Branding by Advertising approach. One we have already touched on is that much advertising, far from being creative, is rather conventional and formulaic. Are we really sure the football players are the stuff of our brand, even if they do get attention as celebrities?

Note, too, that here advertising comes late in the marketing process. Even if the ads do help define the brand, it may be too late to bring the power of the brand to other functional areas. Ideally, the brand should help guide product design, distribution, pricing, and other decisions. It may be too late to do so with Branding by Advertising.

This approach has almost exactly the reverse problem as the Branding by Marketing Planning approach. There the description of brand meaning can be overly abstract and not sufficiently executable. With the Branding by Advertising approach, the meaning is often too concrete. It is already locked up in a set of executions. As Backer points out, the execution must be separated from the underlying idea. Again, are the football players a communications device or do they literally capture the meaning of the brand? With this approach, we may not see that the brand could have a larger, richer meaning than that conveyed by a particular set of ads.

THE BRAND DESIGN APPROACH

If there are practical limitations to approaching the brand as part of marketing planning just as there are practical limitations to approaching the brand as part of advertising execution, how should we approach it? Our view is that a third way is needed. It preserves the advantages of the two existing approaches and extends beyond them in at least three ways. First, it is fully *consumer focused*. It starts with the consumer, not with what the company wants for its strategy or with how creatives want to do ads. Second, the approach results in a description of brand meaning that is neither too abstract nor too concrete, executable but not overly encompassing. The approach shows how meaning is to be attached to the product. It results in a *design*. Third, the approach involves the entire organization, not just marketing or communications, in a process of *internal dialogue*. In short, the objective is a *consumer-focused design negotiated after internal dialogue*.

Consumer Focus

Branding is an effort to make products more meaningful to consumers. The place to look for potential sources of meaning is in the consumer's life.

By life we mean some part of the consumer's everyday experience. Something happens, then something else happens, then something else. These observations may occur over a long period of time or a very brief encounter. It may be at home or at work (especially if we are in search of meaning for business products). Or, it may involve a combination of places.

In looking at the consumer's life, we want to look for narrative threads. There are things that happen, then are connected, and ultimately come to some kind of ending. It is useful to think of this sequence as a story, a play, or a movie. There are scenes, events unfold, and the narrative plays out. But remember, we are usually looking at ordinary life as played out by large numbers of people (whom we call consumers or customers).

In any story with a narrative thread, there is a certain amount of dramatic tension. Things could turn out for better or worse in the end. Therefore, when we look at the consumer's life for stories there are three possibilities: (1) stories where things are already turning out well, (2) stories that are unresolved, and (3) stories that are turning out poorly. The latter two offer more potential because there is always the possibility of making things turn out better. A story is of interest if we see the potential for a better ending.

Things that affect the consumer's life are, by definition, meaningful and relevant. And things that make for a better ending are also valuable. Thus, any story in which we see the possibility for meaningful, relevant value is a potential branding opportunity—if we can attach the product to this meaningful, relevant value.

A consumer story for hamburgers? Try this one. Once upon a time, there was a Dad, a Mom, and 2.3 little kids. The kids loved to go out to fast-food restaurants. They liked hamburgers, but really liked fries and shakes. Best of all they could fidget and get up and down and even play around during the meal without getting yelled at.

Dad liked to go out, too. It was fun to be with the kids when they were having fun. And you could really fill up on the burgers and splurge on the kids ("Thank you, Daddy!"). All for not much money.

But Mom was not happy. She resisted when Dad and the kids suggested going out for fast-food hamburgers. The food did not appeal to her and she did not approve of what her family ate. By the time they returned home, she was in a bad mood, often saying that no one appreciated her cooking.

How could this story have a better ending? How about Dad and the kids taking Mom out for a break so that she could relax and the family could have fun and enjoy each other. The hamburgers would not be the main point. The meaning lies in family, fun, and Mom being appreciated and appreciating the family having fun.

With the brand design approach, we focus on the consumer's life and look for stories to which we can add meaning—meaning that is relevant and adds value to the consumer's life. If we can find a good story and attach meaningful relevant value to our product, we have the start of a brand.

Design as Brand Expression

There are always many versions of a story and alternative sets of characters (just as Hollywood can make the same movie many times). The role of the story in the Brand Design approach is to help us see meaningful, relevant value and to give it a more concrete form by grounding the meaning in the life experience of the consumer. We still need to make this meaning more concrete and executable. *We need to figure out how to express the meaning so that it attaches to the product.*

What we need is a design for the brand. A design is not the same as an execution, nor is it a blueprint. It is a look, a feel, a sensibility that captures an underlying meaning. Think of famous designers. Many different things from clothes to food could reflect Ralph Lauren. (Yes, there could be a Ralph Lauren hamburger). Ralph Lauren is a design that can be imposed on many more things—it is no accident that Ralph Lauren is a brand. Do not think, however, that design must mean high fashion. The use of script lettering on a can of Coca-Cola, or the image of the glass bottle, is no less design. Again, a design simply expresses meaning.

Meaning can be expressed in many ways. It can be expressed *verbally* through words (and sounds). Or it can be expressed *visually* through pictures and images. Touch and smell are also possible, though more for the future when it comes to branding. The Internet carries the possibility, for instance, of at some point mixing a unique smell (just as with RGB color) for release from a computer. So every time a brand of charcoal-broiled hamburgers is encountered, the consumer gets not just verbal and visual images, but an olfactory one as well—a whiff of hamburgers cooking on the outside grill.

In thinking through how to express meaning, it is useful to divide the verbal and the visual to give them equal attention and then to distinguish among major ways of expressing verbal and visual meaning. Such a division shows distinct differences.

Verbal

- *Naming.* Giving descriptive or figurative names to the product and company to reflect meaning (e.g., "I Can't Believe It's Not Butter").

- *Wording.* Developing a lexicon of words that become a vocabulary having special meaning (e.g., "Super size it").
- *Describing.* Composing phrases and sentences that uniquely capture meaning (e.g., "Good to the last drop").

Visual

- *Picturing.* Illustrating meaning with photographs or drawings of actual things (e.g., "Hot dogs on the grill").
- *Symbolizing.* Signifying meaning through more abstract images and graphics, including fonts (e.g., "A red-white-blue globe").
- *Animating.* Conveying meaning by the movement and morphing of objects (e.g., "A pin dropping").

The schematic diagram in Figure 3.3 brings these elements together. By working out the expression of the central meaningful, relevant value, in any or all of the forms, we have devised a design for the brand. This design can be used as an executable idea that can be reflected in many ways.

Figure 3.3
Brand Design Schematic

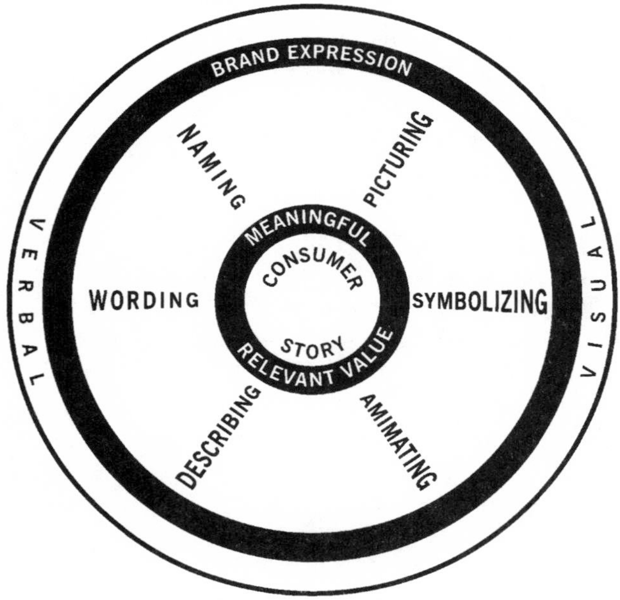

It can certainly be used as a standard for evaluating all marketing communications (a point to which we will return). The design is a standard to aspire to in making sure the meaning of the brand is communicated.

Let us return to our story about hamburgers and Mom, Dad, and the kids. If meaningful relevant value lies in a break for Mom with a fun family experience, how can we express this scenario? With a bow to the history of a very successful brand, the design might be laid out as in Figure 3.4. (Our purpose here is not to get into the current situation of the brand, but to capture the design that expresses the brand in terms of the original meaningful, relevant value.) McDonald's, the brand, is a combination of verbal and visual images that express meaning. Figure 3.4 provides a sense of this tessellation through collage.

Dialogue

Any organization contains many groups. Each of these groups relates to the company's product(s) in different ways. Many of the groups will care,

Figure 3.4
McDonald's Brand Design

some may even care passionately, about the meaning of a product: engineers in a technical company, medical people in a health care organization, editorial staff in a newspaper, the family in a private company, all come to mind. These groups have their own stories and their own values tied to their meaning of the product. If brand meaning is approached in a way that excludes them, these groups will usually ignore branding in the decisions they make and may even actively resist branding efforts.

R&D groups within a company are a good example of this phenomenon. These groups are charged with developing products and as such are ordinarily concerned with technical issues about how the product performs. In the case of a paint product, for example, R&D may be captivated by the fact that a particular formula dries faster than a current product or a competitor's product. Indeed this may represent an engineering breakthrough. Marketing on the other hand may have concluded that the best consumer meaning for the product revolves around the paint's retaining its color "like new" over time. Emphasizing that the paint dries faster might actually detract from this meaning by making the paint seem cheaper or more for casual use. The R&D people, however, may well see this as a failure to appreciate the technical merits of the product, which may lead them to resist cooperating with the marketing people.

One of the major problems with Branding by Marketing Planning or Branding by Advertising is that both approach branding as the provenance of a small group of marketing or communications people in the company. These approaches can thus aggravate conflicts with other groups in the company who approach the product from a different perspective. Attention may be given to general communications issue such as corporate identity in the event of a merger. But such broader thinking is by no means the norm and certainly does not engage other internal constituencies in branding. R&D and other groups feel that they must compete with marketing for a voice in product decisions. With these approaches, branding is likely to be viewed as only the narrow concern of the marketing or communications group.

An *internal communications process* is integral to Brand Design. The final brand design must be consumer-focused. It should, however, take into account internal constituencies that attach different meanings to the product. Ideally, these meanings can be adopted to, or made compatible with, the consumer meaning of the product as a brand.

Doing so will require a dialogue among members of different groups and consumers. Consumers may actually be part of the dialogue or may be represented by someone who can play the role of dialogue participant for them.

Daniel Yankelovich provides an excellent examination into the nature of dialogues as a communication process.[2] Dialogues are not debates or discussions. They represent an effort to listen with empathy to other groups where all groups are on an equal footing and each group makes its assumptions clear. Depending on the level of mistrust among the groups, the process may be more or less elaborate. When there is passionate commitment to product meanings that define a culture within the organization, an extended dialogue over many sessions is required. When dialogue is more about examining the meaning of the product from several points of view (including the consumer's), one or two sessions may suffice.

The crucial point is this: It is only after the dialogue process is completed and people have clarified their assumptions and listened with empathy and equality, that branding is addressed. At this point, negotiation takes place around the brand design. If there are compromises to be made, they are made in full understanding of the different points of view. Branding is freed from misunderstandings and turf wars.

Branding may require a little dialogue or a lot. In either case, the expectation is that the brand design will be something that the entire company can understand and embrace. While the final brand design must be consumer-focused, an internal communication process is essential. Negotiating the meaning of the brand so that whenever possible the point of view of internal constituencies is represented in the consumer meaning of the brand will ensure that decisions are not made that undermine the brand in the minds of consumers. In our paint example, perhaps the final brand meaning is something like this: A paint retains color in part because it dries faster to lock in color.

Integrated Marketing/Communications

Our third approach to branding results in a *consumer-focused design negotiated through internal dialogue.* This approach has definite advantages over Branding by Marketing Planning or Branding by Advertising. It provides even more consumer focus around the actual lives of consumers and defines relevance in terms of consumer lives rather than by reference to product attributes. It is more executable because it expresses meaning in terms of underlying core imagery rather than leaving this to advertising execution. And it is likely to be synergistic with other product constituencies within the organization rather than provoking turf wars between marketing and other groups. Moreover, there is an additional, more compelling, reason for considering the Brand Design approach.

The way in which consumers learn about the brand meaning of products is changing. Consumers do not learn about products via any single medium. Seeing it on television, reading about the promotion in the newspaper, buying it at the store are only some of many possibilities. Consumers use a growing array of media to learn about products. Audiences are becoming more fragmented across media. Increasingly consumers expect to have nonmedia contacts with products and companies. How to market and communicate in an integrated way so that the brand is not lost in all this complexity is the challenge of the future.

The Brand Design approach provides a mechanism for achieving integration. As depicted in Figure 3.5, the Brand Design can serve as a core protocol for contacts with the consumer. Any communication that follows the design should let the consumer see the meaning of the brand. The different elements of the Brand Design serve as the basis for communication through any medium. The specifics of any one communication are integrated with all other communications through the overarching meaning of the brand.

Figure 3.5
Integration through Brand Design

CHANGING THE BRAND WITH TIME

One further issue to keep in mind: Branding is about change. You only have to look at hamburgers and McDonald's to be convinced. As eating in fast-food restaurants becomes more and more a routine of daily life, consumers find less relevance in the nonfood experience. Thus McDonald's has, at this writing, been forced to give more attention to the food product, making it hotter, better, fresher. All the same, it will remain a fast-food chain. Its goal has to be to move beyond memories of the fun family outing to find new relevance in the way food is cooked and presented.

Branding is an act of "creative destruction" that changes the meaning of relatively more stable products as the lives of consumers change with time. The more things change, the more they stay the same. It is the meaning that is different.

Notes

1. Bill Backer, *The Care and Feeding of Ideas* (New York: Times Books, 1993).
2. Daniel Yankelovich, *The Magic of Dialogue* (New York: Simon & Schuster, 1999).

CHAPTER 4

CREATING AND MANAGING BRANDS

ALICE M. TYBOUT and GREGORY S. CARPENTER

Brands are one of the most universal aspects of modern markets. Nearly every company, whether or not it competes in consumer markets, has a brand—an identity, a name, a reputation. Goldman Sachs, USX, and Cargill are all focused on business-to-business transactions and have brands that are recognized by their buyers, just as Coca-Cola or Mercedes-Benz are known to their consumers. Every business that has customers, implicitly or explicitly, has a brand in one form or another. Similarly, nearly every consumer has seen, used, or purchased brands, and has experience with brands. As a result, brands play an important role in buyers' lives; brands provide functionality, images, and experiences, as in the case of Tide, Ralph Lauren, and Disney, respectively.

The value brands deliver to buyers has evolved as consumers and competition have changed. When competition was less intense, product quality and the value products offered varied to a degree unknown in most markets today, creating substantial risk for consumers. The quality of automobiles, restaurant meals, and even coffee varied widely. In such markets, brands served primarily as a means of signaling a consistent level of quality that one could expect to receive from a product. McDonald's, Holiday Inn, and Toyota all grew to be important symbols of consistent quality and consistent value. Since markets have become more competitive and the product quality more consistent, brands have evolved to offer yet different value. For many consumers, life has become more complicated, time too short, and the array of alternatives bewildering. At the same time, new technologies have created unfamiliar new markets and redefined familiar markets. Mobile telephones, the latest technology in a nearly century-old market, are progressing at an incredible pace, merging with the Internet, and requiring consumers to choose between CDMA, TDMA, iDen, or even

GSM format phones. Brands such as Motorola or Nokia instantly convey valuable information about what to expect from otherwise complex products. Brands serve consumers by saving time, assuring a level of quality, and simplifying choice. But brands have evolved to mean even more. In many product categories, the brand name, rather than the product, is now the primary basis for choosing one product over another. In the auto industry, for example, benchmarking and intense competition have resulted in near parity products, and the brand name is the primary characteristic distinguishing, say, a Lexus from a Toyota.

The power of brands with consumers translates directly into profits for those who own them. Indeed, Harry Silverman, CEO of Cendant, built his company on the premise that the brand is the *only* thing worth owning—everything else should be sold off. Cendant owns a variety of brands, including Days Inn, Super 8, Howard Johnson, Ramada, Century 21, Coldwell Banker, and Avis. When Silverman bought each of these companies, the first thing he did was to sell the assets to firms that were willing to manage the day-to-day operations of these businesses. Cars crash, buildings burn, but brands endure, Silverman reasons. Why own depreciating assets when someone else will? Instead of focusing on tangible assets, Silverman spends his time and energy building, extending, and milking brand names.

Silverman's faith in the power of brands is borne out by a recent assessment of the *World's Most Valuable Brands*.[1] The 1998 results of this study, which is conducted annually by Interbrand, reveal that the most valuable brand, Coca-Cola, is worth $84 billion. This figure is the value of the *brand,* apart from the remaining assets of the Coca-Cola Company. By way of comparison, the market capitalization of Home Depot is $88 billion. Moreover, the results indicate that the value of many well-established global brands accounts for more than half the entire market capitalization of the companies that own them (see Table 4.1). Specifically, 77 percent of Nike's, BMW's, and Apple's market value can be attributed to the value of these brands, while a full 59 percent of Coca-Cola's market capitalization reflects the value of its brand. The observation that many dot.com companies are spending heavily in an effort to build their brands indicates the continued appreciation of the power of brands in the so-called new economy. Several of these newer Internet brands (e.g., AOL, Yahoo!, and Amazon.com) made the $1 billion cut for Interbrand's list of the *World's Most Valuable Brands*. As yet, the value of these brands is low relative to their market capitalization. However, a recent study conducted by Corporate Branding, suggests that e-brands are rapidly rising in value, and doing so at the expense of established brands such as Coca-Cola and Disney.[2]

Table 4.1
Brand Value and Market Capitalization

Brand	Industry	Market Capitalization (billions)	Brand Value (billions)
Coca-Cola	Beverages	$142.2	$83.8
Disney	Entertainment	52.5	32.3
McDonald's	Food	40.9	26.2
BMW	Autos	14.6	11.2
Nike	Sporting goods	10.5	8.1
Apple	Computers	5.5	4.3
AOL	Software	24.0	4.3
Ralph Lauren	Clothing	2.5	1.6
Yahoo!	Software	12.7	1.8
amazon.com	Books	18.5	1.4

In this chapter, we examine how brands create such value. We begin by elaborating on the questions: What is a brand? How are brands created? We then turn to an examination of three different types of brands: functional brands, image brands, and experiential brands. We consider how each type of brand is best managed and how it may be leveraged through brand extensions. Finally, we explore three branding strategies; corporate, family, product, and relate these alternative approaches to the types of brands.

WHAT IS A BRAND?

Despite almost universal experience with brands, they remain poorly understood. When queried about why they buy brands such as Coca-Cola, Ralph Lauren, or Mercedes-Benz, consumers' responses typically reflect little insight into the appeal of brands. "Coca-Cola tastes better than Pepsi," some will argue. "Ralph Lauren's clothes fit me best and, besides, they're well made." "Mercedes-Benz is an incredibly well-engineered car; it will last forever." These reasons may or may not be true, but few consumers can reliably distinguish between brands of soft drinks, and most consumers in the United States keep their cars for only a few short years. Rather than deriving value from the product, buyers often seek and gain much more value from the brand, whether it is Coca-Cola, Ralph Lauren, or Mercedes-Benz. But what is that value?

On the most basic level, a brand is a name or some symbol or mark that is associated with a product or service and to which buyers attach psychological meanings. Salt in a jar is a simple chemical substance, sodium chloride. Buyers have few associations with this substance, except perhaps for some recollections from chemistry class. Morton's Salt, on the other hand, may evoke memories of childhood, baking with Mom, and dependability. Many will easily recall, for example, that "When it rains, it pours." Likewise, a brown, fizzy, sweet soft drink is a product that many find difficult to identify correctly in a blind taste test. Coca-Cola, however, is much more than a product. It is a brand that, as it turns out, consumers feel so passionately about that they resist any effort to change it as a matter of principle; something the company learned when it introduced New Coke. Without associations and without emotion, Coca-Cola would be just water, sugar, and some spices.

The number and combination of associations that can be attached to any product to create a brand is infinite. Consider bottled water, for instance, another simple product (although slightly more complex than salt). Perrier is seen as French, with all that implies: European, sophisticated, refined, if expensive. Poland Springs, on the other hand (owned, interestingly enough, by Perrier), has as its brand equity some of the associations conveyed by its Maine heritage: honest, independent, and reasonably priced. Looking at another product category underscores the range of meanings that brands in the same product category may have. In sports utility vehicles, Toyota offers dependability, quality, and value. BMW offers driving excitement, performance, and fine engineering.

A brand can be represented visually as a network of thoughts or associations in the consumer's head. For example, consider Ralph Lauren. Through his Polo line of fashion, Ralph Lauren has created a modern expression of the English country life, the landed gentry and all that it implies—sophistication, tradition, refined taste, and understatement. This is the essential brand equity of Polo Ralph Lauren (see Figure 4.1). By contrast, another clothing brand, Levi's blue jeans, has established quite a different set of associations: American, rebellious, rugged, and youthful. Still other brands have a simpler set of associations, but these may be no less powerful. Wal-Mart is first and foremost a store with the lowest everyday prices. For decades, IBM was known primarily as being the "safe choice" for computers.

A brand's associations can be remarkably valuable to buyers. Water can be obtained easily and inexpensively in most of the world. Being French, to those not lucky enough to be so born, is more difficult. Living the English country life, though not impossible, is unlikely for most buyers. Rather than simply bottling water or manufacturing fine clothing, Perrier and Ralph Lauren make what is the privilege of the few available to the many. For that they are handsomely rewarded.

Figure 4.1
Consumer Associations to the Ralph Lauren Brand

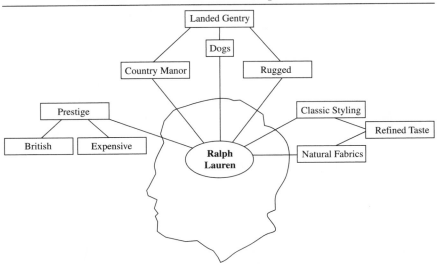

For a brand to have value, these associations must become part of buyers' lives. When a consumer walks into a grocery and sees Coca-Cola or Morton's Salt, if there is no evocation of the brand equity, then the brand has none. Brand equity—though created through product design, advertising, distribution, and all other ways the organization touches the buyer—must ultimately reside in the minds of buyers. Without that, a brand is a product with a meaningless name attached to it.

The distinction between a product and a brand is expressed well by Stephen King of WPP Group, London:

> A product is something that is made in a factory; a brand is something that is bought by a customer. A product can be copied by a competitor; a brand is unique. A product can be quickly outdated; a successful brand is timeless.

HOW DO YOU BUILD A BRAND?

A common misconception is that building a brand is simply a matter of developing some clever advertising to create a desired set of associations. Certainly advertising plays an important role in building many brands, especially those that seek to differentiate from competitors on the basis of their image. However, to be successful, even image brands must have a product, a price, and a distribution channel that support the image communicated through advertising. Advertising is simply a more central component of marketing mix for some brands compared with others, as we shall discuss in greater detail later in the chapter.

To understand better the process of building a brand, consider a brand that was built from scratch, Saturn.[3] The goal for Saturn was quite ambitious: Saturn was conceived with the goal of being a world class product; a compact vehicle developed in the United States that would be a leader in quality, cost, and customer satisfaction. Saturn began by designing a strong product and offering it to the market at a reasonable price. High product quality was communicated by offering a money back guarantee within 30 days or 1,500 miles. This support for the claim that Saturn was a high quality product was important, perhaps necessary, in light of consumers' perception of the parent company, GM. However, while the car was well-designed and offered a great value, Saturn, wisely did not make functional aspects of the car the basis for brand differentiation.

Saturn quickly become known as a unique, American car company that marketed no-nonsense, reliable cars. These associations might have been used to build a brand based on the car's image. Consumers who view themselves as practical and patriotic, might have been invited to choose Saturn as a means of communicating these values to those around them. Saturn, no doubt, attracted many such consumers, but it resisted the temptation to build its brand based on this imagery.

Instead, Saturn built its brand around a key insight regarding American consumers. It recognized that for most consumers, buying a car is a distinctly unpleasant experience, as are most interactions with car dealers. Saturn sought to change all this. The essence of the Saturn idea was to invite customers into a relationship with a car company that treats them as a friend—with regard and respect. Sadly, this idea is seen by many as truly innovative in the auto industry. In contrast to the typical car buying experience, Saturn created a pleasant shopping environment. Salaried sales consultants, many of whom were hired from outside the auto industry to avoid perpetuating traditional selling tactics, were well-informed and helpful. The company's fixed price policy eliminated unpleasant haggling over price and reduced the buyer's anxiety about overpaying due to being a poor negotiator. When recalls were necessary, dealers sponsored events such as barbecues and outings to baseball games to entertain customers while their cars were serviced and washed. Dealer-sponsored gatherings of Saturn owners and tours of Saturn plants personalized the experience of owning a Saturn.

Advertising played a critical role in capturing the corporate personality, as reflected in the people who created and consumed the brand. Early ads featured employees talking about how they came together to build the Saturn culture and the pride that they felt in seeing the first car roll off the assembly line. Later ads shifted attention to customers and their passion for their cars. In all advertising, the people who were associated with the product were central, rather than the product. Advertising summarized the central concept underlying the Saturn brand with the tag line, "A different kind of company, a different kind of car."

Did Saturn build a product that was a leader in quality, cost, and customer satisfaction? Yes, it did. But that description fails to capture the essence of a brand that prompted nearly 100,000 owners from places as far away as Alaska to drive to Spring Hill for the Saturn Homecoming at the plant in June of 1994. One couple attending got married during the event, with the president of Saturn giving the bride away!

The answer to the question, "How do you build a brand?" is complex. The building of a brand is guided by a vision of the desired positioning (see Chapter 2), and is implemented by *all* the decisions related to the marketing mix. The relative importance of different elements of the marketing mix may vary, however, as a function of the type of brand that the company hopes to create. Had Saturn wished to create a *functional brand*, the focus would have been on creating associations based on the physical features of the car and the benefits that they provided. Had the goal been to build an *image brand*, greater emphasis would have been given to creating a personality for the car via advertising and other communications.

Saturn chose to create an *experiential brand*. Doing so entailed designing a strong product and pricing it fairly. And the brand undoubtedly came to have a personality—that of a thoughtful, friendly, unpretentious person. But the central associations were not to the car, but rather to the larger experience of owning a Saturn and to the relationship that owners felt with the company. In the next section, we consider these three types of brands and how they are best managed in greater detail.

TYPES OF BRANDS

Functional Brands

Functional brands are bought by consumers to satisfy functional needs—to wash their clothes, to relieve pain, to transport one's family. Many of consumers' associations with these brands are, as one would expect, related to the physical features and basic functions of the product. Successful functional brands are closely tied in buyers' minds to specific product categories and they often share many associations with other brands in the same product category. Tide is nearly synonymous with clean clothes, for instance. Beyond serving basic needs, many functional brands differentiate from their competitors, which offer much if not all of the same functionality, by offering *superior performance* or by providing *superior economy*.

Superior Performance. Gillette and its razor brands, MACH3, Sensor, Atra, Trac II, are functional brands. Gillette is strongly linked to the wet shaving category and to the function of products belonging to that category: providing a close, comfortable shave. When each Gillette brand was launched, it was positioned as offering superior performance relative to the brands that went before it. Currently, MACH3, with its triple-bladed system, claims to provide the closest, most comfortable shave available. Consumers may also have more general associations to Gillette's shaving products. For example, MACH3 may be viewed as masculine and futuristic, but first and foremost, it is a shaving system. Gillette created and maintains its position of the leading shaving company by investing heavily in R&D.

Detergents such as Tide (United States) and Ariel (Europe) are also strong functional brands that compete on the basis of superior performance. Tide and Ariel are strongly associated with the detergent category and these brands strive to differentiate from other detergents in terms of providing the cleanest wash. Like Gillette, P&G focuses considerable resources on improving these brands to retain their leading position in the detergent category.

Many business-to-business brands are functional brands. Two classic examples are IBM and Caterpillar (for earth-moving equipment). Both built extraordinary brands by using customer service as the basis for creating superior performance. When IBM entered the market, competitors such as RCA were focused on making larger, faster computers and they offered products that out-performed IBM's computers. However, customer service was relatively neglected. As a result, customers experienced significant downtime. IBM addressed this issue by offering excellent customer service. This service enhanced the product performance by increasing computer uptime. The more abstract benefit, confidence that customers could count on the equipment that they purchased from IBM, was communicated through advertising, which showed a pillow with the IBM logo on it. The caption simply read, "What people want from a computer is a good night's sleep." Thus, the safe choice was born.

Caterpillar earth-moving equipment has built an incredibly loyal group of users through a similar strategy. While competitors like Komatsu offer greater performance or lower price, Caterpillar provides unequaled service in the form of providing parts. If a Cat breaks down anywhere in the world, Caterpillar will deliver the necessary parts within 48 hours. Performance is incredibly important to companies that own earth-moving equipment. However, the best performing and lowest priced machine is dead weight if parts are unavailable. Cost is important, but productivity is essential. Through excellent service, Caterpillar ensures its customers' productivity. Other equipment, however attractive it looks, thus carries with it greater risk. Like IBM, Caterpillar built its brand on the realization that superior performance can delivered in innovative ways by thinking beyond the product.

Superior Economy.   An alternative approach to differentiating a functional brand is in terms of how economically the basic functions associated with the product category are performed. Superior economy may be provided by saving time and reducing hassle or by saving money. McDonald's is a functional brand that offers superior economy. When someone says "McDonald's," consumers think "fast food" and "good value." Few think "superior taste." McDonald's is known the world over as the source of a quick, predictable, inexpensive, hot, hassle-free meal. McDonald's competes by striving to satisfy consumers' appetites more consistently and faster than any other fast-food franchise. Dell Computer is also a functional brand that offers superior economy by making the purchase of a computer easy and inexpensive. Sustaining the position of a functional brand that offers superior economy implies the discipline of operational excellence. (See Chapter 1 on Segmentation and Targeting in this volume for a discussion of this and other disciplines.)

Functional brands connect with consumers by helping them achieve basic goals related to physical needs, such as the need for food, shelter, health, or safety. Because consumers vary in their focus on these needs and in their ability to pay for products, both functional brands that focus on superior performance and those that focus on superior economy may succeed in a product category. Some consumers may favor the brand of razor that provides the closest, most comfortable shave, whereas others may prefer the brand that performs adequately and is the least expensive.

Managing Functional Brands

As the foregoing discussion suggests, building functional brands requires focusing resources on either the product (for superior performance) or the place and price elements of the marketing mix (for superior economy). The role of advertising is one of reinforcing the connection between the brand

and the product category and communicating what makes the brand superior to competing products. Advertising itself is not the basis for differentiation, as may be the case for image brands.

To sustain a strong position in the marketplace, functional brands must win the race to provide the best functionality or the lowest cost or both. In many instances, improving performance is taken to mean doing what the brand does currently even better. Thus, Gillette razors have evolved from one to two to three blades, with each additional blade increasing the closeness of the shave without compromising comfort. In the case of semiconductors, quality has continually been raised by Motorola, which now produces products that meet the extraordinary six-sigma standard of excellence.

However, sustaining a point of difference is becoming increasingly difficult. Product life cycles are shortening because competitors can imitate any product performance or economic advantage that a firm creates relatively rapidly. In recent years, this imitation has taken the form of private label or "store" brands. Retailers, whose close contact with customers gives them insight into their desires, contract with manufacturers to produce versions of popular products that bear the retailer's rather than the manufacturer's name. In many categories, private label brands offer quality similar to that of national brands, but at a lower retail price. Some private label products, such as Loblaw's President's Choice Decadent Chocolate Chip Cookies, are actually regarded as being of higher quality than many manufacturer's brands. Overall, private label brands account for roughly 15 percent of U.S. supermarket sales and as much as 36 percent in supermarket sales in countries such as the United Kingdom. In some categories, private label brands in the United Kingdom, such as Marks & Spencer, account for 80 percent of sales!

An alternative strategy is to innovate by adding new functionality to a brand. For example, Gillette might modify MACH3 to not only provide a close, comfortable shave, but also to dispense a skin bracer. Such a strategy would be similar to P&G's approach of combining a shampoo and conditioner in its Pert Plus brand. In essence, a new brand is developed that bundles functionality previously associated with two or more separate product categories.

Expanding functionality may be an attractive strategy in light of several consumer trends. The delineation of roles that consumers play is blurring (e.g., parents take children along on business trips and conduct business via a cell phone while observing a daughter's soccer game) and many consumers report experiencing "time famine." Thus, products that help them cope with these changes are likely to be well-received. Many new technology-based products, such as Smart Phones and PalmVII, are based on the assumption that more functionality in a single product is just what consumers need. However, the challenge will remain one of sustaining any competitive advantage that is created. Already there are multiple brands of smart phones and PDAs. Moreover, there is a risk that some consumers may feel overwhelmed or intimidated by products that seem smarter than the user!

Yet another strategy for growing a functional brand is to extend it into a new product category. Conventional wisdom is that brand extensions should involve a new category that is closely related to the core brand so that the extension will be viewed as appropriate. For functional brands, this implies that extensions should be to product categories that have similar features or that relate to the same need or function at a more abstract level. Thus, MACH3 might appropriately offer a woman's shaver or a line of shaving creams and gels. Similarly, Tide might launch a line of stain-treatment products for the laundry. However, extensions that contradict core associations or that are based on more peripheral associations are likely to fail and, thus, are potentially damaging to the core brand. For example, abrasive scrubbing is a core association for SOS cleaning pads, making the brand extension into a window cleaner (SOS Glassworks) inappropriate.

Image Brands

Image brands create value principally by projecting an image. While they may be based on an extraordinary product, these brands are distinguished from competitors because buyers see them as offering a unique set of associations or image. Image brands are often created in categories where products are relatively undifferentiated or quality is difficult to evaluate (i.e., fine wines, medical, or consulting services), or where consumption of the product is highly visible to others (e.g., cars, shoes, clothing, alcoholic beverages). Under such circumstances, the images attached to the brand add value in terms of distinguishing it from other brands or by serving as a "badge" informing others of one's group membership or accomplishments. In either case, it is the set of images attached to the brand that define the brand's uniqueness and create symbols that are highly valued by buyers. Some brands that begin as functional brands may evolve into image brands if efforts are made to make functional features more abstract and link them to more emotion-laden consumer goals.

Image brands have become increasingly important as competition in many markets has eliminated meaningful differences in products. In autos and mobile phones, for instance, reliability, durability, prices, and even styling have become more similar. Faced with a lack of differentiation, consumers have driven prices down and, in response, organizations have turned to image and the broad array of the options this branding approach affords. Image brands may be created in many ways—by adding product features that evoke images, or make an emotional connection with buyers, by associating a brand with particular types of users, or by clever advertising campaigns. Moreover, image brands may be built for business-to-business products and services, as well as for consumer products and services.

Feature-Based. Some brands create their images by using distinctive product features to create imagery. One such classic example is the Mazda Miata sports car. For many buyers, the British brands MG and Triumph represent the prototypical sports car. The design of the cars, the sense of speed when driving one, and even the sound of the exhaust have had a powerful influence on buyers' view of the ideal sports car. The Mazda Miata is designed to capture the imagery associated with the MG and Triumph sports cars. For example, to re-create the sound of the British sports cars, Mazda tested over 100 different exhaust systems. All were designed to function well, but they varied in terms of the sound that they produced. The goal was to identify the system that would best reproduce the MG/Triumph sound. To re-create the driving feel, Miata speedometers are calibrated so that the sense of speed associated with the MG/Triumph sports car is mimicked. In all, Mazda made a wide variety of product design decisions to collectively evoke the image of the British sports car.

Another good example of feature-based image building is Viking kitchen ranges. As a result of intense competition, fine kitchen ranges are available at a wide range of prices. All of these ranges generate heat in a sufficiently consistent, reliable way to cook well. Viking is no different in this respect. What truly distinguishes Viking ranges is their restaurant style design. Viking ranges are stainless steel and have little, if any, painted surface. They offer an industrial look and are priced at a premium level, out of "range" of many consumers' pocketbooks. Viking has enjoyed huge success. Ironically though, those who purchase Viking and other premium ranges typically do little cooking. The appeal of a restaurant-style range is to make a personal statement to those who visit the home that the owner truly appreciates food—indeed, only the best in food and food preparation.

Waterman pens offer yet another example of image differentiation. Waterman pens certainly perform the writing function, but that alone would not be adequate to justify purchase of a pen in the new $400 Edson line. Choosing an Edson pen is a means of conveying status and refined taste. Indeed, the pen is depicted as being of heirloom quality, something that might be handed down from one generation to the next. Further, by offering a broad array of finishes, Waterman pens enable the users to express their personality in a subtle, sophisticated manner. "Which Waterman are you?" they ask in their advertising. A Waterman pen is more than a fine writing instrument; it is a statement about the user's taste and style.

User Imagery.   Brands also create images by focusing on who uses the brand. Characteristics of the users represent the value of the brand in the minds of buyers. Three companies offer classic examples of branding through user imagery. Nike, founded in the mid-1970s as the Blue Ribbon Sports Company, made an art of the athlete's endorsement. Nike created its images of personal performance, winning, and uniqueness through the endorsements of athletes like Michael Jordan, John McEnroe, and Bo Jackson. The individuals represented the images Nike sought to associate with its brand.

Like Nike, Giorgio Armani has used individuals, in this instance well-known actors and musicians, to personify the Armani brand. An early break for Armani came when Richard Gere wore Armani clothing in the blockbuster "American Gigolo." The movie, one writer noted, was essentially a "two-hour fashion show modeled by Richard Gere's character, Julian Kaye." At the close of the movie as most of the credits rolled by, one credit stood, alone on the screen, frozen for a brief but valuable moment: Giorgio Armani. Since that success, Armani has aggressively pursued celebrities to build his brand. Warren Beatty, Robert DeNiro, Jeremy Irons, Eric Clapton, Tom Hanks, Mel Gibson, Matt Damon, Ricky Martin, and Leonardo DiCaprio have all worn and helped to define the Armani brand—its modern elegance and celebrity. Armani manufacturers little; most of the clothing is made by others. The brand, on the other hand, is perhaps the most successful and enduring Armani creation yet. Armani himself has proclaimed that "it is no longer fashion that matters, but rather the fashion name. The product is secondary."

Apple Computer offers yet a third example of how user imagery can affect brand image. Apple launched as a "different" computer with a novel operating system, challenging IBM, a symbol of corporate America. Although distinguished functionally by an operating system, Apple has become the brand of computer for the iconoclast, someone who worked smarter rather than harder and got ahead by creating the rules, not playing by them. This is reflected in their recent advertising tag line: "Think Different." It draws an interesting, if unintentional contrast to the classic IBM saying: Think.

Advertising.   The classic way to create image brands is through advertising, which often manages to create vivid associations with little reliance on either product features or celebrity users. Brands of bottled water, automobiles, and cigarettes have historically been heavily advertised using images that appeal to the emotional needs of buyers. The elegance of San Pellegrino, the power of the Corvette, and the rugged individuality of the Marlboro Man are enduring images created through advertising.

Pepsi serves as a good illustration of an image brand built through advertising. As a follower in the market to Coca-Cola, Pepsi sought at first to steal share from the leader through a low-priced, me-too strategy. "Twice as much for a nickel," was one advertising slogan that focused on greater value for the same price. These efforts only served to reinforce the dominance of Coca-Cola. Pepsi subsequently adopted a strategy of asserting that it is the beverage for the younger consumer though advertising campaigns such as "The Choice of a New Generation" and, more recently, "Generation Next." By creating the image of being associated with younger users, Pepsi cast Coca-Cola as the beverage of older consumers, thus gaining an advantage.

Brands built solely on advertising can be remarkably successful. Creating them, however, requires heavy, sustained spending of advertising dollars. When new consumers enter the market, if current users do not reinforce the images of the advertising, more advertising dollars must be spent to educate these new buyers. That constant education process is expensive. However, the rewards can be a sustained uniqueness, a price premium, and a larger market share.

Business-to-Business Brands.   While image brands are more commonplace in the consumer realm, they are not absent in the business-to-business world. Business-to-business brands that are based on image fall into two categories: those built exclusively for business customers (i.e., other firms) and those that are focused on end-users or consumers, who are the customers of the firms to which the company's products are sold.

Many business brands are built with an eye on customers. IBM and Caterpillar are two such functional brands discussed previously. Other visible and enduring business-to-business brands are found in the realm of professional services. McKinsey & Company, Boston Consulting Group, and Goldman Sachs are powerful brands, each having unique associations in customers' minds. For such brands, image is often a central concern. In investment banking, image may be created in many ways—through user imagery (their clients), the parent company location (Wall Street, the City of London), how employees dress, and even the firm's stationery. Together these cues tell customers that a firm is powerful, confident, a thought leader, or very stable. Advertising in the form of "tombstones" in the financial pages, listing the deals that the firm has successfully consummated with prestigious clients, reinforces these associations. The tactics used by management consulting firms to create their images are similar.

Other business-to-business brands are directed toward end-users or consumers rather than customers. One of the most successful business-to-consumer brands is Intel. Intel sells microprocessors to firms such as computer manufacturers. As already mentioned, computers are a risky purchase. Without brands to guide buyers' choices, consumers are confronted with an expensive purchase (over $1,000) and no way of knowing whether the computer will perform well. Intel addressed this issue by creating and aggressively marketing the Intel Inside brand. The promise is that if you buy a computer with Intel inside, you've made a safe choice; you'll have the power that you need to run the programs you want. While Intel's competitor, AMD, produces a very competitive microprocessor, many consumers are willing to pay a price premium for the safety and quality assurance that the Intel Inside logo provides. Interestingly, Intel's success may erode the value of computer brands: if a computer has Intel Inside, the brand of the computer becomes secondary. (One exception is Apple.) As a result of greater leverage with customers—created through giving consumers a safe choice—Intel has prospered by branding a product that, in one sense, consumers cannot and would not want to purchase alone.

Although Intel is one of the most visible and successful business-to-consumer brands, it is not alone by any means. DuPont, Nutrasweet, and Perdue all sell their products to other businesses, but they are marketed to consumers. Like Intel, these brands convey valuable information to buyers. The DuPont Stainmaster logo assures a carpet buyer that the product will resist stains and retain its new look. The Nutrasweet brand conveys valuable information about the caloric content and taste of many foods. And, the Perdue brand indicates that the chicken in the package will taste fresh and juicy.

Managing Image Brands.   Image brands succeed when they make an emotional connection with consumers. They address consumers' desire to belong to a larger social group, to be held in esteem by others, or to define one's self according to a particular image. Advertising and other forms of communication (e.g., publicity, event sponsorship, promotions) play a prominent role in developing image brands because the value of these brands stems, in large measure, from a shared interpretation of what using the brand represents rather than the product features.

An examination of consumer trends may reveal opportunities for creating new image brands. As noted earlier, many contemporary consumers experience time famine. Often this means that there is limited opportunity to express certain aspects of their personality or self-identity. Image brands may allow signaling that that part of the self remains alive. For example, driving a Sports Utility Vehicle (SUV) may allow soccer moms and dads to express their desire for an adventurous lifestyle even though they never leave the streets of suburbia.

Building image brands takes time and considerable resources. The images that define these brands must be created in the minds of consumers. In the case of a global brand like Coca-Cola, this means creating images that are meaningful and valuable to consumers around the world; a challenging and endless task. New consumers are born every day who have never heard of Coca-Cola. For the brand to have continued success, those new consumers must somehow be introduced to and accept the images that Coca-Cola offers.

If a firm is successful in building and maintaining these images, its image brands can enjoy considerable competitive advantages. The most obvious benefit is that duplicating the images associated with one brand is difficult, expensive, and of questionable competitive value. Why would a competitor seek to copy the Ralph Lauren image when an infinite array of alternative images that might provide a meaningful basis for competitive distinction can be created? Image brands, thus, offer a considerable degree of insulation from competitors. Moreover, once established, image brands can create some insulation from price competition. When buyers value a brand's image, price becomes less of a consideration in the purchase decision.

A key threat to an established image brand is that its future success is tied to the continued attractiveness of the associations that have been built. Michael Jordan has retired from basketball. While he is still familiar and held in high esteem, his market power as an outstanding athlete fades as his seasons off the basketball court increase. Conspicuous consumption in the form of $400 pens, BMWs, or fur coats is viewed less favorably when economic conditions are tight than when the economy is booming. Further, images related to badge products often have limited appeal across generations. Ralph Lauren's taste of the English country life may come to be seen as outdated and be rejected by youth in favor of an alternative, contemporary perspective. As a case in point, Toyota is suffering a bit as a result of its success with the baby-boomer generation in North America. It has come to be seen as Mom's and Dad's car. As a result, younger car buyers are seeking a more modern alternative; some are turning to Honda, others to Volkswagen. Toyota's challenge is to retain its positioning as dependable but as relevant to the lives of younger buyers. If Toyota fails to achieve this balance, it may suffer the same fate as Buick.

One strategy for growth that can be effective for image brands is to launch brand extensions. A strong image brand may be extended to any product that might be linked to the general image that the brand portrays. Ralph Lauren, for example, has successfully extended his brand from clothing to furniture, linens, and most recently, a restaurant. All of these products depict a common lifestyle and, thus, reinforce the Ralph Lauren image. Of course, extending image brands can be carried too far. Neither Donna Karan bottled water nor Bill Blass chocolates were able to generate significant sales. And, brand extensions that contradict core associations, such as Crystal Pepsi, seem doomed to failure.

The Internet provides an opportunity for image brands to allow consumers a greater level of affiliation with the brand and with like-minded others. This opportunity for two-way interaction may deepen consumers' passion for the brand and move it in the direction of the type of brands that we discuss next, experiential brands. For example, Martha Stewart wannabes can log on to MarthaStewart.com where they can ask questions, share ideas, buy products, and generally learn more about how to emulate their idol.

Experiential Brands

Experiential brands differ from image brands in terms of their emphasis. Whereas image brands focus on what the product represents, experiential brands focus on how consumers feel when interacting with the brand. The brand experience is co-created by the brand and the consumer at the time of consumption and, consequently, it is unique and highly personal. Indeed, such a brand may be experienced differently by the same individual at different times.

An experiential brand may include a tangible product, but this is not required. Moreover, if a product is part of an experiential brand, ownership of it may never be transferred to the consumer. Instead, products, environments, and services are combined to create temporary multisensory encounters with the brand. These encounters may be recurring or may involve extended contact with the customer. Consequently, the "place" and "people" components of service delivery are particularly important in creating strong experiential brands.

Disney is a classic example of an experiential brand. Visitors to Disney World buy the experience of seeing delight on the faces of their children and, perhaps, a chance to regress to the carefree fantasies of their own childhood. Souvenirs may be purchased but they are valued primarily for their ability to evoke memories of the larger experience and not in and of themselves.

On a more everyday level, Starbucks has built a powerful experiential brand. Starbucks stores are much more than a place to purchase a jolt of java. They offer a brief reprieve in a hectic day; a chance to inhale the rich aroma of fresh coffee and listen to relaxing music, while tasting a rich, specially prepared brew in the company of like-minded coffee addicts. One hallmark of the Starbucks' experience, and any great experience really, is consistency. Delivering a consistently good experience is a challenge in the retail coffee business. Making a consistently high-quality café latté, for instance, requires, first, brewing two ounces of coffee. Starbucks' guidelines require this to be drawn in 18 to 23 seconds at 90 degrees Celsius and 9 bars of pressure to produce excellent espresso.

Second, the milk must be steamed to 160 degrees Fahrenheit. Most Italian espresso machines contain a single boiler that both heats the water for coffee and makes steam to foam the milk. As a result, drawing the steam for milk affects the heat of the remaining water, which can produce an inconsistent espresso. If the water is too hot, the espresso will taste burnt; water that is too cold will not extract all the flavor from the ground coffee. This does not pose a significant problem in Italy because Italians and other Europeans prefer espresso to café latté and other coffee-based beverages, so little milk is drawn. By contrast, Americans favor milk in their coffee. In fact, Americans drink 500 times more milk than Europeans in their coffee.

Starbucks' solution is to use La Marzocco espresso machines. These machines cost twice as much as more conventional espresso makers because they contain two boilers (one for steam and another for water). Having two boilers, however, ensures that steaming milk does not affect the temperature of the water used to brew coffee. Thus, every Starbucks' café latté can have the perfect ingredients: 2 ounces of coffee brewed at 90 degrees Celsius, under 9 bars of pressure, for 18 to 23 seconds, combined with 10 ounces of milk steamed to 160 degrees Fahrenheit. Such standards produce a remarkably consistent product yet uniquely personal experience.

Dimensions of Experiential Brands.   While it is always important that a brand offer consistency, the range of experiences around which a brand may be built is enormous. Experiences can be viewed as varying on three dimensions: *valance* (positive, negative), *potency* (mild, intense), and *activity* (passive, active).[4] The valence associated with many experiential brands is positive. Brands such as Disney, the Chicago Symphony, and Elizabeth Arden compete by offering pleasurable experiences. However, some brands focus on experiences that are less pleasant. For example, bungee jumping or roller coaster rides may strive to outdo competitors by offering the most frightening, death-defying experience.

Experiential brands also differ in terms of the potency of the experience. While a stop at the local Starbucks' cafe may evoke mild, positive feelings, a massage and facial at Elizabeth Arden may lead to more intensely pleasurable feelings. Likewise, a horror film may create a mild fright whereas a ride on the world's largest roller coaster may create a heart-stopping experience. The potency of an experiential brand may be affected by both the intensity with which a single sense is engaged and by the number of senses that are stimulated.

Finally, experiential brands vary in terms of whether the consumer is a passive observer or an active participant. Brands associated with traditional venues of entertainment, such as movies, concerts, and theater, historically have offered a relatively passive experience. The consumer reacts to the material being presented rather that interacting with it. However, driven in part by advances in technology, these forms of entertainment are now increasing consumers' involvement. An audience may provide input that changes the outcome of a play or may participate in a commercially staged event. In 2000, the "Bud Bowl" (a battle between Bud and Bud Lite), migrated from being relatively passive "advertisement" during the Super Bowl to being an engaging, interactive Internet experience. This shift both reduced costs (the cost of building the interactive Web site was in the tens of thousands of dollars versus $1.2 million dollars just to air 30 commercial during the Super Bowl), and increased sales because participants in the event ordered brand-related merchandise while they were online.

Other experiences go beyond heightening consumers' mental involvement and engage their bodies. Snow boarding and extreme sports require such active participation that uncoordinated or mature consumers are at high risk of bodily harm should they choose to participate.

Experiential brands connect with consumers' desire to move beyond a self-presentation and focus on self-enriching experiences and causes. Interacting with the brand is an end in itself, rather than being a means to some other goal. Situational and individual differences are likely to moderate the consumers' affinity for different types of experiential brands. Most consumers may seek positive experiences most of the time. However, segments of consumers who need to test and to define themselves (e.g., young adults), or who are deprived of control in other aspects of their lives (e.g., economically disadvantaged), may embrace negative and extreme experiences because surviving such experiences creates feelings of mastery and control. Similarly, the constraints of work and family obligations may prevent consuming intense and active brands on a daily basis. Instead of an afternoon of snow boarding or a trip to Disney World, consumers must settle for more mild (and often more affordable) experiences, such as a manicure or a trip to Starbucks, to indulge themselves on an everyday basis.

Our examples of experiential brands have all been business-to-consumer products or services. Business-to-business firms certainly incorporate experiences into their marketing tactics. For example, Silicon Graphics has a Visionarium Reality Center at its corporate headquarters in Mountain View California. Here, customers can create and interact with three-dimensional product visualizations. As another example, Andersen Consulting has a center in Windsor, England, that allows clients to see Andersen's view of the retail shopping experience of the future. This "store of the future" places potential Andersen clients, many of whom sell their products through grocery stores, in the role of observers of shoppers in this new world, highlighting the challenges these companies will face and Andersen's suggestions for coping with those challenges.

Similarly, the strategy of bringing potential clients to the company's plant to experience, firsthand, aspects of the manufacturing process is a common and effective selling tool. However, while experiences are useful tactics for business-to-business firms, such tactics should be distinguished from building experiential brands. Aside from, perhaps, executive training and education programs (i.e., Outward Bound programs), it is difficult to think of many experiential brands in the business-to-business realm.

Transforming a Functional or Image Brand into an Experience. As brand differentiation on the basis of product features becomes more difficult to sustain in the face of rapid competitive imitation, companies may avoid commodity status by conceiving of their brands as representing a larger experience. Consider the category of electricity providers. One company's kilowatt is indistinguishable from another's. As a result, differentiation (and, thus, the ability to charge a price premium) might seem impossible in this industry. However, an upstart energy company, Green Mountain Energy Resources, has proven that an experiential energy brand can be created and that consumers will pay a price premium to purchase it. Capitalizing on deregulation and the fact that electric energy production is the single greatest source of pollution, the Green Mountain brand offered consumers an ecologically superior alternative—electricity generated by capturing the energy created by the wind, water, and sun. While the electricity that is delivered to a Green Mountain customer's home is no different from that received by a customer of a traditional electricity provider, by choosing Green Mountain energy, customers ensure that a greater portion of overall energy production is done in an environmentally friendly manner.

Switching to a new energy company is just one aspect of the Green Mountain experience. The company has sponsored free "Know Your Power" music festivals with popular entertainers such as Shawn Colvin, Kenny Logins, and James Taylor, who are known to be concerned about the environment. In attending these concerts, consumers have an opportunity to learn more about how they can help to protect the environment while they enjoy the company of like-minded individuals. Further, to ensure that brand is meaningful and relevant to consumers in their everyday lives, Green Mountain offers "eco credits" when consumers use less, rather than more energy. Eco credits can also be earned by engaging in other environmentally friendly activities, such as riding a bicycle to work or planting a vegetable garden. When a community earns sufficient eco credits, Green Mountain will build or refurbish a neighborhood playground using recycled materials. In states where Green Mountain is available (initially California and Pennsylvania), the brand has enjoyed considerable success, proving that viewing a product as a commodity is more a matter of a lack of imagination than a matter of fact.

Marketers of many image brands also are trying to increase the degree to which their brands represent experiences. Niketown expands associations to the Nike brand beyond those that are based on status or the image of athletic excellence. Visiting Niketown is an experience. While Niketown does not charge admission, tacitly acknowledging its function as a retail outlet rather than just a destination, it might be possible for it to do so, particularly if the store were to stage events that enabled visitors to interact with star athletes.[5] Similarly, Pleasant Company (now owned by Mattel) does not charge admission to its American Girl Store. However, if it did, there are undoubtedly many girls and parents who would be willing to pay for the experience of viewing all the artfully displayed dolls with their period furniture and accessories (all for sale, of course).

Managing Experiential Brands.   Experiential brands face two key challenges. The first is the ability to create the brand experience consistently, as noted earlier in discussing Starbucks. Experience brands are typically labor-intensive. Without careful recruiting, clear standards, training, and the right incentive system, employees will lack the ability and motivation to create the brand experience reliably. As a result, companies with successful experiential brands spend a disproportionate amount of their time hiring and training their personnel. Virgin Atlantic Airways is a good example. Virgin provides air transportation, but the brand is based on creating memorable experiences that extend well beyond the flight. For the upper class passenger, the Virgin experience starts with a ride to the airport via motorcycle or chauffeur-driven limousine. It continues in the Clubhouse lounge, where the guest may visit the hair salon, library, or game room while enjoying complementary beverages and snacks. The in-flight experience may include surprises, such as discovering that a masseuse is available or that ice cream sundaes accompany the movie. And, upon arrival, the Virgin passenger may visit Arrival Clubhouse and freshen up with a sauna and shower, or work off jet lag in the swimming pool and gym. At every stage, Virgin employees play a critical role in ensuring not only that the operation runs smoothly, but that even the most mundane activities are instilled with a bit of fun and theater. Accordingly, rather than hiring those who aspire to a career in the airline industry, Virgin recruits outgoing individuals, such as aspiring actors.

The second challenge to experiential brands is the potential for satiation to occur. Can the third trip to Disney World possibly match the first one? One strategy for addressing this issue is to continuously expand and enhance the experience. The danger with this strategy is that expectations may rise along with the experience, making them ever harder to meet. If Nordstrom's continues to upgrade the level of service, can it meet the expectations that it creates reliably and profitably?

An alternative strategy is for a firm to create multiple, maximally different experiential brands within a category. Lettuce Entertain You Enterprises Inc., which owns more than 30 restaurants in the Chicago area, has enjoyed considerable success with this strategy. Want to be transported to Italy, try Lettuce's Scoozi. Have an urge for Chinese, try Lettuce's Ben Pao. Longing for Paris, visit Lettuce's Mon Ami Gabi. Wishing for a romantic evening in a classic restaurant, make a reservation for dinner at a table near the dance floor at Lettuce's Pump Room. In each instance, the experience will be authentic, unique, and memorable because the décor, menu, and wait staff will embody the particular theme.

Experiential brands are easily extended into tangible reminders of the consumption experience (as in the case of Disney), and may also succeed in other brand extension efforts that are unified by a common target audience and understanding of that audience (Disney with movies, theme parks, and video games). However, experiential brands cannot stray outside the bounds of the type of experience they have created. Disney suffers when adult themes or too suggestive clothing appear in its movies and, therefore, it uses a different brand, Touchstone Pictures, for motion pictures targeted at adult audiences.

Experiential brands may benefit from judicious use of the Internet to extend and enrich the consumption experience. Certainly the Internet has been an important venue for enriching the Star Trek experience among the show's fans. Trekkers, as avid fans of the television show are called, gather online in a variety of chat rooms to discuss the television show episodes and movies, engage in interactive role play, and buy and sell memorabilia. For these devoted fans, Star Trek represents a philosophy or religion and the Internet is a valuable means of integrating the show into their everyday lives.[6]

SUMMARY OF TYPES OF BRANDS

We have discussed three types of brands that vary the terms of their basis for differentiation and, thus, the emphasis placed on elements of the marketing mix. As a result, these brands connect with different consumer needs and evoke different levels of consumer involvement. Moreover, sustaining these brands presents unique challenges to management. The brand matrix in Table 4.2 summarizes these distinctions.

For the purposes of exposition, the types of brands have been presented in terms of three discrete categories. However, it is also useful to think of these types of brands as lying on a continuum ranging from a focus on the product to a focus on the consumer. At one extreme are functional brands, which are created at the factory and may be purchased by consumers for consumption at whatever time they might desire. At the other extreme are experiential brands, which are created at the time of consumption with the active participation of those who consume them. Image brands fall in the middle. They are created in the factory but their value stems, in large measure, from their display by consumers.

Further, while we have classified specific brands into one of the three categories, it is also important to recognize that brands may evolve in ways that shift their categorization. Consider, for example, Volvo. Volvo began as a functional brand that focused on features such as reinforced steel beams in the car's roof and side panels, which offered drivers a higher level of crash protection or safety than cars without such features. However, over

Table 4.2
The Brand Matrix

Brand Type	Basis for Differentiation	Marketing Mix Emphasis	Consumer Needs and Involvement	Management Challenges
Functional (e.g., Tide, Mach III, McDonald's, Dell Computer)	Superior performance or superior economy	Product, price, and/or place	Physiological and safety needs, relatively low involvement	Sustaining the basis of superiority
Image (e.g., Miata, Waterman, Nike, Apple, Coke, Pepsi)	Desirable image	Communications	Social and esteem needs, moderate to high involvement	Balancing the brand heritage with the need for relevance in a dynamic environment
Experiential (e.g., Disney, Saturn, Elizabeth Arden, Virgin Atlantic Airways)	A unique, engaging experience	Service delivery (place and people)	Self-actualization needs, moderate to high involvement	Consistency in delivery, risk of consumer satiation

time, by design or by default, Volvo evolved into an image brand. It became the car for caring parents. This association was reinforced when the company aired an advertisement in which, as a means of informing her husband that she was pregnant, a young woman announces that she purchased a Volvo. The image of Volvo as the car for caring, well-educated, affluent parents served the company well for many years. But eventually this image proved to be limiting; Volvo was tied to a generation (baby boomers) and a lifestyle (conservative) that excluded or did not appeal to many car buyers. In an effort to reconnect with a broader target of consumers, particularly Generation X buyers, Volvo has recently launched a campaign with an experiential theme. Volvo claims to provide cars that would "save your soul." Of course, this claim would not be credible without significant modification of the car's physical features. The lines of the classic Volvo "box" have been softened and there is even a Volvo convertible (hardly a design that reinforces the association to safety). Thus, not only has the meaning of the Volvo brand moved from being functional to being more experiential, but the physical features of the car have evolved as well.

A final point worth noting is that while the general population may view a brand as belonging to one of our three categories, this view need not be universally held. Whatever the brand and the product category, heavy users of it are likely to be more emotionally involved and, thereby view the brand as having more image or experiential characteristics than do light users of the brand.

BRANDING STRATEGY

When building a brand, the marketer must also determine the optimal branding strategy. Here we focus on the three strategies that are commonly employed: (1) corporate branding (using one corporate brand for all products), (2) family branding (using multiple brands in a product category and linking them to a common family name), and (3) product branding (using unrelated brand names for several products in the same product category). Each of these three branding strategies can be considered in light of the three types of brands discussed in the previous section. Some examples are shown in Table 4.3.

Corporate branding focuses attention on the company. This strategy may be particularly attractive for experiential brands because the brand represents a relationship with the company rather than with the product. The Saturn example discussed earlier illustrates this point.

Image brands, such as Ralph Lauren and Andersen Consulting also may find the corporate branding approach appealing. Having multiple products with a common name may help to define and enrich the brand image. Certainly, the availability of both English-styled furnishings and clothing reinforces the notion that the Ralph Lauren brand is about a way of life, rather than about the functional properties of the products. Launching a line

Table 4.3
The Relationship between Type of Brand and Branding Strategies

Type of Brand	Corporate	Family	Product
Functional	BIC, GE	Gillette (Mach3, Sensor, Atra)	Tide, Cheer, Era (P&G)
Image	Ralph Lauren, Andersen Consulting	GM (Chevy, Olds, Buick, Cadillac), BMW (3, 5, 8 series, Z-3, X5)	Coke, Sprite (Coca-Cola)
Experiential	Saturn, Starbucks, Green Mountain	Lettuce Entertain You (Scoozi, Ben Pao, Mon Ami Gabi, The Pump Room)	Ritz Carlton, Fairfield Inn (Marriott Corp.)

of very inexpensive or funky clothing would best be done under another label to avoid confusing consumers about the brand meaning and, thereby, dilute its equity.

Even functional brands, such as BIC and GE, may successfully adopt a corporate branding approach. Often companies are attracted to a corporate branding approach for the efficiency that it provides; advertising expenditures can be concentrated on building a single brand name. However, this efficiency carries a price. All products under the corporate brand must be compatible with the associations that the brand evokes, a lesson that BIC learned when it launched a line of perfumes bearing the BIC name.

An alternative approach is to adopt a family branding strategy. Under this approach, a corporate or umbrella brand name may be combined with more specific product-based names. Traditionally, auto manufacturers have used this branding strategy. For example, GM markets Chevy, Olds, Buick, and Cadillac, each targeted to a different segment of consumers and each having unique associations, but all sharing an affiliation with GM. The corporate affiliation may impose a constraint on the range of meanings that can be created at the product level, which is why Saturn was launched as a separate company, rather than an additional GM product line.

Gillette also takes a family branding approach, but does so for a line of functional products. Lettuce Entertain You Enterprises Inc. adopts a family branding strategy for its set of experiential brands. In general, the family branding approach works best when relatively distinct segments of users, or use occasions, exist and thus the common affiliation is not likely to increase cannibalization markedly. Instead, the familial affiliation provides an assurance of a certain level of quality.

The final approach to branding is to market multiple product brands without any common affiliation to the parent company. P&G uses this approach in marketing its line of laundry detergents. Few consumers think of Tide, Cheer, and Era as related brands though they are all produced by the same company. Coke uses a similar strategy in marketing Sprite and Coke, as does Miller Brewing in marketing Red Dog versus the Miller brands. Finally, experiential brands may also be marketed using a product approach. Few consumers are aware that the Ritz Carlton and Fairfield Inn, brands that are at opposite poles of the hotel price spectrum, are both owned by Marriott Corporation.

A product branding strategy can enable a firm to attract distinct segments of consumers who may not wish to be affiliated with each other. For example, some beer drinkers may prefer the image associated with small microbreweries and disdain mass market brands, such as Miller and Bud.

In launching the Red Dog brand, Miller sought to attract beer drinkers seeking a microbrew image, while continuing to serve the mass market with its mainstay Miller-branded products. Product branding can be highly successful. However, it requires deep pockets to build multiple, unrelated brands. It is no accident that P&G, which pursues a product branding approach, was second in the world (GM was first) in terms of advertising spending in 1999. Of course, no matter how much a company spends, it cannot prevent consumers from learning about the parentage of brands, as Miller discovered when the press publicized the fact that Red Dog was a Miller brand. Such disclosures are more likely to be damaging when the brand is based on image rather than function.

Corporate mergers, such as recent ones in the auto industry (Daimler-Chrysler, Ford-Volvo-Jaguar) raise questions about the tradeoffs between the different branding strategies. Efficiencies may emerge from a more integrated, corporate approach, but the ability to appeal to specific segments may be reduced.

In business-to-business settings, it may be difficult to pursue a product branding strategy because direct contact between the seller and buyer makes the corporation a salient aspect of the product irrespective of how it is branded. In such situations, if a firm wishes to market products that are incongruent with the corporate brand, it may be necessary to create a separate legal entity. In the telecommunications industry, for example, AT&T spun off Lucent, its former equipment division, to avoid a conflict of interest with customers. Unencumbered by the AT&T relationship, Lucent has flourished, outgrowing its parent. As of April 2000, the market capitalization of Lucent is $217 billion while AT&T's market capitalization is $173 billion. Similarly, IBM spun off Lexmark as an independent maker of computer printers and other equipment.

Short of spinning off a division, an organization may undertake a joint venture. Power PC was the result of collaboration between IBM, Motorola, and Apple. Because joint ventures are motivated by the desire to explore strategic options that are unavailable to any one company, it is appropriate to create a unique identity—a brand, essentially. However, as Power PC demonstrated, ensuring the success of a joint venture requires much more than a new brand name.

CONCLUSIONS

Brands are a ubiquitous part of modern markets. They exist because they provide value to consumers. Brands assure a level of quality, simplify choice, and help consumers achieve a wide range of goals, ranging from meeting basic, functional needs to self-actualization. Brands also benefit the companies that create them. They support higher margins than strict product differences might permit and, thereby, protect firms against competitors who imitate their products. Brands also may allow the firm to gain leverage over its customers, as in the case of Intel. In sum, brands serve as a bridge between a company and its customers—they are symbols of the value that the company creates.

Brands must be built, and this is a time consuming and costly process. When first launched, many brands are names with no inherent meaning—Sony, Mercedes-Benz, or Ben & Jerry's meant little at first. Over time, these names and the brands that they symbolize come to represent a rich set of associations in consumers' minds. At their core, powerful brands reside not with the company, but rather with consumers. The thoughts, memories, and feelings that people have about a brand are, at an individual level, the essence of brand equity. How that equity is created and maintained, our focus in this chapter, is overlooked by organizations that believe that value arises only from products, or that value is created in the factory. The companies that we have discussed illustrate that success requires creating value in the factory *and* in the minds of buyers. This process of creating and maintaining brand equity can simultaneously enrich consumers' lives and the company's bottom line.

Additional Reading

David A. Aaker, *Managing Brand Equity* (New York: Free Press, 1995).

David A. Aaker, *Building Strong Brands* (New York: Free Press, 1996).

Gregory S. Carpenter, Rashi Glazer, and Kent Nakamoto, *Readings on Market Driving Strategies: Towards a New Concept of Competitive Advantage* (Reading, MA: Addison, Wesley Longman, 1997).

Stephen J. Hoch, "How Should National Brands Think About Private Labels?" *Sloan Management Review,* vol. 37, no. 2 (winter 1996), pp. 89–102.

Jean-Noel Kapferer, *Strategic Brand Management: Creating and Sustaining Brand Equity Long Term* (London: Kogan Page, 1997).

John A. Quelch and David Harding, "Brands versus Private Labels: Fighting to Win," *Harvard Business Review,* vol. 74 (January/February 1996), pp. 99–109.

John F. Sherry Jr., *ServiceScapes: The Concept of Place in Contemporary Markets* (Lincolnwood, IL: NTC Business Books, 1998).

Notes

1. For a detailed discussion of the procedure that Interbrand uses to calculate a brand's value, see Kevin L. Keller, *Strategic Brand Management: Building, Measuring, and Managing Brand Equity* (Upper Saddle River, NJ: Prentice Hall, 1998),

pp. 361–363. This reference also provides a description of other methods for assessing the value of brands.

2. Ron Alsop, "Blue Chips Lose 'Brand Power' to Lower-Tier Firms, Survey Says," *Wall Street Journal* (March 20, 2000), B1.

3. This discussion of the Saturn brand is based on David A. Aaker, "Building a Brand: The Saturn Story," *California Management Review,* vol. 36, no. 2 (winter 1994), pp. 31–50.

4. For a related discussion of these dimensions in the context of attitudes, see Charles E. Osgood, George J. Succi, and Percy H. Tannebaum, *The Measurement of Meaning* (Urbana: University of Illinois Press, 1957).

5. For a more detailed discussion of this and other experience brands, see B. Joseph Pine II and James H. Gilmore, "Welcome to the Experience Economy," *Harvard Business Review,* vol. 76 (July/August 1998), pp. 97–105.

6. For a rich discussion of Star Trek fandom both online and off, see Robert V. Kozinets, "Utopian Enterprise: Articulating the Meaning of *Star Trek*'s Culture of Consumption," a manuscript to appear in *Journal of Consumer Research* (2000).

CHAPTER 5

MARKET-DRIVING STRATEGIES: TOWARD A NEW CONCEPT OF COMPETITIVE ADVANTAGE

GREGORY S. CARPENTER, RASHI GLAZER,
and KENT NAKAMOTO

Creating competitive advantage is the central goal of competitive strategy.[1] As the marketing concept has been widely adopted in the last decade, it has become the dominant conceptual foundation for the development of competitive strategies.[2] According to that view, buyers know what they want, and the objective of competitive strategy is to give it to them. Competitive strategy, in other words, is *customer driven*. Competitive advantage arises from satisfying customers better, faster, or more cheaply than rivals. As markets evolve more rapidly, however, buyers face a growing array of novel products—home robots, digital organizers, Internet service providers—about which they know little. In response, individuals draw on their experience and observations to learn about what they want. Their experience and observations, however, are heavily dependent on the strategies brands advance. Thus, rather than *giving* customers what they want, competitive strategies are increasingly designed to help buyers *learn* what they want.

Although consumer learning is most obvious in rapidly advancing markets, careful observation suggests that every consumer learns in every market, no matter how fast technology advances. Consider the evolution of a buyer over his or her life. At some point, he or she will have no knowledge of how to be a buyer—no perceptions of any product, no preferences, and no experience making choices. Product by product, category by category, buyers amass the knowledge to be consumers. Over our lives, we continually encounter new product categories, sometimes as new-to-the-world products, but in other cases we encounter very old products that are simply novel to us. Although espresso is an "old" beverage, for instance, it was once new to everyone who enjoys it today. Thus, in all markets, whether technology advances or remains stable, buyers learn.

Traditional concepts of competitive strategy are ill-equipped to guide the creation of competitive strategy when buyers learn. When buyers learn, what they want depends on what they experience, and what they experience depends on the strategies brands advance. Thus, what buyers want depends on brand strategies. How, therefore, can you "give customers what they want," as suggested by the marketing concept, if what buyers want depends on what you give them? We propose, in this chapter, a new concept for developing competitive strategy. We argue that when buyers learn, competitive strategy takes on a long-understood but little practiced role: teaching buyers. Brand strategies define buyer experience—through the products offered, the advertising messages conveyed, indeed through every interaction between an organization and a buyer—and through that experience buyers develop an understanding of brand differences (perceptions), form judgments about the value of brand differences (preferences), and create a logic for choosing among brands (brand choice strategies). We refer to strategies that teach buyers as *market-driving strategies*.

The consequences of this concept of competitive strategy and the consumer learning implied by it are profound. Buyer knowledge—more specifically, perceptions, preferences, and logics for choosing among brands—define the essential rules of the competitive game. Every competitor must understand and play by these rules. If buyers learn, the rules of the game evolve, depending on the strategies brands advance. Competitive strategies, therefore, drive the evolution of the rules of the competitive game. Hence, the term market-driving strategies. In contrast, traditional customer-focused strategies assume that buyers know what they want, which implies that the rules of the competitive game are established by buyers and remain unchanged as brands compete. The objective of competitive strategy is to give buyers what they want, and at competitive advantage—faster, more effectively, or for less than rivals. Market-driving strategies, however, create competitive advantage in an entirely different way. Competition is a battle over the rules of competition that result from consumer learning. Competitive advantage is created by shaping the rules of the game to the advantage of one player over another.

Market-driving strategies can yield competitive advantage that is both powerful and enduring. Some of today's most successful organizations drive the market—Cisco, General Electric, and Motorola are all examples of organizations that have created change, carved out successful positions, and created value in novel ways. Figure 5.1, for example, shows the market capitalization of six organizations in mid-2000. Cisco's success is remarkable but more understandable given its role in the Internet. GE and Wal-Mart, on the other hand, are remarkable because they too operate in very mature, less attractive markets. In its aircraft engines business, General Electric has redefined its concept of value by shifting from simply supplying parts and service to working to create closer relationships with airlines to increase their asset utilization and redefine value in the process. In a similarly mature business, Wal-Mart has redefined value to buyers through its everyday-low-price program, offering customers consistently low prices, excellent selection, and good service. Similarly, Motorola has made a tradition of redefining existing markets and inventing new ones, such as cellular phones, paging, and mobile radios. Disney has redefined the theme park, and Amazon is reinventing the bookstore and perhaps retailing more generally. Each of these organizations is driving its markets and being rewarded for it.

In this chapter, we explore how market-driving strategies can create remarkable value. We describe the buyer learning process, the role of competitive strategy in shaping it, and its role in creating competitive advantage. We explore how buyers develop their perceptions and the nature of those perceptions. We discuss how, based on those perceptions, buyers form their concepts of value and how buyers learn to make choices. We explore how competitive strategy plays a role in the buyer learning process. We illustrate the impact market-driving strategies can have with two instances in which buyer learning plays an important role—the creation of new-to-the-world markets and the differentiation of established brands in mature markets.

Figure 5.1
Market Capitalization of Some Market-Driving Firms

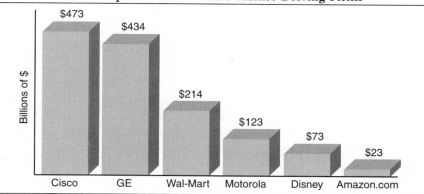

WHEN DO BUYERS LEARN?

New-to-the-World Products

The most obvious case of buyer learning is when consumers are introduced to a new-to-the-world product, such as a home robot, a digital organizer, or an Internet service provider. The first brand to successfully launch a new-to-the-world product, often dubbed the *pioneer,* faces a difficult challenge. Buyers have no knowledge of the product, no concept of value, and no experience in choosing one. Key objectives of the pioneer are to teach buyers about important aspects of the product (that is, to establish brand perceptions), create a concept of value (that is, to help buyers form preferences favoring it), and to help buyers create a logic for choosing the pioneer's brand (that is, to develop a brand choice strategy). From the consumers perspective, to become a buyer, learning is required. Successful pioneers engage buyers in the learning process and create an enduring impact on the market as a result. For example, pioneers often become perceptually distinctive. We easily recall them, and we often associate their brand names with the entire product category (Jello, Xerox, Levi's, and Coca-Cola). Moreover, the pioneer often establishes the concept of value that prevails, sometimes for decades. Levi's established, for example, that jeans ought to be long lasting, rugged, and not change year to year. This concept defined the product category of blue jeans for over a century, and brands continue to be judged by it today.

Product Evolution

After a market becomes established, competitors enter, technology advances, brands reposition, and products evolve. With that evolution, buyer learning continues, if at a modest pace. Automobiles continue to undergo such ongoing, modest evolution. Every year's new models are introduced and brands often seek to reposition, to occupy a somewhat different space in buyers' minds. For years, Volvo sought to be known as the safe car. Volvo crashed their cars to demonstrate their crashworthiness, told of families whose lives had been saved, and emphasized their safety features relentlessly. It worked. Volvos are seen as safe cars. But now, as other maker's cars are increasingly seen as safe (Mercedes-Benz and Lexus are two of note), Volvo hopes to change its image—to be seen as more sporty, more fashionable—but still, of course, safe.

As brands evolve, so do products, and product changes can lead to more dramatic changes in buyer knowledge. Buyers must learn how to value different product features and incorporate that valuation into their brand choice decision. Cadillac is including a satellite-based system, On Call, for instance, that can pinpoint a car's location to send aid or provide directions to its driver. As On Call and its rivals become more commonplace, buyers will reach a judgment about the value; they will form preferences for such systems. As they do, their preferences for cars more generally may be affected. As a result of this shift in value, a buyers' car-choice process can change. Buyers may ignore traditional decision factors such as styling if Cadillac's On Call system comes to be seen as sufficiently valuable.

Thus, whether prompted by a desire to reposition, to differentiate through offering novel products, or simply because of the entry of new competition, brand strategies evolve. With that evolution, buyers learn; their perceptions of brands change, their concepts of value evolve, as do the bases of brand choice.

Value Innovation

More dramatic, though less frequent than market evolution, is the case where one firm redefines value of the product through either a breakthrough technology or a breakthrough strategy. The mobile phone is an example of a value innovation that has lead to profound changes in competitive strategies and thus consumer learning. Prior to the creation of the cell phone, mobile phones existed, but each mobile phone, essentially a two-way radio, operated over a large geographic area. Radios were powerful, and hence bulky (mostly operating as car phones), and with few radio frequencies available, few people had access to mobile communications. The breakthrough that created today's cell phone business is the idea that one large geographic area can be divided into a number of smaller cells, and that a mobile phone needs only to operate within one cell. As a result, a small number of frequencies can be shared by a large number of users (multiple individuals can use the same frequencies in different cells), and phones can lower power and hence be small and portable. Based on this new technology, consumers are developing perceptions of the phone makers and carriers (Motorola, Nokia, Sprint, AT&T, etc.), and learning how valuable a mobile phone can be in their lives.

Although we often associate value innovation with technological breakthroughs, strategic innovations can also be a vital source of value innovation. Starbucks offers an excellent example. Coffee is one of the world's oldest commodities. The rituals surrounding it are well established in many countries as are buyers' preferences. For instance, more darkly roasted coffee beans are preferred in southern Europe while a somewhat lighter roast is preferred in the north. Americans have strong preferences for coffee, too; lighter roasts are preferred to darker roasts and drip brewing is common, yielding a weak brew by southern European standards. Despite these preferences, Starbucks is redefining coffee in North America, using that typically southern European brew—espresso. The technology to brew espresso is well established, but its appeal in North American has been limited. But through the concept of the coffee bar, Starbucks is reeducating North Americans about coffee and is creating a coffee culture. As a result, many people are abandoning their old concepts of coffee—as a weak, drip-brewed beverage—and replacing it with the Starbucks-crafted concept of the Italian coffee bar.

New-to-the-Market Buyers

The least obvious case of consumer learning is when products and competitors remain stable, unchanging for years, perhaps decades. A lack of innovation and the absence of new competitors may lead you to believe that there is no buyer learning occurring. In both laundry detergent and ice cream, for instance, product benefits have remain unchanged for years, there have been few innovations, and virtually everyone is familiar with major brands in both categories. Despite that constancy, buyers continue to learn. Every day buyers who have never heard of Tide or Surf, Breyers or Häagen-Dazs enter this world. These buyers do not even know what ice cream or detergents are. They will learn, perhaps quietly, but they will learn. As buyers age, they continually enter new markets as they enter new stages of life. Adolescence brings with it a fresh set of challenges—insecurity, awareness of the opposite sex, the discovery of clothing—that require learning to address. All the years between adolescence and retirement bring with them some of life's most significant experiences—college, marriage, children, middle age, perhaps divorce, new job, expanding family, aging parents, and many others. As we face some of these challenges for the first time we learn, and our perceptions, our concepts of value, and how we make decisions change, based on our experience. In other words, buyer learning is a life-long process.

WHAT DO BUYERS LEARN?

Whether buyers face a new-to-the-world product or simply face an age-old choice for the first time, the process of buyer learning is similar. Consider the case in which a consumer is entering an established market, graduate business education, for the first time. Suppose a 27-year-old, college-educated advertising executive enjoys work, but recently senses a growing interest in seeking more responsibility, perhaps more money, and more challenging professional opportunities. To satisfy these personal goals, he considers a number of alternatives: a head-hunter, a personal network of colleagues, or an MBA. He may explore all three options, and in the process review brochures from different schools, chat with friends who have MBAs, and those who have made other choices, and read articles in the popular press to learn the advantages of business school and differences among schools. Deciding to pursue the MBA further, he applies for and gains admission to a set of schools. To make a choice, he will develop a clearer sense of the difference between schools, the value of those differences relative to his goals, and ultimately identify some logic for selecting one school. After graduation, and throughout his career, he will assess whether his choice did in fact help him achieve his goals.

That simple process, illustrated in Figure 5.2, is one that buyers engage in many times throughout their lives. The buyer learning process is initiated when we identify goals that we believe we can satisfied, to some degree, by becoming a buyer. With those goals in mind, we seek a set of alternatives that, based on the strategies observed, we perceive can help us achieve our goals. Once buyers engage in a search, reading about business schools or talking to friends for example, the buyer learning process begins. Ultimately, based on what buyers learn, they make a choice and evaluate whether that choice did in fact help them achieve the goals sought. Buyers may, for a particular product category (such as graduate business education), engage in this process only once. In the case of automobiles, they may engage in it every few years, and in the case of wine, buyers may engage in this process more frequently.

Figure 5.2
Buyer Learning Process

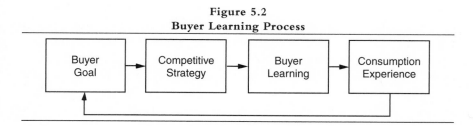

Buyer Learning and Competitive Advantage

Competitive strategies play a central role in the buyer learning process. The competitive strategies brands pursue create the buyer experience and, based on this experience, buyers learn three key things—how to perceive brands, how to value the differences among brands, and how to make a choice among the alternatives. These perceptions, preferences, and choice strategies become the essential rules of the competitive game. Those rules, however, are continually updated as buyers continue to learn. In contrast, under the conventional view of buyers—that they know what they want—the rules of the game remain fixed, or at least they are beyond the influence of competitors' strategies. In that case, competition between two rivals, Coca-Cola and Pepsi or Toyota and Daimler Chrysler, is like a chess match. The rules are clearly established, beyond the control of the players. Competitive strategies are crafted subject to those rules. Competitive advantage, in that case, arises from playing by the rules that buyers establish and creating unique value in the minds of buyers.

But if buyers learn, competitive strategies plays a fundamentally different role in the competitive process. Buyer knowledge still defines the rules of the competitive game. But those rules are the *outcome* of the competitive process. Rather than a chess match between rivals, a better analogy might be a poker game where the game is dealer's choice and the selection of the dealer is up for grabs. The dealer defines the winning hand, and competition determines who deals. Unlike poker, however, the dealer defines the rules *after* the cards have been dealt, and as long as the dealer can retain the dealer's chair, he or she can continue to control the game. A brand that can similarly drive the market, such as Starbucks, is essentially setting the rules of the game for as long as it can retain the initiative. By defining the rules, the market-driving firm gains an edge over its rivals. That edge produces competitive advantage.

The process by which market-driving strategies create competitive advantage is shown schematically in Figure 5.3. Through competitive strategy—the market segments targeted, the brand positions adopted, the products offered, the advertising messages crafted, and the prices chosen—the firm influences the buyer learning process. Some of the key differences between traditional customer-focused approaches and the proposed market-driving approach are listed in Table 5.1. Essentially, according to the conventional approach, buyers evaluate brands on some common perceptual dimension, they judge their value according to fixed preferences, and they select the brand that offers the highest utility. Considering consumer learning

Figure 5.3
Buyer Learning and Competitive Advantage

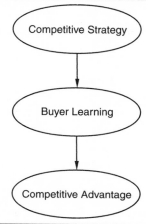

and market-driving strategies reveals that perceptions, preferences, decision making by buyers, and the nature of competitive advantage change as shown in Table 5.1 and are discussed next.

Brand Perceptions

Brand perceptions are the thoughts, feelings, and ideas we associate with a brand. Initially, buyers have no perceptions of any brands. All brands are at some point novel to us, and all the brand perceptions we have are learned. Buyers base their perceptions on many different factors; we perceive differences in product features, different associations are created through advertising or product design; different uses lead us to draw different conclusions about a brand. For instance, thinking of a Montblanc pen, we might associate *luxury, beautiful design,* and *prestige.* These perceptions

Table 5.1
Customer-Focused versus Market-Driving Strategies

Customer-Focused Strategies	Buyer Behavior	Market-Driving Strategies
Common dimensions	Perceptions	Network of associations
Fixed preferences	Preferences	Learned value concepts
Utility maximization	Decision making	Context dependent
Respond to buyers	Competitive advantage	Shape buyer learning

may be due to the design of the pen, its high price, the people we see using one, or where they are distributed, or some combination of all these factors.

Whatever the source, buyers remember or recall brand perceptions as *networks* of thoughts or associations. These networks are simply the associations that a buyer maintains that are linked, at its core, by the brand. One possible such network is illustrated in Figure 5.4 for Volvo. Buyers have some primary perceptions of Volvo: It is a safe car, but boxy and unexciting. Buyers may also hold secondary perceptions. In the figure, unexciting is a complex perception, with both a positive and negative connotation: On the one hand, unexciting is boring, but on the other hand, unexciting suggests dependability. Any perception can be viewed positively or negatively. Boxy, for instance, suggests a lack of stylishness, but it also suggests safety. As this Volvo example suggests, our perceptions typically are logically consistent. Boxy, safe car, and unexciting form a logically consistent view from a buyer's perspective. Collectively, the perceptions that buyers associate with a brand are its *brand equity*—the unique set of associations that distinguish it from competitors, the meaning of a brand to buyers.

Brand perceptions, like those shown in Figure 5.4, have a number of important properties. Perceptions for brands in the same category are not necessarily of equal dimension or of equal perceptual intensity. We may have a richer, more complex set of associations for Volvo than we do of Saab, for example. This may be due to the fact that we have more experience with Volvo than Saab, due to Volvos greater sales or more intense advertising spending, or we may know more people who drive Volvos than Saabs. Whatever the

Figure 5.4
Buyer's Perceptual Network

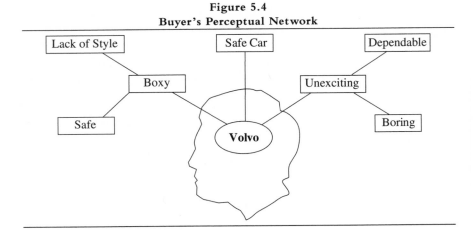

reason, a richer set of associations with a brand can increase the ease with which we recall it, affect our feelings toward the brand (increasing trust or confidence, for example), and affect our price sensitivity. It is hard to justify a price premium for a brand about which we know little.

A different perceptual network is the fundamental basis for brand differentiation. The objective of brand strategy is to create vast differences in perception. Any difference can be valuable, even differences that, at first blush, seem to be negative (as we had noted regarding Volvo's boxiness, implying lack of style, but also safety).

Even if brands have similar associations, differences between brands can still exist in the minds of buyers due to differences in the vividness of brand associations. Levi's and Lee jeans have many of the same associations. Both are American, rugged, associated with the American west, and similarly designed and priced. Despite these similarities, the perceptions of Levi's are more powerful, more vivid. These differences are the result of the experience buyers have with Levi's, the role Levi's have played as a symbol of youth, ruggedness, and independence. Those differences greatly favor Levi's in any competitive situation.

Perceptual Distinctiveness. One of the most powerful sources of competitive advantage is simply being perceptually distinctive—standing out among the alternatives. Perceptual distinctiveness can be achieved in a number of ways. But fundamentally it depends on creating a unique set of brand perceptions or a more vivid set of brand associations. Some brands achieve a perceptual distinctiveness by defining the product category. Jello, Xerox, and Coca-Cola all pioneered their markets and in the process became strongly associated with the product category. Being so perceived has a number of important competitive advantages. When buyers consider buying any brand in the product category, whether it is gelatin or duplicating equipment, the pioneering brand comes to mind. As a result, it is considered more frequently that others and, in many cases, chosen more than others—even if it has no inherent advantage in terms of the product. Its advantage arises from being more memorable, easier to recall, and possibly more trusted. In some special cases, a brand and a product category become inseparable. It is hard, for example, to describe the product that is branded as a Tootsie Roll without using the brand name. The name and the product are inseparable.

Without being synonymous with the category, a brand can still be distinctive. Distinctiveness can be achieved by simply creating a particularly vivid association. BMW is strongly associated with performance. That unique association has been created over 30 years through consistent product development and advertising. The very first advertisements for BMW in North America labeled BMW as "The Ultimate Driving Machine." That description remains true to the products and the entire experience of driving a BMW. It thus provides a powerful basis for being distinctive in a market where important differences between brands are quickly disappearing. Häagen-Dazs is another example of a highly distinctive brand. It too has consistently provided a luxurious, rich dessert. Even so, it is not synonymous with super premium ice cream, nor is BMW synonymous with luxury cars. But within their categories, each has a unique association that distinguishes it from others.

A unique association is competitively valuable. By being linked so strongly with performance, BMW enjoys an advantage by implicitly defining competitors as lacking the very strength BMW enjoys. Similarly, Häagen-Dazs perceptually overshadows other brands that offer equivalently delicious ice cream. With the same perceptual distinctiveness, however, trial of rivals is lower, comparisons less frequent, and thus other brands suffer by comparison, even if in blind taste tests, they might perform on par with Häagen-Dazs.

Some brands achieve distinctiveness by creating networks of associations that, collectively, are unique and memorable. *Brand personalities,* as these are called, consist of a set of associations that individually may be shared with other brands but collectively are unique. The term derives from the human personality; we may share traits with parents or siblings, but every personality is in one sense unique. Consider Levi's once again. Levi's personality is defined by a set of five associations—it is *American, rugged, youthful, rebellious,* and *authentic.* Other brands are *American* (Coca-Cola), *rugged* (Wrangler), *youthful* (MTV), and *rebellious* (Harley-Davidson). But none shares that same mix of associations, that unique personality. Many of the most successful brands of all time have perceptually rich, unique personalities—Apple Computer, Coca-Cola, Marlboro, McDonald's to note just a few. Brands with vivid personalities can be distinctive, competitively unique, more easily recalled, and more positively viewed. As a result, brands with distinctive personalities have advantages as long as the personality remains distinctive.

Preference Formation

In every category, buyers learn their preferences. In some categories, such as wine, this is an "acquired taste." In other categories, such as petroleum jelly, this is less obvious, but nevertheless just as common. In every category, our knowledge of what we like is learned. Individuals enter this world with no preferences for coffee over tea, Coke over Pepsi, BMW over Mercedes-Benz. We learn to prefer one to the other. Initially, buyers have no idea how to value product attributes and thus no way to evaluate alternative brands. Buyers *learn* how to value brands *through experience*. As buyers experience more brands, buyers find some they like, some they do not. This can trigger the process of consumer inference: What are the characteristics of the ones I like and the ones I don't like? Obvious differences in brand or attributes are assumed to be the "cause" of these differences, and one logical inference is that you have a preference for a brand or some combination of attributes. If you prefer Starbucks' coffee to other brands, you might conclude that you do so because of the darker roast and particular blend of beans. Our preferences *are formed*.

To some degree, we form preferences for every product that we buy. Buyers construct their preferences based on their perceptions of each alternative they consider and the goals they seek. For example, suppose the luxury car buyer shown in Figure 5.5 wishes to assess the value of each Volvo to him. He must perceive the key aspects of a Volvo and determine the value of each given his goals. He must, in other words, form preferences for a Volvo.

Figure 5.5
Buyer Valuation Problem

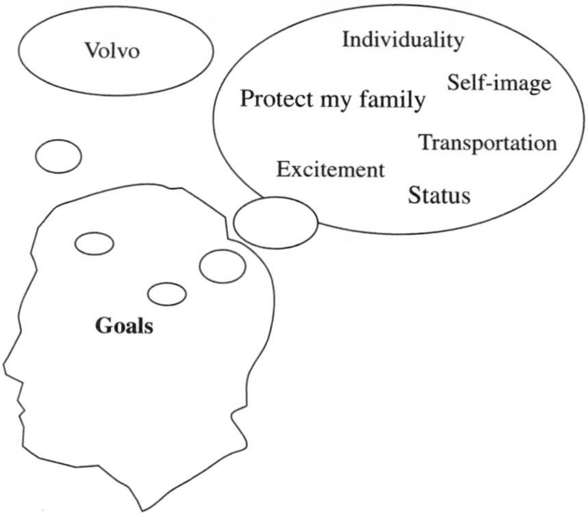

One way to represent the output of that process is with a *brand value network* as shown in Figure 5.6. On the left, are shown the buyer's perceptions of Volvo—safe, boxy, dependable. The buyer in this case seeks a car that will enable him or her to protect his or her family, have a positive self-image, retain a degree of individuality, some status, and enjoy a certain degree of excitement. Of all the goals sought, Volvo is relevant for three (family protection, self-image, and transportation). The dotted lines between associations and buyers goals on the right indicate how buyer perceptions of Volvo contribute to buyer value. For example, the safe perception of Volvo links directly to buyer's desire to protect his or her family, as does the perception of Volvos as boxy. Being perceived as dependable and safe, the Volvo will, buyers believe, provide reliable transportation, and being perceived as dependable, if boring, contributes to a certain self-image. Volvo's perceptions do not contribute to the other goals buyers seek—individuality, status, and excitement.

A brand value network provides a simple yet clear summary of the value buyers derive from the perceptions they observe. It shows importantly that buyers seek multiple goals in making a purchase. It is these multiple goals that often times make being a buyer so difficult. Different brand, being perceived differently, will contribute to a largely dissimilar set of goals beyond basic functionality, making functionally comparable products, in fact, largely incomparable in terms of value. Once established, a buyer's brand

Figure 5.6
Brand Value Map

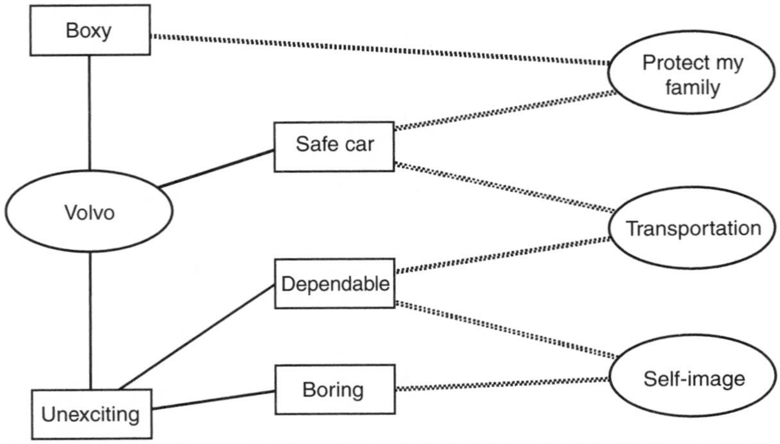

value network can evolve as does the buyer's perceptions of the brand (e.g., Volvo being seen as more sporty, less boxy), or as the buyer evolves, adding or changing the goals sought. Differences across buyer segments can also be captured as different goal structures, so that brand value networks can be constructed for different market segments.

Preference Advantages.   Powerful and enduring competitive advantages can be created in the preference formation process. This is most obvious in the case of a pioneer that defines a new product category, as in the case of Levi's, Xerox, and Coca-Cola. By defining the category, these brands begin the process of linking brand perceptions with buyer goals. As noted earlier, the pioneer can define its perceptions first, and thus become better known and more vividly recalled. But the pioneer can also begin the process of preference formation first. It can define the type of value associated with the product. Levi's for instance, chose to focus on creating functional rather than fashion value (the pants were, after all, designed for gold miners). But by helping buyers understand the nature of value, they help buyers form their concepts of value. In essence, pioneers have the opportunity—sometimes taken, sometime squandered—to define value. Value can be redefined as well, as GE has successfully done in its aircraft engine business and as Wal-Mart continues to do with retailing. The family car, in fact, has gone through two recent revolutions, pushed largely by Chrysler, changing from the station wagon, to the minivan, to the current sport utility vehicle. Throughout these changes, while the concept of the family car has evolved to include four-wheel drive, the use of the family car has changed little.

Defining value creates enormous competitive advantages. In the poker analogy used earlier, the dealer defines the winning hand. In many cases, one brand establishes a standard for value. Starbucks in coffee, Häagen-Dazs in ice cream, Jeep in sport utility vehicles have all defined value in their markets. Coca-Cola, remarkably, defined value and continues to do so over a century later. In the high-technology markets, the notion of an architectural standard has become commonplace. The VHS-Beta battles are legendary, as are the Window/Intel-Apple wars. A key to winning these battles is to establish the technological standard. In markets with no architectural control points, there are perceptual control points, psychological standards with much the same effect. By creating a market standard, a market-driving firm owns these control points in the minds of buyers. In many cases, this creates problems for rivals. Consider Coca-Cola. To gain advantage, a competitor might reason that it would need to differentiate, be distinctive. But how? By being different, with a sweeter beverage, for instance, the competitor might be seen as inferior. Copying Coca-Cola, on the other hand, a rival may be seen as a weak alternative, a poor substitute. Thus, the advantages of defining the standards of value are enormous. What are the options for competing with a brand that drives the market? Essentially, there are three:

1. *Dethrone the leader.* The most obvious, though not always the best, is to displace the established leader, at least among a segment of buyers. The classic example of a successful challenger is Pepsi. For decades Pepsi competed with Coca-Cola using a "me-too" strategy, offering more cola for less money. It failed by most accounts. Finally, Pepsi thought the unthinkable: to challenge Coca-Cola on the core aspect of the product—taste—in Coca-Cola's strongest markets. The purpose of the challenge was to demonstrate the superiority of Pepsi to loyal Coca-Cola drinkers in terms of taste and, through a buyer re-education process, replace Coca-Cola with Pepsi as the standard. Pepsi targeted younger consumers, whose preferences were less well-formed than older buyers who were more loyal to Coca-Cola. Thus, the "choice of a new generation" was born and Pepsi established itself as a standard, at least among younger buyers.

2. *Shift the standard.* If the leader cannot be displaced, another common strategy is to shift the standard slightly but significantly to disadvantage the leader. MCI successfully shifted the nature of value in long-distance service in the United States, long dominated by AT&T, a monopoly known for great customer service. In contrast, MCI (founded as Microwave Communications Inc.) used low price to generate customers and call volume. They fought to deregulate the industry and have consistently been innovative in pricing, offering programs like MCI Friends and Family. As a result of their efforts and the efforts of later entrants like Sprint, prices have dropped, and price has become a more important factor in buyers' decisions. Prices have fallen dramatically to nearly the cost of billing and customer acquisition (about two cents per minute). In response, AT&T has dropped prices to meet rivals, while they are launching an effort to once again shift the nature of the game, this time toward bundling services (to lower billing and customer acquisition costs) and thus regain control of the value standard.

3. *Establish a new standard.* The most dramatic and perhaps risky strategy is to redefine the standard entirely. One way to create a new standard is through product innovation. Gillette has built a powerful position in the razor market through product innovation, enabling Gillette to overtake the market pioneer, Star, and other later entrants.[3] Innovation plays a central role in low technology markets as well as high technology markets—the laundry detergent market, pioneered by Dreft, is dominated by Tide, and Eveready dominates the battery pioneer, Bright Star. In all these cases, late entrants were able to displace the pioneer as the standard of comparison and create a new standard. Gillette has even challenged the standards it established, choosing to replace them with newly created Gillette products. As the newly established market standard, Gillette, Tide, and others like them enjoy many of the advantages previously associated with pioneers. Strategic innovation, as already noted, is a similarly powerful means to redefine value in a market.

Brand Choice

Consider our hypothetical luxury car buyer discussed earlier in the context of Volvo. Suppose that in addition to a Volvo, he also considers a BMW, Range Rover, Lexus, and Mercedes-Benz. Each has a unique set of brand perceptions, and each offers unique value through its own value network. As a result, making comparisons across all the choices is difficult; none are directly comparable. But ultimately, some comparison needs to be made so that a decision can be reached. Brand choice, thus, can be a daunting task. Which brands will best enable the buyer to achieve his goals of individuality, self-image, transportation, excitement, and safety for the family?

The conventional view is that buyers consider all the alternatives, value their differences, making the necessary trade-offs, and ultimately choose the brand that maximizes self-interest. For example, in the case of the luxury car buyer shown in Figure 5.7, the buyer would, based on his or her perceptions of each brand, rate the importance of each difference, and for each brand calculate a total value score (or utility). Choice, then, becomes a simple matter of selecting the highest scoring brand. But coming to that choice is a difficult task indeed. As a result, consumers often adopt a simplified version of this strategy, the equally weighted rule, in which all perceptions are given equal weights to reduce the mental cost of comparisons.

In many situations, buyers abandon that systematic process in favor of simpler choice strategies. Consumers are adaptive. People select brands using a whole variety of strategies. The decision rules buyers adopt depend on the strategies brands pursue and have significant impact on the nature of competition. If all brands deliver value based on the same goals (e.g., video cassette recorders), and comparison between brands is easy, buyers may exhaustively compare alternatives to uncover the best value. In a more

Figure 5.7
Buyer's Valuation Problem

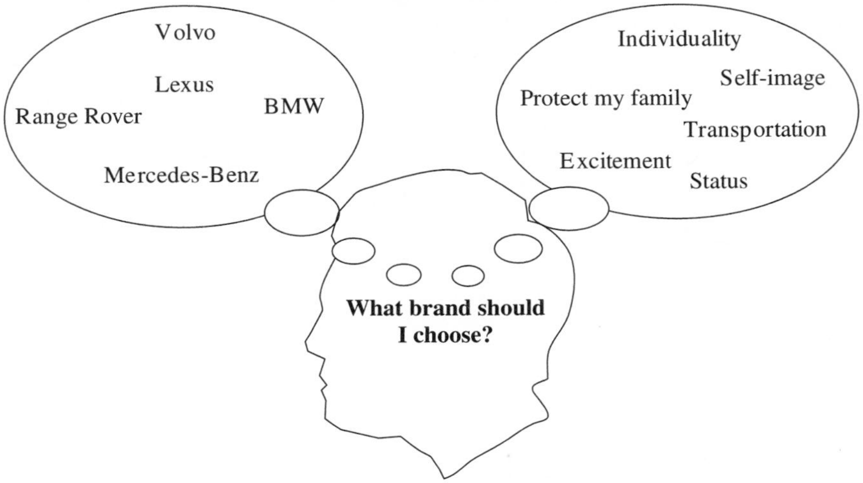

complex situation, buyers may resort to strategies to simplify their choice and use simple choice rules—buy the brand on special, or the one recommended by a friend. Through experience—driven by the strategies brands pursue—we learn how and when to apply these rules.

One common strategy is the *lexicographic choice rule:* Buyers identify the most important goal and then select the alternative that delivers most on that one goal, ignoring all others. In our luxury car example, if excitement is the most important goal, then BMW might be the logical choice. If family protection is the most important goal, then Volvo would be chosen. In selecting a graduate school of business for instance, a prospective student might select the one whose graduates earn the highest starting salaries. By using the lexicographic choice rule, the buyer is ensuring that he gets what is most important and doing so with a minimum of effort. If buyers are using this strategy, it is important not to try to compensate for a weakness on the key dimension with some other rationally valuable but ignored perception of value.

The *elimination-by-aspects heuristic* is a multistage decision rule. In the first stage, the buyer selects the most important goal, determines a cut-off, and eliminates all alternatives that do not meet the cut-off. With a reduced set of alternatives, the buyer then identifies the second most important goal, sets a cut-off level for it, and eliminates those alternatives that do not satisfy the second cut-off. This process continues until only one alternative remains. In the case of luxury cars, for instance, all presumably must provide reliable transportation. Perhaps this leads to the elimination of some brands in the construction of the alternative set. Next, buyers might screen safety, again eliminating some brands. Third, excitement might be most valuable, leading to a choice of BMW.

In some cases, consumers combine different strategies in a phased process. Consumers may use a screening process to create a subset of seriously considered brands and then apply a different decision strategy to select one alternative from the subset. In our luxury car example, for instance, buyers might screen first on safety, eliminating all alternatives that do not meet some minimum level of safety, and then apply a compensatory rule over the remaining choices. Alternatively, a buyer could screen on multiple dimensions, say safety and price, and then choose lexicographically over the remaining alternatives based on excitement or prestige.

Competitive Advantage

Competitive advantage can be created in the choice process by helping buyers resolve their dilemma: How do I choose among the available alternatives? The answer to that question is learned, category by category, buyer by buyer, depending on the strategies brands pursue. Consider a simple case, one in which all brands deliver value on the same goals, brands are perceived as similar, and comparisons between brands are easy (e.g., videocassette recorders). Introducing differentiation in markets such as these can lead to a change in decision strategies by consumers. By innovating, for instance, consumers may have to re-evaluate their choice strategies that ignore everything but price. Eliminating the equivalence on everything but price can prompt buyers to rethink *how they choose* and, as a result, *what they choose*.

One of the best examples is Intel's effort to brand its microprocessor used in personal computers using the *Intel Inside* brand. Makers of computers have traditionally focused on making faster, less expensive, more powerful computers. For most buyers, a computer is a substantial purchase, involving significant risk. Moreover, many computer manufacturers have invested comparatively little in building their brand names, although that is changing, and few computer retailers offered extensive customer service, believing low price is more important. As a result, many buyers face an expensive purchase of largely unknown brands with little retail support. *Intel Inside* offered customers assurance about the computer they were buying, whatever the brand name of the manufacturer. As a result, buyer decision strategies shifted from evaluating the brand of the *computer maker* and the associated technical characteristics to the brand of the *microprocessor maker,* creating a powerful competitive advantage for Intel, all the while reducing the perceived risk for the buyer.

Market Pioneering

Market pioneering illustrates how market-driving strategies create enduring competitive advantage. As mentioned earlier, the pioneer is typically followed by others, some similar to the pioneer, others different. As brands enter the market sequentially, buyers learn about them. The pioneer plays a special role in the buyers' learning process. Being the first entrant, the pioneer has the unique opportunity to become perceptually distinctive, defining buyer notions of value for the entire category and influencing the choice process. To see the impact the pioneer has on the learning process, consider the situation before the pioneer enters. At that point, the category does not exist in the minds of buyers. As a result, no rules of competition have yet been established. This creates an opportunity for the pioneer to establish the basic notion of value—the value proposition of the pioneer's brand and indeed the entire category—and in so doing create perceptions of the pioneer's brand and establish a logic for brand choice.

Perceptions.   Prompted by the strategy of the pioneer and combined with buyer experience, buyers begin to develop their perceptions. But their experience is limited to the pioneer, so the pioneer becomes more memorable, more vivid, and often the pioneer and the product category become closely related in buyers' minds, sometimes synonymous. Having more vivid perceptions of the pioneer, buyers more easily recall it and, as a result, the pioneer is more often chosen.[4] That is, we simply think of the pioneer more easily, more often, and we recall more positive thoughts about it.

Preferences.   As the first brand, the pioneer can define the category and thus the nature of value. Until later brands enter, buyer experience and learning is limited to the pioneer. A buyer could, therefore, very logically come to view the pioneer as the definition of value, the ideal, the standard against which all others are judged. In two studies, we demonstrated this effect.[5] Individuals were exposed to six different brands of software differing in term of characteristics; some individuals saw one brand first, call it A, others saw a different brand, call it B, first. Subsequently, all buyers saw all six brands. Those who saw A first, however, retained a preference for brand A and for its characteristics. Those who saw B first, on the other hand, preferred the characteristics of brand B most. Thus, buyers come to like what they learn about. Advertising and repeat purchase can reinforce the links buyers form.[6] Thus, buyers learn through trial how to value perceptions, but because this trial is limited to the pioneer, the pioneer defines value. Having defined value, the pioneer occupies the ideal position in the category and, being perceptually distinctive, it overshadows others that might try to challenge it.

Choice. Being vivid and seen as ideal, the pioneer is recalled more often and more frequently. Being strongly associated with the category, later entrants are often compared to the pioneer. Thus, the pioneer plays a central role in the valuation of all brands in the category. When we consider a pair of blue jeans, we may implicitly or explicitly compare it to Levi's. Thus our comparison process is heavily influenced by our learning. The impact of the pioneer on our perceptions and preferences has an impact on our choice strategies as well. If the pioneer created a value network, for instance, in which price plays no role, then price sensitivity will be low. By defining preferences, the pioneer can define the choice strategies used by buyers to value later entrants.

The introduction of Vaseline petroleum jelly illustrates these advantages. Vaseline was introduced in 1880 and advertised as a healing agent of unsurpassed purity. It defined in many buyers' eyes the category of petroleum jelly as a translucent, highly pure gel. Sampling Vaseline, buyers learned that a translucent, highly pure gel produced an effective wound preparation and, generalizing from this observation, inferred that the effectiveness of petroleum jelly lies in its translucence and purity. At the time, other wound preparations were based on black coal tar derivatives, lacking both purity and translucence. Subsequent trials and advertising confirmed buyers' conjecture about the superiority of Vaseline. Thus, translucence came to be favored over opacity and gained more importance in brand evaluation. Moreover, because Vaseline pioneered the product, all later brands were compared to it and found wanting even if identical, simply because they were not Vaseline. Brands that attempted to copy Vaseline suffered similarly because they were seen as less distinct.

The advantages created by pioneering can be remarkable. In many cases, market pioneers outsell their rivals for decades. Although some are not strictly the first to enter their markets (e.g., Miller Lite was preceded by Rheingold's Gablinger's by 15 years) and many early entrants fail (e.g., Bowmar in calculators), the first *successful* brand appears to outsell later-entering *successful* entrants systematically. Empirical studies show that this market share difference, dubbed *pioneering advantage,* creates a significant barrier for later entrants to overcome.[7] For example, Figure 5.8 shows the relative market share earned by later entrants compared to the pioneer in a study of consumer goods, adjusted for differences in positioning, pricing, and advertising. After making these adjustments, researchers have shown that the second entrant earns roughly 75 percent of the market share of the pioneer, the third entrant earned about 60 percent of the pioneer's market share, and so on, until the sixth entrant earns less than half the share of the pioneer.[8] In other words, early entry creates an advantage; to overcome that advantage requires pricing below the pioneer, offering a superior positioning, or outspending the pioneer on advertising. While these actions can be taken, all are costly and, more important, they are actions the pioneer need not take to earn its larger share. Other studies report similar ratios.[9]

The advantage created by pioneering can be remarkably enduring. This is well illustrated by Wrigley's chewing gum, which dominated its market in 1923 and continued to dominate its market six decades later, despite low-price attacks, innovation, new entrants, and changing consumer tastes.[10] Looking back at some of the brands that dominated their markets in the 1920s, it is remarkable how many continued to dominate those same markets six decades later (Table 5.2). Not all retained their number one market position, but a surprising number retained leading positions in their market and most did remain market leaders.

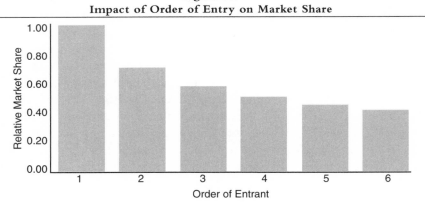

Figure 5.8
Impact of Order of Entry on Market Share

Table 5.2
Market Position of Leading Brands:
1923 and 1983

Brand	1923	1983
Wrigley's chewing gum	1	1
Ivory soap	1	1
Kellogg's Corn Flakes	1	3
Coca-Cola	1	1
Crisco shortening	1	2
Campbell's soup	1	1
Colgate toothpaste	1	2

Brand Differentiation

Brand differentiation provides another illustration of how market-driving strategies create competitive advantage by influencing buyer learning. The conventional view of differentiation is that successful differentiation requires distinguishing a product or brand from competitors on an attribute that is meaningful, relevant, and valuable to buyers. Observation, however, reveals that many brands successfully differentiate by introducing an attribute that *appears* valuable but, on closer examination, is *irrelevant*. For example, Alberto Culver differentiates its Alberto Natural Silk Shampoo by including silk in the shampoo, and advertising it with the slogan "We put silk in a bottle" to suggest a user's hair will be silky. A company spokesman, however, conceded that silk "doesn't really do anything for hair."[11] Consumers apparently value these differentiating attributes even though they are, in one sense, *irrelevant*. We refer to this strategy as an *irrelevant attribute strategy*.

How can an irrelevant attribute be a meaningful basis for differentiation, particularly if buyers become aware that it is in fact irrelevant? The buyer learning process suggests three ways in which an irrelevant attribute can be valued by buyers:

1. *Brand distinctiveness.* If only one brand offers an irrelevant attribute, it will be unique. Buyer perceptions will be different, creating differences in its value network. Being different makes a brand more memorable, and a more memorable brand will be chosen more frequently. The impact of distinctiveness can persist *even if buyers are aware that the irrelevant attribute is irrelevant*. In one study, we found that adding an irrelevant attribute increases preference for a brand—even though buyers know that the distinguishing characteristic is irrelevant.[12] The value, in this case, arises from the distinctiveness of the differentiated brand. The relevance of the differentiating attribute is, quite simply, irrelevant.

2. *Value signal.* Buyers may value an irrelevant attribute because they believe that an irrelevant attribute reveals something about the underlying properties of the product—its quality, its durability, or its effectiveness, for instance—even if the attribute itself is not valuable. During that brief moment when we are looking at the shampoo shelf and the silk catches our eye, we might hypothesize that silk in shampoo is indeed valuable. Why else, one might reason, would they include it? Using the shampoo with a successful outcome would lead us to "confirm" our hypothesis. Buyers may even come to believe that the silk *causes* the shampoo to work well. Even without trial, its existence suggests that it is valuable. A consumer might reason, "If they added silk to the shampoo, spent money advertising it, it must be valuable."

3. *Pricing.* The perception of value conveyed by an irrelevant attribute depends on the price of the differentiated brand compared to competitors. In another study of irrelevant attributes, we examined the impact of pricing strategy on preference for the differentiating brand. When individuals were unaware that the irrelevant attribute was irrelevant, *increasing price* led to *increasing impact.* Buyers appear to reason that the attribute could be valuable and a higher price similarly signals higher value. The signal given by the attribute is reinforced by the signal given by the higher price, making the differentiating attribute quite valuable.[13]

Simplify Brand Choice.   An irrelevant attribute can simplify choice. Consider a consumer facing a set of three effectively identical brands of shampoo. If one brand offers silk and the consumer knows that it is irrelevant, would that affect or simplify his or her choice? The consumer can ignore the information. By doing so, he or she still has no basis to choose among the alternatives. Instead, the consumer can *use* the irrelevant attribute—knowing that it is irrelevant—to help make a choice. Constructing a positive "reason" for why the attribute is attached to the brands (e.g., "at least I am getting something extra") means that the consumer can ignore the other two and make a choice. Thus, an irrelevant attribute can simplify choice even though a consumer may be aware that it is irrelevant. Buyers construct these reasons, even when they know the irrelevant attribute is irrelevant.[14]

Empirical analyses demonstrate that differentiation can have a substantial impact on competitive advantage and can lead to successful late entry. In one study, researchers examined the entry of innovative late entrants into two pharmaceutical markets.[15] In all, 13 brands entered the two markets; among them were innovative, differentiated later entrants along with brands pursuing other strategies. By differentiating their brands, the innovative late entrants were able to overtake the pioneers in three ways: First, they were able to expand the market, drawing a larger pool of buyers who had little experience with the pioneer. Second, they achieved a higher rate of repurchase than any other brand in the market. Third, they grew faster than the pioneer and, in fact slowed the growth of the pioneer appreciably. Non-innovative later entrants were not able to affect the pioneer's growth rate, in addition to having lower rates of repeat purchase, and facing smaller potential markets.[16]

The timing of entry can be important in achieving a successfully differentiated position. In another study of six pharmaceutical markets, researchers examined the impact of the timing of entry on the success of the late mover.[17] They examined, in particular, the stage of the product life cycle in which the brands enter—pioneer, growth-stage entry, and mature-stage entry. The results showed significant advantages for growth-stage entrants. Compared to pioneers and mature-stage entrants, growth-stage entrants grow faster in terms of sales, they are not hurt by increases in sales of competitors, and their buyers are more responsive to changes in their product quality. Pioneers do enjoy advantages, in addition to those already discussed: Buyers are most responsive to pioneer's marketing activities, Mature-stage entrants, however, are more disadvantaged than previously recognized: they grow more slowly than all other entrants, have lower response to product quality, and have the least responsive buyers in terms of marketing spending.

CONCLUSIONS

Recognizing buyer learning reveals new dimensions to the process of competition and new concepts for creating competitive advantage. Buyers learn throughout their lives as buyers. Three elements of the buyer learning process are crucial to understand:

1. Buyers learn their perceptions, and they recall these as networks of associations.
2. Buyers learn how to value the differences in these brand perceptions based on experience.
3. Buyers learn how to make decisions based on the context of the decision they face.

This buyer learning creates a largely different process of competition. Rather than a race to give customers what they want, competition is a battle over the rules of competition.

Successful market-driving strategies reshape markets and define powerful images and enduring concepts of value. The growing recognition of the power of buyer learning is reshaping the practice of marketing. Today, good companies listen to customers and satisfy their needs. Great companies are creating markets, ones that buyer cannot imagine, shaping their evolution, and producing competitive advantage unattainable by ignoring the buyer learning process and the role of competitive strategy in it.

Notes

1. Gregory S. Carpenter, Rashi Glazer, and Kent Nakamoto, *Readings on Market-Driving Strategies: Towards a New Concept of Competitive Advantage* (Reading, MA: Addison Wesley, 1997) and Gregory S. Carpenter, Rashi Glazer, and Kent Nakamoto, *Market-Driving Strategies* (Reading, MA: Addison Wesley, forthcoming).

2. George S. Day and Liam S. Fahey, "Putting Strategy into Shareholder Value Analysis," *Harvard Business Review,* vol. 68 (March/April 1990), pp. 156–162; Philip Kotler, *Marketing Management: The Millennium Edition* (Upper Saddle River, NJ: Prentice Hall, 2000).

3. Peter N. Golder and Gerard J. Tellis, "Pioneering Advantage: Marketing Logic or Marketing Legend," *Journal of Marketing Research,* vol. 30 (May 1993), pp. 158–170.

4. Frank R. Kardes and Gurumurthy Kalyanaram, "Order-of-Entry Effects on Consumer Memory and Judgment: An Information Integration Perspective," *Journal of Marketing Research,* vol. 29 (1992), pp. 343–357.

5. Gregory S. Carpenter and Kent Nakamoto, "Consumer Preference Formation and Pioneering Advantage," *Journal of Marketing Research,* vol. 26 (August 1989), pp. 285–298; and Gregory S. Carpenter and Kent Nakamoto, "Competitive Strategies for Late Entry into a Market with a Dominant Brand," *Management Science,* vol. 36, no. 10 (1990), pp. 1268–1278.

6. Stephen J. Hoch and Young-Won Ha, "Consumer Learning: Advertising and the Ambiguity of Product Experience," *Journal of Consumer Research,* vol. 13, no. 2 (1986), pp. 221–233; and Stephen J. Hoch and John Deighton, "Managing What Customers Learn from Experience," *Journal of Marketing,* vol. 52 (April 1989), pp. 1–20.

7. William T. Robinson and Claes Fornell, "Sources of Market Pioneer Advantages in Consumer Goods Industries," *Journal of Marketing Research,* vol. 22 (August 1985), pp. 305–317; and Glen L. Urban, Theresa Carter, Steve Gaskin, and Zofia Mucha, "Market Share Rewards to Pioneering Brands: An Empirical Analysis and Strategic Implications," *Management Science,* vol. 32 (June 1986), pp. 645–659.

8. Glen L. Urban, Theresa Carter, Steve Gaskin, and Zofia Mucha, "Market Share Rewards to Pioneering Brands: An Empirical Analysis and Strategic Implications," *Management Science,* vol. 32 (June 1986), pp. 645–659.

9. E. Berndt, L.T. Bui, D.H. Reiley, and Glen L. Urban, "Information Marketing and Pricing in the U.S. Anti-Ulcer Drug Industry," *American Economic Review, Papers and Proceedings,* vol. 85, no. 2 (1994), pp. 203–223; and G. Kalyanaram and Glen L. Urban, "Dynamic Effects of the Order of Entry on Market Share, Trial Penetration, and Repeat Purchase Rates for Frequently Purchased Consumer Goods," *Marketing Science,* vol. 11 (summer 1992), pp. 235–250.

10. "Study: Majority of 25 Leaders in 1923 Still on Top," *Advertising Age* (September 19, 1983), p. 32.

11. Gregory S. Carpenter, Rashi Glazer, and Kent Nakamoto, "Meaningful Brands from Meaningless Differentiation: Dependence on an Irrelevant Attribute," *Journal of Marketing Research,* vol. 31 (August 1994), pp. 339–350.

12. Ibid.

13. Ibid.

14. Christina Brown and Gregory S. Carpenter, "Why is the Trivial Important? A Reasons-Based Account for the Effects of Trivial Attributes on Choice," *Journal of Consumer Research,* (forthcoming).

15. Venkatesh Shankar, Gregory S. Carpenter, and Lakshman Krishnamurthi, "Late Mover Advantage: How Innovative Late Entrants Outsell Pioneers," *Journal of Marketing Research,* vol. 35 (February 1998), pp. 54–70.

16. See note 3.

17. Venkatesh Shankar, Gregory S. Carpenter, and Lakshman Krishnamurthi, "The Advantages of Entry in the Growth Stage of the Product Life Cycle: An Empirical Analysis," *Journal of Marketing Research,* vol. 36 (May 1999), pp. 269–276.

CHAPTER 6

MANAGING NEW PRODUCT DEVELOPMENT FOR STRATEGIC COMPETITIVE ADVANTAGE

DIPAK JAIN

New goods and services are essential both for maintaining the existing health of an organization and enhancing its future growth and profitability. At the same time, launching new products is a risky activity with an average failure rate of 40 percent across consumer and industrial products.[1] (In this chapter, the generic term, *products* will be used to refer to goods or services.) A more recent study reports that new product introduction failure rates for consumer products are as high as 95 percent in the United States.[2] In Europe, according to a recent study, 90 percent of all new product introductions fail within two years of launch.[3] A set of reasons behind new product failure is listed in Table 6.1.

Customers today have access to a considerable amount of information about products that makes them more sophisticated, knowledgeable, and also demanding. On the other hand, products are becoming less differentiated because organizations have readily and easily available technology to launch new products rapidly with diminishing quality differences.

A review of the current dynamics of the marketplace and the common reasons behind new product failure listed in Table 6.1 reveals that marketing a new product is becoming increasingly challenging. Some examples of product failures include Market/marketing failure—Crystal Pepsi; financial failure—Concorde; timing failure—Ford Edsel; technical failure—Newton by Apple; organizational failure—dress suits for men by Levi's; environment failure—ethical drugs in countries where government changes the reimbursement policy.

For a new product to be successful, it needs to be launched proactively in the "right" market at the "right" time with the "right" marketing plan.

Table 6.1
Causes of New Products Failure

Causes of new product failure fall under the following categories:

1. Market/marketing failure
   Small size of the potential market
   No clear product differentiation
   Poor positioning
   Misunderstanding of customer needs
   Lack of channel support
   Competitive response
2. Financial failure
   Low return on investment
3. Timing failure
   Late in the market
   "Too" early—market not yet developed
4. Technical failure
   Product did not work
   Bad design
5. Organizational failure
   Poor fit with the organizational culture
   Lack of organizational support
6. Environmental failure
   Government regulations
   Macro economic factors

The key is to create strategic competitive advantage that can be sustained over time.

To address the issue of creating sustainable competitive advantage, organizations need to follow a systematic new product development and marketing process as presented in Figure 6.1. The discussion in this chapter is organized around the steps of this process.

IN-COMPANY ANALYSIS: IDEA GENERATION AND SCREENING

At the first step of the process, it is useful to consider three factors for screening new product ideas.[4] These factors are: the reasons for the new product, the extent to which it is new, and the opportunity cost and development risk. We discuss each factor in turn.

Figure 6.1
New Product/Service Development and Marketing Process

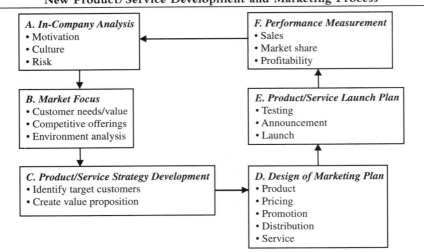

A. In-Company Analysis	F. Performance Measurement
• Motivation	• Sales
• Culture	• Market share
• Risk	• Profitability

B. Market Focus	E. Product/Service Launch Plan
• Customer needs/value	• Testing
• Competitive offerings	• Announcement
• Environment analysis	• Launch

C. Product/Service Strategy Development	D. Design of Marketing Plan
• Identify target customers	• Product
• Create value proposition	• Pricing
	• Promotion
	• Distribution
	• Service

Reason for the New Product

Any organization needs to have a clear idea about why it is developing the new product and how it fits with its strategic vision. Figure 6.2 shows a set of forces that motivate organizations for developing new products. These forces are characterized as being internal or external to an organization.

Figure 6.2
Key Motivating Forces Driving New Product/Service Development

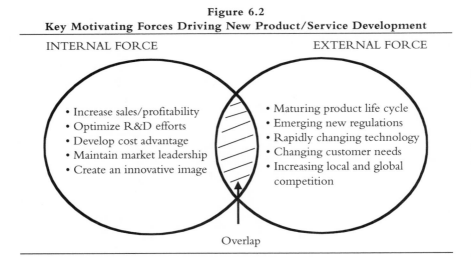

INTERNAL FORCE   EXTERNAL FORCE

• Increase sales/profitability
• Optimize R&D efforts
• Develop cost advantage
• Maintain market leadership
• Create an innovative image

• Maturing product life cycle
• Emerging new regulations
• Rapidly changing technology
• Changing customer needs
• Increasing local and global competition

Overlap

The greater the overlap between these two types of forces, the higher the chance of success for the new product/service should be.

Extent of Newness

Once the motivation behind the new product is clear, the organization needs to evaluate the extent of "newness" along the two dimensions depicted in Figure 6.3, namely newness to the market and newness to the organization. The categories presented in Figure 6.3 include:[5]

- *New-to-the-world product.* Products that are breakthroughs and create an entirely new market; change the existing behavior of customers (e.g., Sony Walkman, FedEx, Internet).
- *New-product lines.* Products that are new for an organization but not for the marketplace, an organization's first entry into an established market (e.g., GM credit card, AT&T's cable service).
- *Additions to existing product lines.* Products that extend the current line of products (e.g., Diet Coke, caffeine-free Coke, diet caffeine-free Coke; Fidelity's online investment service).

Figure 6.3
Types of New Products

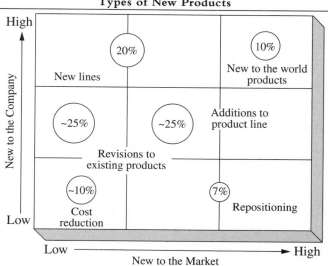

Source: Figure based on *New Product Management for the 1980s* (New York: Booz, Allen & Hamilton, 1982).

- *Improvements in revisions to existing products.* Products that are made better in terms of performance or value and/or replace existing products (e.g., Windows 2000, Economy Plus seats by United Airlines).
- *Repositioning.* Products that are targeted to a new customer segment or positioned for a new use/application (e.g., Arm & Hammer baking soda, Rogaine).
- *Cost reductions.* Products that provide similar benefits at lower cost (e.g., generic drugs, private-label consumer goods, online air travel services).

The set of marketing issues varies depending on a product's extent of newness. A better understanding of these issues is critical to designing an effective marketing plan for the new product.

Opportunity Cost and Development Risk

Opportunity cost refers to the loss in profits due to a delay in product launch. Development risk is the cost of introducing a "poor" product. A major issue in launching a new product is: To be the first or to be the best. Ideally, it should be both. The challenge for organizations is therefore to launch better products faster (i.e., focus on the speed to market for a clearly differentiated and superior new product).

An analysis of these three factors would help in addressing how well the product fits with the capabilities and the vision of the organization. We proceed to the second stage in the process.

MARKET FOCUS: IDENTIFY CUSTOMER NEEDS AND TEST NEW PRODUCT CONCEPTS

In this phase, we focus on identifying markets that offer the best opportunity for an organization. Specifically, we attempt to answer the following question, "How well does the product fit the market needs?"

To answer this question, we first need to define the market for which the new product is being considered. For this, we follow a customer-oriented definition of a product market:[6]

A product market is the set of products judged to be substitutes within those usage situations in which similar pattern of benefits are sought, and the customers for whom such usages are relevant.

This definition clearly emphasizes the link between the set of product features and benefits and the target customer needs. Given that an organization possesses the knowledge about the features and benefits associated with its product offering, a relevant piece of information for the organization is to appropriately identify target customers needs (i.e., listen to the voice of the customer). Figure 6.4 depicts a framework for identifying the two types of customer needs.

Existing Needs

Exiting needs are those currently in the minds of the customers which can be easily expressed. Traditional market research methods such as in-depth interviews, focus groups, and market surveys can be used to identify such needs and to test new product concepts. Examples include the launch of New Coke by Coca–Cola and the introduction of Saturn by General Motors.

Figure 6.4
Identifying Customer Needs

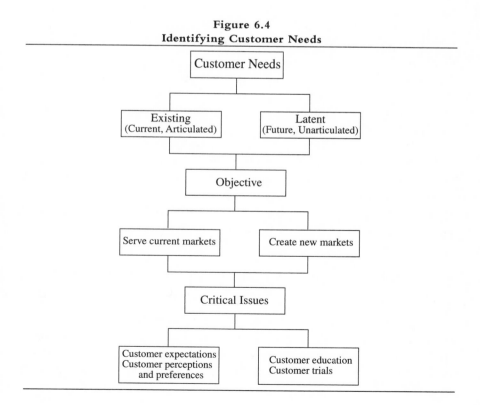

Latent Needs

Latent needs are those that customers either do not realize today and therefore are not able to express or are unwilling to express. For example, consumers did not see any need for a Walkman until Sony launched it and drove the market toward it. Patients with sexual dysfunction do have a need for a drug (e.g., Viagra) but they would not feel comfortable in acknowledging that they have such problems in a standard market survey. Consequently, estimating the size of the potential market for such a drug is not easy with traditional market research techniques.

Recalling the categories of new products presented on pages 133–134, the category of new to the world products primarily relates to addressing latent needs of customers while the other five categories are meant for satisfying existing customer needs.

There is considerable debate in the marketing literature regarding the inadequacy of currently available market research methods in uncovering latent needs and testing new to the world product concepts. Customers are unable to articulate such needs because of their lack of familiarity with the features or benefits of the new product. This is particularly true for most high-tech products.[7] Practitioners feel that conducting standard market research for such products is not useful.[8] Therefore, there is a need for new tools and techniques that would focus on educating customers by either showing them a prototype or an actual demonstration of the product.[9] The key is to get appropriate inputs for designing market-driving strategies for such new-to-the-world products.

A bulk of new products are customer-driven, that is, the needs are expressed by the customers. For such products, market research is needed to gain a better understanding of customer expectations and their satisfaction with current offerings. This information helps in designing a market-driven strategy for the new product by clearly differentiating it and appropriately positioning it relative to other available alternatives.

STRATEGY DEVELOPMENT: CREATING SUSTAINABLE COMPETITIVE ADVANTAGE

Having identified the customer needs and defined the target market, the next step is to physically design the product and appropriately position it in the minds and hearts of the target customers. To do this, it is essential to have a deeper understanding of customer value perceptions and preferences.

The notion of customer value became very popular in the eighties. A comprehensive field study was conducted over the period from 1988 to 1992 to assess customer value in business markets.[10] Based on in-depth field interviews, they proposed the following definition of customer value:

> Value is defined as the perceived worth in monetary units of the set of economic, functional/technical, and psychological benefits received by customer in exchange for the price paid for a product offering taking into consideration the available competitive offerings and prices.

This definition implies that customer value is perceptual, multidimensional, and contextual in nature. In other words, when choosing a new product, customers compare it to other available alternatives along the three dimensions—economic, functional, and psychological benefits (see Figure 6.5) and then make the final choice. We explain these dimensions in turn.

Economic Value

For economic value, customers equate the perceived quality of various products with the price they have to pay using a heuristic like the ratio of perceived quality and price. If a customer perceives the quality of competing products to be similar, the lowest price offering would be chosen because it will provide maximum savings to this customer. MCI entered the long-distance telephone market by emphasizing the savings not only to the users but also to their friends and families.

Figure 6.5
Dimensions of Customer Value

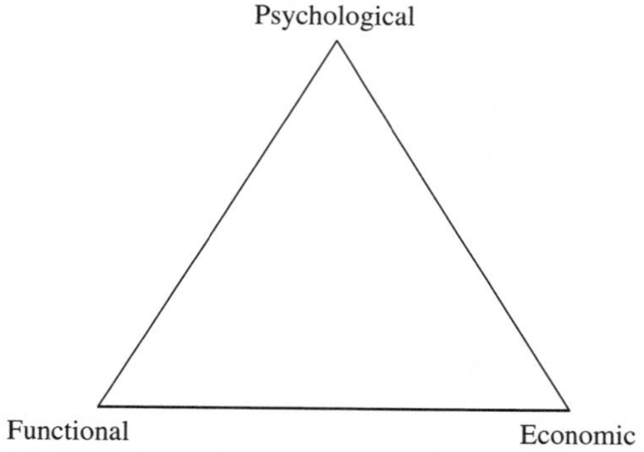

Psychological

Functional

Economic

Technical/Functional Value

Technical/functional value is computed by evaluating products in terms of the set of features or applications they possess. A functional value driven customer would prefer a product with the most sophisticated set of features. The initial positioning of Sprint in the long-distance telephone market was on sound-quality demonstrated through a pin-drop.

Psychological Value

Psychological value is mostly driven by intangibles such as service, brand name, trust, relationship, and reputation. Customers seeking these benefits care about total satisfaction with the product and desire peace of mind. AT&T differentiated itself from competitors like MCI and Sprint by focusing on its excellent customer service, reputation, and an emotional relationship—reach out and touch someone.

Meaningful differentiation of a new product cannot be sustained over time through a value proposition based purely on economic or functional value. It is easy for a competitor to either match or lower its price to capture economic value driven customer segment. Also, given the availability of technology, the competition can develop a product with similar functional benefits. In order to create a sustainable meaningful differentiation, it is essential to offer some psychological benefits in addition to economic and functional benefits.

Consider the launch of Lexus by Toyota. It provided economic value to the customers by pricing its 300 Model lower than competing Mercedes and BMW models. But it also realized that this economic saving was not sufficient to sustain its competitive advantage and therefore introduced a separate dealership for Lexus. The rational is that Lexus dealers would provide a higher level of service than Toyota dealers. This positioning has contributed significantly toward the strong positive perceptions of Lexus in the marketplace. The following propositions create value for a new product:

- *Proposition 1.* Reduce customer overall costs and efforts in terms of time involved in searching, acquiring, and using the new product. Simplify the purchasing process, make it convenient and a pleasant or entertaining experience overall.
- *Proposition 2.* Increase customer cost of switching to competitors' offerings. Develop customer loyalty programs (e.g., frequent flyer programs offered by airlines) or other customer relationship programs

that would help in retaining customers of the new product. Creating cost of switching also enables organizations to raise prices over time.

DESIGNING AN EFFECTIVE MARKETING PLAN

Designing an effective market plan requires an explicit measurement of customer preferences for the three types of benefits discussed previously. Conjoint analysis[11] is a useful technique for estimating customer preference parameters such as part-worths, that is, the importance each customer assigns to various parts of a product offering. Such estimates would help us in designing marketing plans for different customer segments and also in calculating preference shares of the new product and other competitive offerings.

From an organizational perspective, an alternative set of customer value disciplines are thought to be:[12]

- *Operational excellence.* Providing customers with reliable products or services at competitive prices and delivering them with minimum difficulty or inconvenience.
- *Customer intimacy.* Segmenting and targeting markets precisely and then delivering products or services that completely meet their needs.
- *Product leadership.* Offering customers leading-edge products and services that consistently enhance their use or application of the product, thereby making rivals' good obsolete.

This suggests that for an organization to sustain competitive edge in the marketplace, it should excel in one of these three disciplines and maintain parity with competitors on the other two.[13]

We now discuss these value disciplines from a strategic perspective in the context of designing marketing plans for new products. We also show that there exists a clear one-to-one mapping between the macro-level value disciplines presented here and the three micro-level customer value dimensions discussed previously in Figure 6.5.

Operational Excellence

In striving for operational excellence, the focus is on price and convenience. For any organization to be price competitive, it needs to have a cost advantage (i.e., it needs to have efficient operating, manufacturing, and distribution systems). Being operationally excellent reduces the cost of producing a product or providing a service and therefore offers economic value to the target customers. One way to achieve such excellence is to think in terms of standardization: providing new products that share a substantial number of features or components with other offerings of the organization. An example is Southwest Airlines which has grown considerably over the years. It has launched various new services and penetrated new markets but with a clear focus on standardization—all its planes are Boeing 737s. This standardization enables Southwest Airlines to keep its cost structure under control and also offer attractive prices to its customers.

Another example is Lexus. Initially, its 300 Model had the same engine that went into a V-6 Toyota Camry. This standardization provided Toyota with substantial economies of scale advantage. We now make the following proposition:

- *Proposition 3.* Consider standardization on those dimensions that are not critical determinants of choice for the target customers.

Type of aircraft is not a critical factor in choosing an airline. Similarly, customers of Lexus would evaluate the overall quality of the car and not just compare its engine to that of Toyota Camry.

Customer Intimacy

This value discipline emphasizes the concept of being customer-focused. An extreme form of it is to eventually create market segments of size one— true customization. A useful approach is to calculate the lifetime value of each customer, and then design individual level marketing plans based on lifetime values. Although doing so is feasible in principle, it may not be cost effective in practice.[14]

Today, many organizations are targeting customers on a one-to-one basis through Internet-based services. Examples include Peapod, WebVan, and Amazon.com. The critical success factor from an operational viewpoint is scalability such that online services become more cost effective and provide attractive returns on investment for the extensive distribution system. From a customer retention perspective, a critical issue for organizations is maintaining his or her privacy. Accordingly, we propose:

- *Proposition 4.* Focus on the total experience of each customer (before, during, and after the product is bought and used) and think of customization on those aspects of the total experience that are critical to his or her choice.

Lexus is an example of maximizing customer intimacy. Dealers of Lexus try to make sure that each customer is totally satisfied with the quality of service offered, a psychological value.

Given the importance of customer intimacy in creating sustainable competitive advantage, there is a paradigm shift in the marketing of new products: moving from managing products to managing customers or customer relationships. The central idea is that if an organization treats its customers as assets and is successful in retaining them, it can offer those customers more new products over time. By establishing a long-term relationship an organization reduces the risk and uncertainty associated with the new product in the minds of their target customers.

Product Leadership

Product leadership means creating a competitive edge through new offerings in the marketplace. Organizations therefore should focus on continuous innovations and have a rapid product development process. Many organizations are able to launch better new products faster by pursuing an integrated product development process as shown in Figure 6.6.

Figure 6.6 demonstrates a cross-functional team approach to new product development. By working as a team, cycle time can be substantially

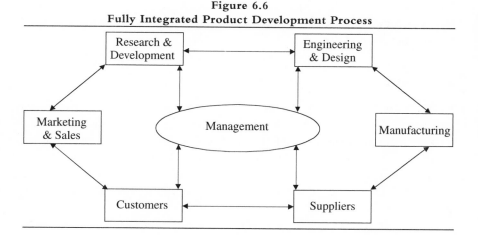

Figure 6.6
Fully Integrated Product Development Process

reduced.[15] Furthermore, success factors such as technical feasibility, economic viability, component availability, and manufacturing capability can be jointly discussed. The following quote by Frank Shrontz, ex-chairman and CEO, Boeing Co., regarding Boeing 777 illustrates very well the merits of an integrated product development process:

> It is a very exciting day for all of us. It's great to see a product of working together with our customers and suppliers turn out so well.

Other examples include Reebok's Pump shoe and Chrysler's Neon, both are results of an excellent team effort. In general, through continuous innovations organizations can keep offering more sophisticated products and thereby enhance the technical and functional value of their offerings. As a result, consider the proposition:

- *Proposition 5.* Product/market leadership requires an innovative mindset and a clear focus on continuous innovations taking into consideration economies of scale, scope, and skills.

Organizations may also consider strategic outsourcing and strategic alliances or partnerships as other ways to achieve product and market leadership. In addition, they can also leverage their current product line and create synergy making the new product globally competitive and attractive.

PRODUCT LAUNCH PLAN

There are two key decisions organizations make at this phase of the product development process: product or market testing, and product announcement and rollout.

Product or Market Testing

Before a product is rolled out in the marketplace, it is critical to test it at some level. The common practice for consumer products has been test marketing, launching the product with a full marketing plan in a couple of cities or metropolitan areas. Doing so enables organizations not only to estimate consumer response to the new product but also to evaluate the trade response. The danger of test marketing is the premature exposure of the product to competitors.

An alternative approach is to conduct pretest marketing (in the form of a simulated test marketing), which is relatively expensive, less time consuming and can be kept confidential. Although fairly accurate, pretest marketing does not provide estimates of trade response. Researchers have proposed various pretest marketing models such as Assessor, Bases, News.[16]

Product Announcement and Rollout Plan

When to announce that a product is going to be launched is an important strategic decision. The timing of the announcement decision can create barriers to competitive entry in the same product market.[17]

The next decision is the timing of the actual product launch. There have been several studies that have analyzed the strategies for market pioneers and late arrivals.[18] In spite of having a good product, delay in the launch decision may seriously affect the market performance of the new product. In addition to the time dimension, geography is also an important decision variable (i.e., where to launch—regional vs. national rollout).

PERFORMANCE MEASUREMENT

The final stage consists of measuring the performance of the new product. Commonly used metrics are tracking sales or market shares over time, computing the return on investment, or focusing on the bottom-line (i.e., profits). A comparison of the actual results with the preset criteria provides necessary action steps regarding continuing with the current marketing plan, making revisions to the plan, or deciding to pull out of the market.

Sometimes the deviation from the expected performance may not be due to the elements of the marketing plan associated with the product but due to changing market conditions. Currently, there have been major shifts in the marketplace because of the evolution of Internet and e-commerce activities. We now discuss the implications of these changes.

CHANGING MARKETING ARCHITECTURE WITH E-COMMERCE/INTERNET

The recent evolution of the Internet is changing the way organizations are marketing their products and services. Some implications of the differences noted in Table 6.2 are that we are moving:

1. From market segments to segments of size one.
2. From "brick and mortar" channels to "click and mortar" channels.
3. From traditional marketing communication campaigns to permission-based marketing.[19]

Table 6.2
Changing Marketing Architecture

Industrial Age (Past) →→→→ *Information Age (Current and Future)*	
Customer needs driven	Customer value driven
One-way	Interactive
Finite reach	Infinite reach
Time delay	Time saving
Information constraints	Information abundance
Fixed/restricted product bundles	Flexible—create your own bundle

These changes lead us to rethink the managing of new products in the Information age. As discussed previously, value-driven customers think in terms of their total experience with an activity (e.g., buying a car, traveling by air). Activities that are logically connected in customer cognitive space may be spread across diverse and disconnected markets in the physical marketplace. This disconnection creates market inefficiencies.[20] Inefficiencies lead to increased customer search cost and customer cost of thinking. Therefore, it is important for organizations to create market efficiencies by realigning suppliers in the marketplace with customers' cognitive space. We suggest two options:

1. Suppliers start providing a one-stop shopping experience for their customers by extending their product offering.
2. New players, called *mediators,* enter the market that serve as a single point of contact between customers and suppliers and provide them a one-stop shopping experience. They realign the marketplace with cognitive space.[21]

Therefore, we would see more new products offered, both in business-to-business and business-to-consumers markets. A major challenge for organizations would be to coordinate and integrate their online and offline offerings such that customers overall have a pleasant experience irrespective of the channels they used to purchase the product.

CONCLUSIONS

New product development and marketing is risky but it is a risk worth taking. Risk of failure can be minimized by following the formal process discussed in this chapter. Each phase of the process can be treated like a check-gate for deciding whether to continue or not with the product. This chapter attempts to provide a specific framework at each stage that would help organizations in making such decisions.

A brief summary of the key concepts for creating sustainable differentiation are:

- Understanding customer needs and what customers value.
- Focusing on customers' total experience with the product and making it pleasant and entertaining.
- Simplifying customer purchasing process by reducing their costs and efforts.
- Creating customer switching costs.
- Establishing barriers to competitive entry.

The marketplace is changing rapidly which makes managing new products more challenging and interesting. The emergence of e-business increases the complexity in designing business models for new products. Organizations need to develop strategies that are adaptive to the changing environment and consistent with the new marketing architecture.

APPENDIX A: HIGH-TECH PRODUCT WITH INDIRECT NETWORK EXTERNALITIES

The utility that consumers derive from some high-tech products (e.g., High Definition Television, HDTV) often depends on the availability of complementary products and services (e.g., programming availability). The greater the availability of programming (the "software") the more attractive the HDTV set (the "hardware") for the consumers. This effect is called an indirect network externality, because the demand for the hardware product is indirectly affected by the increased supply of complementary products.[22] Indirect network externalities result in a coordination problem commonly called the "chicken-and-egg" problem, when hardware and software products are supplied by different sets of firms.

The chicken-and-egg problem in HDTV market arises because hardware firms want the networks to offer a wide selection of high-definition programs but the networks in turn want to wait till the new HDTV sets have achieved significant market penetration. Neither the HDTV manufacturers nor the networks want to move first to invest in market creation. Some other contemporary markets where the chicken-and-egg problem exists are electric vehicles (sales versus the availability of changing stations) and smart cards (adoption versus card acceptance in retail stores).

Gupta, Jain, and Sawhney[23] present a conceptual and operational model for the evolution of markets with strategic interdependence. They apply the model to the U.S. Digital Television industry. Their results suggest that networks' actions play an important role in the acceptance of HDTV, thus forecasts based on diffusion models[24] that ignore the influence of indirect network externalities may be seriously biased.

Notes

1. C. Merle Crawford, *New Products Management* (Boston, MA: Irwin, 1994).

2. Deloitte and Touche, "Vision in Manufacturing Study," Deloitte Consulting and Kenan-Flagler Business School (March 6, 1998).

3. A.C. Nielsen, "New Product Introduction—Successful Innovation/Failure: Fragile Boundary," AC Nielsen BASES and Ernst & Young Global Client Consulting (June 24, 1999).

4. Discussed in Robert J. Dolan, "Matching the Process of Product Development to Its Context," Harvard Business School case (1991), pp. 592–609.

5. Philip Kotler, *Marketing Management, The Millennium Edition* (Englewood Cliffs, NJ: Prentice Hall, 1999).

6. G.S. Day, A.D. Shocker, and R.K. Srivastava, "Consumer Oriented Approaches to Identifying Product Markets," *Journal of Marketing,* vol. 43, no. 4 (1979), pp. 8–19.

7. Some high-tech consumer durables have strategic interdependence with other products.

8. Justin Martin, "Ignore Your Customer," *Fortune* (May 1, 1995), pp. 121–125.

9. Vijay Mahajan and Jerry Wind, "Rx for Marketing Research," *Marketing Research* (fall 1999), pp. 7–13.

10. James Anderson, Dipak C. Jain, and Pradeep Chintaguta, "Customer Value Assessment in Business Markets: A State-of-Practice Study," *Journal of Business-to-Business Marketing,* vol. 1, no. 1 (1993), pp. 3–29.

11. Paul E. Green and V. Srinivasan, "Conjoint Analysis in Marketing: New Developments with Implications for Research and Practice," *Journal of Marketing,* vol. 54, no. 4 (1990), pp. 3–19.

12. Michael Treacy and Fred Wiersema, "Customer Intimacy and Other Value Disciplines," *Harvard Business Review,* vol. 71 (1993), pp. 84–93.

13. In reality, it is possible to excel in more than one value discipline. An organization should start with focusing on one of the disciplines. After having excelled in it, it can move to the next one over time.

14. Mass customization is an effective compromise between achieving customer intimacy and operational excellence. Joseph B. Pine II, "Mass Customization" (Boston: Harvard Business School Press, 1993).

15. Steven C. Wheelwright and Kim B. Clark, *Revolutionizing Product Development: Quantum Leaps in Speed, Efficiency, and Quality* (New York: The Free Press, 1992).

16. A detailed discussion of test and pretest marketing models is available in Glen L. Urban and John R. Hauser, *Design and Marketing of New Product* (Englewood Cliffs, NJ: Prentice Hall, 1993) and Crawford in note 1. For testing industrial products see Dolan in note 4.

17. The work by Robertson, Eliashberg, and Rymon (1995) is a useful study in this regard.

18. Glen L. Urban, Theresa Carter, Steve Gaskin, and Zofia Mucha, "Market Share Rewards to Pioneering Brands: An Empirical Analysis and Strategic Implications," *Management Science,* vol. 32 (June 1986), pp. 645–59; Gurumorthy Kalyanaram, William T. Robinson, and Glen L. Urban, "Order of Market Entry: Established Empirical Generalizations, Emerging Empirical Generalizations, and Future Research," *Marketing Science*, vol. 14, no. 13 (1995), pp. 212–223.

19. Mohanbir Sawhney and Philip Kotler, "Marketing in the Age of Information Democracy," chapter in this volume.

20. Mohanbir Sawhney, "Making New Markets," *Business 2.0* (May 1999), pp. 5–6.

21. Ibid.

22. Jeffrey Church and Neil Gandal, "Network Effect, Software Provision and Standardization," *Journal of Industrial Economics,* vol. 40, no. 1 (1992), pp. 85–103

23. Sachin Gupta, Dipak C. Jain, and Mohan Sawhney, "Modeling the Evolution of Market with Indirect Network Externalities: An Application to Digital Television," *Marketing Science,* vol. 18, no. 3 (1999), pp. 396–416.

24. Barry Bayus, "High-Definition Television: Assessing Demand for a Next Generation Consumer Durable," *Management Science* (November 1987), pp. 1319–1333; and Dipak C. Jain, Frank M. Bass, and Trichy Krishnan, "Modeling the Marketing Mix Influence on Single Product Diffusion," in *Growth, Diffusion, and Market Penetration Models,* eds. Vijay Mahajan, Eitan Muller, and Yoram Wind (Norwell, MA: Kluwer, 2000), pp. 116–121.

INTELLIGENCE: LEARNING ABOUT THE CUSTOMER AND MARKETPLACE

CHAPTER 7

UNDERSTANDING CONSUMERS

BOBBY J. CALDER

The goal of understanding consumers always reminds me of a favorite joke. The joke is about a bartender. One day a dog walks into the bar. The dog jumps up on a barstool.

Dog: I'll have a draft beer.

Bartender (pouring): That'll be $4.

Bartender (pausing): Gee, I have to ask . . . We don't get many talking dogs in here?

Dog: At these prices, I'm not surprised.

As only humor can do, the joke jolts us with a truth that ordinarily is too uncomfortable to admit. The truth here is how different one point of view can be from another. And how our point of view can make us oblivious to another's.

To many companies, consumers or customers seem as strange as "talking dogs." To many consumers, the only remarkable thing about a particular product is its price. Seller and buyer have inherently different points of view. The difference may be more or less, but the gap is always there.

Yet successful marketing requires bridging this gap. It could even be said that successful marketing *is* the bridging of this gap. To market successfully, a company must transcend its own internal point of view to understand what the product means, and could mean, to consumers who have their own points of view. Only a product that is meaningful from their point of view will seem relevant to consumers, will seem different from other products, will seem to be reasonably priced. Thus, the goal of understanding consumers is fundamental. Understanding consumers is not just using "marketing research" as an information source, nor is it just performing a staff activity. It is a vital, and may well be *the* vital, resource factor for marketing.

Even when its importance is appreciated, understanding consumers is often approached through a conventional wisdom that needs rethinking. In this chapter, I reexamine this conventional wisdom and some orthodox views that come with it. My goal is to make suggestions for improving the way companies approach consumer understanding.

MARKETING RESEARCH–CONVENTIONAL WISDOM

Suppose that we wanted to market a new cooking appliance. The appliance is designed to substitute for a conventional oven. Among other things, it cooks meats twice as fast as an oven. How might we go about understanding consumers? The following approach would be typical.

We might well begin by examining available data about consumer behavior from syndicated panel surveys and the like. We might look into how often consumers are using their ovens. (That frequency is down.) Or how much time they are spending preparing dinner. (Dinner preparation time is less.) Or how the sales of other specialty cooking appliances are doing. (Sales are up.)

We would, however, probably also want primary research information specific to our product. First, we might do a series of focus groups to explore reactions to cooking with a new appliance. Hearing consumers talk about meal preparation would give us a feel for what questions to ask and the language used by the consumer. But it would be important not to make any decisions based on this information. Focus groups are qualitative. Responses are not precise, reports only cover the general things people had to say, with perhaps a few idiosyncratic quotes. Moreover, the sample size, which may be only 40 people or so, is too small. And, besides, everyone knows that one or two people tend to dominate a focus group discussion and the other participants go along with what is being said. So the focus groups may be useful "directionally" but we would not want to rely on them.

Ideally, we would need to do a consumer survey to obtain a quantitatively valid understanding of consumers. The answers to questions would be quantified and the sample size large enough to generalize. By surveying hundreds of consumers we would be assured of statistical validity.

Our quantitative survey research might well take the form of asking consumers to rate the importance of various attributes of our appliance on a 1 to 10 scale, with 10 being very important. Key results might be:

Speed of cooking	8.2
Quality of food	7.1
Ease of cleaning	6.5
Counter space	4.8

We could even do analyses to explore the relationship of these attributes with questions about things such as price sensitivity. We might find that price sensitivity goes down with increases in the importance of speed of cooking. In any case, the final results of the survey would provide the understanding to make decisions. Our appliance would become the Speed Cooker and be marketed accordingly.

The thinking underlying this case scenario is what I call *marketing research-conventional wisdom* (MR-CW). Its hallmark is that data is primary, quantitative data is preferred, and that the ability to generalize from data comes from large samples. Its mantra is: How big is the sample size?

THE PROBLEM WITH MR-CW

There is nothing wrong per se with MR-CW thinking about understanding consumers. Quantification is powerful; more data and larger samples are desirable. The problem is that there is more to understanding consumers than is grasped by the MR-CW mentality.

Conventional wisdom falls into the trap of simply assuming that understanding increases with the amount of data available. The more data, and in particular data from more people, the greater the validity of research results and the better the understanding. The MR-CW fixates on achieving understanding through *data*. Regardless of their involvement or sophistication with research, the thing managers under the sway of MR-CW care the most about is "How big is the sample size?" Assured on this score, research results tend to be accepted as equaling understanding.

This fixation on data in general and sample size in particular is, unfortunately, misplaced. Understanding is not just a matter of data. It is first and foremost a matter of *explanation*. To understand something is to explain how it happens. Part of this is to make a prediction about what will happen. But explanation is more than prediction. An explanation is about why something will happen, how it will come about. In the case of our new appliance, what we are looking for is an explanation for why and how consumers might use the appliance.

In looking for explanations, the important thing to realize is that explanations are never *in* the data. Explanation is always separate from the data. Let's digress to take a close look at this point. Consider the following little parable (adapted from Bertrand Russell). Suppose we are in the food service business. We do a survey of a certain demographic group. We find that 85 percent of the consumers in this group have eaten chicken at least four times in the week surveyed. Our survey sample of 400 consumers seems like a lot but it is not statistically representative. We do a second survey and get the same results for a probability sample of 2,000 people. We conclude that our understanding is quantitatively precise and statistically valid. These consumers are chicken eaters!

This may seem about as simple and straightforward a case of consumer understanding as we could possibly hope for. Certainly it would seem this way from the MR-CW perspective. Here is the problem: Where is the explanation? We could predict that these consumers would keep eating chicken (and therefore it should be a bigger part of our menu). But this is a prediction, not an explanation. We could say that the explanation is simply the extrapolation, if so many eat chicken now, many will probably eat chicken in the future. But how do we know we can extrapolate in this way? Can we say it is because such extrapolation often works? This amounts to using extrapolation in general to justify extrapolation in particular, that is, to justify itself, and, with thanks to Bertrand Russell, the logic is not good.

Sampling statistics help us to generalize survey data to a larger population that could have been surveyed but was not. Statistics do not help with the larger problem of extrapolating data into a prediction about the future. A survey may indicate that people are eating (or say they are eating) chicken but extrapolating this behavior into the future because such extrapolation sometimes works in an act of faith, not logic.

Things are even more complicated than this, however. The fact is, you have to have an explanation *before* you can extrapolate from data. One explanation, a simple one, for why our consumers are eating so much chicken is that they like the taste of chicken. This explanation would lead to the prediction that they will eat chicken in the future. Note that it is the explanation that generates the prediction. Our consumers will eat chicken in the future because they like its taste and will want more. The prediction is not mere extrapolation of the data.

We can see this another way. Consider that other explanations are possible. Perhaps our consumers are concerned about their weight and are eating chicken to diet. Or maybe they are eating it to save money. With an explanation along either of these two lines, one could predict that, after accomplishing, or tiring, of their goal, consumers will no longer eat chicken. Our data, people eating a lot of chicken, could lead to either prediction: that they will keep eating or that they will stop. The same data can fit either of the two opposite predictions. Thus, the prediction depends only on the explanation, not the data. The explanation is not in the data, and therefore the prediction is not in the extrapolation of the data.

Explanations are primary. They are independent of data. The only way to predict is to have an explanation. Predicting from data alone is not logically justified.

This conclusion is not as obtuse as it may seem. The point to remember is that one ought not to take market research data, check the sample size, and then extrapolate the data. Sample size and sampling statistics have nothing to say about whether people will eat chicken in the future.

If explanation is primary, it follows that data is not really useful without explanation. You have to come to data with an explanation in mind. Data does not tell you what to think. You have to think in advance of the data.

So where do explanations come from? Logically, they cannot come from data, because they are not in data to begin with. But, if not from data, where *do* they come from? Explanations come from creativity. Explanation is the creative act of figuring out what is going on with consumers. Such creativity may be inspired by data, looking at patterns of data until one gets an idea about what is going on. Or it may follow from other creative impulses, including experience and intuition.

The crucial thing is to have an explanation, to always have an explanation in mind, to start with an explanation. Once an explanation occurs to you, regardless of where it comes from, it is primary. You think about explanation first and data second. The problem with MR-CW is that it thinks only about data or about data with explanation assumed somehow to be in the data.

THE RELATIONSHIP OF EXPLANATION TO DATA

If you have an explanation in mind, data can play a very important role in the process of understanding consumers. The role of data is to make you more confident in the explanation you hold *or* to make you give up that explanation and look for a better one. Data is the most powerful way of *critiquing* an explanation.

Return to the case (simplified, but very real) of the new cooking appliance. Discarding the MR-CW mentality, we realize that our 2,000 consumer sample is impressive, but we need to approach consumer understanding more broadly. First, we need to focus on explanation. If we have data, it can be an inspiration for explanation, but one way or another we need to start with an explanation. In this case, one explanation that might occur to us is that what is going on is that people simply value speed more than quality. People are more and more rushed in their meal preparation and therefore willing to sacrifice quality just to get food on the table.

We can now use data to critique our explanation. For starters, does the consumer survey data we have in hand fit the explanation or not? It turns out that it does. Speed of cooking is rated as more important than the quality of the food. This finding makes us more comfortable with the explanation.

However, despite the 2,000 consumer sample size, the survey should not make us too confident. The reason is that the survey is also consistent with many other explanations that would imply higher ratings for speed of cooking. Consumers might, for example, be thinking that speed is something that companies can easily accomplish with technology, whereas quality is more difficult. The explanation then revolves around consumers' expectations about what is technically possible and therefore should realistically be important to them.

One can see that a stronger test of the first explanation is in order. Can we obtain data that would challenge the "satisfaction/sacrifice" explanation relative to the "technology expectations" explanation. A simple test would be this: Tell consumers to assume that there are no technological limits on either speed or quality and ask them to rate importance based on this assumption. If we obtained the same importance ratings, this would support the "satisfaction/sacrifice" explanation. People are after speed more than quality. But, if ratings of the importance of quality increased relative to speed, this would refute the "satisfaction/sacrifice" explanation and support the "technological expectations" explanation.

There are two principles at work here. One is that the severity with which data tests an explanation is important. The amount of data, including the size of the sample, is not irrelevant, but it is the overall degree to which the data poses a challenge to the explanation (the severity of the test) that matters most. It is the survival of an explanation by the challenge of data that increases our confidence in the explanation.

The second principle, and an even more important one to my way of thinking, is that we learn even more when data causes us to *reject* an explanation. The rationale for this is as follows. If the data are consistent with an explanation, our confidence in it may increase. But it is still possible that other data, from another, more severe test that we have not yet done, or even thought of, would reject the explanation. Thus we cannot know for sure that an explanation is right. *We can never prove an explanation.* We can only have provisional explanations that we accept and use at a point in time. And, in fact, it is not our confidence that increases with consistent data, it is just that we continue to accept an explanation as the preferred one.

Now, if data cause us to reject an explanation, we have learned something new. We know that the explanation we have is not acceptable and that we need a new one. Thus we can use rejection to evolve better explanations. We never have *the* explanation. (The objective, factual certitude of MR-CW is illusory.) The explanation that forms our understanding of consumers is accepted, based on existing data, and, provisional, subject to new data.

It cannot be emphasized enough that data by itself is meaningless. There is no explanation inherent in data. Data can only help in finding an acceptable explanation.

The consequences of this logic have significant practical implications. Many managers approach consumer understanding with the idea that they must *begin* by looking at data. Only by looking at data will they know what to think about consumers. The truth is that data can be inspirational, but so can general experience and intuition. In any event, you have to think something. And this cannot be so simple as making hypotheses about the data, if this means mere prediction, with no explanation. You have to think through what might be going on, you have to have an explanation in mind, before data can help. A report stuffed with data put before managers who themselves have thought very little about consumers equals another decoration for someone's office, another file that no one remembers in a few months.

LEVELS OF EXPLANATION

All explanations are not created the same. They are created, inspired by data, experience, or intuition. But explanations can vary in important ways, too.

Explanations vary along two dimensions that are important for the present discussion. Both are continuums that are most easily thought of as dualisms. One dimension can be termed *particularistic-universalistic*. A particularistic explanation is one that is specific to a given circumstance. That is, the explanation applies only to certain people in a certain setting of time and place. Obviously, this specificity can be more or less. But a particularistic explanation has clear limits on its scope. The explanations brought to bear for our new cooking appliance are particularistic in this way. They apply only to certain consumers (although we have not gone into it, profiled by geography, demographics, and socioeconomic status) in a certain setting (meal preparation). Particularistic explanations contrast with universalistic explanations. The later hold across a range of people and settings.

The second dimension explanations can vary on is *everyday-scientific*. An everyday explanation is stated in terms of the perspective of the people involved in the settings to which the explanation applies. The explanation may in fact be the one participants would themselves give for their behavior (termed a naive explanation). Or it may be one that we can formulate in terms that would be familiar to participants but that they could not articulate themselves. The explanations created for our appliance are everyday explanations couched in terms of peoples' own experience. The *satisfaction/sacrifice* explanation may well be one that the people would themselves express.

Everyday explanations contrast with scientific explanations which are not meant to represent the experience of actual consumers. This type of explanation is formulated in its own terms that are invented for the purposes of explanation. These terms are sometimes referred to as constructs. The main point is that a scientific construct does not depend on anyone's everyday understanding. (Just as general relativity does not depend on anyone thinking about space-time distortions when they drop something.)

It is useful to combine these two dimensions into a matrix as in Figure 7.1. Two of the four combinations are of special interest here. One is labeled *Commonsense Explanation*. The explanation is particularistic in scope and stated in everyday terms. The other is the diagonal contrast. It is universalistic in scope and stated in scientific terms, and consequently I refer to it as *Theory*. The other two types of explanation are possible approaches that have received academic attention but need not concern us here.[1]

In typical marketing practice, managers are usually concerned with Commonsense Explanation. As with our appliance, the objective is to understand specific consumers in a setting of interest in terms that they would themselves understand. I find it useful to lay out such explanations as a story that follows the actual life experience of the consumer. The important thing

Figure 7.1
Types of Explanation

	Particularistic	Universalistic
Everyday	**Commonsense Explanation**	Interpretation
Scientific	Grounded Theory	**Theory**

to realize is that this is the type of theory that we are working with, particularistic and everyday.

Theory has a bad connotation in some business circles. To many managers, it means not proven and abstract. And this is true. The rub is that no explanation is proven and that Theory is necessarily abstract because it has universalistic ambition. Moreover, Theory is generally a powerful type of explanation because it is usually the province of academics that are in the business, and only the business, of subjecting such explanations to data.

Our main point is that, if we are using Commonsense Explanation, we should take this into account in testing our explanations. I turn to this issue in the next section. It is useful as an aside, however, to consider the relationship between Theory and Commonsense Explanation.

Managers who have looked at a Theory article in an academic journal are likely to have wondered whether such work could have any practical value. This value is much easier to see, along with the difficulty of the work, if we keep in mind the distinction between Commonsense Explanation and Theory. Beyond this, however, it is important to realize that there are potential synergies between the two types of explanations.

One synergy is especially important. Theory can help with the construction of Commonsense Explanations. The latter are frequently heavy with content, the experience of everyday life. Because they are abstracted, Theory is much better with process—how people process information, how culture affects people. By linking, at least in a broad way, our Commonsense Explanations to Theory, we can reflect process better and make our Commonsense Explanations more complete.

Back to our cooking appliance. As is often the case with Theory, even if we think we are not using it, we often are. Usually we are using, in Keynes' words, the work of some long-dead, and best-forgotten, theorist. Recall our satisfaction/sacrifice explanation. People get more satisfaction out of speed of cooking than the quality of the food—a Commonsense Explanation if ever there was one. But an explanation is implicitly framed in terms of a Theory. The Theory, briefly, postulates that people are motivated by *needs* that are satisfied when an underlying biological requirement is satiated. In some cases the needs are not based on biological mechanisms but function in the same way. In these cases, they are *wants*.

"Needs and wants" is a Theory that helps in creating our more particularistic and everyday satisfaction/sacrifice explanation. Unfortunately, this use of Theory can be for better or worse. It turns out that not many scientific researchers today would employ the construct of "wants." The construct does not make clear what the connection is to a biological need. There is little explanation in the vague analogy. Theory becomes tautological rather than explanatory. Consuming anything can be explained by simply postulating a want for that thing.

But Theory can help and there is an opportunity for synergy here. More powerful constructs such as beliefs and attitudes can make Commonsense Explanations more complete. Our "technological expectations" explanation, for instance, could well be formulated in terms of beliefs.

RESEARCH METHODS

Given the present state of progress with Theory, we probably should be using Commonsense Explanations for most business problems. That said, we should recognize that we *are* using Commonsense Explanations, and take this into account.

With MR-CW, large consumer surveys are the ideal. They supply quantitative data that can be generalized because of their sample size so that the data holds for an entire population of interest. In my opinion, such surveys can be extremely useful. But MR-CW goes too far in implying that qualitative data and smaller samples are inherently inferior and to be regarded with suspicion. I have argued against the second class status of qualitative methods in the past.[2] Here I will address these methods in the larger context of explanations and data.

Qualitative Methods

There are many kinds of qualitative methods. Focus groups and one-on-one in-depth interviews are the most common. All necessarily involve small samples for reasons of cost and time. Given more resources, one would normally prefer bigger samples for qualitative methods. This is all a matter of practicalities.

But there is more at issue here than practical limitations. If we break through the MR-CW mindset, the most important thing to consider is that we are trying to create Commonsense Explanations and to pit them against data to find the one that is most acceptable. It is crucial to keep this in mind in evaluating qualitative methods.

Consider the focus group. As I have pointed out elsewhere,[3] it is possible to use focus groups in an exploratory way in keeping with MR-CW. It is also possible to use focus groups as a *phenomenological* method. By this I mean "a method that has one overriding objective: to allow the researcher to share, participatively, the experience of a group of people.[4] The focus group is used as an instrument for describing what it is like to be a person in a particular setting.

The very name *focus* group reflects this phenomenological purpose.[5] Originally called the "focussed interview" in the 1940s by Robert Merton and Paul Lazersfeld, the explicit goal was to focus people, individually or in groups, on a specific stimulus so that their comments would reflect their experience of the stimulus. My supposition is that this method wound up as our "focus group" because of the natural focusing properties of a group discussion. Even without a stimulus (though one is often used), people in a group must focus on a topic if they are going to interact with each other. Their comments are, therefore, more rooted in the actual experience (the phenomenon) of what they are discussing, thereby making this experience easier to describe. Groups have the advantage of focusing people on common experience; one-on-one interviews are preferable when more control is desired over what people focus on.

With this background, come back to the main issue here. For any type of data, whether produced by a "qualitative" or a "quantitative" method, we need to have an explanation in mind that the data can support or reject. In many cases, that explanation will be a Commonsense Explanation. Given that a Commonsense Explanation is couched in terms of particularistic everyday experience, it makes eminent sense to use qualitative research to test the explanation. In practice, both focus groups and one-on-one interviews lend themselves to confronting Commonsense Explanations with data.

In the case of our cooking appliance, the "technological expectations" explanation was easily refuted. The quotes below, from 10 one-on-one interviews, are typical:

> "It will always take some time to prepare food. But in the future I'm sure all you'll have to do is program a machine and get Mother's meatloaf."

> "There is no such thing as instant food. I bet that somebody will figure out how to get gourmet food with much less bother. That'll happen soon."

With even 10 interviews (which is a sample size I find useful for a test in cases like this) the "technological expectations" explanation, that consumers of the kind targeted believe that quality is less technically possible than speed, received a strong test. With a Commonsense Theory that is rooted in everyday experience, qualitative data can be extremely powerful.

But 10 interviews? Would not 100 or 1,000 have been better? Yes, in a sampling sense. Remember the broader issues, however. We need to go beyond MR-CW. If our explanation is that people have a particular belief about technology and if we see that a set of people who ought to have that belief do not manifest it in their everyday life, this is strong evidence against our explanation.

We can always say that it may be that some other people would have manifested the belief. But this is not fundamentally a matter of sampling. It is a call for considering the inclusion of individual differences in the explanation. We could do 100 or 1,000 more interviews and this might by chance be helpful if we saw that some people had the belief and others did not. Nonetheless we would be back in the same place, needing to revise the explanation to account for differences in people and needing to test the revised explanation.

Sample size is *an* issue, the big issue is getting data that constitute a severe test and changing explanations, if required by the data. In this case, the data from the sample of 10 caused us to reject the explanation. The fact that some consumers did not fit the explanation, when the explanation says they should, is the big issue. This is what tells us we need to modify the explanation (perhaps by including individual differences) or replace the explanation with a new one.

It turns out that in the case of the cooking appliance, an entirely different explanation needed to be created. I will leave it to the reader to figure out what it might have been. Suffice it to say that when the new Commonsense Explanation was pitted against qualitative data, the explanation clearly fit the description of peoples' experience from the interviews.

Certainly this explanation, and any other, can only be provisionally accepted and would ideally be exposed to further testing. Merely adding sample size, however, would not in itself be the best use of resources for further testing. Increasing the severity of the test, for example by directly observing behavior in the setting of interest, would be more powerful.

Quantitative Methods

Surveys are rightly associated with numbers and being more quantitative. Despite the real advantage of quantification for analysis, it is nonetheless true that quantitative analysis requires abstraction. If we are dealing with a Commonsense Explanation that is very particularistic and stated in everyday terms, it is often much easier to relate such an explanation to the data of focus groups or one-on-one interviews than to survey responses. Surveys, by virtue of being more quantitative, are better suited for mid-range explanations that are more abstract.

MR-CW treats surveys as inherently superior to focus groups and one-on-ones. From a broader perspective, surveys do have the advantage of quantitative analysis but this advantage is contingent on the type of explanation being tested. Many Commonsense Explanations, as we have seen, are a better fit with qualitative methods. They can in fact become trivialized in survey testing. *Qualitative data is not necessarily subordinate to quantitative data.*

You should realize too that, as you move to more general, less particularistic everyday explanations (which a company might do over time), and quantitative analysis becomes more appropriate, this entails its own difficulties. Content validity (the relationship of explanatory terms to actual settings) becomes less important and issues of internal and construct validity become paramount. Even the issue of how explanations are to be applied becomes more vexing.[6] I will only note here that it becomes increasingly apparent on consideration that MR-CW surveys have real disadvantages when it comes to analyzing cause and effect (internal validity) and the relationship of specific measures to the constructs they are associated with (construct validity). Surveys coming out of MR-CW are typically woeful in this regard, and certainly no paragons of sophisticated analysis, regardless of how "quantitative" they may seem.

CONCLUSIONS

We need to broaden our thinking about understanding consumers beyond the perspective of MR-WC. Understanding is an active process. It is not a matter of static information.

Above all else, understanding is hard. We are trying to explain why people do what they do. It is difficult enough to explain anything, explaining people's behavior is harder yet. Moreover, it is difficult enough to explain the behavior of people we know well and who are like us. Explaining consumers, who may seem as different as "talking dogs," is even more challenging.

To meet this challenge, I believe that we must keep these points in mind. Contrary to MR-CW:

- Understanding consumers is not about data and the superiority of one method over another.
- The amount of data we collect, or the number of interviews we conduct, is not the critical success factor.
- Understanding consumers is about creating explanations that can be inspired by data but equally well come from experience and intuition.
- The critical success factor is the ability and willingness to confront explanations with data so that the data poses a severe test of the explanation.

- If an explanation survives testing, it is accepted, but not proven.
- If an explanation fails, we must create a better explanation and test it so that explanations can evolve over time.
- This process should produce, not marketing research reports, but knowledge.

We may have been able to avoid this complexity in the past. The future, however, is the knowledge economy and the learning organization. Consumer, or customer, knowledge is one of the most important types of knowledge a company can have and it is crucial that companies learn how to get better at understanding consumers.

Notes

1. Bobby J. Calder and Alice M. Tybout, "What Consumer Research Is," *Journal of Consumer Research,* vol. 14 (1987), pp. 136–140.

2. Bobby J. Calder, "Qualitative Marketing Research," in *Principles of Marketing Research,* ed. Richard P. Bagozzi (Cambridge, MA: Blackwell Publishers, 1994), pp. 50–72; Bobby J. Calder, "Exploratory, Clinical, and Interaction Centered Focus Groups," *Journal of Data Collection,* vol. 26 (1986), pp. 24–27; and Bobby J. Calder, "Focus Groups and the Nature of Qualitative Marketing Research, *Journal of Marketing Research,* vol. 14 (1977), pp. 353–364.

3. See note 2.

4. See note 2, Calder (1994), p. 54.

5. Ibid., p. 51.

6. Bobby J. Calder and Alice M. Tybout, "A Vision of Theory, Research, and the Future of Business Schools," *Journal of the Academy of Marketing Science,* vol. 27 (1999), pp. 359–366; Bobby J. Calder, Lynn Phillips, and Alice M. Tybout, "Designing Research for Application," *Journal of Consumer Research,* vol. 8 (1981), pp. 197–207; Bobby J. Calder, Lynn Phillips, and Alice M. Tybout, "The Concept of External Validity," *Journal of Consumer Research,* vol. 9 (1982), pp. 240–244; Bobby J. Calder, Lynn Phillips, and Alice M. Tybout, "Beyond External Validity," *Journal of Consumer Research,* vol. 10 (1983), pp. 112–114; John Lynch Jr., "On the External Validity of Experiments in Consumer Research," *Journal of Consumer Research* vol. 9 (1982), pp. 225–239; John Lynch Jr., "The Role of External Validity in Theoretical Research," *Journal of Consumer Research,* vol. 10 (1983), pp. 109–111; Brian Sternthal, Alice M. Tybout, and Bobby J. Calder, "Experimental Design: Generalization and Theoretical Explanation," in *Principles of Marketing Research* ed. Richard P. Bagozzi (Cambridge, MA: Blackwell Publishers, 1994), pp. 195–223; Russell S. Weiner, "Experimentation in the Twenty-First Century: The Importance of External Validity," *Journal of the Academy of Marketing Science,* vol. 27 (1999), pp. 340–358; and William D. Wells, "Discovery-Oriented Consumer Research," *Journal of Consumer Research,* vol. 19 (1993) pp. 489–504.

CHAPTER 8

QUALITATIVE INQUIRY IN MARKETING AND CONSUMER RESEARCH

JOHN F. SHERRY JR. and ROBERT V. KOZINETS

Let's begin this methodology chapter on an ontological note and distinguish, as Shweder does, between the nature of the objects (and the subject matter) we as researchers explore.[1] Quantitative researchers seek to reduce, if not remove entirely, the presence of the "merely subjective," so that illusion will not impede the measurement of the "really real." These researchers pursue *quanta,* that is, things as they "really are," phenomena that exist independently of our attention.

Qualitative researchers chafe at the restrictive notion of the "merely objective," and use the self as an instrument of interpretive understanding to discern the meanings arising in interpersonal interaction. These researchers pursue *qualia,* that is, the irreducibly local phenomena as experienced (sometimes uniquely) by individuals, that enlarge our conception of the "really real." *Qualia* are distinctive, situated objects which are underspecified or undetermined by *quanta.*[2] Qualitative researchers agree with Vladimir Nabokov, who jibed that " 'reality' is one of the few words in the English language that should never be used without quotation marks."

Qualitative marketing and consumer researchers quest for qualia in the everyday, lived experience of consumers, managers, public policy makers, activists, and countless other stakeholders—and, yes, via systematic introspection, including themselves—who contribute to the maintenance and change of marketplace behavior. By attempting to understand from the actor's perspective, and by striving to represent that understanding

The authors thank Dawn Iacobucci, Stephen Brown, and Alladi Venkatesh for constructive comments on earlier versions of this chapter.

authentically, these researchers complement the work of their quantitative counterparts.

This complementarity cannot be overemphasized. Just as the notion of "interpretive" research is a spurious, or, at least, a misleading one—both qualitative and quantitative approaches demand interpretation[3]—so also must it be noted that problem-driven multimethod inquiry is gaining in popularity.[4] Thus, practitioners of ethnographic, contextual, or naturalistic inquiry, while employing a standard battery of qualitative techniques, may also incorporate quantitative measures into their regime. Perhaps the diagnostic feature of these types of inquiry is their quest for *data* as opposed to the *capta* yielded by their quantitative counterparts.[5] That is, qualitative researchers elicit information in context, as a gift, rather less invasively than excising it for examination out of context, as a fact. The theory-ladenness of facts[6] is a qualitative preoccupation. Unfortunately, hard/soft, natural/social, qualitative/quantitative oppositions are pre-eminent symptoms of our cultural era; methodological hegemony has impoverished our understanding of the singularity of the particular.[7]

This chapter is not intended as a disciplinary history,[8] a methodological tutorial,[9] a managerial manifesto[10] or philosophy of science debate.[11] Rather we strive to frame some of the salient issues in the field, and explore some of the managerial implications of this particular approach to research.

ORIENTATION

In a recent study of the worldwide marketing research industry,[12] investigators discovered that ad hoc qualitative research comprises the largest growth segment of inquiries into consumer behavior. The proliferation of qualitative tools in the manager's toolkit is apparently accelerating.[13] As functional parity is achieved among products and services across more and more industries, and marketers are compelled to devote greater attention to understanding and enhancing the experiential dimension of their offerings,[14] we can expect qualitative research to undergo a renaissance. Zaltman's recent admonition to "rethink" market research by "putting people back in" to our design may herald just such a rebirth.[15]

Innovative qualitative research is diffusing widely across companies and categories. Published accounts of this diffusion are suggestive, even if unpublished proprietary reports remain the norm.[16] Firms in the high-tech area such as Hewlett Packard, Intuit, Microsoft,[17] Xerox,[18] AT&T Labs,[19] and Intel[20] are avid proponents. Consumer package goods companies such as General Mills[21] and Kimberly Clark[22] are similarly sold. In the automotive field, Harley Davidson,[23] Toyota, and Nissan[24] employ the latest qualitative methods. White goods manufacturers such as Whirlpool[25] and clothiers such as Patagonia[26] have benefitted from current developments in qualitative research. Enterprises as wide-ranging as servicescape redesign—Borders,[27] Urban Outfitters,[28] and Hallmark[29] being notable beneficiaries—and segmentation sounding—qualitative interest in teenagers among such firms as Coca Cola, Levi Strauss, and Microsoft[30] being especially "hot"—fall within the purview of this trend. Media companies such as Turner Broadcasting Systems are carrying qualitative research methods forward into cyberspace.[31] Customer visits,[32] espoused by firms such as IBM, Raychem, Polaroid, Cigna, Metropolitan Life, and DuPont, foretell the spread of ethnography to business-to-business markets. Motorola has created a board of anthropologists to advise senior management on a host of issues. Specialized research providers, whether small or medium size firms or independent consultants, are flourishing. Chicago, for example, is home to such firms as E-lab, the Doblin Group, BRS Associates, and Teenage Research Unlimited, as well as to agencies such as DDB Needham, Young and Rubicam, Ogilvy & Mather, Leo Burnett, J. Walter Thompson, Kramer Crasselt, and others, who provide innovative qualitative research to clients. Market-oriented ethnography[33] is a going concern.

While these qualitative methods have not diffused as rapidly through the academic disciplines of marketing and consumer research—arguably academics do not depreciate intellectual capital as rapidly as managers alive to practical applications of theories-in-use—they have established themselves as a viable niche in business schools, professional societies, and scholarly journals, usually under the (maddeningly misleading) rubric of "interpretive" or "postmodern" research. Here, researchers from a host of disciplines from anthropology to literary criticism have conspired to produce a view of marketing and consumption that is distinctly different from conventional wisdom. Academic niches are flourishing within U.S. business schools such as Kellogg, Harvard, Sloan, Smeal, Eccles, Eller, Wisconsin, Nebraska, and U.C.-Irvine, as well as outside them, in allied schools such as the Advertising department of the University of Illinois. Professional societies such as the Association for Consumer Research and the American Marketing Association are devoting more conference space to qualitative concerns. Scholarly journals, such as the *Journal of Consumer Research,* the *Journal of Marketing,* the *Journal of Marketing Research,* the *Journal of Advertising,* the *Journal of Business Research,* the *International Journal of Research in Marketing,* and *Culture Markets and Consumption* are fielding more articles in this burgeoning area. Perhaps more encouraging is the increasing incidence of consumption—and marketing-related articles being published in social science journals beyond the conventional business school purview.

DISTINCTIVE FEATURES OF RECENT QUALITATIVE RESEARCH

Given the proliferation of techniques and approaches in recent years, as well as adaptations to traditional methods, any attempt to summarize, synthesize, and integrate the facets of qualitative research will appear absurdly reductionist, if not misleading, in light of such space limitations as this chapter imposes. Nonetheless, an overview should be instructive, and orient the reader to some key features of current inquiry. We encourage the reader to consult authoritative sources for expanded treatments.[34]

Naturalistic observation is the hallmark of much recent effort. Immersion in a field setting, and prolonged engagement with informants (whether consumers, marketers, or other stakeholders) are common practices. Researchers often employ an *emergent design,* in an effort to capture as comprehensively as possible the minimal parameters of a phenomenon. Inquiry has an alternately expanding and contracting focus. Analysis is hermeneutic and iterative, and proceeds via a constant comparative method. Thus, data collection and analysis are conducted in tandem. A dialectical relationship between library research and field research characterizes the inquiry. Researchers sample until saturation and redundancy are achieved, at which time they either conclude their inquiry, or adopt different techniques that may permit the transcending of the limits of researchers' habitual tools of choice.

Progressive contextualization is another important research strategy. Researchers grapple with the nesting and embedding of understanding. Because meaning is always situated, a heightened attention to the context in which a phenomenon unfolds is amply repaid. Contextual inquiry is a way to elicit some of the unarticulated, tacit knowledge, emotion, motivation, and understanding that people possess. Thus, researchers will often strive to understand how behavior will ramify beyond an individual to a household, a community, and, ultimately, to a society itself. Embeddedness is a critical concern.

In keeping with their desire to probe a range of behavior patterns, researchers attempt to make *maximized comparisons.* They use variation as a perspective for plumbing similarities and differences among phenomena. Thus, researchers roam across cultures, times, or situations to provoke variance. While the representativeness of a phenomenon is clearly of interest, researchers are equally—and often, perhaps even more—concerned with outliers. Outliers are embraced (rather than rejected) for the distinctive insight their marginality can contribute. A marginal perspective is often incisively illuminating.

Qualitative inquirers quest for *sensitized concepts*. They are interested in the lived experience of their informants and in representing that experience authentically. Capturing the worldview and ethos of informants, as distinct from an analytic framework imposed by the researcher, is at the heart of the inquiry. Often such investigation is idiographic, the goal being for the researcher to develop systematic intuitions about informants' lifeworlds. Thus, informants are increasingly regarded as collaborators and consultants in the research enterprise, which itself becomes a co-created, jointly negotiated undertaking. The ultimate result of close attention to sensitized concepts is a so-called "thick description"[35] of the phenomenon under investigation.

Perhaps the most controversial hallmark of qualitative research is the notion of *intraceptive intuition*.[36] Simply stated, the researcher is the pre-eminent instrument of research. Believing that it is both impossible and undesirable to eliminate the impact of the inquirer upon the phenomenon, researchers attempt to increase their own acuity as an instrument through a variety of strategies (multimethod training, broad reading, wide experiential exposure, interpersonal skill development, psychoanalysis, introspection, personal disclosure in published research accounts, etc.) that both exalts and harnesses their idiosyncrasies. They strive to develop both wide cognitive peripheral vision[37] and broadly resonant emotional depth as indispensable aids to interpretation.

A final distinctive feature of current qualitative research is its emphasis on *grounded theory*.[38] Simply stated, theory is expected to emerge from the data. Because a researcher cannot approach a project with no a priori theories or hypotheses, and as a consequence of the rejection of a so-called objective or disinterested "fact," an inquirer strives to specify and disclose existing personal biases, but hold them in abeyance (in effect, "bracket" them) as the research regime unfolds. The posture adopted toward theory development is essentially an agnostic, eclectic one, which allows for the discovery and construction of broad, truly rival hypotheses.

The thrust of much recent qualitative work in marketing and consumer research has been critical, culturological, and communicative.[39] Researchers have explored extraeconomic and normative dimensions of behavior. They have worked steadily to unpack, dismantle, and banish the notion of "externality" from the literature. Finally, they have accelerated investigation into the nature, transmutation, and translatability of "meaning" as these issues bear upon marketing and consumption.

SPECIFIC TECHNIQUES

Because of space constraints, we have been selective in our discussion of particular qualitative research techniques without being entirely reductionist. In this section, we describe these techniques which currently enjoy cutting-edge status—participant observation, interview, and projective tasking— among academics and practitioners. We also describe the practice of "close reading" or "hermeneutic tacking" that characterizes each of these techniques.[40] Finally, we consider the extension and application of techniques developed for use "in real life" to phenomena evolving in cyberspace.

Participant Observation

Properly speaking, participant observation is a cluster of techniques employed to discover, interpret, and represent phenomena comprehensively and holistically. Thorough analysis often depends on a negotiated understanding of informant and researcher's perspectives. Participant observation born of prolonged field immersion is the hallmark of ethnography. Alternately obtrusive and unobtrusive, the ethnographer apprehends, with as many sensory modalities and through as many experiential channels as required, the lifeworlds of the informant. The ethnographer is, in effect, acculturated or resocialized by informants, once a rapport is established, to apprehend the strange as familiar, or, more commonly in market research settings, the familiar as strange. Intimacy with stakeholders, achieved through trust evolved over time in context of the round of life, opens a window for ethnographers on the lifeworlds of informants.

Participant observation circumvents many of the problems associated with faulty recall, limited ability to articulate (whether tacit knowledge or the unthought known), and social desirability in self-disclosure. It is invaluable in mapping the ecology of consumer behavior and in providing inferential stimuli for probing its social structure and ideology.[41] It is especially useful in harnessing the marketer's offerings—products, services, advertisements, retail outlets, and so on—into projective stimuli to be used in conjunction with other techniques to unpack the production of consumption. Confronting informants with real time aspects of their lifeworlds in context is a powerful eliciting device.

Increasingly, photography, videography, and audiotaping are used as aids to participant observation. These tools are employed actively by the researcher to capture emergent behavior and create a visual inventory. Just as often, the tools are deployed passively to record material in the researcher's absence. Informants are deputized to photograph, audiotape, and videotape their own lifeworlds, with equipment provided by the researcher (or to behave "as usual" in front of recording equipment fixed and mounted in their personal environments). Such informant-produced insight is a productive complement to the researcher's inquiry.[42] Photos, videos, and audiotape diaries can then be used as projective vehicles to elicit additional informant commentary, in a practice called *autodriving*.[43]

Interviews

Interviews comprise a broad continuum of focused inquiry. At one end, interviews may be informal, unstructured, nondirective, and conversational. On the other end, they may be formal, highly structured, entirely directive, and administered identically across all informants. Interviews may be conducted with individuals or with groups. Interviews may be used to elicit sheer or mere information, in an actuarial or inventory sense. They are also used to enter the phenomenological-existential world of informants. Interviews depend for their success on the forging of bonds of trust between actors, the eliciting skills of the interviewer, and both the insightfulness and desire for disclosure of the informant.

An especially crucial practice for construing the interview is the temporary suspension of the researcher's voice of judgment. Imagining the question to be something more than a simple interrogatory is the key to this suspension. A question is an invitation to creativity, a point of departure; it is the search for a playmate, a form of seductive foreplay.[44] Ultimately, a question is a jointly negotiated quest for understanding, a partnership in an adventure. Learning to listen deeply is essential for the interviewer, since being heard is one of the most profound, humane gifts an individual will ever receive; listening deeply is the symbolic equivalent of holding the informant.[45]

It is our belief that the group interview is the most overused and misused arrow in the qualitative quiver. Focus groups often provide the illusion of human contact and the occasion of pyrotechnics that efficiently satisfy the prematurely narrowed imagination of clients and researchers behind the one-way glass. To exploit fully the potential of the group interview,[46] it may be necessary to conduct archival analysis, participant observation, and depth interviewing before convening a focus group. Briefing participants in advance of the session, or requesting "homework" of them prior to convening the group may yield dividends. Conducting a variety of tasks during the group is often productive.[47] Altering conventional spatial and temporal boundaries of the session may also be indicated; groups can be conducted *in situ,* over hours and even days. The so-called moderator is simultaneously an over-used and underutilized resource. The moderator must facilitate interaction, alternately guide and probe the discussion, and analytically attend, in real time, to the verbal and nonverbal cues that enable systematic unpacking of the clients' interests as embodied in the group. Further, the moderator develops a theory in-use-on-the-fly to direct each subsequent group in the project. Finally, the moderator must deliver an interpretive analysis replete with managerial implications. Such demands require that we empower moderators to be more active (yet not more intrusive) than convention dictates, and that we partner them with confederates (on either side of the glass) to aid in the iterative process of data collection and analysis. This is easily enough accomplished in academic research, and could be routinized in proprietary research by deputizing and training client personnel.

Projective Tasking

It is instructive to consider the tension animating the multiphrenic self in postmodern society[48] from an evolutionary perspective. As a species, we have achieved distinction in no small measure thanks to the tension that modulates our principal personae: *homo faber* versus *homo narrans.* In our former aspect, we are tool-making creatures, and in our latter aspect, storytellers. While these two aspects co-exist and interact synergistically, they serve distinctive adaptive ends. Traditionally, marketers have treated primarily (indeed, have been) makers; only recently have they treated (indeed, become) storytellers. The webs of significance in which stakeholders are suspended[49] are becoming a focal interest.[50] How best to tap such meaning making?

Projective tasks engage our storytelling impulse. Such tasks permit the asking of questions in an indirect fashion and encourage the least restraint in their answering. Projectives invite informants to respond in ways that are distinctively personal and ostensibly personally meaningful. Projectives empower informants to respond in more creative, insightful, and revealing ways than might otherwise be possible. Inquiry is cast in dramatic form, and the drama essentially poses the question. Indirection is used in the service of illumination. Projectives plumb unconscious material, socially objectionable motivations, and informant fantasy; they elicit responses to issues informants may find too trivial or too sensitive to address directly.[51]

Although evolved in a clinical setting for use as a triangulating perspective to assist diagnoses in context, projectives have migrated into marketing and consumer research predominantly as stand-alone measures, modified to suit a nonclinical population. Recently, some researchers have cautioned against the a-contextual use of projectives.[52] Thematic apperception tasks have been most widely used. Sentence completion, figure drawing, word association, structured fantasizing, and collage creation have also proven popular. Often, these individual techniques are combined in a single study to enhance depth and richness of response, as well as to triangulate among techniques. For example, the Zaltman Metaphor Elicitation Technique[53] combines informant-selected images, depth interview, laddering, photo and art therapy techniques, sensory inventory, structured fantasizing and collage creation as eliciting frames.

Close Reading

A common analytic posture across the qualitative methods, tied intimately to intraceptive intuition, is the practice of close reading[54] or hermeneutic tacking.[55] Whether the analyst uses ethnography,[56] existential phenomenological interview,[57] projective tasking,[58] literary criticism[59] or introspection,[60] relentless attention to detail and painstaking relation of part to whole are key features of the enterprise. Working with a textual metaphor in the case of behavior, or with a literal text in the case of interview verbatims, the analyst attends in minute detail to the systematic unpacking of meanings present in the text. Recognizing that meaning is often polysemic, the analyst seeks to reveal—in dialogue with both "text" and "author"—as exhaustively as possible the levels and nuances of meaning embedded in the text. Some or much of the meaning thus wrested from the text may be opaque or transparent to the informant at the time of text production. For example, recently we have seen a shift from a close reading of advertising text[61] to text in reception;[62] we can imagine a longer term inquiry that moves from production through reception to re-production.

Ideally, a close reading produces the richest possible understanding of a "text" because all relevant information—internal and external—to the "text" is carefully considered. Relevance is broadly construed. That is, initial attention is riveted on the content, rhetoric and structure of the "text," and then this analysis ramifies to related "texts," which in turn both extends and amplifies the original analysis. The researcher tacks between and within internal and external information sources, in hermeneutic fashion, in search of enlightenment.

INTERPRETIVE SUMMARY

It is apparent how complementary and overlapping these techniques can be in their nature and application. Participant observation helps the analyst limn the informant's lifeworld, and permits the acquiring of systematic intuitions about worldview and ethos. Participation helps the researcher embody this knowledge and experience. Interviews take the researcher deeper into the phenomenal realm of the informant, allowing for a systematic exploration of the informant's physical and metaphysical experience. Projective tasking helps the analyst transcend his or her observational and elicitation skills, and affords access to unarticulated realms of informant experience. Each technique amplifies, reinforces, extends and challenges the others.

Given the evocative power of things (i.e., products, services, brands, servicescapes, trust relationships, advertising, and anything else in the marketing environment) and our human penchant for meaning mongering, qualitative methods used in consort can be powerfully illuminating. In this situation, consumer ethnographies[63] or customer visits[64] are most productive. Imagine a project conducted over time in sites significant to the customer, where all the artifacts in a given situation are meaningful to the customer. These artifacts (e.g., a brand, a relationship) are fundamental eliciting devices, set as they are in the consumption context. The artifact can be used as a projective task and contextual cues in evidence can be marshaled to elaborate, clarify, contest, and revise the customer's interpretations systematically via interview. Imagine further the analyst debriefing the customer systematically, sharing analytic interpretations of observations, interviews, and projectives, so that the customer might react constructively and critically and thereby improve the "final" interpretation. Such creative triangulation in contextual inquiry and collaboration in analysis is becoming more common.

EXPORTING QUALITATIVE TECHNIQUES TO CYBERSPACE

If part of our goal in using qualitative research is to enlarge our concept of the "really real," what better place to stretch than in the virtual reality of cyberspace? As a society we are consuming cyberspace as diversionary delight and wellspring of communitas and illumination. We are employing the expanded scope and resources of infotech to open and explore a vast range of market relations[65] and consumption servicescapes[66] in the marketspace[67] of cyberspace. Resolved by a one-hour sale on AOL that drove over half a million customers through the digital door of an online retailer—a feat unimaginable in the "real" world—is the fact that informational networks are changing the shape of marketing and consumption forever.[68] No doubt marketing and consumer researchers, including qualitative inquirers, are impelled to follow in their wake. But, upon venturing forth into the contextual frontier of cyberspace, what ecology do we face?

Early research into the medium of *computer-mediated communication* (or CMC) found that its limitations forced an unnatural style of communication, reduced relational cues and impoverished the interpersonal environment.[69] Its anonymity and apparent privacy seemed to erode social structures by equalizing status and encouraging a less inhibited form of communication.[70] Early scientific voyages, then, found cyberspace to be like outer space: cold and inhospitable.[71] Yet field researchers have found it to be a much more generative medium when filtered into the phenomenological stream of lived experience. Cyberspace seen not as computer-mediated communication but as community is an organic entity, diverse, dynamic, and multitendrilled, a carnival of personally-enriching social worlds.[72] Ever-adaptable, the human animal has developed the new communicative tools and abilities to turn the cold online environment into a hearth of sociality.[73] New software and hardware tools and sophisticated avatars advance digitally upon perfectly real and perfectly fantastic simulations of face-to-face. In the meantime, an "electronic paralanguage" captures a range of affection, affiliation, social relational and metacommunicative cues.[74]

In cyberspace, human interaction must cope with (to borrow and fracture Milan Kundera's beautiful turn of phrase) an "unbearable textuality of being." The relationships change as a result of this intrusive and liberating filter on embodiment.[75] Communication that is *technologically mediated* is also radically textualized.[76] Whether our words are converted into ASCII or carried in (still crude) digital sounds and images, the intrusiveness of cyberspace communication channels is instantly obvious. While the medium is challenging us to overcome it and communicate in ways that feel more natural,[77] it is also opening opportunities.[78] Implied privacy and textuality confers experiences of *anonymous search and expression* that can be liberating in the extreme.[79] The leveling of a variety of social playing fields confers *social accessibility* that results in much wider participation than in almost any other social channel.[80] On the Internet no one knows you're a dog—or a kid, or white, or disabled, or living in Timbuktu. Being digital also means that social *information is inscribed and archived,* automatically[81] *and widely accessible.* With search costs vastly reduced, problem sets across the board change from the collection of information to management of the hypertext cascade ensuing from even the most cursory search.

Cyberspace is a liminal locale, providing a placeless space and what anthropologist Victor Turner called a "time out of time." For the human species, the move into the altered time and space horizon of cyberspace presents a radical temporal and environmental discontinuity.[82] According to some, this change is an evolutionary one in which the thinking animals that make tools increasingly blur the distinction between tool and thinking animal. The result is a *cyborg ecology*[83] in which abstract being and embodied being, mind and AI, organism and machine comfortably coexist.[84] To help understand this ecology, qualitative inquiry can evolve along with it.

Netnography

From the raw material of bits and icons, people construct meaningful social communities. But whether called "virtual communities,"[85] "brand communities,"[86] "communities of interest"[87] or "Internet cultures,"[88] these groups use common marketplace interests as the social cement to form their foundation.[89] While, to a marketer's eye, some of the symbolic cues they use may look familiar, the challenge in cyberspace's twisted social arenas is often one of disentangling the message from the medium, and making familiar the strange and tortured dances of social cyberia. Encompassing online community, *netnography* has been developed as a naturalistic technique for capturing conduct in cyberspace.[90]

Netnography is an amalgam of qualitative techniques, adapted for cyberspatial environs.[91] Like participant-observation, it can be simultaneously obtrusive and unobtrusive. The act of "lurking" in online fields[92] offers an unobtrusiveness that blurs telepresence[93] to near invisibility. Yet netnography holds online participation to be a beneficial investigative movement.[94] Like its offline counterpart, it seeks *immersion,* a profound experiencing of digital sociality. Access to a wealth of data may make it easy to confuse breadth for depth, and mistake quantity for quality. But being acculturated into bravely evolving new social spheres requires *prolonged engagement.* This infers naturalizing the techno–environment and rules of engagement of the overall realm of cyberculture.[95] The body language of emoticons, intentional misspellings, lexical surrogates for vocal segregates, spatial arrays, grammatical markers, absence of corrections and capitalization, as well as visual ASCII art[96] will be essential gadgets in the netnographic inquirer's kitbag. Then, there are more specific codes to learn that pertain to your communities of choice, their personnel, their history and rules,[97] their relations to the offline servicescapes[98] of markets and consumption.[99]

In furtherance of this goal, trust is an essential catalyst. Honesty, a legitimate purpose, and a genuine firsthand knowledge of the community offer entrée modes of solid basis. Specifying the nature of quid pro quos and a common interest can fuel ongoing participation and ever-increasing access.[100] All the while, the ethics of the inquiry are double-edged and very real. Investigators must vigilantly attend to ever-evolving online privacy concerns.[101]

Through this endeavour, the adept cybernaut will be chronicling the journey through field or journal notes. The bulk of these notes will be self-transcribing—digital captures of the social flow. Introspection and the testing and elaboration of theory will be greatly assisted by additional fieldnotes which are reflective, analytical and which point to interesting directions for future investigation. Even as the technology's mediation textualizes and occludes researcher insights, it similarly places limits on what informants (consumers, marketers, other stakeholders) are able to articulate. Tacit knowledge is thus a difficult but essential prize to be sought in cyberspace. Gaining it requires discriminating and empathic elicitation, and can be greatly assisted by incorporation of two other techniques: the cyber-interview, and digital projectives.

Cyber-Interview

In a sense, the interview already permeates cyberspace. An almost unbounded interactional space, newsgroups, chat rooms and e-mail messages are filled with the interpersonal dialog of questions and answers. Informants expound and explore, sharing personal histories, anecdotes, urban myths and legends. Decoding and finding the common and the particular in the stories these people tell[102] is one important source of netnographic insight. Others are more proactive.

As prelude and adjunct to the cyber-interview, *e-profiling*[103] leverages cyberspace's unprecedented access to social information to bolster inquiry effectiveness. E-profiling entails gaining publicly-available information on an informant's public Internet social activities. Reading samples of an informant's postings and visiting the newsgroups to which they post regularly—or their personal Web-pages or profiles—can confer precious perceptions of their social situation, interpretive communities,[104] life themes and life goals,[105] and overall experiential multidimensionality.

Cyber-interviews offer a means of altering the conventional spatial and temporal boundaries of focus group sessions. In cutting-edge university and corporate labs around the globe, software and groupware is being tested for deployment in electronic focus groups. The focus group conducted through teleconferencing software has been heralded as the major trend in focus group development.[106] As it by now may be obvious, cyber-interviews, like their offline counterparts, can be group-based or individual, formal or informal, structured or unstructured. The medium's technological characteristics are, however, directive. Particular interview styles fit particular cyber-forums better than others. So the synchronous, real time realm of chat rooms—with its conversational tone and its unfettered nature—is more suited to the informal interview that hopes for insight through heat-of-the-moment disclosure.[107] Posted newsgroup or e-mail questions offer a foundation of carefully considered answers often more appropriate to the aims of a formal interview.[108] "Persistent conversation" in any cyberspace forum can, nevertheless, lead to revelationary personal and emotional discovery.[109] Coupled with researcher genuineness, trust-building and heart-felt confession, these interviews—which can often seem a synthesis of penpal-like enthusiasm and ongoing tutelage[110]—can provide much disclosure and enlightenment. Coupling cyber-interviews with techniques that deploy digital projectives can enable access to more of the unknown and tacit levels of cultural knowledge.

Digital Projectives

Postmodernist Jean Baudrillard has coined the term *hyperreality*[111] to refer to the contemporary blending of simulation and reality, the place where the artifice and the authentic merge, and where the synthetic illusion is often deemed preferable to the concrete original. Although Baudrillard's is an often pessimistic view,[112] the information economy seems almost custom-built to blur boundaries[113] offering nearly limitless alternatives for losing oneself in simulation. The stream of prospective multimedia stimuli that online informants engage with encompasses ASCII texts and other representational codes, visual imagery such as logos and photos, sound bits and video bytes, avatars and live teleconferencing images. As with Baudriallard's creeping hyperreality, almost every "thing" in the physical world is coming to have, in cyberspace, at least one and usually a multitude of virtual doppelgangers.

With multifarious choices arraying everything from Scientology and UFO conspiracies to V-chip technical standards and the latest lampshade fashions, in some ways, cyberspace itself might be construed as a gigantic projective task. In anonymous and accessible telespace, it affords a forum for the articulation of the previously inexpressible. Turkle says that the Internet has become "a significant social laboratory" in which people experiment

with "the constructions and reconstructions of self" which characterize contemporary life.[114] Postmodern identity has been conceived as consisting of
endless acts of refashioning and re-creating our selves.[115] In the play of cyberspace, a virtual playground is constructed. Netnographers in this space
are lurkers on the side and fellow playmates. Qualitative inquiry delves into
the revelatory possibilities of this serious site of play and identity creation,
observing the multiplicity, heterogeneity, and fragmentation of the multiphrenic consumer in action.[116]

Cyberspace is said to be based on an "attention economy," in which the
scarcest resource is not money or any other resource, but human attention.[117]
Capturing and holding the attention of cyberspace informants is thus a central challenge. Formally instituting the projective properties of cyberspace,
a *Web-based intrication strategy*[118] can help capture the attention and imagination of informants. A research homepage that provides detailed visual and
textual material on topics targeted to the particular interests of cultural informants can be an invaluable means of intrication. Open-ended questions,
word completion tasks, even requests for scanned artworks and doodles can
also appear. This strategy can also make use of computer-translations of existing projective tasks, for instance, autodriving.[119] Zaltman's aforementioned Metaphor Elicitation Technique has already been digitized.
Consumers use magazine photos to synthesize paper-based collages expressing brand or product hypostasis. The collage is digitally scanned, pol-
ished by a graphic designer and drafted into service as a powerful projective
probe. Sensibly customized, the technique easily transports to cyberspace.
In summary, the artifacts used as projectives by the qualitative inquirer in cyberspace are abstract renditions, representations once removed. But through
the online construction of sociocultural reality,[120] these digital images, Web-
page, or content elements of a Web-page undergo a psychological and ontological transmutation. They achieve a status considered—within limits—
"real," thereby becoming useful tools of cultural exploration.

Nuance and Compromise

In the context of cyberspace, contextual inquiry morphs to accommodate
its technological mediation, radical textualization, anonymous search and
expression, and accessible information and social arenas. Tradeoffs are critical to netnographic inquiry. Cyberspace decontextualizes by removing
physical facets of identity we naturalize as useful.[121] Self-selection and representativeness are sticky and difficult issues. A textualized way of knowing reduces the number of observable cues, and the opportunities to discern

tacit knowledge. In exchange, it recontextualizes identity by infusing it with fantasy, play and interactivity.[122] Paradoxically, a realm of deception can increase disclosure. A home-based excursion into virtual reality can offer not only a more dynamic and accessible context than a laboratory but a far less artificial one. In keeping with our theme of complementarity between methods of investigation, netnography—with its cyber-interviews and digital projectives—must be understood as adding to, not replacing, offline research (of both the qualitative and quantitative persuasions). In addition, information technology transforms qualitative inquiry in a myriad of other ways. It changes the nature of in-person inquiry and recording, data analysis, triangulation, member checks, and research representation.[123] It can provide fresh perspectives for triangulating upon cultural actors as they engage in new forms of expression and experience. These methods may thus assist our understanding, not only of the virtual, but of the human reality.

CRISIS OF REPRESENTATION

As qualitative research evolves into the next historical epoch—the so-called sixth moment[124]—it is animated by a number of tensions, some of which, like technology, we have explored in detail in this chapter. Issues of reflexivity and legitimization, that is, the situatedness of knowledge claims and authority of interpretation, though broached here, must be deferred for extended discussion to subsequent papers. Polyvocality and representation, the emergence of contrasting stakeholder voices and agendas, and the challenge to depict authentically the lived experience of others,[125] require a ritual bow in our present treatment, however, since they form collectively one of the most interesting challenges to the marketing imagination.

Having spent so much time trying to achieve intimate understanding of marketplace behavior through communion with consumers and managers via methodological means, qualitative researchers have now turned their attention to the vehicles used to represent their interpretive efforts. Recall our earlier discussion of the foundational importance of storytelling, then note its neglect in our disciplines' research stories. Not only are we slow to plumb the possibilities of text, let alone hypertext, or of dialogic let alone polylogic discourse, but also we are just beginning to imagine the shape a nonlinear, nondiscursive, nonliterate representation might assume.

Consumer researchers have begun asserting[126] that conventional journal articles are insufficient vessels for conveying a holistic understanding of the lived experience of stakeholders. We have seen the emergence of genres such as "messy texts," autoethnography, poetry, performance texts, ethnographic fictions and narratives of the self[127] in consumer research. Photography, videography and painting have also emerged as research vehicles. Exemplars of such experimental representation are proliferating.[128]

Managers as well as academics have responded to the crisis of representation by embracing new expressive strategies. With a shift toward interpretive management, companies such as Levi Strauss, Intel, Motorola, Nokia, and Chiron have sought to enfranchise polyvocality in everyday operations, and promote multistranded discussions of the future among stakeholders and constituents.[129] 3M invokes storytelling in the service of business planning, exploiting narrative logic to plumb the places that bullet points can't reach.[130] Arguably, the increasing emplacement[131] of brand essence in vehicles such as retail theatre and Web sites is a creative response to the crisis of representation.

With its holistic, often visual qualities, qualitative research is, in many ways, cinematic in its gaze.[132] To represent findings, the interactive multimedia formats afforded by information technologies are not only ideal, but also alter the nature of representation itself. Hypertext and hypermedia (links to audio and visual information) change the relationship between researcher and reader in ways eerily attuned to the concerns of the crisis of representation.[133]

Described by some as a relatively unproblematic change in reporting opportunities,[134] this change is viewed by others as a radical departure in which the research writer "disappears, receding into the background."[135] From this perspective, final authority is conferred upon the text's new author, the point-and-click *bricoleurs* who, "in the electronic spaces of hypertext . . . construct the text out of the bits and pieces and chunks of material left for them by the writer" (ibid). Others emphasize the accessibility of the entire cyberspatial modality by envisioning hypertext netnographies linked to myriad Web-pages, Web-ring and chat rooms.[136] Hypertext netnographies are data rich, and provide opportunities for "open" textual construction,[137] real-time cultural observation, and unmediated contact with informants. They can transcend the uniformity and voyeurism of traditional ethnography's thick description, transcription and even inscription[138] to approach the stimulation of sociosimulation.[139]

CONCLUSIONS

As cultural life transforms, becoming more fragmented and diverse, so also do the methods of researching it. Marketing and consumer researchers are increasingly thinking about their task in terms that are naturalistic and holistic, and that deftly combine complementary methods. They blend (and apply) their art and science in ways that seek to reveal the sophisticated configurations, the constellation of lifeways and interests that undergird markets and consumption. In some cases, these configurations can be observed simply by watching what people do with artifacts such as products, advertisements or brands. For others, watching someone surf the net, observing the way their lifeways intersect with cyberspaceways can provide provisional clues. Almost always, the complementarity of multimethod techniques provides more comprehensive perspectives. Extending our knowledge into the lifeworlds of human beings in interaction means following them, seeing with their eyes as well as our own.

Branching out into real spaces and cyberspaces is empowering. Viewing markets and consumption holistically means opening vistas that encourage interdisciplinary, multidisciplinary and even transdisciplinary thinking. Setting our sites on longer term inquiries will allow researcher to scope out new cultural processes in the production, reception and the reproduction of meanings.[140] Many companies are just beginning to use virtual communities for lead user analysis[141]—blurring the bounds between production and consumption as customers serve as fountainheads of corporate innovation. The new questions and problems these processes propose are far from simplistic. Indeed, the intersection of cultures, markets and cyberspace are bound to become the source of the most pressing ethical and moral issues of the next few decades. Perhaps some of these techniques and ideas might be helpful in the investigations that will inform these urgent and important debates.

As it unfolds in cyberspace and IRL, we believe the future of qualitative inquiry in marketing and consumer research hinges upon the posture adopted toward the practice of "deep hanging out." The social sciences are simultaneously relinquishing[142] and re-embracing[143] the tradition of prolonged local immersion that results in nuanced interpretation of field data. At this point in their intellectual evolution, our disciplines require the kind of deep hanging out that permits researchers to infuse our databases with soul. Deep hanging out—the kind of loitering with intent that positions the marketer to become the marine biologist (not simply the fisherman) to the consumer's fish[144]—is a necessary corrective to premature closure and the rush to generalization. We hope we have provided enough guidance in this chapter to provoke our readers to dwell for awhile among the deep hangers-out, in search of more intimate understanding of marketplace behavior.

Notes

1. Richard Shweder, "Quanta and Qualia: What is the Object of Ethnographic Method?" in *Ethnography and Human Development,* eds. Richard Jessor, Anne Colby, and Richard Shweder (Chicago: University of Chicago Press, 1996), pp. 175–182.

2. Ibid., p. 180.

3. John F. Sherry Jr., "Postmodern Alternatives: The Interpretive Turn in Consumer Research," in *Handbook of Consumer Behavior,* eds. Thomas Robertson and Harold Karsarjian (Englewood Cliffs, NJ: Prentice Hall, 1991), pp. 548–591.

4. Ajay Sirsi, James Ward, and Peter Reingen, "Microcultural Analysis of Variation in Sharing of Causal Reasoning and Behavior," *Journal of Consumer Research,* vol. 22, no. 4 (1996), pp. 345–372.

5. Donald McCloskey, *The Rhetoric of Economics* (Madison, WI: University of Wisconsin Press, 1985).

6. See note 3.

7. Marjorie Garber, *Symptoms of Culture* (London: Penguin, 1998); and John F. Sherry Jr., "Heresy and the Useful Miracle: Rethinking Anthropology's Contributions to Marketing," *Research in Marketing,* vol. 9 (1987), pp. 285–306.

8. Russell Belk, "Studies in the New Consumer Behaviour," in *Acknowledging Consumption: A Review of New Studies,* ed. Daniel Miller (New York: Routledge, 1995), pp. 58–95; Norman Denzin and Yvonna Lincoln, eds., *Handbook of Qualitative Research* (Thousand Oaks, CA: Sage, 1994); and Sidney Levy, "The Evolution of Qualitative Research in Consumer Behavior," paper presented at the 26th International Conference on Marketing Research at La Londe des Maures, France (June 4, 1999); and see note 3.

9. Russell Belk, John F. Sherry Jr., and Melanie Wallendorf, "A Naturalistic Inquiry into Buyer and Seller Behavior at a Swap Meet," *Journal of Consumer Research,* vol. 14, no. 3 (1986), pp. 449–470; Russell Belk, Melanie Wallendorf, and John F. Sherry Jr., "The Sacred and Profane in Consumer Behavior: Theodicy on the Odyssey," *Journal of Consumer Research,* vol. 16, no. 1 (1989), pp. 1–38; Bruce Berg, *Qualitative Research Methods for the Social Sciences* (Boston, Allyn and Bacon, 1998); Russell H. Bernard, ed., *Research Methods in Anthropology* (Walnut Creek, CA: Altamira Press, 1995); Russell H. Bernard, ed., *Handbook of Methods in Cultural Anthropology* (Walnut Creek, CA: Altamira Press, 1998); and John Lofland and Lyn Lofland, *Analyzing Social Settings: A Guide to Qualitative Observation and Analysis* (New York: Wadsworth, 1995); and see note 7.

10. John F. Sherry Jr., ed., *Contemporary Marketing and Consumer Behavior: An Anthropological Sourcebook* (Thousand Oaks, CA: Sage, 1995).

11. Stephen Brown, *Postmodern Marketing* (New York: Routledge, 1995); Norman Denzin, *Interpretive Ethnography: Ethnographic Practices for the 21st Century* (Thousand Oaks, CA: Sage, 1997); Richard Jessor, Anne Colby, and Richard Shweder, *Ethnography and Human Development* (Chicago: University of Chicago Press, 1996); George Marcus, *Ethnography Through Thick and Thin* (Princeton, NJ: Princeton University Press, 1998); and Barbara Stern, *Representing Consumers: Voices, Views, and Visions* (New York: Routledge, 1998).

12. Cantar Group, "Market Research Industry," *The Economist,* vol. 22 (July 1995), pp. 60–63.

13. Dominique Desjeux, Anne Monjaret, and Sophie Taponier, *Quand les Francais Déménagent* (Paris: Presses Universitaires de France, 1998); Dominique Desjeux,

Cécile Berthier, Sophie Jarraffoux, Isabelle Orhant, and Sophie Taponier, *Anthropologie de l'Électricité* (Paris: Harmattan, 1996); Dorothy Leonard-Barton, *Wellsprings of Knowledge: Building and Sustaining the Sources of Innovation* (Boston: Harvard Business School Press, 1995); and see note 10.

14. Joseph Pine and James Gilmore, *The Experience Economy* (Boston, MA: Harvard Business School Press, 1999).

15. Gerald Zaltman, "Rethinking Market Research: Putting People Back In," *Journal of Marketing Research,* vol. 34 (November 1997), pp. 424–437.

16. Paco Underhill, *Why They Buy: The Science of Shopping* (New York: Simon & Schuster, 1999).

17. Dorothy Leonard and Jeffrey Rayport, "Spark Innovation Through Empathic Design," *Harvard Business Review* (November/December 1997), pp. 102–113.

18. Joan Blomberg, Jean Giacomi, Andrea Mosher, and Pat Swenton-Wall, "Ethnographic Field Methods and Their Relation to Design," in *Participatory Design: Principles and Practices,* eds. Douglas Schuler and Aki Namioka (Hillsdale, NJ: Lawrence Erlbaum, 1993), pp. 123–155.

19. Amanda Crawford, "Computers Not Made for Kids, Study Says," *Baltimore Sun* (May 8, 2000), p. 1D.

20. Katie Hafner, "Coming of Age in Palo Alto," *New York Times* (June 10, 1999); and Dean Takahashi, "Doing Fieldwork in the High-Tech Jungle," *Wall Street Journal,* vol. 27 (October 1998), B1, B22.

21. See note 17.

22. Ronald Lieber, "Storytelling: A New Way to Get Close to Your Customer," *Fortune,* vol. 3 (February 1997), pp. 102–108.

23. James McAlexander and John Schouten, "Brandfests: Servicescapes for the Cultivation of Brand Equity," in *Servicescapes: The Concept of Place in Contemporary Markets,* ed. John F. Sherry Jr. (Lincolnwood, IL: NTC Business Books, 1998), pp. 377–401.

24. See note 17.

25. Tobi Elkin, "Product Pampering," *Brandweek,* vol. 16 (June 1998), pp. 28–29, 32, 34, 36, 40.

26. See note 22.

27. Patty Kerr, "Borders," *Advertising Age,* vol. 24 (June 1996), S22.

28. Justin Martin, "Ignore Your Customer," *Fortune,* vol. 1 (May 1995), pp. 121–126.

29. Nancye Green, "Environmental Re-engineering," *Brandweek,* vol. 1 (December 1997), pp. 28–29, 32.

30. Michael McCarthy, "Stalking the Elusive Teenage Trendsetter," *Wall Street Journal,* vol. 19 (November 1998), B1–B10.

31. B.X. W, "Online or Off Target?" *American Demographics* (November 1998), pp. 20–21; and Sara Browne, "The Chat Room as a 'Third Place,'" *Brandweek,* vol. 14 (April 1997), pp. 24, 26.

32. Edward McQuarrie, *Customer Visits: Building a Better Market Focus* (Newbury Park: Sage, 1994).

33. Eric Arnould and Melanie Wallendorf, "Market-Oriented Ethnography: Interpretation Building and Market Strategy Formulation," *Journal of Marketing Research,* vol. 31, no. 4 (1994), pp. 484–504.

34. See for example, Clifford Christians and James Carey, "The Logic and Aims of Qualitative Research," in *Research Methods in Mass Communication,* eds. Guido Stempel and Bruce Westley (Englewood Cliffs, NJ: Prentice Hall,1981), pp. 342–362; and see note 3.

35. Clifford Geertz, *The Interpretation of Cultures* (New York: Basic Books, 1973).

36. Henry Murray, *Thematic Apperception Test Manual* (Cambridge, MA: Harvard University Press, 1943); see note 3; and Howard Stein, Listening Deeply: *An Approach to Understanding and Consulting in Organizational Culture* (Boulder, CO: Westview Press, 1994).

37. Gerald Zaltman, "One Mega and Seven Basic Principles for Consumer Research," in *Advances in Consumer Research,* vol. 18, eds. Rebecca Holman and Michael Solomon (Provo, UT: Association for Consumer Research, 1991), pp. 8–10.

38. Barney Glazer and Anselm Strauss, *The Discovery of Grounded Theory* (New York: Aldine, 1967); and Anselm Strauss and Juliet Corbin, *Basics of Qualitative Research* (Newbury Park, CA: Sage, 1990).

39. See note 3; and Alladi Venkatesh, "Ethnoconsumerism: A New Paradigm to Study Cultural and Cross-Cultural Consumer Behavior," in *Marketing in a Multicultural World,* eds. Janeen Costa and Gary Bamossy (Thousand Oaks, CA: Sage, 1995), pp. 26–67.

40. Clifford Geertz, *Local Knowledge* (New York: Basic Books, 1983); John Schouten, "Selves in Transition: Symbolic Consumption in Personal Rites of Passage and Identity Reconstruction," *Journal of Consumer Research,* vol. 17, no. 3 (1991), pp. 412–425; Linda Scott, "The Bridge from Text to Mind: Adapting Reader-Response Theory to Consumer Research," *Journal of Consumer Research,* vol. 21, no. 3 (1994), pp. 461–480; Linda Scott, "Images in Advertising: The Need for a Theory of Visual Rhetoric," *Journal of Consumer Research,* vol. 21, no. 2 (1994), pp. 252–273; John F. Sherry Jr. and Eduardo Carmargo, " 'May Your Life Be Marvelous': English Language Labeling and the Semiotics of Japanese Promotion," *Journal of Consumer Research,* vol. 14, no. 3 (1987), pp. 174–188; Barbara Stern, "Literary Criticism and Consumer Research: Overview and Illustrative Analysis," *Journal of Consumer Research,* vol. 16, no. 3 (1989), pp. 322–334; and Barbara Stern, "Feminist Literary Criticism and the Deconstruction of Ads: A Postmodern View of Advertising and Consumer Responses," *Journal of Consumer Research,* vol. 19, no. 4 (1993), pp. 556–566.

41. See note 10.

42. John Collier and Malcom Collier, *Visual Anthropology: Photography as a Research Method* (Albuquerque, NM: University of New Mexico Press, 1986); and Melanie Wallendorf and Eric Arnould, "We Gather Together: The Consumption Rituals of Thanksgiving Day," *Journal of Consumer Research,* vol. 18, no. 1 (1991), pp. 13–31.

43. Deborah Heisley and Sidney Levy, "Autodriving: A Photo Elicitation Technique," *Journal of Consumer Research,* vol. 18, no. 3 (1991), pp. 257–272.

44. Michael Ray and Rochelle Myers, *Creativity in Business* (New York: Doubleday, 1986).

45. Howard Stein, Listening Deeply: *An Approach to Understanding and Consulting in Organizational Culture* (Boulder, CO: Westview Press, 1994).

46. Bobby Calder, "Focus Groups and the Nature of Qualitative Marketing Research," *Journal of Marketing Research,* vol. 14, no. 3 (1977), pp. 353–364; and Prem Shamdasani and David Stewart, *Focus Groups* (Thousand Oaks, CA: Sage, 1990).

47. Susan Douglas and C. Samuel Craig, *International Marketing Research* (Englewood Cliffs, NJ: Prentice Hall, 1983).

48. Kenneth Gergen, *The Saturated Self* (New York: Basic Books, 1991).

49. See note 35.

50. Susan Fournier, "Consumers and Their Brands: Developing Relationship Theory in Consumer Research," *Journal of Consumer Research,* vol. 24, no. 4 (1998), pp. 343–373; John F. Sherry Jr., "Some Implications of Consumer Oral Tradition for Reactive Marketing," in *Advances in Consumer Research,* vol. 11, ed. Thomas Kinnear (Provo, UT: Association for Consumer Research, 1984), pp. 741–747; and Craig J. Thompson, "Interpreting Consumers: A Hermeneutical Framework for Deriving Marketing Insights from the Texts of Consumers' Consumption Stories," *Journal of Marketing Research,* vol. 34 (November 1997), pp. 438–455.

51. John F. Sherry Jr., Mary Ann McGrath, and Sidney Levy, "The Disposition of the Gift, and Many Unhappy Returns," *Journal of Retailing,* vol. 68, no. 1 (1992), pp. 40–56; and Mary Ann McGrath, John F. Sherry Jr., and Sidney Levy, "Giving Voice to the Gift: The Use of Projective Techniques to Recover Lost Meanings," *Journal of Consumer Psychology,* vol. 2, no. 2 (1993), pp. 171–191.

52. Ibid.

53. Gerald Zaltman and Robin Coulter, "Seeing the Voice of the Consumer: Metaphor-Based Advertising Research," *Journal of Advertising Research,* vol. 35, no. 4 (1995), pp. 35–51; and Gerald Zaltman, "Metaphorically Speaking," *Marketing Research,* vol. 8, no. 2 (1996), pp. 13–20.

54. John F. Sherry Jr. and Eduardo Carmargo, " 'May Your Life Be Marvelous': English Language Labeling and the Semiotics of Japanese Promotion," *Journal of Consumer Research,* vol. 14, no. 3 (1987), pp. 174–188; and see note 40, Stern (1986).

55. Clifford Geertz, *Local Knowledge* (New York: Basic Books, 1983); and see note 40, Schouten.

56. See note 10.

57. Craig J. Thompson, William Locander, and H. Polio, "The Lived Meaning of Free Choice: An Existential-Phenomenological Description of Everyday Consumer Experiences of Contemporary Married Women," *Journal of Consumer Research,* vol. 17, no. 3 (1990), pp. 346–361; and Craig J. Thompson, William Locander, and H. Polio, "Putting Consumer Experience Back in Consumer Research: The Philosophy and Method of Existential-Phenomenology," *Journal of Consumer Research,* vol. 16, no. 2 (1989), pp. 133–146.

58. Sidney J. Levy, "Dreams, Fairy Tales, Animals and Cars," *Psychology and Marketing,* vol. 2, no. 2 (1985), pp. 67–81.

59. Linda Scott, "The Bridge from Text to Mind: Adapting Reader-Response Theory to Consumer Research," *Journal of Consumer Research,* vol. 21, no. 3 (1994), pp. 461–480; Linda Scott, "Images in Advertising: The Need for a Theory of Visual Rhetoric," *Journal of Consumer Research,* vol. 21, no. 2 (1994), pp. 252–273; Barbara Stern, "Feminist Literary Criticism and the Deconstruction of Ads: A Postmodern View of Advertising and Consumer Responses," *Journal of Consumer Research,* vol. 19, no. 4 (1993), pp. 556–566; and Barbara Stern, "Literary Criticism and Consumer Research: Overview and Illustrative Analysis," *Journal of Consumer Research,* vol. 16, no. 3 (1989), pp. 322–334.

60. Morris Holbrook, "The Retailing of Performance and the Performance of Service: The Gift of Generosity with a Grin and the Magic of Munificence with Mirth," in *Servicescapes: The Concept Place in Contemporary Markets,* ed. John F. Sherry Jr. (Lincolnwood, IL: NTC Business Books, 1998), pp. 487–513.

61. Linda Scott, "The Bridge from Text to Mind: Adapting Reader-Response Theory to Consumer Research," *Journal of Consumer Research,* vol. 21, no. 3 (1994), pp. 461–480; and Barbara Stern, "Literary Criticism and Consumer Research: Overview and Illustrative Analysis," *Journal of Consumer Research,* vol. 16, no. 3 (1989), pp. 322–334.

62. David Mick and Claus Buhl, "A Meaning-Based Model of Advertising Experiences," *Journal of Consumer Research,* vol. 19, no. 3 (1992), pp. 317–338.

63. See note 10.

64. See note 34.

65. See for example, Joseph Alba, John Lynch, Bart Weitz, Chris Janiszewski, Rich Lutz, Al Sawyer, and Stacy Wood, "Interactive Home Shopping: Incentives for Consumers, Retailers, and Manufacturers to Participate in Electronic Marketplaces," *Journal of Marketing,* vol. 61 (July 1997), pp. 38–53; and Donna Hoffman and Tom Novak, "Marketing in Hypermedia Computer-Mediated Environments: Conceptual Foundations," *Journal of Marketing,* vol. 60 (July 1996), pp. 50–68.

66. John F. Sherry Jr., "The Soul of the Company Store: Nike Town Chicago and the Emplaced Brandscape," in *Servicescapes: The Concept of Place in Contemporary Markets,* ed. John F. Sherry, Jr. (Lincolnwood, IL: NTC Business Books, 1998), pp. 109–146.

67. Jeffrey F. Rayport and John J. Sviokla, "Managing in the Marketspace," *Harvard Business Review,* vol. 72 (November/December 1994), pp. 141–151.

68. See for example, Joseph Alba, John Lynch, Bart Weitz, Chris Janiszewski, Rich Lutz, Al Sawyer, and Stacy Wood, "Interactive Home Shopping: Incentives for Consumers, Retailers, and Manufacturers to Participate in Electronic Marketplaces," *Journal of Marketing,* vol. 61 (July 1997), pp. 38–53; Donna Hoffman and Tom Novak, "Marketing in Hypermedia Computer-Mediated Environments: Conceptual Foundations," *Journal of Marketing,* vol. 60 (July 1996), pp. 50–68; and Robert V. Kozinets, "E-Tribalized Marketing?: The Strategic Implications of Virtual Communities of Consumption," *European Management Journal,* vol. 17, no. 3 (1999), pp. 252–264.

69. See for example, Richard L. Daft and Robert H. Lengel, "Organizational Information Requirements, Media Richness and Structural Design," *Management Science,* vol. 32, no. 5 (1986), pp. 554–571; and Sara Kiesler, Jane Siegel, and Timothy McGuire, "Social Psychological Aspects of Computer-Mediated Communication," *American Psychologist,* vol. 39, no. 10 (1984), pp. 1123–1134.

70. See for example, Lee Sproull and Sara Kiesler, "Reducing Social Context Cues: The Case of Electronic Mail," *Management Science,* vol. 32 (1986), pp. 1492–1512.

71. Sara Kiesler, Jane Siegel, and Timothy McGuire, "Social Psychological Aspects of Computer-Mediated Communication," *American Psychologist,* vol. 39, no. 10 (1984), pp. 1123–1134; Ronald E. Rice, "Evaluating New Media Systems," in *Evaluating the New Information Technologies: New Directions for Program Evaluation,* ed. Jerome Johnstone (San Francisco: Jossey-Bass, 1984); Lee Sproull and Sara Kiesler, "Reducing Social Context Cues: The Case of Electronic Mail," *Management Science,* vol. 32 (1986), pp. 1492–1512; and Joseph B. Walther, "Interpersonal Effects in Computer-Mediated Interaction," *Communication Research,* vol. 19 (1992), pp. 52–90.

72. See for example, Nancy K. Baym, "The Emergence of Community in Computer-Mediated Communication," in *Cybersociety,* ed. Stephen G. Jones (Thousand Oaks, CA: Sage, 1995); Luciano Paccagnella, "Getting the Seats of Your Pants Dirty: Strategies for Ethnographic Research on Virtual Communities," *Journal of Computer-Mediated Communications,* vol. 3 (June 1997). Available: www.ascusc.org/jcmc/; John Paolillo, "The Virtual Speech Community: Social Network and Language Variation on IRC," *Journal of Computer-Mediated Communication,* (June 4, 1999). Available: www.ascusc.org/jcmc/; Russell Spears and Martin Lea, "Social Influence and the Influence of the Social in Computer-Mediated Communication," in *Contexts of Computer-Mediated Communication,* ed. M. Lea (Hemel-Hempstead: Harvester Wheatsheaf, 1992), pp. 30–65; and Joseph B. Walther, "Interpersonal Effects in Computer-mediated Interaction," *Communication Research,* vol. 19 (1992), pp. 52–90.

73. Ronald E. Rice and G. Love, "Electronic Emotion: Socio-emotional Content in a Computer-Mediated Communication Network," *Communication Research,* vol. 14 (1987), p. 89.

74. Joseph B. Walther, "Interpersonal Effects in Computer-mediated Interaction," *Communication Research,* vol. 19 (1992), pp. 52–90.

75. N. Katherine Hayles, *How We Became Posthuman: Virtual Bodies in Cybernetics, Literature, and Informatics* (Chicago: University of Chicago Press, 1999); and Robert V. Kozinets, "E-Tribalized Marketing?: The Strategic Implications of Virtual Communities of Consumption," *European Management Journal,* vol. 17, no. 3 (1999), pp. 252–264.

76. See note 74.

77. Richard L. Daft and Robert H. Lengel, "Organizational Information Requirements, Media Richness and Structural Design," *Management Science,* vol. 32, no. 5 (1986), pp. 554–571; and Sara Kiesler, Jane Siegel, and Timothy McGuire, "Social Psychological Aspects of Computer-Mediated Communication," *American Psychologist,* vol. 39, no. 10 (1984), pp. 1123–1134.

78. Susan Herring, "Interactional Coherence in CMC," *Journal of Computer-Mediated Communication,* vol. 4, no. 4 (1999). Available: www.ascusc.org/jcmc/

79. John Short, Ederyn Williams, and Bruce Christie, *The Social Psychology of Telecommunications* (New York: Wiley, 1976); and Diane F. Witmer, "Risky Business: Why People Feel Safe in Sexually Explicit On-Line Communication," *Journal of Computer-Mediated Communication,* vol. 2 (March 1997). Available: www.ascusc.org/jcmc/

80. Brittney G. Chenault, "Developing Personal and Emotional Relationships via CMC," *CMC Magazine,* (May 1998). Available: www.december.com/cmc/mag/1998/may/chenault.html

81. Judith Donath, Karrie Karahalios, and Fernanda Viégas, "Visualizing Conversation," *Journal of Computer-Mediated Communication* (June 4, 1999). Available: www.ascusc.org/jcmc/

82. Arturo Escobar, "Welcome To Cyberia: Notes on the Anthropology of Cyberculture," *Current Anthropology,* vol. 35 (June 3, 1993), pp. 211–231.

83. Donna J. Haraway, *Simians, Cyborgs, and Women* (New York: Routeledge, 1991).

84. N. Katherine Hayles, *How We Became Posthuman: Virtual Bodies in Cybernetics, Literature, and Informatics* (Chicago: University of Chicago Press, 1999).

85. Howard Rheingold, *The Virtual Community: Homesteading on the Electronic Frontier* (Reading, MA: Addison-Wesley, 1993).

86. Albert M. Muniz Jr., "Brand Community and the Negotiation of Brand Meaning," in *Advances in Consumer Research,* vol. 24, eds. Merrie Brucks and Deborah J. MacInnis (Provo, UT: Association for Consumer Research, 1997), pp. 308–309.

87. Arthur Armstrong and John Hagel III, "The Real Value of On-Line Communities," *Harvard Business Review,* vol. 74 (May/June 1996), pp. 134–141.

88. Stephen G. Jones, ed. *Cybersociety: Computer-Mediated Communication and Community* (Thousand Oaks, CA: Sage, 1995).

89. Robert V. Kozinets, "E-Tribalized Marketing?: The Strategic Implications of Virtual Communities of Consumption," *European Management Journal,* vol. 17, no. 3 (1999), pp. 252–264.

90. Robert V. Kozinets, " 'I Want to Believe': A Netnography of The X-Philes' Subculture of Consumption," in *Advances in Consumer Research,* vol. 24, eds. Merrie Brucks and Deborah J. MacInnis (Provo, UT: Association for Consumer Research, 1997), pp. 470–475; Robert V. Kozinets, "On Netnography: Initial Reflections on Consumer Research Investigations of Cyberculture," in *Advances in Consumer Research,* vol. 25, eds. Joseph Alba and Wesley Hutchinson (Provo, UT: Association for Consumer Research, 1998), pp. 366–371; and Robert V. Kozinets, "The Field Behind the Screen: Using the Method of Netnography to Research Market-Oriented Virtual Communities," J.L. Kellogg Graduate School of Management Working Paper (1999). Available: www.kellogg.nwu.edu/faculty/kozinets/htm/research/

91. Robert V. Kozinets, "On Netnography: Initial Reflections on Consumer Research Investigations of Cyberculture," in *Advances in Consumer Research,* vol. 25, eds.

Joseph Alba and Wesley Hutchinson (Provo, UT: Association for Consumer Research, 1998), pp. 366–371; and Robert V. Kozinets, "The Field Behind the Screen: Using the Method of Netnography to Research Market-Oriented Virtual Communities," J.L. Kellogg Graduate School of Management Working Paper (1999). Available: www.kellogg.nwu.edu/faculty/kozinets/htm/research/

92. Henry Jenkins, "Do You Enjoy Making the Rest of Us Feel Stupid?: alt.tv.twin-peaks, The Trickster Author and Viewer Mastery," in *'Full of Secrets': Critical Approaches to Twin Peaks,* ed. David Lavery (Detroit: Wayne State University Press, 1995), pp. 51–69.

93. Taeyong Kim and Frank Biocca, "Telepresence via Television: Two Dimensions of Telepresence May Have Different Connections to Memory and Persuasion," *Journal of Computer-Mediated Communication,* vol. 3 (September 1997). Available: www.ascusc.org/jcmc/

94. Robert V. Kozinets, " 'I Want to Believe': A Netnography of The X-Philes' Subculture of Consumption," in *Advances in Consumer Research,* vol. 24, eds. Merrie Brucks and Deborah J. MacInnis (Provo, UT: Association for Consumer Research, 1997), pp. 470–475.

95. See for example, Margaret L. McLaughlin, Kerry K. Osborne, and Christine B. Smith, "Standards of Conduct on Usenet," in *Cybersociety: Computer-Mediated Communication and Community,* ed. Stephen G. Jones (Thousand Oaks, CA: Sage, 1995), pp. 90–111.

96. See note 74.

97. John Paolillo, "The Virtual Speech Community: Social Network and Language Variation on IRC," *Journal of Computer-Mediated Communication,* (June 4, 1999). Available: www.ascusc.org/jcmc/

98. John F. Sherry Jr., *Servicescapes: The Concept of Place in Contemporary Markets* (Lincolnwood, IL: NTC Business Books, 1998).

99. See for example, Robert V. Kozinets, " 'I Want to Believe': A Netnography of The X-Philes' Subculture of Consumption," in *Advances in Consumer Research,* vol. 24, eds. Merrie Brucks and Deborah J. MacInnis (Provo, UT: Association for Consumer Research, 1997), pp. 470–475; Robert V. Kozinets, "E-Tribalized Marketing?: The Strategic Implications of Virtual Communities of Consumption," *European Management Journal,* vol. 17, no. 3 (1999), pp. 252–264; and Robert V. Kozinets and Jay M. Handelman, "Ensouling Consumption: A Netnographic Exploration of Boycotting Behavior," in *Advances in Consumer Research,* vol. 25, eds. Joseph Alba and Wesley Hutchinson (Provo, UT: Association for Consumer Research, 1998), pp. 475–480.

100. Robin Hamman, "Cyborgasms: Cybersex Amongst Multiple-Selves and Cyborgs in the Narrow-Bandwidth Space of America Online Chat Rooms," unpublished Master's dissertation (1996), University of Essex; and Luciano Paccagnella, "Getting the Seats of Your Pants Dirty: Strategies for Ethnographic Research on Virtual Communities," *Journal of Computer-Mediated Communications,* vol. 3 (June 1997). Available: www.ascusc.org/jcmc/

101. See for example, Jim Thomas, "Introduction: A Debate about the Ethics of Fair Practices for Collecting Social Science Data in Cyberspace," *Information Society,* vol. 12, no. 2 (1996), pp. 107–117.

102. Craig J. Thompson, "Interpreting Consumers: A Hermeneutical Framework for Deriving Marketing Insights from the Texts of Consumers' Consumption Stories," *Journal of Marketing Research,* vol. 34 (November 1997), pp. 438–455.

103. Robert V. Kozinets, "The Field Behind the Screen: Using the Method of Netnography to Research Market-Oriented Virtual Communities," J.L. Kellogg Graduate School of Management Working Paper (1999). Available: www.kellogg.nwu .edu/faculty/kozinets/htm/research/

104. Stanley Fish, *Is There a Text in This Class?* (Cambridge, MA: Harvard University Press, 1979).

105. See note 62.

106. Daniel Clapper and Anne Massey, "Electronic Focus Groups: A Framework for Exploration," *Information and Management,* vol. 30 (1996), pp. 43–50; and Thomas L. Greenbaum, "Focus Groups by Video Next Trend of the '90s," *Marketing News,* vol. 30 (July 1996), p. 4.

107. See for example, Robin Hamman, "Cyborgasms: Cybersex Amongst Multiple-Selves and Cyborgs in the Narrow-Bandwidth Space of America Online Chat Rooms," unpublished Master's dissertation (1996), University of Essex; and Diane F. Witmer, "Risky Business: Why People Feel Safe in Sexually Explicit On-Line Communication," *Journal of Computer-Mediated Communication,* vol. 2 (March 1997). Available: www.ascusc.org/jcmc/

108. Robert V. Kozinets and Jay M. Handelman, "Ensouling Consumption: A Netnographic Exploration of Boycotting Behavior," in *Advances in Consumer Research,* vol. 25, eds. Joseph Alba and Wesley Hutchinson (Provo, UT: Association for Consumer Research, 1998), pp. 475–480.

109. See note 80.

110. See note 103.

111. Jean Baudrillard, *Simulacra and Simulations,* trans. Paul Foss, Paul Parton, and Philip Beitchman (New York: Semiotext(e), 1983).

112. Compare to A. Fuar Firat and Alladi Venkatesh, "Liberatory Postmodernism and the Reenchantment of Consumption," *Journal of Consumer Research,* vol. 22 (December 1995), pp. 239–267.

113. Stan Davis and Christopher Meyer, *Blur: The Speed of Change in the Connected Economy* (Reading, MA: Addison-Wesley, 1998).

114. Sherry Turkle, *Life on the Screen: Identity in the Age of the Internet* (New York: Simon & Schuster, 1995).

115. See note 48.

116. Robin Hamman, "Cyborgasms: Cybersex Amongst Multiple-Selves and Cyborgs in the Narrow-Bandwidth Space of America Online Chat Rooms," unpublished Master's dissertation (1996), University of Essex; and Sherry Turkle, *Life on the Screen: Identity in the Age of the Internet* (New York: Simon & Schuster, 1995).

117. Seth Grodin and Don Peppers, *Permission Marketing* (New York: Simon & Schuster, 1999).

118. See note 103.

119. See note 43.

120. See note 88.

121. Sara Kiesler, Jane Siegel, and Timothy McGuire, "Social Psychological Aspects of Computer-Mediated Communication," *American Psychologist,* vol. 39, no. 10 (1984), pp. 1123–1134; and John Short, Ederyn Williams, and Bruce Christie, *The Social Psychology of Telecommunications* (New York: Wiley, 1976).

122. Robin Hamman, "Cyborgasms: Cybersex Amongst Multiple-Selves and Cyborgs in the Narrow-Bandwidth Space of America Online Chat Rooms," unpublished Master's dissertation (1996), University of Essex; and Diane F. Witmer, "Risky Business: Why People Feel Safe in Sexually Explicit On-Line Communication," *Journal of Computer-Mediated Communication,* vol. 2 (March 1997). Available: www.ascusc.org/jcmc/

123. For a more comprehensive treatment of some of these topics see T. Richards and L. Richards, "Using Computers in Qualitative Analysis," in *Handbook of Qualitative Research,* eds. Norman Denzin and Yvonna Lincoln (Thousand Oaks, CA: Sage, 1994), pp. 445–462.

124. Norman Denzin, *Interpretive Ethnography: Ethnographic Practices for the 21st Century* (Thousand Oaks, CA: Sage, 1997).

125. Yvonna S. Lincoln and Norman K. Denzin, "The Fifth Moment," in *Handbook of Qualitative Research,* eds. Norman K. Denzin and Yvonna S. Lincoln (Thousand Oaks, CA: Sage, 1994), pp. 575–586.

126. See note 3.

127. See note 124.

128. Russell Belk, "Hyperreality and Globalization: Culture in the Age of Ronald Mc-Donald," *Journal of International Consumer Marketing,* vol. 8, no. 3 and 4 (1995), pp. 23–28; Russell Belk, Melanie Wallendorf, and Deborah Heisley, *Deep Meaning in Possessions,* Video, Marketing Science Institute, Cambridge, MA (1987); Stephen Brown, *Postmodern Marketing* (New York: Routledge, 1995); Deborah Cours, Deborah Heisley, Melanie Wallendorf, and Dylan Johnson (1998), " 'It's All in the Family': A Performance Presentation," performance presented at the twenty-sixth annual conference of the Association for Consumer Research, Montreal, Canada. [subsequently published as "It's All in the Family, But I Want It," in *Advances in Consumer Research,* vol. 26, eds. Eric Arnould and Linda Scott (Provo, UT: Association for Consumer Research, 1999), pp. 253–259; Morris Holbrook and Takeo Kuwahara, "Probing Explorations, Deep Displays, Virtual Reality and Profound Insights: The Four Faces of Stereographic Three-Dimensional Representations in Marketing and Consumer Research," in *Advances in Consumer Research,* vol. 26, eds. Eric Arnould and Linda Scott (Provo, UT: Association for Consumer Research, 1998), pp. 240–250; Robert V. Kozinets, "Desert Pilgrim," Multimedia Ethnography presented at the Heretical Consumer Research conference, Columbus, OH (September 30, 1999); Richard Mead, "Where

is the Culture of Thailand?," *International Journal of Research in Marketing,* vol. 11, no. 4 (1994), pp. 401–404; John Schouten, "When a Rose Is Eros: A Demi-anagramatical Study of Brand Names," *Consumption, Markets and Culture,* vol. 2, no. 4 (1999), pp. 449–456; John F. Sherry Jr., "The Soul of the Company Store: Nike Town Chicago and the Emplaced Brandscape," in *Servicescapes: The Concept of Place in Contemporary Markets,* ed. John F. Sherry, Jr. (Lincolnwood, IL: NTC Business Books, 1998), pp. 109–146; John F. Sherry Jr., John Schouten, and George Zinkham, "Capturing Consumption Through Poetry," poems presented at the twenty-sixth annual conference of the Association for Consumer Research, Montreal, Canada (1998); and Craig J.Thompson, Barbara Stern, and Eric Arnould, "Writing the Differences: Poststructuralist Pluralism, Retextualization, and the Construction of Reflexive Ethnographic Narratives in Consumption and Market Research," *Consumption, Markets and Culture,* vol. 2, no. 2 (1998), pp. 105–160.

129. Richard Lester, Michael Piore, and Kamel Malek, "Interpretive Management: What General Managers Can Learn From Design," *Harvard Business Review* (March/April 1998), pp. 86–96.

130. Gordon Shaw, Robert Brown, and Philip Bromiley, "Strategic Stories: How 3M is Rewriting Business Planning," *Harvard Business Review,* vol. 76 (May/June 1998), pp. 41–50.

131. John F. Sherry Jr., "Bottomless Cup, Plug-in-Drug: A Telethnography of Coffee," *Visual Anthropology,* vol. 7 (1995), pp. 351–370; and John F. Sherry Jr., "The Soul of the Company Store: Nike Town Chicago and the Emplaced Brandscape," in *Servicescapes: The Concept of Place in Contemporary Markets,* ed. John F. Sherry, Jr. (Lincolnwood, IL: NTC Business Books, 1998), pp. 109–146.

132. Patricia Ticineto Clough, *The End(s) of Ethnography: From Realism to Social Criticism* (Newbury Park, CA: Sage, 1992); and Norman Denzin, *The Cinematic Society: The Voyeur's Gaze* (Thousand Oaks, CA, 1995).

133. James Clifford and George E. Marcus, eds., *Writing Culture: The Poetics and Politics of Ethnography* (Berkeley: University of California Press, 1986); Robert V. Kozinets, "The Field Behind the Screen: Using the Method of Netnography to Research Market-Oriented Virtual Communities," J.L. Kellogg Graduate School of Management Working Paper (1999). Available: www.kellogg.nwu.edu/faculty /kozinets/htm/research/; and Yvonna S. Lincoln and Norman K. Denzin, "The Fifth Moment," in *Handbook of Qualitative Research,* eds. Norman K. Denzin and Yvonna S. Lincoln (Thousand Oaks, CA: Sage, 1994), pp. 575–586.

134. See note 123.

135. See note 125, p. 583.

136. Robert V. Kozinets, "The Field Behind the Screen: Using the Method of Netnography to Research Market-Oriented Virtual Communities," J.L. Kellogg Graduate School of Management Working Paper (1999). Available: www.kellogg.nwu.edu /faculty/kozinets/htm/research/; and Robert V. Kozinets, "E-Tribalized Marketing?: The Strategic Implications of Virtual Communities of Consumption," *European Management Journal,* vol. 17, no. 3 (1999), pp. 252–264.

137. James Clifford, *The Predicament of Culture* (Cambridge, MA: Harvard University Press, 1988).

138. Clifford Geertz, *Works and Lives: The Anthropologist as Author* (Stanford, CA: Stanford University Press, 1988); and Eric Arnould and Melanie Wallendorf, "Market-Oriented Ethnography: Interpretation Building and Market Strategy Formulation," *Journal of Marketing Research,* vol. 31, no. 4 (1994), pp. 484–504.

139. See note 103.

140. Cary Nelson, Paula Treichler, and Lawrence Grossberg, "Cultural Studies: An Introduction," in *Cultural Studies,* eds. Lawrence Grossberg, Cary Nelson, and Paula Treichler (New York: Routledge, 1992), pp. 1–22; John F. Sherry Jr., ed., *Contemporary Marketing and Consumer Behavior: An Anthropological Sourcebook* (Thousand Oaks, CA: Sage, 1995); and John F. Sherry Jr., "Nothing But Net: Consumption, Poetry and Research Pluriculture (in the Sixth Moment)," Presidential Address presented at the twenty-sixth annual conference of the Association for Consumer Research, Montreal, Canada (1998).

141. Mohanbir Sawhney and Emanuela Prandelli, "Beyond Customer Knowledge Management: Customers as Knowledge Co-Creators," J.L. Kellogg Graduate School of Management Working Paper (1999).

142. James Clifford, *Routes: Travel and Translation in the Late Twentieth Century* (Cambridge, MA: Harvard University Press, 1998).

143. Clifford Geertz, "Deep Hanging Out," *The New York Review of Books* (October 22, 1999), pp. 69–72.

144. William Tucker, *Foundations for a Theory of Consumer Behavior* (New York: Holt, Rinehart and Winston, 1967).

CHAPTER 9

QUANTITATIVE MARKETING RESEARCH

DAWN IACOBUCCI

"**M**arket sensing," "listening posts," "data mining," "customer connections," "competitive intelligence" . . . all of these currently used buzzwords express aspects of marketing research. Data availability and opportunities have exploded in recent years. Yet in the presence of vast data, managers simultaneously express the urgent need for information. Good marketing research methods are those that transform data into useful information. The definitions of marketing research that we at Kellogg find most useful in teaching are those that emphasize the role of research in assisting managers in making optimal decisions.[1] The business world is moving increasingly faster, with multitudes of marketplace decisions requiring resolution every day, and well-conducted marketing research tools are valuable in asking and answering the right questions.

Accordingly, in this chapter, we explore a number of marketing decisions that can be illuminated through analysis. We focus on two new research tools: first, the relatively new class of *network data* and its requisite models, and second, *collaborative filtering* which is the novel application to e-commerce of cluster analysis. Researchers can use both of these methods to derive insight regarding customers and competitors. To demonstrate the utility of these new data and methods and put their potential contributions into perspective, we begin by presenting a brief framework to give an overview structure of marketing research analytics.[2]

EXPLORATORY, DESCRIPTIVE, CAUSAL

Marketing research often progresses from exploratory methods to descriptive techniques to causal manipulations. The focus of inquiry for exploratory methods (e.g., focus groups, interviews, open-ended items on surveys) is depth and richness of understanding, but not detailed numerics to be extrapolated to a broader population. Descriptive methods (e.g., surveys, regression forecasting) seek quantitative summaries of general tendencies in attitudes and behavior from segments of the targeted population. Methods intended to yield causal statements (e.g., simulated test markets, price sensitivity tests, electronic split-cable advertising comparisons) are those in which the manager intervenes in the consumption environment and measures the subsequent customer reaction.

The marketing research process is more iterative than that linear presentation would suggest, particularly given that most industries are dynamic, requiring that managers respond rapidly to changing customer requirements and new competitive offerings. The research process can also be seen to run parallel to a product life cycle: Exploratory methods are used more frequently for new product concept testing, descriptive methods to forecast market demand and sales trajectories, and causal methods to fine-tune the product offering and feature combinations. It is also the case that exploratory methods need not be qualitative, nor descriptive and causal methods more quantitative. For example, conjoint analysis, a special application of regression, is very useful in the early stages of new product design. In this chapter, we focus on quantitative methods, because qualitative techniques will be covered in the chapters by our colleagues, Calder, Sherry, and Kozinets in this volume.

Secondary versus Primary Data

Marketing researchers also distinguish between secondary and primary data sources. The former are those data that already exist (e.g., census data, industry reports, governmental and global economic indicators). Their benefits include their ease of access and hence their relative cost efficiency. A major drawback is that the data were collected with someone else's research needs in mind, hence the data may not address the particular research needs. Primary data are better tailored to addressing the specific current issues because it is research commissioned specifically for the questions at hand. Given that the strengths and weaknesses of primary and secondary data are complementary, any good research project should be comprised of both; researchers begin with secondary data to investigate what is known and to crystalize the research questions and directions, and then they proceed to execute their own new, distinct piece of research to contribute to the knowledge base.

The distinction between secondary and primary data can depend simply on time frame. For example, advertising agencies regularly maintain databases of advertisement copy performance measures that are compared to their internal extant data bank as a benchmark, to facilitate forecasting of the current advertisement's likely effectiveness. The data bank would be classified as secondary data, whereas the results on the focal advertisement being tested would be classified as primary data, at least until the current ad is evaluated, after which the data are aggregated into the larger database to await comparison to future advertisements as secondary data.

The distinction between primary and secondary data also depends in part on industry tendencies. Managers of consumer package goods have available to them an enormous and powerful class of secondary data that have been compiled and sold by an objective external supplier: scanner panel data. Analysis of these data allows for timely estimates of market share, effectiveness tests of marketing mix variables and their observed impact relative to competitive action, sequential analyses of brand loyalty and switching behaviors, and much more. In contrast, given that consulting industries are usually called upon to address immediate concerns, often of a previously unseen nature or a yet unresolved issue, new primary data must be collected to consider the current problem in-depth.

Given these framework dimensions, we may classify the data and techniques that we will discuss in this chapter as follows:

- Network data are new enough that rarely will they already exist, so most such studies involve the collection of primary data. Network data have been used to address causal questions, but are most often used to address exploratory and descriptive issues.
- Collaborative filtering is a cluster method applied to secondary data typically used to address descriptive and causal research questions.

Hence, between the two selections, we intend to show a variety of types of data, methods, and marketing research questions that we hope the reader will recognize as being valuable to the marketing manager in making fine decisions. We discuss networks first, then turn to collaborative filtering later in the chapter.

NETWORKS

For most standard (i.e., non-network) research inquiries, we create data sets that tabulate multiple observations, such as consumers or firms, measured on numerous variables, including perceptions, attitudes, preferences, purchases, and so on. Most analytical methods (e.g., regression or logit models) focus on modeling the relationships among the variables to answer questions such as, "Does customer satisfaction predict repeat purchases?" The units of observations (i.e., the consumers whose satisfaction attitudes and purchase behaviors have been recorded) are assumed to be independent.

However, there are many scenarios for which this assumption of independence does not hold. For example, when work teams interact to produce joint outcomes, their very interactions create interconnections and dependencies that are important and necessary for optimal group performance; the work is not conducted by independent parallel processors. Similarly, at the level of the firm, alliances and corporate partnerships of many varieties are ventures into the marketplace as networked entities that presumably gain net benefits from their mutual transactions.

In situations like these, data can be collected to represent the interconnected ties among the actors in these networks. However, standard statistical models are inappropriate, given the aforementioned assumption of independence. Further, the interconnected structures of networks are not perceived as simply statistical nuisances to be fixed—rather they comprise the core of what is interesting for many phenomena. Thus, the network paradigm, philosophy and analytical methods were born.[3]

Perhaps the best way to motivate this new paradigm is to examine a variety of its possible applications. Let us consider in some detail a few examples of an "intraconsumer network," essentially a mapping of the cognitive associations that a consumer makes among concepts like brands, attributes, and the like. We will then briefly also consider interconsumer networks, and intra- and inter-firm networks.

Intraconsumer Networks

As the phrase, intraconsumer suggests, these networks occur within a single individual. Usually the network of interest is comprised of those associations that a consumer makes between brands and attributes (e.g., when consumers see a televised commercial for Nike, what thoughts are prompted, what pops into their heads? A competitor, like Reebok? An attribute, like good cushioning? A spokesperson, like Michael Jordan? Idiosyncratic thoughts, like their racquetball appointment?). The analysis of networks allows the brand manager to see what people think of when they think of the focal brand.

Consumer Perceptions of Brand-Extensions.   A premier task of the marketer is to communicate various thoughts to the consumer. Marketers use advertisements to initiate positive associations to their brand in the minds of the viewing public. Soft drinks are described as tasty and refreshing, and their consumption is depicted in friendly, social environments. Performance aspects of automobiles are described and demonstrated, and imagery is built around the statements the car purports to make regarding the driver's status in life. Product advertising usually emphasizes the positive aspects of the featured brand, but advertising can also be used to emphasize the negative aspects of the competitor, as with political advertisements. The marketer's goal is to create and reinforce a cognitive network of associations, with positive attributes linked to their brand, and weak or negative associations linked to alternative brands.

Classic and contemporary theorizing in psychology posits cognitive networks as a metaphor for memory.[4] Thus, there may be said to be a soft drink category "node" in memory, which is connected to brand instantiations like Coke, Pepsi, Dr. Pepper, with connections of varying strengths. Connections can also include attribute information, like sweetness and carbonation, current marketing campaigns, and for better or worse, residual former marketing efforts, such as lingering connections between Pepsi and Michael Jackson or Madonna.

When a stimulus node (a brand, an attribute, etc.) is activated, associations that are stronger are those more likely to "come to mind" and to do so more quickly. Connections that are weaker and distal are less likely to result in ready recollection (e.g., a prompting of the brand Pepsi may bring nearly immediate recall of Michael Jackson). In contrast, if an ad for Dr. Pepper were shown, it would take longer and require more thought processing on the part of the consumer to make a link from the brand of Dr. Pepper to the category of soft drink to another brand instantiation such as Pepsi finally to the singer, Michael Jackson.

Cognitive networks may be constructed in a wholly exploratory way to begin to address the marketing manager's question, "Just how do my consumers see my brand?" We recently examined the possibility of using networks to detect the effectiveness of causal interventions.[5] Specifically, a study was designed to measure brand equity and the extent to which brand associations changed after consumers were given information about a forthcoming new product offering. When companies create line and brand extensions, the hope is that the new offering will carry the positive associations from the parent brand. In addition, there is a hope that nothing about the new product will damage the associations linked to the parent brand. In cognitive network-ese, we would expect a strong, positive link between the parent brand and positive associations, and weaker (because they are newer) but still positive links between the new product line and some positive attributes, and the addition of the new product line to the network should not weaken or neutralize nor negate the links to the extant parent product.

As an example, we focused on the category of sports car, with the focal, prototypical brand of Porsche. Previous research had taught us there was consensus in perceptions of Porsches as being fast, sporty, sleek, and expensive; that is, these associations were the ones elicited most frequently and quickly in response to prompting respondents for descriptions of Porsches. We also asked participants to nominate a few other brands in the sports car category, to compare the various brands with Porsche and each other, and to rate each car on the dimensions that they saw as distinguishing among the cars.

In this experiment, we then exposed three different groups to extensive mock advertisements announcing the rollout of a new Porsche: in one case a "family" Porsche, described as having leg room, a trunk, luggage racks, and so on; an "economy" Porsche, priced at $15,000, fuel efficient, and so on; and a control group was told to imagine a new Porsche that was simply "everything you've always thought a Porsche to be." We then re-tested the cognitive associations among the brands and attributes to determine whether any changes had occurred.

We expected the first two product introductions to be incongruent with consumers' perceptions of Porsche's typical positioning. We were interested in testing the associations and affiliation for the new Porsche cars, but we were also interested in seeing whether the new weird cars required the participants to make changes in the associative schemata they had previously held to the parent Porsche.

Figure 9.1 depicts a prototype of results, a simplified version of a comparison of pre- to postnetworks. Note the network to the left, an example of what a cognitive mapping of associations and attribute and brand links might resemble before the interference and shaping by a marketer. The brands of sports cars that came quickly to mind were Porsche, Mercedes, Nissan 300ZX, Camaro, and Corvette. The first few were seen as relatively expensive, the 300ZX and Camaro relatively inexpensive, and the Corvette somewhere in between given that there were no strong ties to either the attribute of "high price" or "low price." Corvette and Porsche are linked given their similarity based on comments regarding their distinctive body shapes. Porsche and Mercedes are similar given their higher status pricing and their perception as being classy automobiles. Where the European sports cars were seen as "classy," the Camaro was seen as lacking the same mystique.

Figure 9.1

Cognitive Networks for Hypothetical Economy-Porsche Line Extension

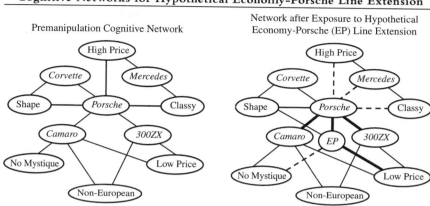

Premanipulation Cognitive Network

Network after Exposure to Hypothetical
Economy-Porsche (EP) Line Extension

The marketer then provides some information to the consumer, and the consumer's schema may begin to shift to something like the cognitive network depicted on the right in Figure 9.1. The economy model Porsche (EP) is strongly linked to its parent brand, sharing the attribute of a perceived distinctive body shape. The manipulation of the economic positioning would be deemed effective, given the strong link to the attribute of low price, and perhaps unfortunately, that positioning has introduced a weak association with a "lack of mystique."

In addition, the presence of this economy Porsche in the cognitive network has shifted the associations held to the parent Porsche. The ties between that classic Porsche and one brand, Mercedes, and two attributes, high price and classy, have weakened (depicted by the dashed, rather than solid, lines), presumably due to the consumer's attempt to resolve the psychological incongruity of the introduction of a cheap Porsche. Furthermore, the similarity of the parent Porsche with the Camaro and 300ZX models has strengthened, given the latter two cars' positions as relatively lower priced.

Network data like these would be a strong indication that such a line extension could have a devastating impact on the parent brand. The new model, the economy Porsche, may fair reasonably well in testing—it is associated with the parent brand, its positioning is clear, and so on. However, the impact on the parent car could destroy its brand equity and strong heritage. Brand and line extensions are but one example of the type of marketing question that might be addressed given representations of consumers' brand associations.[6]

Segmentation on Attitudes and Behaviors. Another fundamental tool in marketing is an understanding of segmentation, and while marketers often speak of segmenting on demographic variables, these are usually simplistic and ineffective in explaining much variance. Rather, it can be superior to segment based on cognitive associations, and networks can help. For example, some consumer behavior researchers have studied the attitudes and motivations of people who made frequent purchases at their local health food store.[7] They developed intricate cognitive maps that delineated two distinct segments of shoppers—those motivated by their concerns for health and fitness, and those who appreciated the store's stance on animal rights activism. These groups converged on the same store, and their behaviors appeared similar. However, those apparently similar behaviors were driven by extremely different aims, as the differences between the two groups' cognitive networks of concepts and associative links demonstrated.

Where the health food store study was one in which the behaviors of two different groups appeared similar, a social marketing study[8] tells a segmentation tale wherein two groups differ with regard to their behaviors—one group engages in a socially attractive behavior, recycling, and the other group is comprised of nonrecyclers. Many psychological theories (heartily embraced by consumer behavior theorists and practitioners) posit that an understanding of a person's attitudes can yield insight into that person's likely behaviors. Accordingly, if we could examine the attitudes, or the cognitive network of attitude structures and beliefs held by the recyclers and that of the nonrecyclers, perhaps there would exist differences that would lend insight as to their different behavior. While the example that follows may be classified as social marketing, the analogy to a typical purchase application is straightforward: If we compared the cognitive networks of those persons who are loyal to one's brand, to those who are frequent purchasers of a competitor's brand, or who are not engaged in the category, similar insights would be available to understand the purchase behavior differences.

In the recycling study, data were obtained using an in-depth interview technique called *laddering,* in which a interviewee is asked, "Why do you recycle?" and upon obtaining a response, pursued with the follow-up questions, "Why is that important," and "why is *that* important," and so on. Results are often described as *means-ends* hierarchical chains, because the reasons elicited earliest are usually fairly concrete compared to the later abstract goals; hence the early-stated reasons serve as means to obtaining the later end goals. For example, one respondent said that recycling "avoids fill-ing-up landfills (and running out of land)" which is important in order to "save resources" which in turn is important in order to "give to future gen-erations," and so on. Note the increasingly abstract nature of the goals cited.

The results indicated that for recyclers, there were strong connections between "avoiding filling landfills," "reducing waste," and "saving the environment," whereas for nonrecyclers, the goal of "avoiding filling up landfills" was simply aesthetic, associated with "avoiding messy trash." Fur-thermore, nonrecyclers did not make the association between the landfills and the goal of "saving the environment." In addition, nonrecyclers thought that the goal of "reusing materials" could contribute toward "saving money." Recyclers did not cluster these goals—they know that while re-cycling is important for a variety of long-term reasons, it does not yet pay for itself. The social marketer seeking to increase rates of recycling can take results like these as diagnostic of the education campaigns necessary to mod-ify how the nonrecycler thinks, enhancing appropriate cognitive links, eliminating errorful associations, and so on, in order to get their cognitive associations resembling those of the recyclers, in an effort toward increas-ing the similarity of their recycling behaviors.

Numerous other studies are beginning to be reported on cognitive net-works (e.g., in services industries including airlines, tourism, health ser-vices, social marketing and nonprofits marketing issues, and religions).[9] In the sections that follow, we briefly present alternative research scenarios in which networks have proven fruitful.

Interconsumer Networks

Interconsumer networks are those that study patterns of connections be-tween individuals. In marketing, the focus of this kind of research is usu-ally on understanding the pattern of communication flows.

Word-of-Mouth. Word-of-mouth is thought to influence purchasers in the marketplace; the so-called early adopters (of a new product) become opinion leaders affecting the later entrants to the category (consumers who try the product subsequent to receiving such advice). Even early models for the diffusion of innovation and information about new product intro-ductions throughout the consumer marketplace included an indicator for word-of-mouth.[10] Research has begun to elaborate upon the nature of the word-of-mouth effect, integrating the diffusion and networks literatures.[11] It is a widely held belief that word-of-mouth is especially important for the success of service providers, and networks are beginning to be used to substantiate these claims.[12]

An untapped arena for following flows of communication and the effectiveness of persuasion is the Internet, particularly in the form of online user-groups and chat rooms. In these vehicles, nominally anonymous consumers are interacting around common goals, exchanging information, as well as experiencing a pseudo-social function. Word-of-mouth should be even easier to study in such constrained and tractable environments compared to the flow of communication in the marketplace at large. Companies are also exploring the ethically dubious practice of installing a confederate in a chat room to speak on behalf of the firm so as to influence the other users' opinions regarding its products, and the effectiveness of such attempts at persuasion could be measured through the use of network techniques.

Multilevel Marketing. Another area in which networks are providing new insights into marketing and consumer behavior is that of multilevel marketing, also referred to as network marketing.[13] In these hierarchical systems, a sales force devotes its time to selling product as well as recruiting new sales personnel. Resources flow down from experienced salespeople in the form of training and assistance and product. The system contracts that a percentage of the new recruit's sales will come back to the supervisor, and a smaller percentage of the new recruit's recruits' sales, and so on, thus each new recruit helps build the supervisor's business. Resources therefore flow upward from the new recruits in the form of time expenditures on business growth and percentages of profits on new sales. These multilayered exchanges are characterizations of networks because the sales force, by definition, is interconnected and interdependent.

Intraorganizational Networks

Intraorganizational networks usually involve the study of the structure of the connections between departments or functions within a firm. Accordingly, such research is usually conducted by an organizational behaviorist,[14] however, a notable exception is a study of the coordination of interdepartmental efforts in buying centers,[15] and the field could benefit from more often pursuing an interdepartmental view. For example, many current-day phenomena require an unprecedented synchronization between departments such as marketing and engineering and research and development, or marketing and operations and customer service frontline personnel (e.g., just-in-time delivery systems, high technology, customer service call-in centers, mass customization, and one-to-one service). Indices that reflect various aspects of the network structures can be used to model the extent to which these interdepartmental exchanges are functioning smoothly, the impact on outcomes such as customer (or employee) satisfaction, and even profitability.

Interorganizational Networks

Managers can use networks to study anything from optimal channels of distribution structures (e.g., which partners act reliably in accordance with agreements, which partners are frequent sources of conflict), to offering guiding principals regarding the selection of business partners (e.g., which of a selection of focal firms brings with it the best portfolio of resource partner firms, determined by considering as resources the indirect alliances of the potential-partner firm).[16] Network indices are easily derived from examination of the network structure to represent the most influential firms, the most centrally located firms, the firms that form tightest interconnections with others, the firms whose links to others are similar and thereby interchangeable as alliance partners, and so on.

Networks as a Marketing Tool

What makes a research question one viable for the network paradigm is interest on interrelationships among entities like firms, department, persons, or concepts. The nature of the links connecting the entities is determined by the research interests and not limited by the methodology (e.g., research reports flowing between departments in an organization or flows of recommendations among friends and family). Network methods allow for the examination of properties of the individuals nodes in the network (e.g., the brands or attributes in Figure 9.1), clusters of nodes (e.g., dyads, or subgroups of larger sizes), or the entire network itself (e.g., to what extent is it largely heavily connected, or are there many isolated nodes or groups). The paradigm is still relatively new, but its promise for addressing numerous perennial marketing issues in a manner that might shed unprecedented clarity is great.

COLLABORATIVE FILTERING

While networks or communities of users on the Internet is an interesting and growing phenomenon, this section of the chapter has little to do with the previous section on networks. In this section, we examine the implicit model underlying the recommendations that Internet sites use to try to customize their offerings to their site visitors in the hopes of enhancing purchases.

It is a function of intelligent agent software used by service providers on the Internet to make recommendations to Internet users based on the data the site has already stored on other Internet users. Both retailers and information search engines use software that compares a user's profile (purchases, preferences, clickstreams, histories of downloaded information, etc.) to their data base that characterizes other users to determine which other users may be similar to the focal user, thereby increasing the precision and relevance of the predicted recommendations (products or information strings) to the focal user. This process has come to be called "collaborative filtering" because similar users collaborate in identifying the products that are most likely to be relevant, filtering out the extraneous.[17]

The current efforts in programming these agents could be greatly enhanced if the Internet modelers were to draw more from the enormous academic literature on the multivariate statistical tool of "cluster analysis." Cluster analysis is ideal to address this class of problem, whereby researchers seek to aggregate discrete units (e.g., consumers) into groups (i.e., segments) based on their similarity (e.g., of past purchases).

The input for a cluster analysis is precisely the sort of data the Internet agents have stored. The data can be binary and behavioral (e.g., a consumer bought a particular book). Or they can be more continuous rating scales of perception or preference (e.g., a consumer rates a CD a "9" on a scale of 1 to 10). The data can be frequencies (e.g., the number of times a consumer visits a certain Web page or downloads a certain information packet). The storage of data is often very large (i.e., millions of consumers and multitudes of SKUs). In addition, the data set is typically quite sparse; while in aggregate, many people buy many products, the likelihood of any particular consumer buying a particular product is low.

The clustering question may be posed as: How does one determine whether two customers/users are sufficiently similar that the one's behavior might be helpful in making suggestions to the other? Hence, there are two decisions that must be made in a cluster analysis: first, how does one measure similarity amongst users; and second, which model or algorithm should be used to find clusters of similar users. Numerous texts on cluster analysis exist to help the modeler make these choices.[18] Such resources would allow researchers unfamiliar with cluster analysis (i.e., the Internet agent programmers) to skip ahead quickly on the cluster analysis learning curve, given that so many of the issues that the Internet agents are dealing with for their first time have been addressed, and many resolved, in the vast clustering literature—texts and journal articles.

Let us discuss an example of some of the issues that arise for both the measurement question and the modeling choice question; first, the measurement of similarity among the Web-site visitors. The cluster analysis literature would caution against the use of the similarity indices that are currently being employed by many Internet agents[19] and offer superior alternatives. Often as not, the similarity index computed between the pairs of consumers is a simple correlation coefficient.[20] This statistic is easily computed and understood, but not a particularly good index of similarity. The statistic standardizes the consumer's purchases, which means that a frequent purchaser is treated as similar to an occasional purchaser, if the purchases of the latter are a subset of those of the former. To standardize in this manner is to make an assumption that may not be suitable for the analytical problem at hand (e.g., any segmentation depending on usage).

An alternative similarity index measures the distance between two users, and may seem desirable because it does not standardize the data as just described; that is, a heavy user would not be indexed as similar to a light user. Nevertheless, in the extensive literature on cluster analysis, it is known that still another index is usually superior.

Generally, the simpler the statistic, the better the findings will be upheld in cross-validation (i.e., to predictions for new consumers, segments, and products). A simple and well-performing index of similarity (the Jaccard coefficient)[21] is formed by the ratio of:

$$\frac{\text{The number of mutually purchased items}}{\substack{\text{The number of items that consumer A bought and consumer B did not}\\ \text{+ the number of items that consumer B bought and consumer A did not}}}$$

Note this index leaves out those items which neither consumers A nor B purchased, since (given the sparsity of the matrix) these observations would overwhelm the statistic, rendering all pairs of consumers spuriously highly similar. This index is straightforward, its computation even for all pairs of consumers is trivial, it has theoretical bases and empirical demonstration of robust performance.

In addition to determining one's preferred similarity index, the Internet modeler will have to choose one of the myriad of cluster analysis algorithms. Once again, the cluster analysis texts and academic journal articles can illuminate the conditions under which one model should perform better than another. We now highlight three models, delineating one dimension of their relative strengths (i.e., some of the objectives for which one would outperform another).

One model is called *single-link clustering* and its criterion for subsuming some consumer into an extant segment of consumers, would be that the new consumer would have to be similar enough to at least one consumer in the intact group. "Similar enough" is somewhat a judgment call, but the important criterion is that the new consumer need not be particularly similar to many or all of the group members, only at least one, the most similar one. That is, it takes only a single link between the new consumer and any member of the group to include the new consumer in the group.

By contrast, in *complete-link clustering,* a new consumer joins the segment if he or she is sufficiently similar to all the members in the group, or put another way, the new consumer must be similar enough to the most dissimilar member in the group. Meeting this criterion means that the new customer will be completely linked to all the other members in the segment.

Average-link clustering is an intermediate algorithm that places a new customer into a segment if he or she is, on average, similar to the other members in the group. The new customer may be different from some and similar to others, but on average, meets the threshold of being "sufficiently similar" on average.

Empirically, these algorithms perform differently on data. Single-link clustering results in *chaining,* a phenomenon where the group gets larger by adding one person, then another, then another. With the addition of each new member, there is created a diversity or heterogeneity among the group, such that any potential new member could be similar to the latter members, who were not all that similar to the group as a whole, but simply sufficiently similar to at least one member in the group.

For applications to Internet modeling, this algorithm would be the best means to obtain a potential "lead." A consumer would have been identified as similar to at least one segment member, so there is a possibility, even if remote, that the prospective consumer would also find utility in the offerings of the firm that has satisfied the larger intact segment. The yield might not be efficient, so the model might not be desirable when there is cost associated with contacting the potential customer.

Complete-link models tend to form tight-knit groups, all highly similar customers. Yields would be more efficient, in the sense that recommendations of products to consumers would more likely result in higher probabilities of adoption. However, there may be fewer cluster segments identified, given that the criteria (all members being similar) is fairly rigorous.

Not surprisingly, the performance of average-link clustering is somewhere in the middle, not as generative as single-link and not as precise as complete-link. Some reasonably good number of prospective cluster members will be identified, like single-link models, and the segments will be somewhat similar, like complete-link models. The e-marketing strategist can determined which scenario (i.e., many leads with poor yield, fewer leads with more efficient yield, or decent leads with decent yields) describes the immediate objectives, and then select from these models the one to be adapted for those stated goals (i.e., achieved via single, complete, or average-link cluster analyses, respectively).

Collaborative Filtering as a Marketing Tool

In sum, we can draw from the extensive literature on cluster analysis to address the questions that Internet modelers are (re)discovering in their quest to derive valued recommendations for their users. We briefly compared similarity coefficients and the logic underlying several cluster analysis models, so the programmer of an intelligent agent may select from them in an informed manner and do so, . . . well, intelligently.

CONCLUSION

In this chapter, we focused on two novel research techniques rather than offering breadth in surveying the entire realm of marketing research methods. Network data are new, and they require some effort at data collection since they do not tend to already exist as secondary data bases, but they show strong potential for addressing important issues in marketing. The prevalence of the collaborative filtering problem and the phenomenon of huge databases of purchases and preferences stored at commercial Internet houses has only begun, so the questions have only begun to be posed. These enormous bodies of information threaten to overwhelm the marketing or brand manager. Hopefully we have provided some insights into how one might raise pointed questions and extract useful answers from this class of data as well. Both techniques were presented not as if learning the methods would be the goal per se, but rather as means for addressing critical questions and choices that marketing managers face daily.

Notes

1. For example, the American Marketing Association's definition of marketing research is: "Marketing research is the function that links the consumer, customer,

and public to the marketer through information—information used to identify and define marketing opportunities and problems; generate, refine, and evaluate marketing actions; monitor marketing performance; and improve understanding of marketing as a process. Marketing research specifies the information required to address these issues, designs the method for collecting information, manages and implements the data collection process, analyzes the results, and communicates the findings and their implications" as reported in "New Marketing Research Definition Approved," *Marketing News,* vol. 21 (January 2, 1987), pp. 1, 14.

2. More background and introductory material is well-covered in marketing research texts, such as Gilbert A. Churchill Jr., *Marketing Research: Methodological Foundations,* 7th ed. (Fort Worth, TX: Dryden, 1999).

3. Compare to Dawn Iacobucci, ed., *Networks in Marketing* (Thousand Oaks, CA: Sage, 1996); Dawn Iacobucci and Nigel Hopkins, "Modeling Dyadic Interactions and Networks in Marketing," *Journal of Marketing Research,* vol. 29 (1992), pp. 5–17; and David Knoke and James H. Kuklinski, *Network Analysis* (Beverly Hills, CA: Sage, 1982).

4. John R. Anderson and Gordon H. Bower, eds., *Human Associative Memory: A Brief Edition* (Hillsdale, NJ: Lawrence Erlbaum, 1973); Allan M. Collins and Elizabeth F. Loftus, "A Spreading-Activation Theory of Semantic Processing," *Psychological Review,* vol. 82 (1975), pp. 407–428; and Henry C. Ellis and R. Reed Hunt, *Fundamentals of Cognitive Psychology,* 5th ed. (Dubuque, IA: Brown, 1992).

5. Geraldine R. Henderson, Dawn Iacobucci, and Bobby J. Calder, "Brand Diagnostics: Mapping Branding Effects Using Consumer Associative Networks," *European Journal of Operational Research,* vol. 111 (1998), pp. 306–327.

6. Ibid.

7. Ajay K. Sirsi, James C. Ward, and Peter H. Reingen, "Microcultural Analysis of Variation in Sharing of Causal Reasoning about Behavior," *Journal of Consumer Research,* vol. 22 (1996), pp. 345–372.

8. Richard P. Bagozzi, Geraldine Henderson, Pratibha A. Dabholkar, and Dawn Iacobucci, "Network Analyses of Hierarchical Cognitive Connections Between Concrete and Abstract Goals," in *Networks in Marketing,* ed. Dawn Iacobucci (Thousand Oaks, CA: Sage, 1996), pp. 367–383.

9. Dawn Iacobucci, "Cognitive Networks of Services," *Journal of Service Research,* vol. 1, no. 1 (1998), pp. 32–46.

10. Frank M. Bass, "A New Product Growth Model for Consumer Durables," *Management Science,* vol. 15 (1969), pp. 215–227.

11. Thomas W. Valente, *Network Models of the Diffusion of Innovations* (Cresskill, NJ: Hampton Press Inc., 1995).

12. Peter H. Reingen and James B. Kernan, "Analysis of Referral Networks in Marketing: Methods and Illustrations," *Journal of Marketing Research,* vol. 23 (November 1986), pp. 370–378.

13. Jonathan K. Frenzen and Harry L. Davis, "Purchasing Behavior in Embedded Markets," *Journal of Consumer Research,* vol. 17 (1990), pp. 1–12; and Kent Grayson and

Dawn Iacobucci, "Network Marketing: Embedded Exchange?" (Manuscript under review, 1999).

14. See for example, Ronald S. Burt and Gregory A. Janicik, "Social Contagion and Social Structure," in *Networks in Marketing,* ed. Dawn Iacobucci (Thousand Oaks, CA: Sage, 1996), pp. 32–49.

15. John R. Ronchetto Jr., Michael D. Hutt, and Peter H. Reingen, "Embedded Influence Patterns in Organizational Buying Systems," *Journal of Marketing,* vol. 53 (October, 1989), pp. 51–62.

16. See for example, Håkan Håkansson and D. Deo Sharma, "Strategic Alliances in a Network Perspective," in *Networks in Marketing,* ed. Dawn Iacobucci (Thousand Oaks, CA: Sage, 1996), pp. 108–124; and Mark S. Mizruchi and Joseph Galaskiewicz, "Networks of Interorganizational Relations," *Sociological Methods and Research,* vol. 22, no. 1 (1993), pp. 46–70.

17. Joseph A. Konstan, Bradley N. Miller, David Maltz, Jonathan L. Herlocker, Lee R. Gordon, and John Riedl, "Applying Collaborative Filtering to Usenet News," *Communications of the Association for Computing Machinery,* vol. 40, no. 3 (1997), pp. 77–87.

18. See for example, John A. Hartigan, *Clustering Algorithms* (New York: Wiley, 1975); or Peter H.A. Sneath and Robert R. Sokal, *Numerical Taxonomy: The Principles and Practice of Numerical Classification* (San Francisco: Freeman, 1973).

19. See for example, Daniel Lyons, "The Buzz about Firefly," *The New York Times Cyber Times* (June 29, 1997), pp. 1–9.

20. Jonathan L. Herlocker, Joseph A. Konstar, Al Borchers, and John Riedl, "An Algorithmic Framework for Performing Collaborative Filtering," Association for Computing Machinery (1999), pp.1–8. Available: herlocker,konstar,borchers,riedl@cs.umn.edu

21. See note 18, Sneath and Sokal.

SECTION III

IMPLEMENTATION: MANAGING THE MARKETPLACE

CHAPTER 10

ADVERTISING STRATEGY

BRIAN STERNTHAL

Advertising often has a critical role in developing a brand's equity. Advertising is particularly effective when a brand is differentiated from its competitors on dimensions important to consumers. For example, in the early 1970s, Life cereal was advertised as a nutritional cereal that tasted so good that even kids would enjoy it. Life's advertising featured Mikey, a young child who disliked most foods, but who liked the taste of Life. As a result, Life cereal's share of the cereal market grew from 1.8 to 2.5 in the six years following the onset of this campaign.

Advertising is also an effective vehicle in stimulating the growth of many parity products. Although different brands of peanut butter, detergent, bottled water, analgesics, and cough remedies do not have unique benefits, they often have quite different market shares. For example, Advil has a dominant share among ibuprofen analgesics, and Jif is the leading brand of peanut butter. Advertising for these largely undifferentiated brands accounts for their market share dominance.

Advertising often has an important role in sustaining brand equity. Long-lived advertising campaigns that presented Marlboro as the masculine cigarette and Pepsi as the soft drink for the young and those who aspired to be young have helped sustain these brands' position and market share. Moreover, consistently advertising a brand's position serves as a barrier to competitive entry. The many years of advertising linking Samsonite to durable luggage, prompts people to think of this brand whenever any brand of luggage advertises this benefit.

In this chapter, we examine strategies for developing effective advertising. Our analysis begins with a discussion of consumer insight, which is the foundation of effective advertising. Two types of insight are important. One relates to what consumers believe about a brand and the category in which it holds membership. The other type of insight pertains to how consumers use advertising information to make brand decisions. This insight is the basis for planning the advertising function: identifying a target and developing a brand position. In turn, targeting and positioning guide the design of creative and media strategies.

APPLYING WHAT CONSUMERS THINK TO DEVELOPING EFFECTIVE ADVERTISING

Consumer insight is the starting point in developing effective advertising. For example, Pantene hair care products found that consumers believed that shiny hair implied healthy hair. This insight was used to develop an advertising campaign that propelled what was a small share brand into the leading hair care product. Similarly, research for Brita water filtration systems suggested that there was a substantial segment who believe tap water or even bottled water is not necessarily pure. These individuals feel that only they could ensure that the water they drank is pure by filtering it themselves. Brita used this insight to develop advertising that promoted water purity. And the "Got Milk" campaign, which focused on the negative outcomes resulting from being out of milk, is based on the observation that consumers consider milk important only when they are deprived of it.

These and other consumer insights emerge from conducting focus groups, depth interviews, and surveys. For example, a survey conducted by Forrester Research was the basis for developing online brokerage services. Forrester Research indicates that there are several consumer segments for brokerage online brokerage services. One segment is what Forrester termed "Get-Rich-Quick." This segment is composed of relatively young (average age 37) and moderately affluent consumers (mean income $56,000) who grew up wired. They spend a substantial amount of time on the Internet and are avid readers of financial magazines. They are self-directed, place relatively little value on outside advice, and are risk tolerant. Get-Rich-Quick consumers make over 10 trades annually. They are interested in an online brokerage that would provide them with low cost transactions as well as market information.

The Get-Rich-Quick segment was the first to be sought by online brokerages such as E★Trade and Ameritrade as well as more traditional brokerages that had a Web presence such as Fidelity and Charles Schwab. Advertising highlighted the low cost of online transactions and used a tone and manner that reflected the aggressive and edgy Get-Rich-Quick consumers' approach to trading and other aspects of their life. This strategy was successful in attracting a substantial number of investors. But it also represented a rather limited opportunity. The problems were that the Get-Rich-Quick segment represents a small percentage of all investors, and that many online firms were seeking these investors.

This scenario prompted a search for alternative targets. One attractive target is what Forrester Research labels "Portfolio Cruise Control" investors. These individuals are older and more affluent than the Get-Rich-Quick segment. They represent about 13 percent of investors. More than half of the Portfolio Cruise Control segment is online, but their online activities are restricted largely to a search for financial information. Only about 3 percent of Portfolio Cruise Control make trades on the Internet. They are individuals who buy and hold their investments and who value the services of financial advisers. As attractive as Portfolio Cruise Control consumers are, their accepted beliefs appear to run afoul of what online only brokerages offer. Firms with both an online and offline presence such as Fidelity and Charles Schwab are more likely to attract the Portfolio Cruise Control customer by advertising the availability of integrated online and offline services.

The analysis of online trading underscores the value of consumer insight. An understanding of what consumers believe is the starting point for developing effective advertising. An understanding of the Get-Rich-Quick segment served as a basis for developing both the brokerage services offered and the type of advertising targeted to this segment.

The brokerage example also hints at a common observation made with regard to advertising strategy. Advertising that is based on accepted consumer beliefs is generally more effective, at least in the short run, than advertising requiring consumers to change a belief. This observation was the basis for online brokerages decision to target the Get-Rich-Quick segment. Advertising performance in other categories also offers support for this premise.

To illustrate the virtue of developing advertising that addresses an accepted consumer belief, consider the marketing of body washes. In the United States, body washes are used primarily by women. Brands of body wash such as Clairol's Herbal Essence and Oil of Olay have made significant inroads in the body wash category by presenting advertising that extends the brand equity of their lines of health and beauty products for women. In contrast, Zest has a heritage as a masculine deodorizing soap. Men prefer bar soap to body wash because they believe that directly applying the soap is the best way to use the product and body wash requires some sort of lathering device if it is to be used economically. Advertising may be able to change these beliefs, but it is generally a slow process. Advertising for Zest body wash used a football player who confronted men with their belief that body washes were for women because they required the use of a lather builder and then asserted that Zest body wash made you cleaner. The hope was that the use of a credible masculine spokesperson would prompt men to change their beliefs about the appropriateness of body wash for men. Despite a substantial expenditure against advertising, after two years Zest remained a small brand while Herbal Essence and Oil of Olay flourished.

In sum, knowing what consumers think provides a starting point for advertising. The preferred approach to using this information is to develop advertising that conforms to accepted consumer beliefs. When this is not possible because a brand's equity is not consistent with consumer belief's, knowledge of these beliefs serves as a basis for developing counterarguments to change consumers' dispositions.

APPLYING HOW CONSUMERS THINK TO DEVELOPING EFFECTIVE ADVERTISING

Insight about *what* consumers think is an important basis for developing effective advertising. No less important is an understanding of *how* consumers think, and more specifically how they process and use advertising information. Advertising influences consumers by prompting them to relate what is said in advertising to their current repertoire of knowledge about the advertised brand and competitive brands. This process is referred to as *cognitive elaboration*.

Strategies for Elaboration

There are a number of different advertising strategies that can be used to prompt consumers to elaborate on message information. Some of the more prominent ones used in TV advertising are examined in the discussion that follows.

Hard Sell. Hard sell is a technique developed by Rosser Reeves of the Ted Bates Advertising Agency after World War II. It involves developing a simple associative bond between a brand and its benefit. The hallmark of the hard sell is "buy this brand, get this benefit." Advertising for Rolaids stating that "Rolaids spells relief" illustrates the approach. Hard sell has the virtue of ensuring that a brand name is linked to its benefit. It is an effective device when a product possesses a point of difference that is important to consumers. When a strong point of difference is not available, other approaches to stimulating elaboration should be considered.

Convergent Attributes—The Big Idea. The big idea approach to facilitating elaboration was pioneered by Leo Burnett. The big idea involves identifying a benefit that is focal to consumers (usually the benefit that defines a category) and over time presenting a variety of attributes that imply the benefit to sustain the presentation of brand news. At the same time, the context is kept constant so that people can readily link the advertising information to the brand.

To illustrate the big idea, consider advertising for Green Giant. Successive generations of ads feature the fact that Green Giant vegetables are fresh frozen, vacuum-packed, and packed in butter sauce. All of these attributes imply that Green Giant is of superior quality. The setting in these ads is always in the valley of the Green Giant. This allows consumers to link the information being presented in the ad to the Green Giant brand. The reliable use of this context, and the fact that the benefit is always superior quality enhance the likelihood that consumers will associate the benefits with Green Giant. By changing the attributes that imply this benefit over time, news is provided to sustain consumer interest.

A variant of the big idea involves the use of an attribute to generate the associative network. Here the goal is to develop the campaign around the different benefits implied by some attribute. For example, a run–flat tire system was recently launched where the air pressure in each tire is monitored and reported to the driver via a dashboard indicator. In addition, the tire runs flat without doing damage for about 50 miles. These attributes imply that low air pressure can be detected quickly and thus increase the driver's safety as well as improve gas economy. The run–flat feature also suggests the benefit of not needing a spare tire, which would offer more useable trunk space and increase gas mileage. By presenting the safety, economy, and space implications in advertising, an associative network is represented in consumers' memory to facilitate the recall of run–flat benefits when tires are purchased.

The big idea works well if a firm has an attribute that implies many benefits or a benefit that is derived from many attributes. These situations are most likely to occur when a brand has leadership in its category and when the benefit is likely to be the one that motivates category use.

Story Grammar. The story grammar approach was popularized by Doyle, Dane & Bernbach (DDB, now an Omnicom brand) in the 1960s and is commonly used in advertising today. It is based on the notion that people store information in memory in the following form: problem, episodes to address the problem, and outcomes. From an early age, children exhibit the ability to process information in story grammar format as manifested by their understanding of fairy tales and nursery rhymes. Advertising takes advantage of this structure by associating the problem solved by the brand with the story grammar. Often doing so involves showing an extreme version of the problem for which the brand is an effective solution. The hope is that consumers will infer that if the product works under the extreme conditions depicted, it will work in the less extreme situations that they face.

A well-known illustration of DDB's approach is the introductory campaign for VW in the early 1960s. In it, the person who drives the snowplow is shown driving through a snowstorm to the snowplow in a Volkswagen. Federal Express advertising offers a more contemporary illustration of a story grammar approach. In one spot, problems are shown that occur when rival next-day delivery services are used, thus establishing the problem. Next, the ad shows the procedures followed by Federal Express, including the use of their unique tracking system, to solve the problem. The ad ends by showing a successful outcome, the on-time delivery of the package.

In some cases, the advertiser offers consumers no reason to believe that they have a superior solution to a consumer's problem. A story grammar that involves just the statement of the problem and the solution can be used in this situation. The hope is that consumers will make the inference that because the advertiser understands their problem, the advertiser can solve it. Along these lines, Lee jeans showed the lengths people had to go to in an effort to get into most manufacturers' jeans. Lee was presented as the solution to this problem. No rationale was provided to prompt consumers to believe Lee's claim. Yet, the campaign was effective because people felt that if Lee understood the difficulty they had buying good fitting jeans, Lee was likely to make ones that fit.

Story grammar typically involves the development of a drama in the advertising. People in dramatic ads are not talking to the audience. They are either carrying out some activity or having a conversation with others in the ad. It is as if the audience is witnessing or overhearing some real life episode. A dramatic format is often effective when the advertiser's goal is to demonstrate product efficacy, or to convey some feeling related to a product or service. A critical element in developing a drama is its *verisimilitude;* that is, the extent to which the scene portrays situations that have the appearance of being real or plausible.

The verisimilitude of dramatic advertising is most often compromised because drama is an inappropriate format for the promotional needs of a product or service. This frequently occurs when the advertiser attempts to use a drama to convey substantial amounts of product or service information. It is difficult to have an actor convey many product facts and still maintain the realism of the drama. For example, to convey the fact that White Rain shampoo performed well but was economical, an ad spot showed a couple discussing the benefits of the brand in front of the shampoo display. Another customer comes over and offers testimony to the virtues of White Rain's performance. At issue is whether this is the way things would actually happen to customers and, if not, will this fact be the focus of attention rather than the persuasive arguments presented in the message.

An alternative is for the advertiser to interrupt the drama, present a lecture, and then return to the drama. While this approach is a device that is often used successfully, the interruption can compromise the persuasive power of the drama.

When there is substantial information that needs to be conveyed to an audience, a lecture format is superior to a drama or other story grammar format. A lecture involves having some spokesperson talk to the audience. The spokesperson may be visible or unseen, and may use audio and visual props to reinforce the information being conveyed. The lecture format is particularly appropriate when the advertiser has significant information to convey. Thus, Gillette used a lecture format to introduce the Mach 3 razor, which was considered to be a substantial innovation. Advertising showed how each of the blades operated to give the user a close shave while the voiceover described why Mach 3 offered a superior shave.

Comparative Advertising.   Another approach to prompting elaboration of a message involves pitting the attributes of a firm's brand against those of competitors' brands. Extensive use of comparison emerged during the late 1960s in response to the FTC urging that advertisers provide consumers with the information necessary to make informed choices. Critics of comparative advertising argue that comparative advertising is in reality free advertising for competitors. There is also a concern that disparaging rival brands will lead consumers to think "let there be a pox on all of your brands." The appropriate question, however, is not whether comparative advertising is effective but when is it likely to be effective.

Comparative advertising is useful when a nonleading brand has a benefit on which it dominates the category leader. Here a comparison identifies a follower brand as a member of the same category as the leading brand. But if a nonleading brand is to invite comparison, it must offer demonstrable superiority on some characteristic that is important to consumers.

Perhaps the most successful use of comparison was the Pepsi Challenge, where Pepsi used a blind taste test to show that it was superior in taste to the category leader, Coke.

A leading brand in a category typically would not compare itself to the competition. The leading brand is already closely associated with the product category, so such a comparison would be unlikely to enhance brand membership in the category. Identifying competition might also legitimize competitive brands that consumers may not have previously considered as alternatives. In effect, when a leading brand does comparative advertising, it runs the risk of doing free advertising for the brand to which it is compared.

Even with these concerns, leading brands sometimes compare themselves to followers. They do so because comparison offers a more powerful way to show superiority on some benefit than is possible by simply presenting the merits of the advertised brand. Thus, it is appropriate for a market leader to use comparison when they believe that the increased power of a comparison offsets the potential liabilities of enhancing a competitor's membership in the category. For example, Fidelity compares its online services to those offered by E★Trade, which has substantially smaller market share. Such comparison enables Fidelity to show the superiority of having both on- and offline services, rather than merely implying it. This advantage would seem to outweigh the concern that Fidelity's comparison would interest people in considering the use of E★Trade. Presumably most consumers know about E★Trade brand and nothing in the Fidelity advertising recommends the use of E★Trade.

Leading brands can also make use of comparative advertising by comparing itself to a brand in a different category that performs a like function in a superior way. Thus, Coffee-Mate, which is the gold standard in nondairy creamers compares itself to cream rather than other creamers. Similarly, Tropicana compares itself to fresh-squeezed orange juice rather than other packaged brands, and DiGiorno compares itself to delivered pizza rather than other frozen pizzas.

In developing a comparative ad, the issue emerges about what should be said about the competitor. For example, when Crest introduced its Multi-Care brand to compete with Colgate's Total, it listed better taste and fresher feeling breath as two factors on which it is superior to Total. MultiCare also listed a series of factors, including helps fight cavities, helps fight tartar, and helps brush away plaque, on which MultiCare was represented as being no better than Colgate. In addition, it was noted that Colgate dominated Crest on the reduction and prevention of gingivitis and on the reduction of plaque dimension.

Is this execution appropriate? Research suggests that consumers expect brands in a category to be compensatory.[1] If one brand dominates a second on some factor, a consumer's expectation is that the second brand is likely to dominate the first on some other dimension. Presenting a large number of common attributes along with the one on which Crest dominates serves to reduce the plausibility of consumers' compensation hypothesis. It tells consumers that in this instance compensation is unlikely. Thus, the evaluation of Crest is expected to be more favorable when parity attributes are present than when they are absent, a prediction confirmed by published data.

Providing a factor on which Colgate dominates Crest also satisfies consumers' belief about compensation and it makes Crest a credible source for the claims that it is superior on the taste and fresher feeling breath dimensions. Whether satisfying consumer's assumption of compensation and the credibility gained by acknowledging a competitor's superior feature results in more favorable evaluations of Crest than if the feature on which Colgate dominated was absent is an empirical question. In the case of Crest Multi-Care, the dimensions on which Colgate Total was superior to Crest were sufficiently important to consumers that Colgate gained substantial market share despite the Crest MultiCare advertising.

Analogy is a particular type of comparison that is commonly used in advertising when the task involves the promotion of services and other abstract entities. Analogies involve the transfer of internal knowledge from a base that is known to a target that is being learned. For example, the assertion that Palm Pilot is a secretary enables people who understand a secretary's function (base) to transfer this knowledge and gain an understanding of how a Palm Pilot might function (target). Analogies are also used to make a brand's low salience feature more salient by relating it to another object where that feature is focal. For example, the assertion that Jergen's skin cream is light like a feather makes the brand's lightness salient by its comparison to a feather where lightness is a key feature. Because analogies require the mapping between a base and target, their effectiveness depends on a message recipient's willingness to expend considerable cognitive effort in processing such appeals.

Color. The use of color can be an effective means of prompting message recipients to elaborate on their feelings about the product or the context of use. Red implies active and lively, blue cool and serene, and yellow implies medicinal and weak. Pastels imply a product is feminine, whereas dark colors and especially dark brown imply masculinity. The use of white lettering on a black background implies high tech.

This use of color cannot always be employed to advantage. Processing color in advertising can be an effortful task. This is a problem when people use their cognitive resources to process the meaning of the color rather than the persuasive content of the message. When complex verbal information is to be transmitted, consideration should be given to using black and white advertising.

Color can also be used to direct attention. Advertisers use color highlighting to have the audience focus on the product or some other element that is critical to the persuasiveness of the message. Thus, 7UP used a black and white ad in which the bottle of 7UP was in red to emphasize that the brand came in a cherry flavor.[2]

Spokespeople.   Advertisers frequently use spokespeople to deliver their messages. In some instances, spokespeople are selected because they are attractive; that is, they are dynamic, likable, or of high status. Bill Cosby advertised Jell-O, Candice Bergen was the spokesperson for Sprint, Jenny McCarthy served as the model for Candies shoes, and Sarah Ferguson, the Duchess of York, advertised the virtues of Ocean Spray's LightStyle drink. Such attractive spokespeople enhance advertising recall. This effect is probably attributable to the fact that message recipients have many associations to celebrities in memory. However, recall of the celebrity who serves as a spokesperson for a brand is often not related to the brand's benefit. When this is the case, the persuasive impact of messages using celebrities is quite modest.

Another concern in using celebrities is that if they are hot properties they may represent multiple sponsors and thus dilute the celebrity's association to the brand. Among the brands that Michael Jordan advertises are Nike, Gatorade, Chevrolet, McDonald's, Rayovac batteries, and MVP.com. Jordan is a powerful endorser for some of these brands. His personal appearances with members of the sales force for the companies that he endorses are undoubtedly motivational for these audiences. However, when a spokesperson has multiple affiliations, confusion often emerges about the brands with which the person is affiliated. For example, when Jordan and Larry Bird played a game of horse for Jordan's Big Mac in a Superbowl ad for McDonald's, many viewers thought the ad was sponsored by Nike. While this disturbed McDonald's, their concern was modest when compared to that expressed by Converse for whom Bird was an athletic shoe spokesperson.

Even if overexposure is not a problem, celebrities may lose their popularity, do something illegal, or die. Any of these outcomes results in campaign discontinuity and often a drop in advertising performance. Or, recognizing the equity they represent, the celebrity may attempt to hold out at contract renewal for a larger fee, more creative control, or both. Clearly, there should be a compelling reason to use celebrities if taking these risks is to be judicious. It is a strategy of last resort when other means of persuasion are not available.

One compelling reason for using attractive spokespeople is that they personify a key product benefit. John Houseman was an appropriate spokesperson for Smith Barney because he personified the firm's hard-working and analytical attributes. Michael Jordan is an appropriate spokesperson for Nike because he personifies superior performance. In effect, the spokesperson acts as another cue that implies the benefit of the brand.

Personification of a brand's benefit is not the only basis for selecting spokespeople. Sources who are credible by virtue of their trustworthiness and expertise are used as spokespeople. This practice is based on the premise that a credible source enhances persuasion, a belief that is qualified by research. Credible spokespeople enhance persuasion among those who are initially opposed to the position advocated in a message advocacy. Credible sources block the retrieval of message recipients' own thoughts, which are composed largely of counterarguments given their opposition to the message. In contrast, less credible sources are more persuasive than highly credible sources when the audience favors the message position. Here, the less credible source stimulates the activation of the audience's own thoughts, which in this case are arguments supporting the message, whereas a highly credible source inhibits such activation. This observation does not give the strategist license to use the least credible source available when advertising to those favorable to a brand. To do so might undermine influence. Rather, the implication is that employing the most credible spokesperson is not always prudent.

It is often difficult to find spokespeople who are credible. Although expert sources are not difficult to find, ones who are expert and trustworthy are rare. This is because consumers perceive people who serve as spokespeople to be acting in their own interests; they are being paid to say favorable things about a product. One way to overcome this problem is to use spokespeople whose integrity is unquestionable. For example, British Telecom used Stephen Hawking to support the notion of communication to better the world.

Spokesperson credibility may also be achieved by using consumer testimonials. People who are like those in the target are often viewed as credible sources. This is particularly the case when their testimonials are spontaneous. Tylenol, for example, used testimonials recorded by a hidden camera in advertising its analgesic. Pepsi Cola used blind taste tests in which consumers chose between Coke and Pepsi to enhance the credibility of their appeal.

Actors too may be viewed as credible spokespeople. Typically, credibility is achieved by portraying the actor as a discerning person or one who is antagonistic to the product category but who endorses the advertised products. As noted earlier, Mikey, a 3-year-old child, who hated cereal but liked Life cereal, helped that brand significantly increase its market share.

Finally, a top corporate officer sometimes is used as the spokesperson for the brand. Charles Schwab's services are advertised by its CEO, Richard Branson has served as spokesperson for Virgin Atlantic Airlines, and Dave Thomas, the founder of Wendy's, is featured in advertising for that fast-food restaurant. While some CEOs, such as Thomas are effective spokespeople, most are better at their day job than they are at acting. Further, it is a short-term strategy that necessarily has to change if something happens to CEO. Along these lines, Wendy's had to change its advertising while Dave Thomas recovered from a cardiac condition.

Brand Linkage

Elaboration of a brand's benefit is effective only if it is linked to the brand name. This observation suggests that the brand name be made prominent to consumers. This can be achieved by presenting the brand name early in advertising and prior to the information about the benefit. In addition, it is useful to introduce information about a brand that is consistent with what people already know about it. When this is not possible, it is important to enhance its recall by creating associations to it in the message. For example, Cutty Sark scotch whisky is a brand that scotch drinkers associate with its tall sailing ship logo. When Cutty Sark began to lose share, a campaign was developed that promoted brand recall and associated it to Cutty Sark's heritage. It was "don't give up the ship." Thus, for Father's Day the Cutty Sark ad stated: "The best advice I ever got from my Daddy was . . . Don't give up the ship," and on New York subways the poster read "When you have had it up to here with graffiti, don't give up the ship." This slogan not only was memorable by virtue of the fact that it was the battle cry during the Revolutionary War, but also because it was closely linked to what consumers knew about the brand. The result was a resurgence of Cutty Sark's sales.

While the importance of developing advertising that links a brand to its benefit seems obvious, there have been a notable number of advertising campaigns where people can play back the message, but link it to a brand other than the one doing the advertising. For example, Schick developed an ad for a man's razor that showed a woman shaving her face and reporting how easy it was with a Schick blade razor. The novelty of this visual prompted the majority of people who saw the ad to remember it. However, many message recipients thought it was an ad for a Gillette razor.

Why is brand linkage difficult to achieve? One reason is that a persuasive advertising message typically has a greater number of connections to people's lives than does the brand name. As time passes, the numerous associations to the message facilitate its recall, while the small number of associations that people have to many brand names make them difficult to recall. The implication is that brands with a rich set of associations in people's minds such as Coca-Cola or McDonald's are less likely to have failures to link the brand name to the message than are brands that are less integral to consumers' lives. However, failures to link the brand and its message occur even when a brand is well known. This outcome results because the message is not related to the brand's equity.

Advertisers sometimes walk away from a brand's equity and weaken brand linkage in an effort to present advertising that is consistent with consumers' beliefs. For example, Special K had a heritage as a brand of ready-to-eat cereal that was a part of a regimen to keep healthy and thin. When women objected to the advertising on grounds that it fostered the pursuit of a goal that ran afoul of contemporary women's values, Special K changed its advertising. The new message was that women should be content with whatever figure they had. While this message resonated with many women, few connected this message to Special K. Why would they given Special K's heritage as a nutritional brand that helped keep women slim? A new campaign was then developed featuring Cindy Crawford that presented Special K's heritage in a modern way. The brand was positioned as being part of a regimen that kept people fit rather than slim.

An absence of brand linkage is even more likely when a brand does not have a strong point of differentiation from its competition. In this situation, the point of difference becomes an understanding of target consumers and their goals rather than some brand benefit. When several competitors use this same approach the linkage between brand and message is weakened. Along these lines, VW, Toyota, and Subaru all target young drivers. Advertising for all of these brands represents the edgy attitude and lifestyle of their target. The result is that advertising for these brands fostered weak linkage to the brands, particularly for Toyota and Subaru who were later adopters of this advertising approach than VW.

In the United States, the late identification (ID) of the brand name in television advertising generally undermines the linkage of the brand to its benefit. For example, advertising for Compaq showed the novel applications that were available. Only at the end of the ad was Compaq explicitly mentioned, resulting in weak brand identification. In the Schick advertising featuring the woman shaving described earlier, the identification of the brand was also forestalled until the end of the ad, undermining brand linkage.

Despite its potential liability, late IDs can serve as powerful persuasive devices. A late ID can be used to encourage people to process the message rather than their own thoughts about the brand advertised. For example, when Tums, an antacid, found that people often responded to their advertising by arguing that such a small tablet could not be as effective as Tums was claiming, a late ID was introduced. The commercial showed an extreme close-up of a green Tums tablet that was revolving slowly as its efficacy was being described. Only at the end of the commercial was the tablet in a position where the brand name could be read. This commercial not only halted brand erosion but resulted in a significant upturn in business. The late ID forestalled the audience's counterarguments until a point when it would have taken too much effort to re-evaluate what had been learned about Tums.

Creative Strategies to Prompt Message Elaboration

Because message elaboration is a cognitively effortful task, devices that motivate or facilitate elaboration are often used in advertising. Here we examine motivational devices that are integral to the message as a means of encouraging elaboration of its contents.

Message Discrepancy. One motivation factor is the discrepancy between the position advocated in a message and people's current beliefs. Precision is needed in using this motivational device. If a communication argues for a position that people currently hold, persuasion will be minimal. At most, this approach will reinforce individuals' current beliefs. If a communication is highly discrepant, it is likely to evoke counterarguments and thus have limited influence. The implication is that messages of moderate discrepancy are maximally persuasive.

Support for these contentions is found in the psychological literature as well as in commercial experience. When Sears introduced its Die Hard battery, advertising showed it starting 12 cars. This commercial was not effective. Many people inferred that they would have to pay a premium for a battery that powerful. By systematically changing the number of cars the battery was depicted as being able to start, Sears found that showing 5 cars being started induced the greatest amount of persuasion. Thus, on both a theoretical basis and empirical grounds there is reason to believe that moderate discrepancy in an advertisement is maximally persuasive. To determine the precise level of message discrepancy that is optimal, trial and error is required.

Threat Appeals. From everyday experience, it might be expected that threat would be an effective means of motivating message elaboration. Admonitions to children such as "don't touch the hot stove or you will be burned" seem to be influential without repetition. However, research findings suggest that threat may not stimulate persuasion, and may even undermine it. Thus, the focal question is when does threat enhances persuasion?

The prevailing view is that threatening information can be processed by one of two systems that operate in a parallel. One system is called *danger control*. As Figure 10.1 shows, the danger control system processes information regarding what constitutes danger, who is in danger, and how to control danger. This information is stored in memory and may stimulate actions that are adaptive in coping with danger.

The other system is *fear control*. It involves the processing of information about the dire consequences of noncompliance with the message

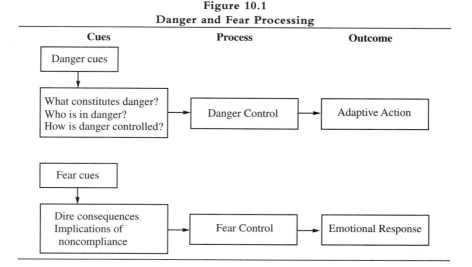

Figure 10.1
Danger and Fear Processing

advocacy. Such information is likely to trigger individuals' repertoire of associations that are pertinent to coping with fear. This repertoire is idiosyncratic: Some people cope with fear by sleeping, others by eating, and still others by smoking. Thus, by triggering fear control emotional responses emerge that may or may not lead to adaptive action.

To clarify this explanation, consider a commercial advocating that people should stop smoking. To induce adaptive action, the audience should be told about what constitutes danger with regard to smoking. Operationally, this might involve telling people that there is danger if they have a hacking cough, or cannot walk up a flight of stairs without getting short of breath. Recommending ways of coping with danger might also stimulate adaptive action. This might include recommendations such as placing cigarettes in inconvenient locations and drawing a circle around the middle of the cigarettes and only smoking them down to that line. In contrast, showing gory illustrations of smokers' blackened lungs or stating dire consequences such as "Be sure you have a lot of insurance; your kids will need it to go to college" should be avoided. Focusing on dire consequences may trigger fear and thus induce an emotional response. This response may or may not be adaptive. Some people might even light up a cigarette as a means of coping with the fear induced.

The foregoing analysis suggests that inducing fear is an inappropriate strategy for persuasion. So-called threat appeals should focus on helping people to recognize danger and to cope with it. This type of information is likely to be used in pursuing an adaptive course of action. Although it may not be possible to eliminate all mention of the dire consequences of noncompliance, information about consequences should be relegated to the background. Otherwise, it is likely to stimulate individuals' own repertoire of thoughts, which may or may not lead to adaptive action.

A threatening ad developed by Lynx illustrates the problem with threatening dire consequences. The goal of this organization is to get people not to purchase fur coats. The ad shows a model dressed in a fur coat walking down a runway during a fashion show. The chic patrons of the show are admiring the fur coat until, blood spewing from the skins starts splattering the runway and the patrons. The ad ends with the slogan, "It takes up to 40 dumb animals to make a fur coat, but only one to wear it." It would seem that those who are already convinced about the virtues of not wearing fur coats would be most persuaded by this appeal.

Humorous Appeals.   Humor is frequently used to motivate message processing. Some form of humor is used in more than half of commercials aired on television. Advertisers use turns-of-phrase, double entendre, slapstick, and the like to stimulate message processing. The available evidence suggests that humor is an effective device for gaining attention and motivating an audience to process a message. However, it is equally evident that humor is not always an effective means of influence. In fact, it may undermine influence.

Several guidelines might be followed to enhance the persuasiveness of humorous appeals. Most important is that the humor is related to conveying the brand benefit. When it does not, humor may induce attention and learning of information that is not germane to promoting the product. Recall of a humorous ad may be substantial, but information that is relevant to motivating purchase may not be available.

Humor should be focused on the product and not the user. Making the product user the brunt of the joke may stimulate counterarguments and thus limit persuasion. If it is not feasible to focus humor on the product, it is preferable to make nonusers of the product rather than its users the brunt of the humor. This approach is illustrated by an ad for Dr. Scholl's. A fisherman is shown sitting on a dock with his feet in the water. Before he can cast, the fish come to the surface, apparently dead from his foot odor. The remedy is Dr. Scholl's foot powder.

Multiple executions are generally required when humor is used. Because initial exposures stimulate attention, repeated exposure to the same humorous appeal quickly causes wearout. To forestall inattention, different ads are required that offer message recipients news about the product.

Critics question the use of humor, even when the above guidelines are followed. They argue that humor usurps time that could be better spent informing people about a product's virtues. This problem is thought to be particularly troublesome because most commercials are only 30 seconds in length. Although it is undoubtedly true that some factual information must be sacrificed in favor of humor, it should be noted that there is nothing inherent in a humorous approach to require substantial time for its development.

Media Strategies to Prompt Message Elaboration

Thus far, we have considered creative strategy approaches to developing effective advertising. Here, we consider media strategies as a means of enhancing the resources available for message elaboration. One media strategy that affects resource availability involves selecting schedules that deliver *reach* or *frequency* against some target. Reach refers to the extent a target has been exposed at least once to an ad during a four week period. Frequency is the average number of times that target people are exposed during this period. Reach and frequency are related such that, for a given ad budget, increasing one requires the reduction in the other. Exposing additional target consumers to advertising, that is obtaining additional reach, requires a reduction in the average number of times target consumers are exposed to brand advertising. (See the Appendix for a description of computations involving reach and frequency.)

Message Exposures.   Advertisers have long debated the tradeoff between reach and frequency. In the 1970s, it was common to favor a reach approach. Budgets tended to be sufficient to ensure reasonable frequency and still get high levels of reach. The preferred number during the 1970s and 1980s was at least three exposures, which is referred to as the three plus frequency rule. This rule was presumably based on a 1979 Association of National Advertisers' (ANA) study. But the investigator responsible for that study, Michael Naples states: "What I said was that each brand should . . . figure out what its own curve was."

A General Electric researcher, Herb Krugman, also advocated three exposures, but what he was referring to was three *types* of exposures. The first type gets people to say "What is it?" This type of exposure can thus be viewed as an effort to establish a brand's membership in a category. The second type of exposure gets people to say "What of it?" Here, the effort is to facilitate the processing of a brand's point of difference. And the third exposure prompts a decision. Thus, Krugman's argument was not that three was the right number of ad exposures, but that consumers responded to mounting exposures in three different ways. The specific number of exposures that make people decisional is an empirical question.

In the late 1990s, a new rule of thumb emerged. Based on research with selected brands, the conclusion is that a single exposure to an ad is the appropriate level of frequency. This is generally referred to as the C-curve because of the shape of the response function (see Figure 10.2). The C-curve implies that reaching another target person is of greater value to the advertiser than reaching the same target person another time.

Evidence for the C-curve has been found in several recent studies. These have been for leading or major brands in their category that have had a stable position and a long-lived advertising campaign. Reach makes sense in this circumstance. However, it is inappropriate to conclude that in general all brands follow the C-curve. In fact, the preponderance of evidence suggests that in most cases some repetition of advertising enhances consumers'

Figure 10.2
The "C" Curve

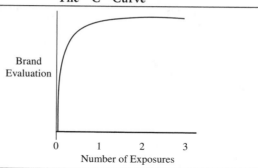

Figure 10.3
The "S" Curve

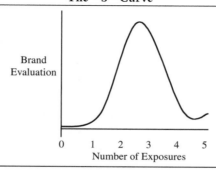

responses. This outcome is not surprising because repeated exposures enhance elaboration and the recency of message processing, the two factors thought to stimulate information accessibility.

While some repetition of a message increases its persuasive impact, very substantial levels of repetition prompt a decline in message impact. Figure 10.3 illustrates this response function—an S-curve. The declining portion of the curve is termed *wearout*. Wearout is thought to occur because once people have learned the information an ad has to convey, they use additional ad exposures as an opportunity to scrutinize the message assertions by comparing it to other things they know. Or, they may simply dismiss the information as old news. In either event, what is in memory is likely to be less favorable than the information presented in the ad, resulting in wearout.

The most common approach used by advertisers to address wearout is to change the context in which advertising is presented while sustaining the same theme. For example, a soft drink producer may emphasize thirst quenching in all of the commercials included in a campaign but use different scenes and actors to deliver this appeal. This approach is often ineffective. What appears to happen is that people process the message information in response to the first few exposures. Thereafter, they activate their own repertoire of product-related associations. Because advertising messages are designed to be highly persuasive, the processing of message information is likely to lead to a more favorable disposition toward the product than the activation of individuals' own repertoire of associations. Thus, wearout occurs. Unless the change in the setting offers consumers insights, it is unlikely to enhance the processing of message information.

Wearout may be forestalled by presenting new information that again stimulates the audience to process the message. Keeping the setting the same provides cues that facilitate the location of information in memory relevant to the advertising issue. Changing the ad content can provide the news needed to sustain audience interest in processing the message. Illustrative of this approach is advertising for Cheer detergent. The same individual and setting are shown in each Cheer television ad. The fact that Cheer cleans in cold water is announced in every spot. However, the information that is conveyed changes over time. In one spot, the fact that clothes will not fade in cold water is highlighted, and in another, the benefit of clothes not shrinking is presented.

Generally, it is useful to think of wearout as a problem that occurs because consumers have more resources available for message processing than are required for this task. Two strategies are available to address wearout. One is to increase the resources required to process the message so that they match the resources available. The Cheer example illustrates the use of this strategy, though any device that increases message complexity might be considered. The other strategy involves reducing the resources available for processing. Some mild form of distraction or increasing the rate of message presentation might be useful in this regard. In using either of these strategies, caution is necessary to ensure that the resources available for message processing are not reduced to such an extent that the audience fails to process the communication content.

Our analysis indicates that a simple rule of thumb about the appropriate level of frequency is unlikely to result in an effective media strategy. There are many considerations that underlie the choice of the reach and frequency level. Reach is appropriate when the purchase is planned, the interpurchase interval is long, interest in the category is high, and the environment is uncluttered by competitive advertising.

Media scheduling involves not only decisions about where to advertise, but also about when to advertise. One alternative is to use a continuity strategy, which entails advertising with about equal weight throughout the year. Or, a concentration strategy could be used where advertising dollars are spent during a single period. Historically, advertisers used a concentration strategy for seasonal products and continuity otherwise. However, as the cost of media began to rise at a faster rate than advertising budgets, two new approaches became common: flighting and pulsing. *Flighting* involves advertising for some period, followed by a hiatus with no advertising and then by a second flight. *Pulsing* involves the same general approach as flighting, except that low levels of advertising replace the hiatuses. The idea in flighting and pulsing is to deliver the impact of concentration with the sustaining value of continuity.

Some informative work regarding the impact of these various strategies has been conducted by Hugh Zielske of Foote, Cone & Belding. He examined the impact of different ways of allocating 1300 Gross Rating Points (GRPs). The Appendix on page 245 illustrates the calculation of GRPs throughout a year. The findings were:

- Concentrating the 1300 GRPs in one quarter with 100 GRPs per week produced the highest recall. Twenty-three percent of the audience recalled the advertising. However, recall was very low in non-advertising quarters.
- Using two flights of 700 and 600 GRPs in two different quarters produced peak recall in those quarters of about 18 percent, with the second flight producing slightly better recall than the first.
- Continuity with 25 GRPs for each of the 52 weeks produced the lowest recall of the strategies tested, an average of 8 percent recall. This level was attained in the first quarter and sustained thereafter.
- Using a strategy of one week in with 100 GRPs and 3 weeks out produced somewhat better recall than continuity by the end of the year— over 10 percent.

This analysis underscores the problem with a concentration strategy. Although it has high impact, there is significant forgetting during the periods when there is no advertising. This state of affairs would seem acceptable only when dealing with a seasonal product, and even then caution is warranted in using concentration. Too often advertisers use concentration in the belief that sales are seasonal, in effect exacerbating seasonality.

To illustrate this point, consider the experience of a soft drink manufacturer about 25 years ago. Category sales were seasonal, with 65 percent of sales occurring during the period May to October. Soft drink advertisers spent the vast majority of their ad budgets against this season. In an attempt to alter this pattern, one soft drink producer experimented with a more balanced budget. The result was increased nonseasonal consumption and sustained seasonal consumption. Apparently there was not a compelling reason for soft drink seasonality. Disproportionate advertising against the summer season became a self-fulfilling prophecy that ensured continued seasonality. Other soft drink manufacturers quickly changed to a more balanced spending pattern. As a result, the six-month soft drink season accounts for only about 60 percent of annual sales today.

Whether concentration or continuity is planned, an important issue in planning a media schedule is how to space repeated exposures to advertising. There is emerging evidence that as you increase the time interval between exposures to an ad, you increase the perception that the information contained in the ad is unfamiliar, and this enhances the likelihood that the audience will pay attention to the advertising. The spacing of repeated exposures operates in the same way as exposures themselves, that is, by affecting the resources available for message processing. Like increases in repetition, increasing the interexposure interval enhances the resources available for information processing. However, there comes a point where the interval between exposures is so large that there is little savings from the prior exposure. In this event, each exposure acts like an initial exposure.

Several other media devices are available to allow an advertiser to outshout competition. For advertisers with large budgets, such dominance can be achieved by outspending competitors. Smaller competitors must resort to other approaches to have their voice heard. Accordingly, a low budget advertiser might narrow the target, reduce the variety of vehicles needed to reach a target, and thus allow dominance of the consumers who are targeted. Reducing the geographical scope of advertising and the times during the year when there is an advertising presence are also useful means of achieving dominance. Selecting less expensive vehicles or using shorter or smaller ads as well as a reduction in the reach and frequency might be considered to gain dominance. In selecting among these strategies, the goal is to have a strong presence among as large a portion of the target as possible by restricting the playing field to a size that allows for media dominance.

ADVERTISING AND INTEGRATED MARKETING COMMUNICATION

During the past several years, emphasis has been on broadening the scope of communications strategy so that advertising is only one element of the communication mix. This recasting of advertising as a less dominant element of the communication mix seems appropriate in light of the growth of other communication vehicles such as publicity, direct marketing, event marketing, and the Internet. Unlike a decade ago, when consumer advertising implied television and magazines or newspapers, today's marketing communication implies a variety of different vehicles. The notion is that these vehicles should offer another point of contact with consumers that deliver the brand position. Such integration is referred to as Integrated Marketing Communications (IMC). The central tenets advanced by proponents of IMC are that (1) television is no longer king and that many media should be considered; and (2) all media should present a consistent view of the brand.

To illustrate the application of IMC, consider the promotion of Marlboro cigarettes. Marlboro uses print advertising featuring cowboys and Marlboro country. It also runs contests where the prizes are caps and jackets with Marlboro logos on them. Another vehicle that is used to market Marlboro is its sponsorship of Formula 1 racecars. The use of cowboys, contests, and racecars are all images that support Marlboro's position as a cigarette for a goal-focused, self-expressive individual. In addition, the use of media beyond print, provide the opportunity for additional reach, that is, exposing people to the brand who might not read the magazines in which Marlboro advertises.

Although it is clear that IMC is a useful approach to communications, as it currently stands, the implications of IMC are tactical rather than strategic. To be strategic would require that IMC analysis provide guidelines about when various media should be used. For example, what is the role of advertising on the Internet in relation to advertising done via broadcast and direct marketing?

One way that this might be done is to assess the role of various media in fostering a particular level of brand/customer intimacy. For example, Doral advertises its cigarette in magazines, which informs consumers about the brand's imagery. We refer to messages that describe the brand as "brand presentation." Doral also invites smokers to spend a day on a ranch, which provides an indication that the brand has a connection to its smokers' interests. We refer to such messages as "brand relation." And, Doral sends their smokers birthday cards, indicating that they relate to their customers as individuals. We refer to such messages as "brand intimacy."

Thus, three different vehicles are employed to attain three different levels of brand/customer intimacy—about the brand, about the brand relation to customers, and the brand relationship with the individual consumer. It is also possible that a single vehicle can achieve all three levels of intimacy. Internet communications are particularly useful in this regard. A Web site, for example, might be used to provide consumers with detailed information about a brand. Indeed, Web sites enable the advertiser to present more information than any other medium. A brand can include interstitials (ads presented without having to leave a site) in sites that relate not only to the advertised brand but also the consumers' lifestyle. This would enable to the brand to communicate brand relations. A Web site can also be specifically tailored to a user and thus deliver brand intimacy. For example, United Airlines can achieve brand presentation by reporting detailed information about its flights, in-flight amenities, and the like on its Web site. It can achieve brand relations by selecting appropriate travel Web sites. Finally, it can promote brand intimacy by retaining personal information such as a passenger's seating preference, frequent flyer number, and special meal requests to facilitate the transaction.

One inference that might be suggested by the above analysis is that because the Internet is capable of delivering all three levels of intimacy, it will replace traditional forms of media. This prospect seems remote. First, some vehicle is needed to attract consumers to a firm's Web site. The main Internet vehicle for this purpose is banners. These are brief ads placed at search engine and other sites. When clicked on, the Web user is taken to another Web location and given a detailed communication. While these devices were effective initially, the sheer number of banners has prompted a decline in banners' effectiveness. Clicks on banners have been falling and are now below one half of a percent, and surveys indicate that consumers' annoyance with banner advertising is increasing. Conventional advertising thus seems an important device to prompt consumers to visit a Web site, particularly when the firm is new and unfamiliar to consumers, as many e-commerce firms are, or when an e-commerce firm is offering a new service such as Edmunds site that offers help in performing various tasks related to car purchase. It is not surprising that there has been a huge increase in the use of conventional media such as television, radio, and magazines to promote Web sites.

There is also likely to be a growth in the use of other vehicles. An already emerging Internet communication device is to rent real estate on existing sites. For example, when consumers purchase say a digital camera from Amazon.com, Eveready has its brand so situated that it prompts the consideration of batteries as part of the camera purchase. As more bricks-and-mortar retailers establish Web sites, manufacturers are likely to use real estate rental as a key vehicle for communicating with consumers. For example, the Sears Web site might include a Maytag store, that is, real estate rented by Maytag to feature its brands. This arrangement is likely to be particularly attractive to Internet novices who can quickly learn to purchase online because of the resemblance to bricks-and-mortar retail operations they are familiar with.

MEASURING ADVERTISING EFFECTIVENESS[3]

Advertisers have substantial choice in the selection of copy-testing services. There is less variety in the type of tests that are used. For television advertising, most services recruit consumers to watch program material such as television programming in which the ads to be tested as well as control ads are inserted. Prior to the viewing of these programs and ads, respondents are asked to indicate their brand preferences in several categories including the ones to be tested. They are then shown the program and advertising material.

When the presentation is complete, the audience is asked to recall the advertising they have seen. If the respondents fail to recall the target ad, they may be prompted with the target ad's category (e.g., "Do you remember seeing an ad for automobiles?"). The recall data are typically available in the form of the respondents' verbatim responses as well as a summary score that reflects the percentage of viewers who demonstrated recall of critical message information. This latter measure is used to establish norms for all advertising that is tested by the service. In addition, respondents are asked to select anew a brand they would prefer in various categories. These responses are compared to the pre-advertising preferences as a means of assessing the switching power of an ad.

A variety of other measures might also be administered, including respondents' prediction of what elements of the advertised information they would remember, their evaluations of the advertising and the brand, and their suggestions for improving advertising. Some services ask respondents to turn a knob or some other device while viewing the materials to indicate their interest or liking of what they are seeing moment-to-moment. Sometimes the viewers' physiological responses to advertising are assessed by examining voice stress, pupil dilation, galvanic skin response, or some other physiological reaction to ad copy.

Clients of these copy-testing services make use of the test results to assess the likely impact of their advertising when it is aired. It is understood that the recall and brand-switching scores do not offer accurate parameter estimates of ad performance. Rather, the scores are used to compare different executions at a point in time, to evaluate current creative relative to its predecessors, or as a variable in a model to predict sales. In addition, the copy-testing services provide norms to be used as benchmarks in evaluating the effectiveness of all the ads being tested. Copy-testing services frequently offer their clients consultation about how copy-testing scores might be enhanced. If moment-to-moment measures have been administered, they are used to eliminate low interest portions of the ad or to suggest what facets of the message should be elaborated upon.

These copy tests can provide valuable insights about consumers' reactions to advertising and how creative executions may be revised. However, there are potentially serious limitations to the current approaches of measuring advertising responses. We examine some of the more popular measures and suggest how the measurement of advertising effectiveness might be enhanced.

Explicit Measures

A majority of the copy-testing measures are based on the assumption that when consumers make purchase decisions they attempt to recall advertising for brands in the relevant category, as well as other brand knowledge. The extent to which this search for advertising information is successful is thought to depend on how well advertising has been learned. Thus, the measure most often used to assess advertising effectiveness is verbatim recall of the advertising message. Consumers are asked to recall an ad for a specific brand and to play back the message content. This measure is referred to as an explicit measure of memory because it reflects the extent to which people retrieve the content of an explicit message. While there is little dispute that recall of the advertising content is a useful indicator of the extent to which message learning has occurred, interpreting the impact of advertising from a measure of explicit ad recall is problematic.

One problem with using what people can remember from an ad as a measure of what they know about a brand is that consumers often have difficulty in tracing the origin of their knowledge. People respond to advertising by relating what they know to the ad content. What is stored in memory is a combination of the message information and recipients' own thoughts. When asked to recall the contents of a specific ad, people conjure up brand-related information. But they often have difficulty in determining whether the information they retrieve is based on the particular message being asked about, some other message they might have seen for the brand, or self-generated knowledge. This difficulty in preserving the origin of one's knowledge explains why misreporting of what people have learned about a brand from advertising is a frequent occurrence.

Even when advertising recipients report accurately on what they learned from advertising, free recall and other explicit measures of memory are likely to be poor indicators of advertising effectiveness. This is because brand evaluations and choice are often not determined by the information recalled but by the associations consumers have to that content. For example, consumers might exhibit good recall of an automobile manufacturer's claim that the car came with a complete tool kit because they associated this claim with the thought that the tool kit would be needed to fix the car's frequent breakdowns. In this event, good advertising recall would be associated with a disinclination toward purchase.

Implicit Measures

Consumers make purchase decisions based on what they know about a brand, rather than on what they remember from an ad. Whereas explicit ad recall reflects what people can remember about information stated in an ad, advertisers are interested in what people know about their brand. Implicit measures of memory are useful in this regard. Implicit measures solicit what people know without making reference to the origins of their knowledge. For example, brand recall is an implicit measure because people are asked to tell what they know about a brand. The impact of exposure on brand recall is a more appropriate measure of the learning prompted by advertising than is ad recall because brand recall is a reflection of what people know rather than what they can remember.

Another useful implicit measure is top-of-mind awareness. This involves using a category cue to prompt the retrieval of brand names. For example, top-of-mind brand recall might entail asking consumers to list the brands of beer they would consider purchasing. An increase in top-of-mind awareness is indicated by the observation that people who have seen an ad for, say, Miller, include this brand in their list to a greater extent than those who have not. This would suggest that the ad was effective in increasing the probability that Miller is included in the consumers' consideration set.

While brand recall and top-of-mind awareness are useful indicators of what people know about a brand, advertisers are generally most interested in consumers' dispositions toward a brand as a result of advertising exposures. To some extent, these measures of learning are useful in making inferences about dispositions. For example, enhancing top-of-mind recall frequently is found to increase preference for a brand. However, because this measure is of limited diagnostic value in efforts to enhance brand purchase, measures specifically designed to reflect people's dispositions are considered.

Perhaps the most frequently used measure of dispositions is attitude. Unlike learning measures, attitude questions probe how people feel about some brand rather than what they know about it. Message recipients are asked to evaluate a brand on general affective items such as like-dislike, good-bad, and superior-inferior as well as more brand specific characteristics such as consumers' feelings about a brand's price and quality. Attitude measures are typically implicit in nature, as no mention is made of prior advertising exposures to the brand. The message has an impact if those who were exposed to an ad for the brand exhibit more favorable disposition toward it than do those who have not been exposed. In addition, attitudinal measures offer some insight about why people have the preferences they do.

Copy tests often include measures of choice. The brand-switching potential of an ad is assessed by the change in brand preference as a result of ad exposure. This measure is of interest when the goal of advertising is to promote brand switching. In many cases, however, the goal is to sustain current user loyalty. When this is the case, the use of choice as a measure of ad effectiveness requires the assumption that the same execution that best promotes switching also best sustains loyalty. At a minimum, it would be useful to develop a procedure that tests this assumption. Alternatively, when the goal is to maintain brand loyalty, it might be useful to examine the extent to which target advertising enhances consumers' ability to combat competitive attack. This would entail evaluating whether brand loyalty was sustained when a target ad was presented in the context of other ads in the same category.

Attitudes and dispositions are likely to be informative indicators of consumers' dispositions toward an advertised product when the advertising presents some substantial news. When the goal of advertising is to maintain a brand's long-standing position in consumers' minds, the effects of advertising may be too small to detect with attitude and choice measures. In these instances, it may be useful to use measures that are likely to be responsive to the advertising execution and at the same time related to consumers' brand attitudes. One measure that might be useful in this regard is consumers feelings induced by the *advertising* for the brand rather than brand dispositions per se. Thus, consumers are asked the extent to which seeing brand advertising was energizing and prompted positive and negative feelings. There is some evidence that feelings toward the advertising are correlated with brand attitudes and yet are more sensitive to small changes in disposition prompted by advertising than measures of brand attitudes.[4]

Some copy tests attempt to bolster attitudinal and choice measures with moment-to-moment measures of consumer response. These measures typically entail having respondents turn a dial to indicate their level of interest moment-to-moment while watching the message. The problem with this indicator is to determine how the changes in response should be analyzed. Often, interpretation proceeds in a literal way where those portions of an ad that yield high interest are considered effective, whereas portions corresponding to weak interest are deemed ineffective. As intuitive as this approach is, there is evidence that other parameters are more useful in interpreting moment-to-moment responses.[5] Indeed, the trend in interest over the commercial and the level of peak interest may be more indicative of ad effectiveness than is the specific response to a portion of the copy. There is also the possibility that providing moment-to-moment responses might prompt respondents to focus on their own thoughts, and thus affect their processing of the advertised information. Or, the respondent might feel that having expressed their thoughts on a moment-to-moment measure, there is little need to repeat this on verbal measures that are administered later, thus affecting the value of these latter measures.

Finally, tests of advertising effectiveness sometimes include measures that require consumers to assume expertise. This takes the form of suggestions where consumers are asked to indicate how they would enhance the impact of advertising. This approach to measurement is problematic because in most instances consumers have little insight about what ad content would have greatest impact. Their responses often take the form of what is generic in the category. If the ad is for a beer, the suggestion might be to add a bar scene or to include women, which if adopted would make the ad indistinguishable from many other beer ads.

Perceptual Measures. The measures discussed thus far are intended to tap consumers' knowledge and beliefs about a brand that would be diagnostic in situations where choice is based on information retrieved from memory. For example, this context emerges when consumers select a restaurant by remembering those they have learned about in advertising.

There are, however, a growing number of situations where the goal of advertising is limited to just making consumers familiar with a brand name. Billboards, signage at sporting events and on vehicles are often used for this purpose.

In these cases, perceptual measures are useful. These measures tap whether advertising enhances the consumers' ability to recognize the brand name. To discern this type of knowledge, measures such as fragment completion are appropriate. This task entails presenting a word with some letters missing and seeing if respondents complete the fragment by spelling the brand name. For example, if respondents complete B_ _ls_ _ _ with "Bullseye" after seeing an ad for this brand, there would be evidence of perceptual learning.

CONCLUSIONS

Advertising operates by prompting consumers to relate the information presented in an ad to their knowledge about a brand or a category. Even when nothing is known about a brand or a category, the impact of advertising depends on the extent to which it resonates with consumers' goals. Thus, much of the persuasive impact of advertising is self-persuasion. This implies that the likelihood of developing effective advertising is enhanced by having insight about consumers' beliefs. The most efficient application of this knowledge is to develop a brand position and advertising that conforms to consumers' beliefs. When this is not possible, advertising can be used to change consumers' beliefs, though this is a more demanding task than communicating information that resonates with what consumers believe.

How consumers use information to make decisions is also fundamental to developing effective advertising. The goal in presenting advertising is to have message recipients learn information about a brand that will prompt them to purchase it. Such learning is enhanced by stimulating consumers to elaborate on brand benefits. This goal can be achieved in many different ways. One approach is to cement the relationship between a brand and benefit using a hard sell. This approach works well when a brand has a strong point of difference. Alternatively, elaboration can be fostered by creating a big idea, where a brand benefit is associated with multiple attributes to create a rich network of associations to the benefit. This network facilitates thinking about advertised information at the time of purchase. The big idea is most effective when the benefit is one that can be readily associated with many attributes. A story grammar that presents the problem, episodes to address the problem, and outcomes is another device that prompts elaboration. It is particularly useful when brand performance needs to be demonstrated. Comparison offers another approach to stimulating elaboration by relating the brand to some other category. Spokespeople can be used to personify the brand benefit and thus stimulate its elaboration.

Whatever the approach to prompting elaboration, it is important that there is strong linkage between the brand and benefit. This can be achieved by developing advertising that builds on the equity of the brand, by distinguishing the brand from competitors in terms of both the benefit and the type of creative execution used, and by identifying the brand early in a television commercial. In addition, because elaboration is an effortful task, devices such as humor, threat, and various media dominance devices should be considered to enhance the likelihood that consumers process message information.

The effectiveness of advertising can be enhanced by rigorous measurement of its outcomes and by using this knowledge to modify the appeal. Verbatim recall of the advertising content is not adequate for this purpose. Measures of brand knowledge and brand disposition offer greater promise in assessing the impact of advertising than does knowledge of advertising content.

APPENDIX: REACH AND FREQUENCY COMPUTATIONS

Consider a television program that has a rating of 30 against some target. This means that a single insertion in the program will expose 30 percent of the audience. If an advertiser decides to place five ads in this program during a month, the result is a total ad weight of 150. This monthly weight is called gross rating points or GRPs. This relationship can be expressed as follows:

$$\text{Rating} \times \text{Insertions} = \text{GRPs}$$

$$30 \times 5 = 150$$

Suppose that this schedule exposed 75 percent of the target during a month. The reach for this schedule, which is estimated using survey data, is 75. The average frequency is 2.

$$\text{GRPs} = \text{Reach} \times \text{Average frequency}$$

$$150 = 75 \times 2$$

Consider a second schedule. Here too, five insertions are placed in a program with a rating of 30, which results in the delivery of 150 GRPs per month. However, for this program the viewers are very loyal and thus the reach is estimated to be 25 percent of the target. Thus, the schedule delivers an average frequency of 6.

This illustration underscores the fact that in developing a media plan, it is necessary to specify both the desired GRPs and the level of reach. Two media plans involving the same level of GRPs delivered quite different levels of reach and frequency.

Notes

1. This research was conducted by Alex Chernev, "The Impact of Common Features on Consumer Preferences: A Case of Confirmatory Reasoning," unpublished paper, Northwestern University (1999).

2. This article discusses the relative merits of color, color highlighting, and black and white in detail. Joan Meyers-Levy and Laura A. Peracchio, "Understanding the Effects of Color: How the Correspondence between Available and Required Resources Affects Attitudes," *Journal of Consumer Research,* vol. 22 (September 1995), pp. 121–138.

3. The following analysis was developed by Angela Lee and Brian Sternthal. A version of this discussion is published in "Putting Copy-testers to the Test," *Financial Times,* Mastering Marketing Series, Part 5 (October 12, 1998), pp. 6–8.

4. Dawn Iacobucci, Bobby Calder, and Brian Sternthal, "Measuring Advertising Effectiveness," unpublished paper, Northwestern University (2000).

5. Hans Baumgartner, Mita Sujan, and Dan Padgett, "Patterns of Affective Reactions to Advertisements: The Integration of Moment-to-Moment Responses into Overall Judgments," *Journal of Marketing Research,* vol. 34 (May 1997), pp. 219–232.

CHAPTER 11

MARKETING CHANNEL DESIGN AND MANAGEMENT

ANNE T. COUGHLAN and LOUIS W. STERN

A marketing channel structure is the set of pathways a product or service follows after production, culminating in purchase and use by the final end-user.[1] The design and ongoing management of marketing channels (sometimes known as channels of distribution) is a perpetual challenge facing corporate managers worldwide. Consider the following two examples, which suggest, respectively, the dynamic pace of change in marketing channel management and the complexity and broad membership that a marketing channel can comprise:

- *Personal computers.* When IBM sold its first personal computers (PCs) in the early 1980s, the company broke a long-standing precedent of selling virtually everything in its competitive arsenal (e.g., mainframe computers, software, minicomputers) through its employee sales force direct to reasonably large business end-users. When IBM decided to use personal computers to target small businesses and homes, however, the personal computer channel quickly changed with value-added resellers (VARs), computer dealers (e.g., companies like Businessland, Computerland, and Entre), and retail stores acting as intermediaries. Dell Computer, founded in 1984, changed the channel formula once again and has focused its channel strategy on direct sales, first through telephone ordering and today also over the Internet. In 1999, Dell surpassed Compaq Computer to take market share leadership in sales to U.S. businesses, with 30.9 percent of that market and 21.2 percent overall market share in the United States to all buyer segments. Worldwide in 1999, Dell had 9.2 percent market share, second only to Compaq with 13.4 percent market share. The data indicate that the direct sales channel is now a well-accepted way of buying PCs.[2]

- *Pharmaceutical products.* Like prescription (or "ethical") drugs, pharmaceutical products reach the end-user in several different ways. The pharmaceutical manufacturer typically has an employee sales force (but may also use contract salespeople who are not employees) that calls on physicians, hospitals, distributors, and insurance companies. Most health insurance companies have *formularies,* lists of approved drugs that may be prescribed for particular conditions, and sales effort is used to convince them to put a company's new drugs on the list (or keep existing ones on it). The ethical drugs themselves may pass through the hands of independent distributors on their way to a retail pharmacy or a hospital pharmacy. Even the physician plays a role, in actually prescribing the pharmaceutical that the patient will use. In cases where the patient's health care coverage includes prescription drug coverage, payment may flow not from the patient directly to the pharmacy, but from the insurance company to the pharmacy.

These examples raise several questions. Why do marketing channels change in structure over time? What role do consumer characteristics and demands play in the appropriate channel design? How should a manufacturer decide what types of intermediaries to use in the channel? What problems can arise in the ongoing management of complex marketing channels?

This chapter discusses what a marketing channel is and what productive purpose it serves in the overall strategy of marketing a product or service. We then turn to the explication of a framework for analysis that is robust, widely used, and helpful in generating insights into both how to build a new channel, and how to modify an existing channel to improve performance in the market. Finally, we discuss some key issues facing marketing channel managers today and provide some insights into how to deal with them.

DISTRIBUTION CHANNELS: DEFINITION AND MOTIVATION

Marketing channels deliver every product and service that consumers and business buyers purchase, everywhere in the world. Yet, in many cases, these end-users are unaware of the richness and complexity necessary to deliver what might seem like everyday items to them. Usually, combinations of institutions specializing in manufacturing, wholesaling, retailing, and many other areas join forces in marketing channels that deliver everything from mutual funds to books, from medical equipment to office supplies, to end-users in both businesses and households. A marketing channel can be defined as follows:

A marketing channel is a set of interdependent organizations involved in the process of making a product or service available for use or consumption.

The definition bears some explication. It first points out that a marketing channel is a *set of interdependent organizations.* That is, a marketing channel is not just one firm doing its best in the market—whether that firm is a manufacturer, wholesaler, or retailer. Rather, many entities are typically involved in the business of channel marketing. Each channel member depends on the others to do their jobs.

What are their jobs? The definition makes clear that running a marketing channel is a *process.* It is not an event. Distribution frequently takes time to accomplish, and even when a sale is finally made, the relationship with the end-user is usually not over (think about buying an automobile and servicing it over its lifetime to see that this is true).

Finally, what is the purpose of this process? The definition claims that it is *making a product or service available for use or consumption.* That is, the purpose of channel marketing is to satisfy the end-users in the market, be they consumers or final business buyers. Their goal is the use or consumption of the product or service being sold. A manufacturer who sells through distributors to retailers, who serve final consumers, may be tempted to think that it has generated "sales" and developed "happy customers" when its sales force successfully places product in the distributors' warehouses. This definition argues otherwise. It is of critical importance that all channel members focus their attention on the end-user.

The marketing channel is often viewed as a key strategic asset of a manufacturer. This view of the channel as an asset was abundantly apparent in the $70 billion merger in 1998 between Citicorp and Travelers Group. Citicorp was one of the world's biggest banks, while Travelers focused on insurance, mutual funds, and investment banking businesses. One of the major stated goals of the merger was the ability of each organization to cross-sell the other's products to its customers and to exploit the two organizations' distribution channels to maximize the penetration of the merged companies' products throughout the world.

Citicorp already had a worldwide distribution network of branch banks, which Travelers lacked. Meanwhile, Travelers had 10,300 Salomon Smith

Barney brokers, 80,000 Primerica Financial Services insurance agents, and 100,000 agents selling Travelers insurance—coverage in these markets that Citicorp could neither match nor easily build on its own. In a joint statement to the U.S. House Banking Committee on April 29, 1998, Mr. Charles O. Prince, General Counsel for Travelers, stated "We believe we will be successful because of the quality and breadth of our products and services and because of each of the company's greatly expanded and innovative distribution channels. Financial products 'manufactured' in various parts of our company will be distributed through a broad range of methods, from the Internet and other technology-based methods to branch office locations in one hundred countries around the world to fully individualized, in-home service."[3] This example makes clear that, whether selling products or services, marketing channel decisions play a role of strategic importance in the overall presence and success a company enjoys in the marketplace.

A FRAMEWORK FOR MARKETING CHANNEL ANALYSIS

The marketing channel challenge involves two major tasks: first, to *design* the right channel, and second, to assure successful *implementation* of that design. The design step involves *segmenting* the market accounting for the service output demands (SODs) of end-users, identifying optimal *positioning* responses to segments' demands, *targeting* the segments on whom to focus the channel's efforts, and *establishing* (in the absence of a pre-existing channel) or *refining* (in the presence of a pre-existing channel) the channels to manage in the marketplace. The implementation step requires an understanding of each channel member's *sources of power and dependence,* an understanding of the potential for *channel conflict,* and a resulting plan for creating an environment where the optimal channel design can be effectively executed on an ongoing basis. This outcome is called *channel coordination.*

Figure 11.1 depicts the important elements in the channel design and implementation process: segmentation, positioning, targeting, and responsive channel establishment or refinement, which together comprise the channel design component, and channel power and channel conflict issues, which comprise the implementation component. This framework is useful both for creating a new channel in a previously untapped market, and for critically analyzing and refining a pre-existing channel. The sections of this chapter that follow amplify these concepts further.

Figure 11.1
Channel Management Schematic

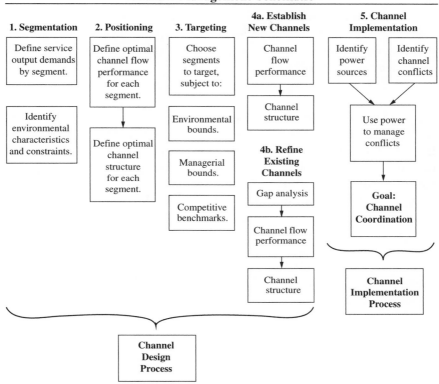

DESIGN OF THE MARKETING CHANNEL

Segmentation

One of the fundamental principles of marketing is the *segmentation* of the market. Segmentation means the splitting of a market into groups of end-users who are (1) maximally similar within each group, and (2) maximally different between groups. But maximally similar or maximally different based on what criterion? For the channel manager, segments are best defined *on the basis of demands for the service outputs of the marketing channel.* A marketing channel is more than just a conduit for product; it is also a means of adding value to the product marketed through it. In this sense, the marketing channel can be viewed as another "production line" engaged in producing not the product itself that is sold, but the ancillary services that define *how* the product is sold. These value-added services created by channel members and consumed by end-users along with the product purchased are called *service outputs*.[4] Service outputs include (but may not be limited to) *bulk-breaking, spatial convenience, waiting and delivery time,* and *assortment and variety*.

End-users (be they individuals purchasing for personal consumption or business buyers) have varying demands for these service outputs. Consider for example two different soft-drink buyers: a family buying for at-home consumption, and an office employee at work, looking for a soft drink during her afternoon coffee break. Table 11.1 outlines the differences in service output demands between the two segments of buyers. The office employee has high demands for all service outputs except assortment and variety (for which her demand is moderate, implying willingness to brand-switch

Table 11.1
Service Output Demand Differences
(An Example of Segmentation in the Soft Drink Market)

	Family		Office Employee	
Service Output	Descriptor	Service Output Demand Level	Descriptor	Service Output Demand Level
Bulk-breaking	"I buy groceries weekly for my family, and all of us like soft drinks."	Low	"I'm on my coffee break and I only have time for one can of soft drink."	High
Spatial convenience	"I drive to the supermarkets in my area to shop."	Low	"I only have 15 minutes for my break, so I need to buy whatever is handy."	High
Quick delivery	"We usually have some extra cans of soft drinks in the house, so I'll just come back the next time if I can't find the soft drinks I want on this trip."	Low	"If I don't get my soft drink right at 3:00 P.M. when my break starts, I'll never have a chance to go back later and get one."	High
Assortment and variety	"My husband and I like Coke and Pepsi, but our kids aren't permitted to drink caffeinated soft drinks. They like caffeine-free fruit-flavored soft drinks."	High	"I can't be too particular about which soft drink I pick. It's important to me to get one, as long as it has caffeine."	Moderate

within reason), while the family has the opposite pattern of service output demands.

Clearly, a different marketing channel meets the needs of these two segments of shoppers. The office employee cannot travel to a grocery store to buy a can of soda during her break, nor does she want to buy a six-pack or more cans of soft drinks. She is willing to pay a slightly higher price for the convenience of getting just a single can of soda close to her office. A vending machine would be an ideal retail outlet for her. The family, on the other hand, would not find the vending machine an attractive retail purchase alternative. The family's demand for assortment and variety may not be met by a vending machine, and other service outputs are offered at too high a level, resulting in a high per-unit price that the family does not want (or need) to pay. A local supermarket does a better job of meeting the family's service output demands for soft drinks.

This example shows how the same product can be demanded with a widely varying set of service outputs, resulting in very different demands for the product-plus-service-output bundle by different segments of end-users. An analysis of service output demands by segment is thus an important input into a manufacturer's marketing plan, and can help increase the reach and marketability of a strong product to multiple market segments.

Positioning

When the market has been segmented into groups of end-users, each of which can be described by a set of service output demands, the channel manager should next define the optimal channel to serve each segment. We call this exercise *positioning* or *configuring* the channel (*positioning* to parallel the segmentation/targeting/positioning paradigm in marketing management). Just as positioning a product means setting its product attributes, price, and promotional mix to best fit the demands of a particular segment, so also positioning in this context refers to the design of the distribution channel to meet the segment's demands. This exercise should be done even if the channel ends up *not* selling to some of the segments in the end. By doing this exercise, the channel analyst may discover that some segments simply do not make reasonable targets because their demands cannot be adequately met with the channel's current resources. Alternatively, the positioning exercise may reveal some unexpectedly attractive segments to target. Unless the optimal channel is defined for each segment, it is impossible to make a thorough decision about what segments to target.[5]

The optimal channel is defined first and foremost by the *necessary channel flows* that must be performed in order to generate the specific segment's service output demands. Channel flows are all the activities of the channel that add value to the end-user. In enumerating the list of channel flows, we go beyond the concept of the mere handling of the product to include issues of promotion, negotiation, financing, ordering, payment, and the like. Table 11.2 shows the costs that are typically incurred in performing eight classic flows. The list is general and can be expanded and customized to a particular channel's situation, but the activities represented are typical of most channel structures.

For example, our office employee looking for a soft drink on her coffee break has a high demand for spatial convenience and minimal tolerance for out-of-stock product. This means that the channel flow of

Table 11.2
Marketing Flows in Channels

Marketing Flow	Cost Represented	Typical Flow of Activity in Channel
Physical possession	Storage and delivery costs	Producer → Wholesaler → Retailer → Industrial and/or Household End-User
Ownership	Inventory carrying costs	Producer → Wholesaler → Retailer → Industrial and/or Household End-User
Promotion	Personal selling, advertising, sales promotion, publicity, public relations costs	Producer → Wholesaler → Retailer → Industrial and/or Household End-User
Negotiation	Time and legal costs	Producer ↔ Wholesaler ↔ Retailer ↔ Industrial and/or Household End-User
Financing	Credit terms, terms and conditions of sale	Producer ↔ Wholesaler ↔ Retailer ↔ Industrial and/or Household End-User
Risking	Price guarantees, warranties, insurance, installation, repair, and after-sale service costs	Producer ↔ Wholesaler ↔ Retailer ↔ Industrial and/or Household End-User
Ordering	Order-processing costs	Industrial and/or Household End-User → Retailer → Wholesaler → Producer
Payment	Collections, bad debt costs	Industrial and/or Household End-User → Retailer → Wholesaler → Producer

Notes: The flows of activity shown here are typical, but can vary from channel to channel. For example, a retailer may take orders for products that are shipped directly from the manufacturer to the end-user, causing physical possession to pass directly from the manufacturer to the end-user. Each channel member who participates in the performance of a channel flow bears a cost.

Producers, wholesalers, and retailers are collectively called the *Commercial Channel Subsystem*. End-users are channel members who can perform channel flows, but they are not considered commercial channel members.

physical possession (the physical holding of inventory) takes on great importance for such end-users. Each product or service selling situation can have its own unique concatenation of service output demands by segment, implying the differential importance of different sets of channel flows.

Further, the channel analyst must identify the optimal *channel structure* to produce the necessary channel flows (which themselves, of course, result in the generation of the required service outputs that are demanded by a particular segment of end-users in the market). The design of the *channel structure* involves two main elements. First, the channel designer must decide *who* are to be the members of the channel. For example, will a consumer packaged-goods manufacturer sell its grocery products through small independent retailers with in-city locations, or through large chain stores that operate discount warehouse stores? Or will it use an outlet like Ethnicgrocer.com, an online seller of ethnic foods and household products that operates no retail stores at all?[6] Moving up the channel from the retail level, it must be decided whether to use independent distributors, independent sales representative companies (called "reps" or "rep firms"), independent trucking companies, financing companies, export management companies, and any of a whole host of other possible independent distribution channel members that could be incorporated into the channel design.

Beyond this decision, the channel manager must also decide the exact identity of the channel partner to use at each level of the channel. If it is deemed advisable to sell a line of fine watches through retail stores, for example, should the outlets chosen be more upscale, like Tiffany's, or should they be family-owned local jewelers? The choice can have implications both for the efficiency with which the channel is run and the image connoted by distributing through a particular kind of retailer. In a different context, if a company seeks distribution for its products in a foreign market, the key decision may be which distributor is appointed to carry the product line into the overseas market. The right distributor may have much better relationships with local channel partners in the target market, and can significantly affect the success of the foreign market entry.

The other main element of the channel structure is the decision of *how many* of each type of channel member will be in the channel; this is the *channel intensity* decision. In particular, should the channel for a consumer good include many retail outlets (*intensive* distribution), just a few (*selective* distribution), or only one (*exclusive* distribution) in a given market area? The answer to this question depends both on efficiency and on implementation factors. More intensive distribution may make the product more easily available to all target end-users, but may create enormous competition among the retailers selling it, resulting in destructive price wars among them. The price wars may negatively affect their margins which may, in turn, cause them to be less interested in promoting or supporting the product.

The channel structure decisions of type, identity, and intensity of channel members all should be made with the minimization of channel flow costs in mind. That is, each channel member is allocated a set of channel flows to perform, and ideally the allocation of activities results in the reliable performance of all channel flows at minimum total cost. This task is nontrivial, particularly because it involves comparing activities across different companies who are members of the channel. Intuitively, an activity-based costing (ABC) sort of analysis is useful to establish the best allocation of channel flows.[7]

This exercise results in one channel profile for each segment that is identified in the market segmentation stage of the exercise. Each of these channel profiles is called a *zero-based channel,* because it is designed from a zero base of operations; that is, as if there is no pre-existing channel in existence in the market. The concept of a zero-based channel means that the segment's service output demands are met, and that they are met at minimum total channel cost.

Targeting

At this stage of the analysis, the channel manager is equipped to decide what segments to target. Note carefully that this also means that the channel manager is now equipped to decide what segments *not* to target! Knowing what segments to ignore in one's channel design and management efforts is very important, because it keeps the channel focused on the key segments from which it plans to reap profitable sales.

Why not target *all* the segments identified in the segmentation and positioning analyses? The answer requires the channel manager to look at the internal and external environment facing the channel. Internally, *managerial bounds* may constrain the channel manager from implementing the zero-based channel (e.g., top management of a manufacturing firm may be unwilling to allocate funds to build a series of regional warehouses that would be necessary to provide spatial convenience in a particular market situation). Externally, both *environmental bounds* and *competitive benchmarks* may suggest some segments as higher priority than others. For example, legal practices can constrain channel design and hence targeting decisions. Many countries restrict the opening of large mass-merchandise stores in urban areas, to protect small shopkeepers whose sales would be threatened by larger retailers.[8] Such legal restrictions can lead to a channel design that does not appropriately meet the target segment's service output demands, and may cause a channel manager to avoid targeting that segment entirely.

The corollary of this statement is that when superior competitive offerings do not exist to serve a particular segment's demands for service outputs, the channel manager may recognize an unexploited market opportunity and create a new channel to serve that under-served segment. Meeting previously unmet service output demands can be a powerful competitive strategy for building loyal and profitable consumer bases in a marketplace. But these strategies are impossible to identify without knowledge of not just *what* consumers want to buy, but importantly, *how* they want to buy it, and the necessary response in terms of channel flow performance and channel structure.

The outcome of this portion of the channel analysis is the identification of a subset of all the segments in the market that the channel plans on targeting, using the segmentation and positioning insights derived earlier.

Establishing or Refining the Channel Structure

At this point, the channel manager has identified the optimal way to reach each targeted segment in the market, and has also identified the bounds that might prevent the channel from implementing the zero-based channel design in the market. If no channel exists currently in the market for this segment, the channel manager should establish the channel design that comes the closest to meeting the target market's demands for service outputs, subject to the environmental and managerial bounds constraining the design.

If there is a pre-existing channel in place in the market, however, the channel manager should perform a *gap analysis*. The differences between the zero-based and actual channels on the demand and supply sides constitute gaps in the channel design. Gaps can exist on the demand side or on the supply side, as Table 11.3 indicates.

On the demand side, gaps mean that at least one of the service output demands is not being appropriately met by the channel. The service output in question may be either undersupplied or oversupplied. The problem is obvious in the case of undersupply: the target segment is likely to be dissatisfied because they would prefer more service than they are getting. The problem is more subtle in the case of oversupply. Here, target end-users are getting all the service they desire—and then some. The problem is that service is costly to supply, and therefore, supplying too much of it leads to higher prices than the target end-users may be willing to pay. Clearly, more than one service output may be a problem, in which case several gaps may need attention.

Table 11.3
Types of Gaps

Cost performance level:	Demand-side gap. (SOD > SOS)	No demand-side gap. (SOD = SOS)	Demand-side gap. (SOS > SOD)
No supply-side gap (efficient flow cost)	Price/value proposition = Right for a less demanding segment!	No gaps.	Price/value proposition = Right for a more demanding segment!
Supply-side gap (inefficiently high flow cost)	Insufficient SO provision, at high costs: Price and/or cost is too high, value is too low.	High cost, but SO's are right: Value is good, but price and/or cost is high.	High costs and SO's = Too high: No extra value is created, but price and/or cost is high.

On the supply side, gaps mean that at least one flow in the channel of distribution is carried out at too high a cost. This situation not only wastes channel profit margins, but can result in prices that are higher than the target market is willing to pay, leading to reductions in sales and market share. Supply-side gaps can result from a lack of up-to-date expertise in channel flow management or simply from waste in the channel. The challenge in closing a supply-side gap is to reduce cost without dangerously reducing the service outputs being supplied to target end–users.

Figure 11.2
Closing Channel Gaps

Types of Gaps

Demand-Side Gaps:	Supply-Side Gaps:
• SOS < SOD • SOS > SOD • Which service outputs?	• Flow cost is too high. • Which flow(s)?

Closing Gaps

Demand-Side Gaps:	Supply-Side Gaps:
• Offer tiered service levels. • Expand/contract provision of service outputs. • Change segment(s) targeted.	• Change flow responsibilities of current channel members. • Invest in new low-cost distribution technologies. • Bring in new channel members.

When gaps are identified on the demand or supply sides, there are several strategies available for closing the gaps, as depicted in Figure 11.2. But once a channel is already in place, it may be very difficult and costly to close these gaps. This scenario suggests the strategic importance of initial channel design. If the channel is initially designed in a haphazard manner, channel members may have to live with a sub-optimal channel later on, even after recognizing channel gaps and making best efforts to close them.

MANAGEMENT OF THE MARKETING CHANNEL

Channel Power

Assuming that a good channel design is in place in the market, the channel manager's job is still not done. The channel members now must *implement* the optimal channel design, and indeed must continue to implement an optimal design through time. The value of doing so might seem to be self-evident, but it is important to remember that a channel is made up of multiple entities (companies, agents, individuals) who are interdependent, but who may or may not all have the same incentives to operate in the desired manner.

Incompatible incentives among channel members would not be a problem if they were not dependent upon each other. But by the very nature of the distribution channel structure and design, specific channel members are likely to *specialize* in particular activities and flows in the channel. If all channel members do not perform appropriately, the entire channel effort suffers. For example, even if everything else is in place, a poorly-performing transportation system that results in late deliveries (or no deliveries) of product to retail stores prevents the channel from succeeding in selling the product. The same could be said about the performance of any channel member doing any of the flows in the channel. Thus, it is apparent that inducing *all* of the channel members to implement the channel design appropriately is critical.

How, then, can a "channel captain" implement the optimal channel design in the face of interdependence among channel partners, not all of whom have the incentive to cooperate in the performance of their designated channel flows? The answer lies in the possession and use of *channel power*. A channel member's power "is its ability to control the decision variables in the marketing strategy of another member in a given channel at a different level of distribution."[9] These sources of channel power can of course be used to further one channel member's individual ends. But if instead channel power is used to influence channel members to do the jobs that the optimal channel design specifies that they should do, the result will be a channel that more closely delivers demanded service outputs at a lower cost.

Channel Conflict

Channel conflict is generated when one channel member's actions prevent the channel from achieving its goals. Channel conflict is both common and dangerous to the success of distribution efforts. Given the interdependence of all channel members, any one member's actions have an influence on the total success of the channel effort, and thus can harm total channel performance.[10]

Channel conflict can stem from differences between channel members' goals and objectives (*goal conflict*); from disagreements over the domain of action and responsibility in the channel (*domain conflict*); and from differences in perceptions of the marketplace (*perceptual conflict*). These conflicts directly cause channel members to fail to perform the flows that the optimal channel design specifies for them, and thus inhibit total channel performance. The management problem is twofold. First, the channel manager needs to be able to *identify* the sources of channel conflict and, in particular, to differentiate between poor channel design (which can also inhibit channel performance) and poor performance due to channel conflict. Second, the channel manager must decide on the action to take (if any) to manage and reduce the channel conflicts that have been identified.

In general, channel conflict reduction is accomplished through the application of one or more sources of channel power. For example, a manufacturer may identify a conflict in its independent distributor channel: the distributorship is exerting too little sales effort on behalf of the manufacturer's product line, and, therefore, sales of the product are suffering. Analysis might reveal that the effort level is low because the distributorship makes more profit from selling a competitor's product than from selling this manufacturer's product; there is a *goal* conflict. The manufacturer's goal is the maximization of profit over its own product line, but the distributorship's goal is the maximization of profit over *all* of the products that it sells—only some of which come from this particular manufacturer. To resolve the goal conflict, the manufacturer might use some of its power to reward the distributor by increasing the distributor's discount, thus increasing the profit margin it can make on the manufacturer's product line. Or, the manufacturer may invest in developing brand equity and thus pull the product through the channel. In that case, its brand power induces the distributor to sell the product more aggressively because the sales potential for the product has risen. In both cases, some sort of leverage or power on the part of the manufacturer is necessary to change the distributor's behavior and thus reduce the channel conflict. Besides obvious bases of power such as coercion and reward, leverage can also be gained through expertise, legitimate authority (e.g., contracts), and the accumulation of valuable information.

Channel Coordination

After following all five steps of the channel management schematic in Figure 11.1, the channel will have been designed with target end-user segments' service output demands in mind, and channel power will be appropriately applied to ensure the smooth implementation of the optimal channel design. When the disparate members of the channel are brought together to advance the goals of the channel, rather than their own independent (and likely conflicting) goals, the channel is said to be *coordinated*. This term is used to denote both the coordination of interests and actions among the channel members who produce the outputs of the marketing channel, and the coordination of performance of channel flows with the production of the service outputs demanded by target end-users. Coordination is the end goal of the entire channel management process. As conditions change in the marketplace, the channel's design and implementation may need to respond; thus, channel coordination is not a one-time achievement, but an ongoing process of analysis and response to the market, the competition, and the abilities of the members of the channel.

CURRENT ISSUES IN MARKETING CHANNEL DESIGN AND MANAGEMENT

The framework we have offered is useful in evaluating currently existing channels as well as in creating new ones. It is also important to recognize, however, that the framework for analysis we propose will be implemented by channel managers operating in a constantly-changing environment. Three aspects or implications of the environment of particular importance for channel management include: (1) an increasingly demanding consumer base; (2) the need to manage multiple channels to reach multiple market segments (including electronic channels); and (3) the globalization of retailing, wholesaling, and manufacturing.

Increasingly Demanding Consumer Base

Particularly in developed countries, consumers are becoming more and more time-constrained. This trend has long been documented in the United

States, with its increasing numbers of working women, single-parent house-holds, and homemakers with part-time jobs.[11] However, the trend is now present in many countries of the world, including Japan, Australia, New Zealand, Britain, Italy, Canada, and most other developed nations.[12] With more time spent in the workplace, less time is available for shopping, cooking, do-it-yourself home improvements, and the like. One working home-maker summarized the situation by saying, "We're desperate for a few minutes of rest. If we didn't have help, we would fall down."[13]

The implication for channel managers is that channels offering more ser-vice outputs—particularly spatial convenience, broad assortments that per-mit one-stop shopping, bulk-breaking, and nonproduct services like home delivery—are likely to find a warm reception with the time-starved con-sumer. Poverty of time also helps explain the popularity of nonstore re-tailing options like catalogs and online shopping. And standard retailers respond by offering more services under one roof to expand the one-stop shopping benefits that consumers crave (e.g., offering bank automatic teller machines in grocery stores).[14]

Another factor leading to escalating service output demands is con-sumers' increasing level of knowledge about characteristics, availability, and pricing. In some cases this knowledge has come with enhanced consumer mobility. For example, as Japanese consumers have traveled more widely outside their country, they have become aware of the sometimes very sig-nificant price differences between identical products sold in Japan and else-where.[15] In other cases, it is increased personal computer literacy that drives greater consumer knowledge. One manager from Procter & Gamble pre-dicts that expectations for service and information as well as product per-formance will increase in the future as a result, making it necessary for the manufacturer and retailer to work with consumers as partners rather than simply selling to them.[16]

The responses by marketing channel managers to increasingly knowl-edgeable consumers can be many. It is crucial to recognize in what arenas the consumer is becoming more knowledgeable. If knowledge is in the area of product usage or ability to service, then the channel need not provide these educational and postsale service functions, and the channel manager can decrease its prices by deleting these services from the channel. Indeed, if prices do not fall as a result of this increased consumer knowledge, lost sales are likely to result as consumers find other alternatives that offer ap-propriate service bundles at competitive prices. However, as the need for basic product education and service dwindles, consumers may maintain or even increase the value they place on other services (e.g., rapid delivery).

In such situations, the right response might involve not only divesting the channel of lower-valued services, but also adding other services that carry relatively higher value to the consumer and can differentiate the channel from its competitors.

For example, as individual travelers' abilities to search for their own airline tickets have increased (due to Internet sites such as Travelocity), the value they place on some travel agent services has fallen. Airlines have progressively dropped the commissions they pay to travel agents to reflect the lower value added by typical agents writing airline tickets. As a result, many travel agencies have actually gone out of business. But those who have survived have emphasized the provision of services that *are* highly valued or have targeted specific segments whose needs for services have not decreased. Thus, boutique travel agencies focusing on travel packages, rather than airline transportation alone, have found they could continue to make commissions for booking entire trips involving cruises or other transportation forms, as well as coordinated hotel and tourism bookings. Both the array of services offered and the very coordination of these services is valued by many leisure travelers. On a segment-specific basis, other travel agencies have focused on the business travel segment. Their clients are not individual business travelers, but companies, and the agencies provide one-stop shopping and controlled pricing for their corporate clients. Thus, what has been a death knell for some agencies has been a call to respond to changes in the market for other agencies. The survivors will be those who both recognize and can respond to the changing demands for service outputs by their customers.

The Need to Manage Multiple Marketing Channels

As an awareness of segmentation in the distribution arena has spread, channel managers have come to realize the need to build and maintain customized channel approaches for each distinct customer or consumer segment in the market. For example, W.W. Grainger, a major distributor of MRO supplies in the United States, offers standard paper catalog sales, outlet sales, telephone sales, and online electronic ordering. On the consumer side, many retailers (both standard bricks-and-mortar retailers and catalog retailers) now believe that offering Internet sales is not just a curiosity but a necessary channel alongside their more traditional methods of reaching the consumer. In any of these cases, the addition of the new channel is not meant to fully replace previously existing ones. Rather, it serves two important purposes. First, it provides an alternative way for current customers to buy and to communicate with their suppliers. Second, it may attract totally new buyers to the products or services that suppliers are trying to sell.

In some cases, the addition of the new channel is also motivated by cost concerns. Some pharmaceutical firms, for example, maintain an employee sales force, independent distributors, and a telemarketing operation jointly. The employee sales force, the most expensive channel, is used only for large customers with big-ticket purchases. Independent distributors sell to smaller customers. And telephone selling and ordering is reserved for the sale of replacement items to already-established customers. In each channel, the cost of serving the customer is matched to the value of the transaction, so that each type of sale is possible to transact profitably.

In any situation where multiple channels are managed together, the potential for channel conflict is great. Direct selling companies like cosmetics firm Avon face the domain conflict challenge inherent in adding an Internet channel to their existing direct selling modes. One "Avon Lady" expressed her worries about declining sales in the face of direct corporation-to-consumer sales on the Internet by saying, "This takes away what Avon has been for many years. . . . We feel we're such a small voice."[17] The expressed threat here is cannibalization of sales through the current channel with sales through the new (in this case, Internet) channel. Cannibalization is not bad if it results in total cost reduction in the channel without a diminution of desired service outputs. But in some cases, it can result in severe enough channel conflicts to lead to the loss of a primary channel of distribution. If access to some consumer segments is lost because the new channel is permitted to replace the old, the result may not be increased sales or satisfaction by all consumers. As an example, Home Depot threatened its suppliers (e.g., Whirlpool, Stanley) with "delisting" if they were to establish Web sites for the purpose of selling directly to end-users targeted by the home improvement giant.

A more reasonable long-term likelihood is that the Internet will take its place as another channel alongside ones that are already well established in both business-to-business and consumer markets. An executive vice president for the department store Bloomingdale's states what most major U.S. retailers (and many non-U.S. retailers) also believe: "You have to be willing to sell and return [unwanted purchases] into all three channels," that is bricks-and-mortar store, catalog, and the online channel.[18] Online selling holds an advantage over standard retailing in spatial convenience and speed of access, but, like catalog shopping, it falls short on delivery time and ease of product returns. Thus, a multiple channel strategy is one way to provide the full array of service outputs that consumers demand in different shopping conditions. However, there is always the possibility that prices may be driven down to the level established by the most efficient channel. In that case, increased volume will have to counterbalance the decline in margins. And whether multiple channels include the Internet or not, the goal of channel management still remains the maintenance of viable channels (and channel relations) to reach all the chosen target market segments the company has identified.

Globalization and Marketing Channel Management

With increasing abilities to communicate quickly and accurately, lowered trade barriers and the establishment of world trading blocs, business—and hence channel management—is a truly global enterprise. In retailing the trend has been particularly pronounced. For example, 132 retailers accounted for 75 percent of Europe's primary market sales in 1980; in 1996 the number had fallen to just 43 retailers, an extremely high rate of consolidation. Carrefour, the French-headquartered hypermarket chain, has networks of stores in Europe, South America, and Asia. Ahold, a grocery retailer originally from the Netherlands, has acquired companies in more than 10 countries since 1995 (including being the seventh largest grocery retailer in the United States). And Wal-Mart operates over 700 stores outside the United States, in Canada, Mexico, South America, Europe, and Asia, even though it only began foreign expansion in 1991. Other more specialized retailers are also following the same path: apparel companies like The Gap, furniture providers like IKEA, toy seller Toys "R" Us, and others have aggressively moved outside their home markets as well.[19]

The result of increased global presence of major retail players is greater competitiveness in markets that once were local enclaves of protected indigenous retailers. Local retailers that do not respond either go out of business or are acquired (e.g., after Wal-Mart's entry into Canada, Kmart's business collapsed within four years, and Wal-Mart acquired the local Woolco chain). Some local retailers respond, and survive, by emphasizing the assets they have that the foreign entrants do not—primarily location and a deep knowledge of local consumer tastes. For instance, the Pao de Azucar grocery chain in Brazil responded to Carrefour's entry into its market by investing in information technology to improve store productivity and by remodeling its local neighborhood supermarkets, which enjoy a locational advantage that Carrefour cannot match. It also offers attractive credit to its shoppers, a popular local custom.[20] In short, successful response by indigenous smaller retailers typically involves a refocusing of the business on the provision of highly valued service outputs on all levels.

Globalization at the retail level also transforms formerly local suppliers. A local manufacturer that can sign a contract for regional or worldwide supply of a particular product with a global retailer like Wal-Mart or Carrefour acquires an enormous sales and profit potential. The manufacturer may have to learn new ways of doing business in order to remain the global supplier, however, including understanding about international shipping, delivery needs for long transportation distances, or even establishing overseas manufacturing capabilities to move along with its retailer. Conversely, the entry of a large retailer like Carrefour into a foreign country can mean a great increase in sales for local suppliers—but only if they offer products at prices and terms competitive with what these global retailers can get from their worldwide supply chains. Even local suppliers are not protected in such a system.

Thus, globalization has an impact not just on the channel partners that actually establish operations across national borders, but also on all of the other channel members that help provide products and services to the worldwide consumers thus served. Further, from a competitive point of view, it is no longer possible to argue that one's business is local, even if the company's operations lie entirely within one country's boundaries. Foreign entrants increasingly impinge on local retailers as well as suppliers, so that the entire supply chain in effect globalizes.

CONCLUSIONS

Creating and managing a marketing channel system is an enormous and strategic undertaking. Once created, it is often extremely hard to change or to dismantle. The "lumpy," high fixed-cost nature of many channel investments necessitates careful consideration of how the channel should be structured and managed when it is initially created or whenever any major change is contemplated.

Creation of the channel structure starts with an understanding of the end-user's demands for the service outputs of the channel. Service output demands are different in different end-user segments of the market, and this suggests the value in developing a customized channel for each segment's demands. The mapping between demanded service outputs and the channel flows necessary to produce those service outputs must be understood, so that the type of channel (e.g., direct to consumer, through independent distributors or retailers) as well as the specific identity of channel members can be established. Finally, each channel member's responsibility for channel flow performance must be clearly delineated and an appropriate management system put into place to guarantee that channel members in fact perform the channel flows with which they are charged.

In the case of pre-existing channels, a channel analysis of the type we have described is still a useful exercise, because it can uncover important channel gaps that inhibit growth of sales and profits. Gaps can exist on the demand side (through insufficient or excessive service output provision) or on the supply side (through excessive cost of performing channel flows). When demand-side gaps exist, the product's sales are likely to experience immediate ill effects. The negative impact of a supply-side gap may be more subtle, but can be just as harmful: Performing adequate channel flows, but at too high a cost, produces a high price for the bundle of product and service outputs that consumers demand. As a result, competitors with better channel management skills may find an opportunity to steal sales by offering comparable (or even superior) levels of service outputs at comparable (or even lower) overall prices.

Even with a good channel structure, the channel members may have difficulty in implementing the design. Channel conflicts can arise from differences in goals, disagreement over domains, or differing perceptions of reality. Any of these can prevent the best channel structure design from succeeding in a market. Judicious application of relevant sources of channel power can reduce channel conflicts to manageable levels. Ideally, channel managers seek "channel coordination," a situation where all channel members strive for the unique goal of providing demanded service outputs at minimum cost.

The channel design process takes place in a complex and ever-changing environment. Three phenomena particularly worthy of recognition are the increasing service output demands of consumers; the need to effectively manage multiple channels of distribution, including online channels; and the global expansion of marketing channels. Channel members that do not recognize important environmental factors such as these may succeed in the short-term, but will face difficulties as the marketplace changes in fundamental ways around them. A constant vigilance and willingness to respond are the keys to successful ongoing channel management.

Notes

1. For greater detail on any of the issues developed here, please refer to Anne T. Coughlan, Erin Anderson, Louis W. Stern, and Adel I. El-Ansary, *Marketing Channels*, 6th ed. (Upper Saddle River, NJ: Prentice Hall, 2001).

2. See for example "Dell Takes Significant Lead in U.S. Corporate Marketplace: Ziff-Davis Study Shows Dell Also No. 1 in All U.S. Business Segments," at

www.dell.com/corporate/media/newsreleases/99/9904/12a.htm; and David P. Hamilton, "PC Shipments Climbed in First Quarter on Strong Demand, but Compaq Slid," *Wall Street Journal* (April 26, 1999), p. A3.

3. Mr. Prince's remarks to the U.S. House Banking Committee are printed in *PR Newswire* 1998. For other information on the Citicorp/Travelers merger and its distribution implications, see for example, Anne Colden, "Insurers Seeking New Niche in Bank Mega-Merger World," *Journal of Commerce* (April 30, 1998), p. 5A; Tracy Corrigan, "Travelers Beats Expectations with $1 Billion," *Financial Times* (April 21, 1998), p. 35; "Finance and Economics: Watch Out for the Egos," *The Economist* (April 11, 1998), pp. 55–56; Gregory J. Hoeg, "Merging Sales Operations Is Key Financial Services," *Best's Review—Life-Health Insurance*, vol. 99 (July 3, 1998), p. 92; "Citibank Eyes 11 New Regional Outlets in Japan," *Jiji Press Ticker Service* (July 3, 1998); "Profitable Partners? Don't Bank on It Yet," *Journal of Commerce* (October 5, 1998), p. 8A; Brendan Noonan, "Poking Holes in the Umbrella," *Best's Review—Property-Casualty,* vol. 99 (August 4, 1998), pp. 65–67; "Citigroup To Begin Trading Today, Following Completion of Merger of Citicorp and Travelers Group," *Business Wire* (October 8, 1998); William Glasgall, John Rossant, and Thane Peterson, "Citigroup. Just the Start?" *Business Week* (April 20, 1998), pp. 34–38; and Rodd Zolkos, "Insurers Starting to Bank on Integration," *Business Insurance* (January 18, 1999), p. 12D.

4. Defined by Louis P. Bucklin, *A Theory of Distribution Channel Structure* (Berkeley, CA: IBER Special Publications, 1966); Louis P. Bucklin, *Competition and Evolution in the Distributive Trades* (Englewood Cliffs, NJ: Prentice-Hall, 1972), pp. 18–31; and Michael Etgar, "An Empirical Analysis of the Motivations for the Development of Centrally Coordinated Vertical Marketing Systems: The Case of the Property and Casualty Insurance Industry," unpublished doctoral dissertation, The University of California at Berkeley (1974), pp. 95–97.

5. Louis P Bucklin (see note 4) originally proposed that a knowledge of service output demands leads to the specification of channel flows, and that channel structure should be chosen to minimize flow costs. George J. Stigler (1951), speaks more generally of allocating business activities to their lowest-cost performers. The discussion here is consistent with and based on these ideas. George J. Stigler, "The Division of Labor is Limited by the Extent of the Market," *Journal of Political Economy* (June 1951), pp. 185–193.

6. We thank Subjash Bedi and Parry Singh, founders of Indiangrocer.com, for information about this online service.

7. For information on activity-based costing, see for example, Bala Balachandran, "Strategic Activity Based Accounting," *Business Week Executive Briefing Service* (1994); Ronald E. Yates, "New ABCs for Pinpoint Accounting," *Chicago Tribune* (January 24, 1993), p. 7; Robin Cooper and Robert S. Kaplan, "Profit Priorities from Activity-Based Costing," *Harvard Business Review,* vol. 69 (May/June 1991), pp. 130–135; and William Rotch, "Activity-Based Costing in Service Industries," *Journal of Cost Management* (summer 1990), pp. 4–14.

8. The Large Scale Retail Store law in Japan requires retailers wanting to open a store larger than 5000 square meters to follow a complicated bureaucratic process that

tends to prevent large stores from opening commercial centers in town. Other legal constraints exist in some European markets, where "green belts" are sometimes created around cities inside of which large retailers may not open stores. For a viewpoint on the perceived threat imposed by outlet mall developers in Europe, see Ernest Beck, "Europeans Fear a Mauling by Outlet Malls," *Wall Street Journal Europe* (September 16, 1997), p. 4.

9. Adel I. El-Ansary and Louis W. Stern, "Power Measurement in the Distribution Channel," *Journal of Marketing Research,* vol. 9 (February 1972), p. 47.

10. See Ernest R. Cadotte and Louis W. Stern, "A Process Model of Dyadic Interorganizational Relations in Marketing Channels," in *Research in Marketing,* vol. 2, ed. Jagdish N. Sheth (Greenwich, CT: JAI Press, 1979); Michael Etgar, "Sources and Types of Intrachannel Conflict," *Journal of Retailing,* vol. 55 (spring 1979), pp. 61–78; Torger Reve and Louis W. Stern, "Interorganizational Relations in Marketing Channels," *Academy of Management Review,* vol. 4 (July 1979), pp. 405–416; Larry J. Rosenberg and Louis W. Stern, "Conflict Measurement in the Distribution Channel," *Journal of Marketing Research,* vol. 8 (November 1971), pp. 437–442; and Louis W. Stern and James L. Heskett, "Conflict Management in Interorganization Relations: A Conceptual Framework," in *Distribution Channels: Behavioral Dimensions,* ed. Louis W. Stern (Boston: Houghton Mifflin, 1969), pp. 288–305.

11. Jan Larson, "The New Face of Homemakers," *American Demographics,* vol. 19 (September 9, 1997), pp. 44–50.

12. Paul Betts, "Big Retail Groups Eye Italian Wallets," *Financial Times* (May 9, 1997), p. 23; Doreen L. Brown, "The Changing Japanese Consumer: New Attitudes, Purchasing Habits on Quality, Value, and Imports," *East Asian Executive Reports,* vol. 18, no. 5 (May 15, 1996), pp. 8, 14; "Retailers and Manufacturers Told—Know Your Customer or Die," *Canada NewsWire* (February 16, 1999); Harriot Lane Fox, "The 1995 British Shoppers Survey (Part 2)," *Marketing* (August 31, 1995), pp. 14–15; and Ang Wan May "Hypermarkets, Lifestyle Changes Bug Dairy Farm," *Business Times* (Singapore) (March 22, 1997), p. 7; "Shop? I'd Rather NAP, Thanks; Six Hot Consumer Trends," *Profit* (September 1998), p. 48.

13. See note 11, p. 47.

14. "Minnesota Grocers Association Grocers Celebrate 100 Years of Answering 'What's for Dinner?' " *PR Newswire* (August 20, 1997).

15. See note 12, Brown.

16. See note 11.

17. Dennis Berman, "Is the Bell Tolling for Door-to-Door Selling?" *Business Week e.Biz* (November 1, 1999), p. EB59.

18. Richard Karpinski, "Retail—Physical, Online Worlds Merging," *Internetweek* (October 25, 1999), p. 42.

19. Denise Incandela, Kathleen McLaughlin, and Christiana Smith Shi, "Retailers to the World," *McKinsey Quarterly,* no. 3 (1999), pp. 84–97.

20. "Survival Skills," *The Economist* (July 12, 1997), pp. 57–58.

CHAPTER 12

PRICING STRATEGIES
AND TACTICS

LAKSHMAN KRISHNAMURTHI

Pricing as a management function has
taken on an important role in many companies. From being viewed largely
as a decision made by the finance and accounting departments, it is now
seen to require the role of marketing. This chapter will cover the strategic
role of price as well as how to organize to set prices.

To price effectively, you must consider the following issues:

- Pricing should reflect strategic objectives (profitability or market share).
- Pricing should reflect the customer target (the *Who*).
- Pricing should reflect product positioning (the *How*).
- Pricing should reflect competitive position (Is the company the market leader? a dominant player? or a weaker player?).
- Pricing should take costs into account, noting that variable cost is the floor and customer value is the ceiling.
- Pricing should take channel considerations into account (Is the channel necessary? How to incentivize the channel? How to price to ensure channel coordination?).
- Pricing should understand the product life cycle.

A good understanding of marketing is necessary to set the price for a product or service. Figure 12.1 emphasizes the macro factors (strategic objective, competitive position, and product life cycle) that affect the pricing decision. Figure 12.2 shows how an understanding of customers and competitors and the market environment is important in segmentation and

This chapter extends article titled "Pricing: Part Art, Part Science" published in *Mastering Marketing, Financial Times*/Prentice Hall (1999).

Figure 12.1
Developing Strategy: A Macro Framework

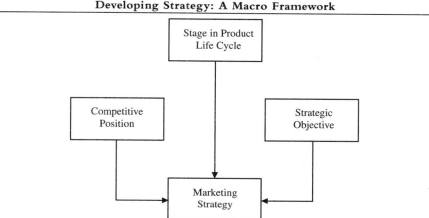

targeting (the *Who*) and positioning (the *How*) and leads to a choice of marketing mix variables, of which price is one.

This chapter first draws a connection between market share and profitability objectives and pricing actions. Next, we discuss the role of costs, customer value, competition, the distribution channel, and regulation in

Figure 12.2
Developing Strategy: A Micro Framework

SWOT Analysis:
Market Analysis
Competitive Analysis
Customer Analysis

```
Conduct
Opportunity
Analysis

Design          Implement        Measure
Strategy        Strategy         Outcome
```

Segmentation	Marketing mix	Sales/market share
Targeting	Customer service	Profits
Positioning	Integration of	Customer satisfaction
Customer advantage	functions	
Competitive advantage		

setting prices. The chapter concludes with a discussion of the sequential process to follow in arriving at a price.

STRATEGIC OBJECTIVE

A large-scale study conducted using the PIMS database noted a fairly strong positive relationship between market share and return on investment, or profitability.[1] Nevertheless, in many industries, smaller players are often more profitable, in relative terms, than larger ones. Although most companies would like to pursue both profitability and market share objectives, these two objectives require different pricing actions as the following examples illustrate:

> Busch Entertainment, a unit of Anheuser Busch, plans to open a park called the Discovery Cove in Orlando, Florida, sometime in the year 2000.[2] Visitors to the park have the opportunity to engage in interactive experiences including swimming with dolphins, snorkeling among tropical fish, as well as relaxing on the beach. The expected entrance fee is $179 per person for the interactive experience and $89 a person if you choose not to engage in these activities. It is also $89 for children under six. In contrast, Disney, Universal, and Busch's own SeaWorld, all in Orlando, charge an admission fee of $44 per person. Discovery Cove's stated objective is to provide the visitors a relaxed, less crowded, less frenzied experience. The daily park capacity will be restricted to 1000 visitors a day, so the objective is clearly not to maximize share. The cost of building the park is reported to be 100 million dollars compared to 1 billion dollars for Universal's Islands of Adventure park. Can Discovery Cove find 1000 visitors a day willing to pay $179 for the experience? Which customer segments should be targeted? How should the park be positioned to justify the high price?

> ★　★　★　★

> Coca-Cola announced that it would raise soft drink prices 5 percent to boost profitability.[3] The article reported that the company plans a major marketing campaign to support the premium positioning of the product. An issue is how Coke's arch competitor Pepsi would react. If Pepsi maintains its price, would it steal some share from Coke? The answer depends on the cross price elasticity. Within a few days, Pepsi announced they would match Coke's price increase.[4]

> ★　★　★　★

> British Airways recently announced that it was going to focus more on business and first-class passengers, move away from aggressively competing

at the lower price range, and reduce the number of seats in economy class to make the airline more profitable. The chief executive conceded that the airline will lose share, but said that it was important to boost profitability by targeting the right customer.[5]

★   ★   ★   ★

General Motors in the last few years has focused attention more on market share. Although they have earned record profits in some of those years, their strategic objective has been to stem market share erosion. Their stated objective is not to fall below 30 percent market share in the United States, implying that they would price aggressively to gain market share or prevent market share from falling. In 1999, they also announced that they would be aggressive in gaining market share in Europe.

★   ★   ★   ★

Boeing and Airbus compete head on for airline customers and price aggressively to gain customers and prevent the loss of customers. The primary objective is market share.

Companies typically have both share and profit objectives. What we are arguing here is that the primary objective has a major role in setting price targets. If your strategic objective is profitability more than market share, you will price less aggressively and seek those market segments that are willing to pay your prices rather than cut prices to appeal to a larger segment. It is not very realistic to expect to maximize both profits and market share in highly competitive markets. In the Web browser market, Microsoft started to provide its Internet Explorer product free two years ago. One cannot beat that strategy for building market share! Netscape, which was charging for its browser at that time, was forced to follow suit, and was then acquired by AOL. Clearly, you have to distinguish between short-term and long-term objectives as well as cross-subsidization. If giving away a product free helps build the customer base for selling other products and services in the future, the short-term revenue and profit shortfall could turn into a long-term bonanza.[6]

Is your primary objective customer satisfaction? Xerox is a strong believer in maximizing customer satisfaction. They believe that satisfied customers will result in share and profits. The pricing implication of this objective is to take a long run view of the customer and realize profits over a longer horizon. A similar view is espoused by USAA which provides casualty and property insurance products to officers of the U.S. military and their dependents. The stage of the product life cycle (PLC) affects price as well. In the introduction and rapid growth stage of the PLC, prices tend to be typically high because of strong demand and fewer competitors. As the product enters the slow growth and mature stages of the life cycle, relative pricing becomes a pressing issue. The only way to grow is by selling more to current customers, by stealing customers from competitors or finding new markets or new uses for the product.

We will now take a closer look at each of the major determinants of the pricing decision.

THE DETERMINANTS OF PRICE

Role of Costs in Setting Prices

The product's variable cost is the pricing floor. The ceiling is whatever the customer is willing to pay. The expected profitability of price increases or price decreases depends substantially on the ratio of variable costs to the price. Figure 12.3 shows the determinants of price. Consider the following example where the price (P), variable cost (VC), and contribution margin (CM) are all on a unit basis.

As depicted in Table 12.1, it is assumed that the variable costs stay the same as a proportion of the *current price,* regardless of the price increase or decrease. How much does sales have to increase in percentage terms to make the same *dollar* contribution as before if price is reduced 20 percent? The formula is

$$\frac{\text{Old \$CM} - \text{New \$CM}}{\text{New \$CM}} \times 100$$

Therefore, sales have to go up

$$\frac{(0.4P - 0.2P)}{0.2P} \times 100 = 100\%$$

Figure 12.3
The Determinants of Price

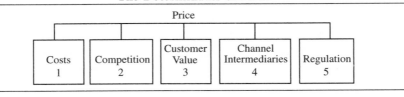

Price				
Costs 1	Competition 2	Customer Value 3	Channel Intermediaries 4	Regulation 5

Table 12.1
The Role of Costs in Selling Prices

Current ($)		20% Price	
		Decrease ($)	Increase ($)
Price	P	0.8P	1.2P
VC	0.6P	0.6P	0.6P
CM	0.4P	0.2P	0.6P

How much of a sales loss can be tolerated when price is increased 20 percent before new contribution becomes less than old contribution? The answer is figured as

$$\frac{(0.4P - 0.6P)}{0.6P} \times 100 = -33.3\%$$

The corresponding sales change for a 10 percent price decrease is 33.3 percent, and for a 10 percent price increase, −20 percent.

Consider the case in Table 12.2 where variable costs are 20 percent of the price. Now sales have to go up only 33.3 percent to make the same dollar contribution as before under the 20 percent price cut, but a sales loss of only 20 percent can be tolerated before the dollar contribution declines. The corresponding sales change for a 10 percent price decrease is 14.3 percent, and for a 10 percent price increase is −11.1 percent. Figure 12.4 graphically depicts the required sales changes for price increases and decreases of 10 percent and 20 percent for different levels of variable costs.[7]

For many manufacturing operations, variable costs tend to be high as a percent of the selling price. In such cases, a price increase may be more profitable than a price decrease because the required sales increase to make the same level of contribution is quite high and possibly unattainable, whereas the company may believe that the price increase will not result in

Table 12.2
The Role of Costs in Setting Prices:
Variable Costs at 20 Percent

Current ($)		20% Price	
		Decrease ($)	Increase ($)
Price	P	0.8P	1.2P
VC	0.2P	0.2P	0.2P
CM	0.8P	0.6P	1.0P

Figure 12.4
Increases and Decreases in Sales to Return the Same Profit

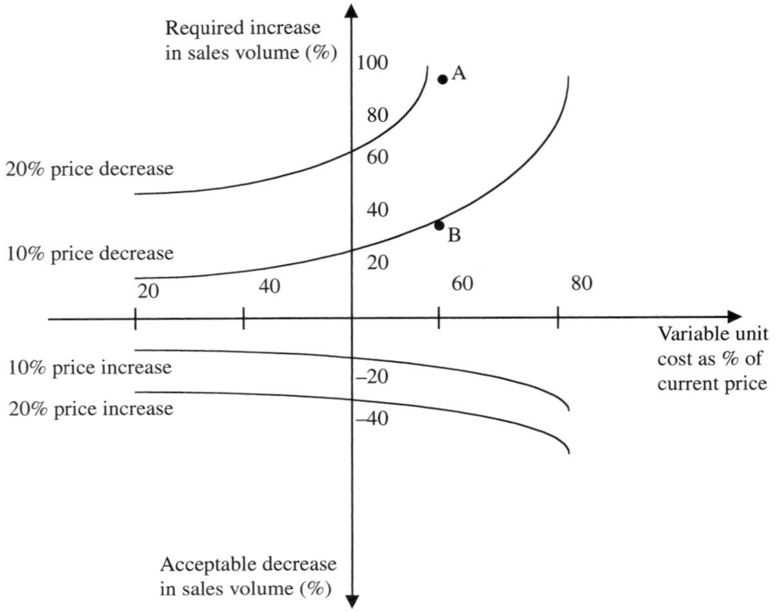

Read as follows: With variable units cost of 60 percent, a 20 price decrease requires a 100 percent volume increase (Point A); a 10 percent decrease requires only a 33 percent volume increase (Point B). See note 7 on page 301.

a sales loss of large enough magnitude to make the decision unprofitable. On the other hand, for many service businesses, variable costs as a percent of the selling price tends to be low. In such cases, like the airlines, price cuts are much more likely. Of course, whether one is able to achieve the necessary sales increase or avoid the sales decrease depends on the price sensitivity of the target customers. We will discuss the price sensitivity issue later in this chapter.

There are different components of costs as the following example demonstrates. Consider a company that manufactures a basic line of cotton pants. Assume it sells 50,000 pairs at $10 a pair. The manufacturing plant has capacity for 80,000 pairs. The total manufacturing cost is $350,000 which includes fixed manufacturing cost of $100,000. Thus, the variable cost is $5 per pair. There is also a fixed selling cost of $50,000. The company gets an order for 20,000 pairs at $6.50 a pair, which is below the manufacturing unit cost of $7 a pair. Should the company accept the order?

Purely from a financial point of view, it should because of the positive contribution of $1.50 for each pair yielding additional profit of $30,000. The company is not going to incur any additional fixed costs because there is excess manufacturing capacity of 30,000 units and the special order is only for 20,000 units.

There are four costs that need to be kept in mind: the *variable manufacturing cost of goods* which is $5/pair and the *fixed manufacturing cost of goods* of $2/pair, the sum of which equaling $7/pair is often called the *absorption cost,* and the fixed selling cost of $1/pair which when added equals the *full cost or fully distributed cost* of $8/pair. If the total fixed costs are allocated on a unit basis, they will change with volume. In this simple, single product example, it is better to treat the fixed costs as a lump sum and subtract them from total contribution to get profits rather than allocating them on a unit basis.

The point of this example is that fixed costs are not relevant when you have to take a pricing decision under existing plant capacity, equipment, and basic operating conditions. Optimizing total contribution is the only way to cover fixed costs to the maximum extent possible. So, if you have an option to manufacture product A or B and if A yields greater *total* contribution than B you should pick A from a financial point of view. Even in cases where additional fixed costs will be incurred, it is better from a decision-making point of view to ignore fixed costs to determine the price and then evaluate whether the resulting contribution covers fixed costs. The fallacy of including fixed costs in setting the price should be clear. The fixed cost per unit is larger when fewer units are sold and smaller when more units are sold. This calls for increasing the price when the firm sells fewer units and decreasing the price when the firm sells a larger number of units. Increasing the price could result in the firm selling even fewer units which will lead to increasing the price further because the fixed cost per unit increases.

What are the practical consequences of accepting this special order? What if the first buyer who paid $10 a pair finds out that someone else paid only $6.50 a pair? The clothing manufacturer must make sure that there is no spill-over from the secondary market into the primary market. Selling to an overseas buyer is one way of achieving this goal. Making sure that the special order is sold under a different brand name is another. Making small modifications to the pants for the special order is a third way. The issue of whether a firm should accept orders that fill capacity that cannot be sold at the regular price goes beyond this hypothetical example. Major companies like Kraft, Kimberly Clark, and others face this problem.

From a financial point of view, it makes sense to fill capacity as long as the order covers variable cost. But this is a very short-term view of the problem. Consider a company that markets a well-known branded product through the retail channel. Suppose this company accepts a special order from a large retailer for a store brand version for which the retailer will pay a lower price than the manufacturer branded product. In turn, the store brand will be sold at a lower retail price than the manufacturer brand. Suppose the store brand version starts to sell very well at the expense of the manufacturer brand. In response, the retailer would like to order less of the manufacturer brand and more of the store brand. Faced with smaller demand for the flagship brand and the possibility of even larger unused capacity, the manufacturer accepts the larger order of the store brand. It is easy to see what will happen if this story unfolds as written. The manufacturer will destroy long-term profits by chasing short-term volume goals.

You cannot ignore the fact that all costs have to be covered in the long run. Otherwise, the firm will become insolvent. Unlike depreciation which is a noncash expense, salaries, advertising costs, and so on, involve cash outlays. For this reason, some argue that you should price the product to cover full costs. Although this has a simple flavor to it, it can lead to overpricing when the firm is inefficient relative to competitors. For new products that have large fixed costs, full costing might result in unrealistic prices. Clearly costs are important because one cannot compute profitability without knowing costs. But costs should only be a starting point; they should not be the determining factor.

To determine the price that maximizes contribution, one has to start with a formulation of the demand curve that relates quantity to price. It can be shown that fixed costs play no role in determining the price that maximizes contribution. Assuming that unit variable costs stay constant, a particular combination of price and quantity will maximize contribution. Subtracting fixed costs yields profit before taxes. A key component of this analysis is the price sensitivity parameter that relates unit changes in price to unit changes in quantity. Price elasticity, on the other hand, is a dimensionless quantity computed as the ratio of percentage change in quantity to percentage change in price.

The usual recommendation is to increase the price when the price elasticity is less than one in magnitude and decrease price when the price elasticity is greater than one in magnitude. These recommendations should not be followed blindly. For example, increasing the price when the price elasticity is less than one can change the reference price of the product and change the competitive set among which the product is being compared. Doing so can increase the price elasticity and result in a much greater loss in sales than suggested by the mathematical model. Strictly speaking, the demand curve assumes that all other things remain fixed as the price is varied. So, the demand curve itself changes in this example. By the same token, reducing the price when the price elasticity is greater than one is not the automatic thing to do; it depends on the relationship between the current price and the profit maximizing price. If the current price is less than the profit maximizing price, the price has to be increased and vice versa. What will be true is that the optimal price is a decreasing function of the price elasticity. The bottom line is that one needs some estimate of how demand is related to price to get an estimate of a profitable price range. A number of ways to estimate price response are suggested later in this chapter.

If you are a low cost producer, should you price your products lower? No! Costs are an internal matter, prices are an external matter. The price you can charge depends on the value your customer segment places on your product and prevailing competitive prices. For industrial raw materials, for machinery, for freight, and so on, costs are the starting point in setting prices. For many services (e.g., consulting services), costs are the starting point. You figure out the number of workforce-days, the mix of personnel that will work on the project, compute a baseline cost, add an overhead burden, and a profit number and arrive at the price. The more unique the service, the harder it is to compare the quotes of different service providers.

The Role of Customer Value in Setting Prices

The first step in understanding the role of customer value is to segment the customer market. The personal computer market, for example, could be divided into the following segments: corporate, business professionals, small office/home office (SOHO), government, military, education, scientific computing, and family/home. To position the product appropriately to each segment (the *How*), it is most instructive to start with the benefits desired by each segment. Understanding customer benefits in each segment should lead to appropriate product design, choice of distribution channels, communication media, and price. For example, you might believe that the corporate segment values connectivity, compatibility, reliability, security, and low total usage cost as key benefits. These benefits call for specific design features like automatic backups, dual processors, universal network compliance, password protection, and so on. Low total usage cost might be delivered by value-added resellers who configure computers to provide the benefits desired. The family/home segment might value ease of use, fun, education, reliability, aesthetics, peace of mind, and low price. The firm will not design automatic backups and dual processors to ensure reliability for this segment. Reliability has to be designed into the system using lower cost means. This segment would like to purchase computers mostly from convenient retail outlets. The more sophisticated members of this segment could use mail order. Unlike the corporate segment, the direct price of the item is likely to be the relevant factor, not low total usage cost.

It is useful to construct a table like Table 12.3 to get an understanding of the importance of price in the purchase decision. Using the computer example illustration, segment 1 could be the corporate segment, and segment 2 the family or home segment. The key benefits that are important to the segments are obtained through marketing research. The features and service levels, the distribution requirements, the communication media, and so on, that are necessary to deliver the benefits complete the table. The relative importance of price among the benefits identified in each segment is critical in determining how to price the product as the following example about Xerox illustrates.

Xerox evaluated the importance of different factors in the equipment purchase decision and the service purchase decision.[8] They conducted research on three segments, namely Fortune 500 accounts, large non–Fortune 500 accounts, and government or educational accounts. Reliability and ease of operation were more important than price in the equipment purchase decision, and technical expertise of the service provider and guaranteed repair time were more important than price in the service purchase decision for both the corporate segments. On the other hand, price was the most important factor in both decisions for the government and education accounts. Does this mean that price is not important for the corporate accounts? Not at all. What the research indicates is that the corporate accounts will make a trade-off between product and service quality and price.

Suppose the Social Security Administration (SSA) wants to buy 500 computers. As in the copier example, price is likely to be the most important factor in the purchase. As a computer manufacturer, you might try to sell them a DVD drive at a small premium over the cost of the drive. The SSA will most likely reject this feature. For them the DVD drive is

Table 12.3
Determining the Importance of Price Relative to
Other Benefits for Different Segments

Segment	Benefits	Product Features/ Service Levels	Distribution	Communication
Segment 1				
Segment 2				

probably worth zero. On the other hand, the same DVD drive can be sold at a high premium when it is packaged in a multimedia computer sold to the family/home segment. The latter segment is also price sensitive but the value derived from the DVD drive is greater than the price of the drive. Suppose instead that you are a consultant who travels extensively. You are likely to highly value portability in a computer, but not just any portable. You want a full-featured but light machine, something that weighs less than 5 pounds. You might be willing to pay a hefty premium for the value you derive from not having to lug a 7-pound portable from airport to airport. (Those 2 extra pounds start feeling like 20 pounds after a while!) Everyone would prefer a lighter machine over a heavier machine but not everyone would want to pay the premium to save on the weight which suggests that the target has to be chosen appropriately.

Price is more complicated than other elements of the marketing mix. It might be helpful conceptually to separate the price from the product. Doing so is typically easier for industrial products than certain types of consumer products, notably luxury goods where a high price could signal high quality. The product, including its functional features and service levels, its brand name, country of origin, mode of distribution, and the communication, creates the value. The price captures the value. Pricing is a complicated decision because value can be manipulated. Everything else remaining the same, you might be willing to pay a higher price for a German milling machine than one made in the United States, for an Armani suit than a Joseph Abboud suit, for online brokerage services provided by Schwab than E★Trade, and so on. In each of these cases, you might feel justified in paying the higher price because the product in question delivers higher value than the competitive product. It is therefore also important to make a distinction between price and value. Everyone wants the best value, but that does not mean the lowest price.

Consider this definition of value: "Value is defined as the perceived worth in monetary units of the set of economic, functional/technical, and psychological benefits received by the customer in exchange for the price paid for a product offering taking into consideration available competitive offerings and prices."[9] Value is the "art" part of pricing. It is idiosyncratic. One person may have high value for a Mazda Miata, another may have no value for it. Value is relative; there are no absolutes. The competitive set affects value. Value is multidimensional as shown in the value triangle in Figure 12.5. The value that a customer derives from a product or service is a function of the quality delivered by the product or service which in turn is obtained from the economic, functional, and psychological benefits provided by the product or service. Economic benefits are driven by price and

Figure 12.5
Three Aspects of Customer Value

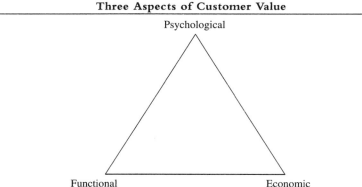

increased productivity. Functional benefits are obtained through product features. Examples of psychological benefits are satisfaction, comfort, reliability, security, peace of mind, control, power, relationships, brand name, and so on.

Among airlines, Southwest provides a clear economic benefit in the form of low prices, whereas United or American Airlines provide more functional benefits relative to Southwest, such as choice of food and movies. Southwest might also provide a psychological benefit of fairness for its target segment. Among athletic shoes, Converse is anchored more on the economic benefit, New Balance on the functional benefit of width sizing and Nike on the psychological benefit (a connection to Michael Jordan).

The three benefits connect neatly with Treacy and Wiersema's three value disciplines.[10] To win through economic benefits, the firm needs *operational excellence*. To win on functional benefits, *product leadership* is key. And *customer intimacy* is the key to win on psychological benefits. In general, the route to psychological benefits is through functional benefits and economic benefits. Nike first competed against Adidas by offering lower priced running shoes, next concentrated on product leadership through waffle-soled shoes, air encapsulated heels, and so on, and then employed superstar athletes like Michael Jordan to build the brand and the psychological image. Lexus entered the market with a car, the LS400, ostensibly positioned against the E-class Mercedes Benz, at a price several thousand dollars cheaper. A key feature of cars in the luxury segment is the engine. By offering a V-8 engine compared to Mercedes' V-6, Lexus raised the quality perception. They achieved product leadership by winning the J.D. Power quality awards. The extraordinary reliability of their cars coupled with superior, intimate, customer service paved the way for psychological benefits of satisfaction, comfort, and peace of mind.

What is the connection between benefits and pricing? Providing economic benefits goes hand–in–hand with lower prices. The target market is broad, unit margins tend to be low, and profits are made through volume. Concentrating on product leadership initially implies a narrower target market that will pay the higher price for functional superiority. Sony, for example, is a leader in consumer electronics. They have a history of building innovative products that are initially released at high prices. Prices are then brought down to reach a wider audience. Customer intimacy requires a high degree of customization. By providing a unique combination of products and services, the firm is able to command a high price. Again, this is a narrow target segment.

Determining Value.   It is not a simple matter figuring out what customers value. A path to understanding value is to estimate price response or price sensitivity. Here are a number of ways that can be used to measure price responses, including:

1. *Managerial judgment.* Assemble a group of decision makers including product managers, salespeople, members of the product engineering team, and so on, and ask them how much in percent terms sales is likely to change to an X percent price increase where X is incremented in some fashion, say 2 percent, 4 percent, and so on up to 10 percent, followed by the same questions for an X percent price decrease. For each price response, the respondents should fill out a source of volume model. For example, for a 10 percent price cut, how much of the sales increase is going to come from increased purchase by our customers, by switching competitive customers, and from new customers. For a price increase, how much are we going to lose to competition, and to whom. Obtain responses from multiple decision makers for each product. Ask them to justify their response briefly. If you have multiple products in the company, it would be very instructive to compare the price response (elasticity) estimates across products. You should be able to relate characteristics of the different products to the varying price elasticity estimates. For example, you would expect that the price elasticities are higher in more competitive markets, when many substitutes are available, when relative marketing spending is low, and when the expenditure outlay by the customer is large.

2. *Use of analogous products.* To understand the evolution of an nth generation product, it is instructive to look at previous generations of the product. This methodology works best for incremental innovations and where the competitive set does not change. The price of a previous generation serves as the benchmark for the new generation.

3. *Benchmarking.* An analysis of price response of competitive products can provide an understanding of how the firm's product might behave.

4. *Focus groups.* Properly conducted, focus groups can be used to obtain price ranges for products and services. These price ranges will be affected by how the products and services are described, and by what these items are compared to. Therefore, a richer understanding of price response can be obtained by changing the descriptions and the reference products across focus groups.

5. *Surveys.* Purchase intention surveys can be used to obtain likelihood of purchase at specific prices. A demand curve can be generated by using different prices with different random samples. Rather than asking the respondent to react to multiple price points and creating an artificial demand effect, it is better to describe the product and ask willingness to pay a single price and rotate the prices across the random samples. The downside is that larger sample sizes would be required.

6. *Experimentation.* Controlled field experiments are an excellent way of assessing price response. Unlike the previously listed ways, however, experiments are costly, time consuming, open to competitive mischief, and difficult to implement. But when conducted properly, management gets a highly reliable measure of price sensitivity.

7. *Analysis of historical data.* With good quality sales and price data on own price and competitive prices, one can estimate a demand curve. If price changes contemplated are in the range of prices in the data and if competitive response does not change, the estimated price elasticity is likely to be a good benchmark.

8. *Economic value to the customer (EVC) or value-in-use analysis.* If your product is going to replace a product that the customer currently uses, a value-in-use analysis can demonstrate the additional benefits. These additional benefits can be translated into monetary terms. The price of the product currently used serves as the reference price. The net benefits, which is the difference between the benefits and the additional costs incurred by using the product (training costs, for example), added to the reference price is the value of your product. The astute marketer returns some of the surplus benefit to the customer and charges a price lower than the value. Combining beta testing and

value-in-use analysis is one way of assessing customer value and the price to charge. For example, Xerox used about 20 beta sites in launching their very successful Docutech Production feeder product. Value-in-use analysis is more practical for business products than consumer products.

9. *Conjoint analysis.* Conjoint Analysis can be used to calibrate trade-offs customers make in terms of price. When price is one of the attributes in the conjoint design, the attribute utilities can be rescaled to reflect how much the customer is willing to pay for specified changes in the attribute levels. Consider the following example. To understand trade-offs among laptop features, a conjoint design was constructed using five features:

Size of the hard disk	2.0, 4.0, or 6.0 GIG[11]
Manufacturer	IBM, COMPAQ, or DELL
Price	Varies from $2250 to $5250
Weight	6 lbs. or 7.5 lbs.
Processor speed	Pentium II CPU of 233 or 300 MHz

The respondents were told to assume that they were paying for the laptop out of their pocket, to focus only on the five features, and not to assume that a computer at a lower price is inferior on some other features not mentioned. For example, it was mentioned that the lower price could be because the computer is on sale. By the same token, they were told not to assume that a high price signals superior quality on a feature that is not listed. They were also informed that all laptops have an Intel Pentium processor, come preloaded with Windows 98 and the same application software, all have a color screen, and are essentially identical on all features other than the five mentioned. Each respondent was given a set of 18 laptop profiles to rank from most likely to purchase to least likely to purchase. A regression was run to obtain the utilities.[12] Dummy variables were used for all the features except for price which was treated as a continuous variable measured in 000's of dollars. Here is one respondent's utility function:

$$Y = \text{Constant} + 4.10\,(6\ \text{GIG}) + 1.47\,(4\ \text{GIG}) + 2.19\,(\text{P300 Mhz})$$
$$+ 0.76\,(6\ \text{lbs.}) + 1.63\,(\text{IBM}) + 2.07\,(\text{Compaq}) - 7.09\,(\text{Price})$$

From this equation, we compute that a $1000 increase in price will reduce the utility by 7.09 units, or one unit of utility is scaled as $141. Thus, a 6 GIG (4 GIG) drive is worth $578 ($207) over a

2 GIG drive, a 300 MHz processor is worth $309 over a 233 MHz processor, a 6 lb. Laptop is worth $107 over a 7.5 lb. Laptop, an IBM (Compaq) branded laptop is worth $230 ($292) over a Dell laptop.

This problem is fairly simple. There are more sophisticated conjoint methods available like Adaptive Conjoint Analysis and Choice Based Conjoint to handle more complex decisions and estimate the price trade-offs.

It is important to understand how to affect price sensitivity. In general, you want to lower customers' *own* price sensitivity and make *cross* price elasticities asymmetric. Several factors that affect price sensitivity are:[13]

1. *The unique value effect.* The more unique the product or service is, the lower the price sensitivity and higher the price that can be charged. Unique value is also embodied in brand equity. Michelin tires are typically higher priced than other tires, Sunkist pistachio nuts are higher priced than generic nuts, clothes at Nieman Marcus are usually at the higher price points, IBM for a long time priced its PCs higher than competitors, Caterpillar tractors are more expensive than comparable tractors, Nike shoes are more expensive than other athletic shoes, and so on. Even though one can search online and find the identical book at a lower price than at Amazon.com, Amazon is the clear leader in selling books online. This is a combination of greater awareness of Amazon and unique value.

2. *The substitute awareness effect.* The greater the number of substitutes the customer is aware of, the greater the price sensitivity. In general, the customer is likely to be aware of more substitutes when search costs are low. Reducing the time available for the customer to indulge in searching lowers price sensitivity, which is one reason why many retailers such as Best Buy and Circuit City announce that they will match or beat the lowest competitive price, or why car dealers tell customers the price is only good for that day. The Web has lowered the cost of search in many cases which does not bode well for sellers, unless they can create unique value in their site or customer interaction as Amazon (see example above) seems to have done.

3. *The difficult comparison effect.* The more difficult it is to compare options, the less the role of price in the decision. Even within a defined class, say luxury cars, it is not simple to compare cars because there are many differences other than price. Sony, for example, produces several variants of its Walkman product as well as several variants of television sets within a particular screen size. The products vary by retailers

making comparisons difficult for the consumer. Full service broker-age companies employ this logic in pricing their services.

4. *The total expenditure effect.* Price sensitivity is greater when the total financial outlay is greater. Creative financing can reduce the impact and lower price sensitivity. This effect is most evident in leas-ing. If the product or service being sold is modular, the total expen-diture can be reduced by selling a base product with the expectation of selling the add-ons later. Typically, customer are less sensitive to the price of add-ons than to the base product. For example, consider a business customer who has purchased or leased a large office copier. Adding options to the product are evaluated less stringently than ne-gotiating the original price of the copier. Unbundling is one way of re-ducing the total expenditure effect. Fast-food restaurants like McDonald's and Burger King periodically run à la carte menu pro-motions which are lower priced than the bundled "value meals."

5. *The shared cost effect.* Price sensitivity is lower if the costs are shared with a third party. Consumers with drug prescription plans are less sensitive to the price of brand name drugs than those without such insurance. Realizing this, insurance companies are now changing the blanket co-payment amount to one that takes into account the dif-ference between the generic price, if a generic alternative is available, and the branded price. Another way of sharing in the cost and re-ducing price sensitivity is through buy-back plans which reduces the risk of obsolescence for the buyer.

6. *The price-quality effect.* It is difficult to disentangle this effect after a while from the unique value effect. Here, price itself positively af-fects the valuation the customer places on the product or service. The obvious examples are luxury goods. In most cases, these manufac-turers provide unique value derived from exotic or precious materi-als, hand crafted labor, elaborate ritualistic selling methods, and so on. Over time, the value embedded in functional benefits but more so in psychological benefits starts to escalate allowing the seller to increase prices and signal quality.

Role of Competition in Setting Prices

The effects of competition are generally as follows:

- Competition forces prices down.
- Competition means more substitutes, giving customers more choices, and raising price sensitivity.

- Competition in the introduction and growth stages of the PLC increases market size and does not put much pressure on prices.
- Competitive price pressure starts to increase when customers become more knowledgeable, and productive and delivery capacity of sellers increase.
- Competitive price pressures increase as market growth slows down, and the players start fighting over market share.
- Price pressures are generally more subdued when market concentration is high.
- Competition forces weaker players out and the better managed companies to improve.

There are several means of responding to competition, including:

- Heuristics that is, matching competition or being higher or lower than competitors depending on competitive position.
- Selectively matching competition based on targeting and positioning, or being selectively higher or lower depending on competitive position.
- Ignore competitors and continue current pricing.
- Gradually withdraw from market by milking.
- Find customer segments which value non-price factors: product quality, service, reputation, prestige, partnering, just-in-time delivery, training, and so on. That is, align your competency with what customers value.
- Understand competitive motivation for the actions. Do not confuse tactics (e.g., a change in price) with the strategy that led to the pricing action.
- Gather competitive intelligence information to help you respond with confidence.
- Understand objective(s) of competitor(s). Price response depends on whether competitor's objective is market share or profitability.
- Understand the role of signaling in communicating price response.
- Recognize that price increases and decreases have ramifications throughout the channel.
- Recognize that despite competitive actions, it is important to protect your price "image."

Remember, competition is only one among several factors that affects your response. No one is immune to competition, at least in the long run.

The extent to which competitors affect your price depends on the following factors:

- What is your brand equity? How loyal are your customers?
- What is the pace of market changes?
- How substitutable are the products?
- What is the extent of market concentration?
- What is the stage of the product life cycle?

If you are the market leader, you are less vulnerable to competitive pricing actions. Compaq is less affected by Gateway than vice versa. That is, the cross price elasticities are asymmetric. Regardless of the asymmetry, however, the higher the cross price elasticity the closer the product is to a commodity. Smaller players are usually the hardest hit when the leader or one of the major players cuts prices. Their "me-too" strategy was founded on the price advantage they have which is now eroded with the price cut announced by one of the major players. The smaller players have to cut their price further but they do not have much of a cushion. Although smaller players generally have lower overhead and administrative costs than larger players, they do not have economies of scale or scope and consequently operate on very small margins. This does not mean all is lost and the smaller players should fold up. The name of the game is differentiation. You may be unable to differentiate on the basic core product but might be able to differentiate on the augmented product. Better response time, reliable delivery, customized services and support are all ways in which one player can build differentiation over another. Smaller players may know their customers better and may be able to react more quickly to changing needs.

In the desktop laser printer market, Hewlett Packard (HP) has a greater than 60 percent market share and its printer prices are a little higher then competition. This status is the power of brand equity. Of course this power did not happen by accident nor did it come cheap. HP has devoted considerable marketing dollars in building the LaserJet brand name. This equity insulates them to some extent from pricing actions by their competitors. By constant innovation and extension of the product line to cover a wide price range, HP has created a powerful position in the desktop laser printer market. Compaq which is so successful in personal computers exited the printer market after only two years when they realized that they couldn't make a dent in HP's share. HP has become the technical and psychological standard when it comes to laser printers. The value that the customer derives from the psychological benefit of owning an HP printer is greater than the higher price of the printer relative to competition and is worth more than the additional functional benefits that competition might provide. Everything else remaining the same, Epson might sell a printer with a print speed of 10 ppm at the same or lower price than an HP printer with a print speed of 8 ppm. Thus, Epson offers a superior functional benefit (and effectively superior economic benefit) but HP offers superior psychological benefit which is the HP name. HP was the first to introduce 600 dpi printers to the home and the SOHO market but this functional advantage lasts no more than a few months. But the psychological advantage properly nurtured can live on for a long time. It is brand equity which makes the cross price elasticities asymmetric and in your favor.

We said value is relative, so obviously competitive prices matter. The customer does not make a choice in a vacuum. The smart marketer builds in differentiation, real or perceived, to try to make comparisons across products more difficult. The smart marketer also finds the market segment that will value these differentiating features. Store brands and generics placed right next to name brand products on U.S. supermarket shelves are quite a bit cheaper yet have not had much success in many product categories. The best examples are in the over-the-counter (OTC) pain relievers and cough and cold remedies market. Generic aspirin is outsold by Bayer aspirin, generic acetaminophen is outsold by its branded counterpart Tylenol, and so on. You are not going to consume the brand name, are you? But the psychological costs of making a mistake is greater than the price difference, so the customer selects the trusted branded product, the one they know will cure their headache.

Such examples exist not just in the consumer domain where perceptions play an important role. In business decisions involving the purchase of machinery, mainframe computers, large copiers, selection of consulting companies, and so on, perceptions are important too. If you are not on the preferred vendor list you are not likely to be selected. In all these cases, particularly when the dollar outlay is large, there is a reluctance to choose the lowest priced vendor or supplier. Why? Should not the decision makers be saving the company money? Yes, they should. But saving money is only one of the three benefits—the economic benefit—that contributes to value. For example, we cited research conducted by Xerox on customers for their large copiers which found that the large Fortune 500 type accounts cited reliability and ease of operation as far more important than price in the equipment purchase decision and technical expertise and guaranteed repair time as far more important than price in the service purchase decision. Government and education accounts, on the other hand, cited price as most important in both decisions. This finding does not mean price is not important to the Fortune 500 type accounts. What it means is that a copier manufacturer who bids low and sacrifices on some functional benefits which impact ease of operation and sacrifices on quality and timeliness of service which negatively affects economic and psychological benefits may not win the account against a higher priced bid.

So, what is the bottom line? Given the targeted market segment, you have to stay within a price range of competition. IBM learned this to their chagrin when prices of their PCs were out of line with market prices in the early 1990s. You have to differentiate your product. It could be through advertising, promotion, publicity, the Internet, endorsements, through tie-ins, and so on. It could be through distribution as Dell has successfully done. It could be through product functionality like the new digital copiers from Xerox and Canon. It could be through low price as Southwest Airlines has done. It could be through an overpowering brand name and ubiquity like Nike. It could be through a passionate embrace of the product as Starbucks has done. It could be through highly personalized service as several stand alone opticians have done despite charging higher prices in the face of enormous competition from operations like Lens Crafters; and so on.

Role of the Channel in Setting Prices

In these days of electronic commerce, close attention is being paid by manufacturers and retailers alike to the impact of the distribution channel on the end-user price. A comparison of Dell and Compaq makes the distinction obvious. Dell sells direct to the end-use customer, while Compaq sells through a variety of distribution channels.[14] Assuming same manufacturing costs and ignoring all marketing costs, Dell can sell a computer to the end-user at the same price as Compaq but make a higher margin than Compaq. Compaq has to share some of its margin with the channel, whereas Dell doesn't have to. It is interesting that Dell which pioneered direct sales of computers has been so successful.

The secondary channel is critical when the products require display and demonstration and after sales service and support to sell them. Prestige products require appropriate display and ambience to assist in the sale. Manufacturers of high-end cosmetics sold through department stores lease space in the stores and staff the counters with their own personnel to provide the high quality service that helps to sell the product. Makers of high-end cookware and kitchenware seek retailers who would add value by demonstrating the products in their stores. This allows the retailers to add a nice margin to the manufacturer's price. Purchase of high-end stereo amplifiers and speakers targeted at audiophiles require retailers to have knowledgeable personnel and acoustically designed sound rooms. Again, these products have high mark ups to justify the value added service. Since computers require after sales service and support, Dell uses extensive telephone and Web support as well as third-party service providers to visit customer sites.

The question to ask is whether the seller benefits from using channel intermediaries or is better of going direct to the end user or should employ both direct and indirect channels. Consider a seller of high-end stereo products. For these products, there is typically a manufacturer suggested retail price (MSRP). This MSRP allows a healthy margin for the retailers. What if the seller were to go direct and sell to end users at a price lower than what the retailer charges? First, the seller faces the possibility that retailers, of which there are likely to be only a few, will stop carrying the product. Second, can the seller reach and sell to the target audience without having a retail presence? How much marketing costs will the seller have to incur? For these high-end products that require auditioning in simulated environments the decision to bypass the retail channel might backfire. The seller recognizes that the retailers require the margin to provide the value-added services to customers but fears loss of volume if the retail prices are too high. How does the seller impress the retailer to lower retail prices? Dual distribution is one way of rationalizing prices but is not feasible in many cases. Alternatively the seller can help the retailer by providing certain services to customers which is cheaper for the seller than the retailer. By sharing in the cost of the services, the seller could influence the retailer to lower prices.

For example, the seller could have a Web site which provides extensive product information including comparisons with competitive products, and so on, as well as direct links to authorized resellers in the customer's area. The seller could also post new, lower MSRPs which makes it difficult for retailers to charge higher prices. Of course, the seller could also charge retailers a lower price with the expectation that the retailers would pass the savings to customers.

The secondary distribution channel is critical for ubiquitous products like soft drinks, chewing gum, an enormous number of grocery products, batteries, light bulbs, and simple hardware products. The secondary channel is far more efficient for distribution of these products than anything the manufacturer can do. What about books, video, software, CDs? Direct retailers, either through mail order or the Web, have made a major impact on prices of these products. What is it about these products that makes the direct channel advantageous? These are non-perishable, relatively higher value per unit weight, and easily packaged and shipped. Without the high overhead costs to cover, Web retailers can sell these products at a small premium over variable costs. The lower prices charged by these retailers impacts the bricks-and-mortar retailers. In many cases, the traditional retailer carrying the identical products is forced to match the Web retailer. With higher costs to bear, traditional retailers are finding it difficult to compete. Manufacturers cannot sell the identical product at different prices to different retailers. It is not the manufacturer's price, or the margin, that is affected by the shift from one form of retail channel to another. As the shift takes place to the lower priced retailer, there will be pressure over time from this channel on the manufacturer to lower their price. One option for the manufacturer is to provide slightly different products to the online and offline channel and that way lessen the price competition between the two.

The manufacturer can also affect retail pricing through advertising. Heavy manufacturer advertising pulls consumers to the stores. This in turn forces more stores to carry the product. This increases retail competition and brings down retail prices, lowering unit margins to the retailer. But total margins can increase because the retailer is now selling more of the product. This outcome is much more likely with the leading brands in the category because they have the greatest pull on consumers.[15] The manufacturer has three points of influence on the end-user. One is indirect through the channel. By providing a higher margin to the channel temporarily through trade promotions, the manufacturer could expect the channel to pass on the lower price to the end-user. The second point of influence is direct through coupons, rebates, free trials, sweepstakes, contests, and so on. The third point of influence is the advertising discussed earlier. Some research has shown that increased mood-type nonprice advertising can reduce price sensitivity, implying the price can be raised.[16] The cost of the advertising must be compared to the increased revenue that can arise from the higher price to evaluate profitability. In other research it was found that although loyal customers select the brand they are loyal to even if the price goes up they decrease the quantity that they purchase. That is, loyal customers are not very price sensitive in the choice decision but price sensitive in the quantity decision.[17]

Role of Regulation in Setting Prices[18]

The involvement of government in business decision making affects pricing directly and indirectly. In certain cases, such as the historic treatment of electric and other utilities, government determines the price that will be charged to the end-user, typically in exchange for granting the seller a monopoly or quasi-monopoly. In other situations, government's effect is indirect, but often significant. Taxation and tariff policies influence pricing, as do the payment of subsidies and the provision of patents and other forms of intellectual property protection. Government can also affect pricing by deciding how much will be produced (e.g., frequently used for agricultural commodities), banning direct sales by producers (e.g., common with respect to alcoholic beverages) and regulating the cost of inputs (e.g., by setting minimum wages), as well as the creation and disposition of outputs (e.g., through environmental laws).

In addition, government can set parameters for how pricing is done. The law of the United States in this regard is particularly well-developed and has served as a model (both positively and negatively) for other parts of the world, including the European Union and Japan. Indeed, federal antitrust law in the United States has evolved substantially over its more than 100-year history to account for marketplace changes. At the same time, particular laws like the Robinson-Patman Act (described shortly) today are viewed by many as archaic.

Price Fixing.   Setting prices to reduce or avoid market risks is instinctively rational behavior that generally has been discouraged by the law, although there has been a substantial softening of public policy in this regard. There are two types of price fixing—horizontal and vertical. The former is where competitors agree on the prices they will charge or key terms affecting price. The latter is where suppliers and resellers agree on the prices the resellers will charge or such terms, but only applies where ownership to the products *changes hands.* In other words, vertical price fixing does not cover consignment sales and those through agents or independent sales representatives.

The primary law in this area is Section 1 of the Sherman Act, an 1890 statute that prohibits "[e]very contract, combination . . . or conspiracy in restraint of trade." The contract, combination or conspiracy requirement necessarily means that there must be an agreement between or among two or more individuals or entities. As a result, the law does not cover unilateral behavior. Moreover, the Sherman Act does not ban imitating a competitor's pricing behavior (something called "conscious parallelism"), unless there is evidence of communication, such as an invitation to act in concert.

Case law has further refined Section 1 to incorporate two kinds of analysis depending on the activities involved. Some offenses are considered to be "per se" illegal, while others are analyzed under the "rule of reason." In general, it is easier to prove a violation under the per se test and more difficult to do so under the rule of reason, because the latter requires detailed economic analysis and a balancing of pro-competitive and anti-competitive effects. Historically, all arrangements affecting price were presumed to be unreasonably anti-competitive and, therefore, per se illegal. However, during the last 25 years or so, the U.S. Supreme Court has placed more emphasis on showing demonstrable economic effect rather than relying on assumptions, so there has been an erosion of per se application to pricing.

In the horizontal arena, both direct price fixing (competitors in a smoke-filled room) and indirect price fixing (ambiguous arrangements where a detailed factual review or market analysis is necessary to figure out that price fixing has occurred) remain per se illegal. However, where a restriction on price is the incidental effect of a desirable activity ("incidental price fixing"), it is now clear that the more forgiving rule of reason applies. This point is illustrated by the 1984 Supreme Court case, *National Collegiate Athletic Association* (NCAA), where the Court applied the rule of reason and noted that NCAA rules regarding equipment and schedules were appropriate, but those that limited the television exposure of member football teams were an unreasonable restriction on output that increased prices.

While vertical price fixing is still considered per se illegal, recent Supreme Court cases have narrowed the application of the per se rule. In late 1997, the Supreme Court in *Khan* unanimously overturned a 29-year-old case, holding that the rule of reason, rather than the per se test, applies to vertical agreements that set maximum or ceiling resale prices because consumers are not always harmed by such arrangements and may be benefitted by them. However, setting minimum (floor) or exact prices by agreement remains illegal on its face.

At the same time, the Supreme Court's *Monsanto* (1984) and *Business Electronics* (1988) decisions make it clear that setting maximum, minimum or exact resale prices without an agreement (i.e., unilaterally) is simply outside the Sherman Act. As a result, a supplier may announce a price at which its product must be resold (ceiling, floor, or exact price) and refuse to sell to any customer who does not comply. Moreover, even when resellers follow the supplier's resale price policy, there is no unlawful agreement. Due to this latitude, many manufacturers of desirable branded products have successfully discouraged the discounting of their products during the 1990's in such industries as agricultural supplies, consumer electronics, appliances, sporting goods, apparel and automotive replacement parts.

Predatory Pricing.   Long-term aggressive pricing that is below marginal cost (or its measurable surrogate, average variable cost) and is aimed at driving rivals out of business can be attacked under Section 2 of the Sherman

Act and other antitrust statutes. However, in 1993, the Supreme Court in *Brooke* made it clear that a violation also requires that the structure of the market be such as to permit the supplier to recoup its losses, an element which limits the applicability of the law.

Price and Promotional Discrimination.   Although economists maintain that the ability to charge different prices to different customers promotes efficiency by clearing the market, U.S. law has focused on insuring the viability of numerous sellers as a means to preserve competition. Consequently, while price discrimination has been unlawful since 1914, the Robinson-Patman Act amended existing legislation in 1936 so this entire area is commonly referred to by the name of the amendment. This complex Depression-era legislation was enacted to protect small businesses by outlawing discriminatory price and promotional allowances obtained by large ones, while exempting sales to government or "charitable" organizations for their own use. At the same time, the emergence of contemporary power buyers through consolidation and otherwise, as well as heightened marketplace competition in general, has forced sellers to offer account-specific pricing and promotions by creatively finding ways through the Robinson-Patman maze.

To prove illegal *price discrimination,* each of five elements must be present:

1. *Discrimination.* This standard is met simply by charging different prices to different customers. However, if the reason for the difference is due to a discount or allowance made available to all or almost all customers (like a prompt payment discount), there is no discrimination, something referred to as the "availability defense."
2. *Sales to two or more purchasers.* The different prices must be charged on reasonably contemporaneous sales to two or more purchasers—a rule that permits price fluctuations. Note that offering different prices alone is not enough. Sales or agreements to sell at different prices must exist.
3. *Goods.* The law applies to the sale of goods only ("commodities" in the statute), so services are not covered. When a supplier sells a bundled offering, such as computer hardware that includes maintenance services, Robinson-Patman is relevant only if the value of the goods in the bundle predominates.
4. *Like grade and quality.* The goods involved must be physically the same or essentially the same. Brand preferences are irrelevant, but functional differences can differentiate products.

5. *Reasonable probability of competitive injury.* The law generally focuses on injury at one of two levels. The first is called "primary line" and permits a supplier to sue a competitor for the latter's discriminatory pricing, but here the law also requires that the discriminating supplier is doing so to drive its rival out of business, and as is the case with predatory pricing, the market structure must allow the recoupment of losses later through higher prices. Not surprisingly, there are few contemporary primary line cases due to this standard. Far more common is "secondary line" injury, where a supplier's disfavored customer may sue the supplier. However, the law is clear that only competing customers must be treated alike. Geographic or other legitimate distinctions permit different prices.

Even if all five elements are present there are three defenses: cost justification (i.e., price disparities are allowed if due to real cost differences), meeting competition (i.e., prices may be lowered to meet those of a competitor), and changing conditions (i.e., special prices may be provided to sell off perishable, seasonal or obsolete merchandise).

Robinson-Patman also bans promotional discrimination in an effort to deny an alternative means of achieving discriminatory pricing. In general, price discrimination covers the initial sale from supplier to customer, while promotional discrimination relates to the resale of the supplier's products by the customer. This distinction is important because different legal standards apply, and there is more flexibility under *promotional discrimination* rules.

As is the case with price discrimination, each of several elements must be present to violate the law:

1. *Provision of allowances, services, or facilities.* Here, the supplier grants to the customer advertising or promotional allowances (like $5 off per case to advertise a product) or provides services or facilities (such as demonstrators or free display racks), usually in return for some form of promotional performance.
2. *Resale of the supplier's goods.* Again, the law does not reach service providers.
3. *Not available to all competing customers on proportionally equal terms.* The services or facilities offered or the performance required to earn the allowances must be usable or attainable in a practical sense by all competing customers, something which may require that alternatives be provided. In addition, proportional equality means that the same total benefits do not have to be given to all competing customers.

In fact, there are three ways to proportionalize benefits: (a) on unit or dollar purchases (buy a case, get a buck); (b) on the cost to the reseller of the promotional activity (a full-page ad in a big city newspaper costs more than that in a neighborhood shopper); or (c) on the value of the promotional activity to the supplier (sales people dedicated to the supplier's brand have more value than those who are not).

Meeting competition is the only defense to unlawful promotional discrimination. Moreover, if the supplier provides promotional allowances to the ultimate reseller, it must also provide them to competitive resellers that buy the promoted product through intermediaries.

The U.S. experience with the regulation of pricing behavior has been a long and evolving one. While mandating ways of doing business in an effort to insure a competitive environment, it also has left considerable flexibility to cope with a changing marketplace.

ORGANIZING TO SET PRICES

Although picking a precise value for the price is finally a judgment call, picking a price range should be based on facts. And, facts are provided by data. Figure 12.6 outlines a process to follow to help set prices. The first step of the pricing process is assembling internal data on product sales, prices, costs, and margins as well as equivalent information on competitive products, customer benefits, environmental factors, and so on.

Figure 12.6
The Pricing Process

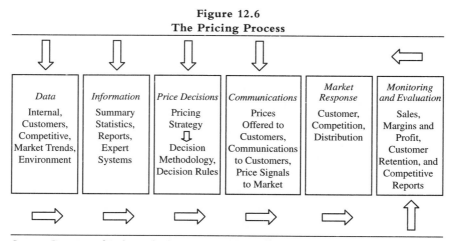

Data	Information	Price Decisions	Communications	Market Response	Monitoring and Evaluation
Internal, Customers, Competitive, Market Trends, Environment	Summary Statistics, Reports, Expert Systems	Pricing Strategy ⇩ Decision Methodology, Decision Rules	Prices Offered to Customers, Communications to Customers, Price Signals to Market	Customer, Competition, Distribution	Sales, Margins and Profit, Customer Retention, and Competitive Reports

Source: Courtesy of Robert Blattberg, Kellogg Graduate School of Management, Northwest University.

The second step is to convert these data into usable information. A critical piece of information is customer response to price changes, embodied in price sensitivity or price elasticity. It is not possible to set price objectively without some measure of price response. We discussed in a previous section different ways of measuring price response. Retention rates, plot of prices paid by customers against total service costs incurred, and plot of customer order size by price paid are useful pieces of information that should be extracted from the data. Using scanner data on the salty snacks category from data providers such as IRI and Nielsen, companies like Frito Lay have computer models to compute the profitability of different SKU assortments. Such data provide objective evidence that Frito Lays sales representatives can communicate to the supermarket chains.

The third step is to formulate a price position or strategy based on the data and actionable information. This can take the form of decision rules such as being the premium pricer in the market, being at a certain price point above or below specific competitors with clear rules on what to do when competitive prices change, being the lowest priced player in the market, and so on. It is important that these decisions are fact-based. When Cadillac priced the convertible Allante in the early nineties at close to the Mercedes SL convertible's price, it was not based on objective evidence. The car has since been discontinued because of poor sales. The current prices of the Cadillac Seville, on the other hand, are much more fact based and reflective of market reality.

The fourth step is to communicate the prices to end consumers, to the channel and signal competition. When resin prices went up, Rubbermaid increased the prices of its plastic housewares products to the channel. Key channel customers felt that they could not pass on the price increases to consumers. Rubbermaid's action created a lot of ill will and some retailers opted not to give prominent shelf space to Rubbermaid products. Proper communication is essential to make channel partners feel included and understanding of why prices had to be increased. At the same time, the partners must believe that the seller is also sharing in the pain; it cannot be unilateral. Wal-Mart and other retailers who adopt an everyday low price (EDLP) strategy are under a disadvantage when promotional retailers have sales on products. Consider a washing machine that is priced everyday at $299 at Wal-Mart. Suppose a washing machine that typically sells for $349 at a competitive promotional retailer is on sale for $299. Consumers might believe that they are getting a higher valued product for the lower price at the promotional retailer whereas they might believe that the machine at Wal-Mart is only valued at $299. To overcome these value connotations,

EDLP retailers usually note that their products are valued at higher prices at competing retailers.

The fifth and sixth steps involve the actual reaction by the market and monitoring and evaluating the response. Sometimes it takes a while for a pricing action taken by the seller to make its way to the customer. Also, price cuts passed on by the seller to the channel may not find its way to the end customer. By the same token price increases taken by the seller may not be fully passed on to the end customer. So, it is important to have a good monitoring system that connects the pricing and other marketing mix changes to sales and market share. In some markets, like the grocery industry, third party data collection agencies provide extensive data. In other markets, it might require the seller in cooperation with channel members to collect the data.

CONCLUSIONS

This chapter has provided some guidelines to consider in setting prices. In some cases, cost-plus pricing is used because it is simple and because all costs have to be covered in the long run. In reality, even cost-plus pricing is not simple because in a multiproduct situation fixed costs have to be allocated. Such allocations are never precise and in some cases can be quite wrong leading to significant over pricing or under pricing of products.

A more common way of pricing is to use a combination of cost-plus and competitive pricing. The logic here is that competitive prices reveal shared wisdom about market place price response. Blindly following competition like lemmings, however, is not strategic, because you are signaling that you have an undifferentiated product.

Using costs and competitive information as a benchmark and making adjustments to reflect your product's differentiating features is what was mentioned previously as value-in-use analysis. This analysis requires an understanding of what customers value. Translating this value to monetary or price terms is difficult. One way to do so is through conjoint analysis. Another way is through experimentation (e.g., if your markets are geographically separated or relatively self-contained, you could experiment in one representative area to learn about price response). If you cannot conduct experiments, see if you can follow one of the ways to measure price response suggested in this chapter. What is important is to get some understanding of customer response to a price change. Theory will get you only so far in understanding the "science" part of pricing; it is learning by doing that gets at the "art" part of pricing.

Notes

1. Robert Buzzell and Bradley Gale, *The PIMS Principles* (New York: The Free Press, 1987).

2. *Wall Street Journal* (November 18, 1999).

3. Ibid. (November 16, 1999).

4. *New York Times* (November 22, 1999).

5. *Wall Street Journal* (November 8, 1999).

6. In highly competitive markets it is difficult for cross-subsidization to work. It is not clear whether giving the Internet Explorer for free helped Microsoft sell more Office Suite products, for example.

7. The idea to depict the relationship graphically was provided in Robert Dolan and Hermann Simon, *Power Pricing* (New York: The Free Press, 1996). Figure 12.4 is based on Figure 2.3 of their book.

8. Melvyn A.J. Menezes and Jon Serbin, "Xerox Corporation: The Customer Satisfaction Program," Harvard Business School case, 9-591-055 (1991).

9. James C. Anderson, Dipak C. Jain, and Pradeep K. Chintagunta, "Customer Value Assessment in Business Markets: A State-of-Practice Study," *Journal of Business-to-Business Marketing,* vol. 1, no. 1 (1993), p. 5.

10. Michael Treacy and Fred Wiersema, "How Market Leaders Keep Their Edge," *Fortune,* (February 6, 1995), pp. 88–93.

11. A GIG represents 1000 mega bytes.

12. The ranks were first converted so that the most likely computer to purchase was ranked 18 instead of 1. Running a regression using rank order data is inappropriate from a statistical point of view. However, in most cases, the procedure works quite well.

13. Thomas Nagle and Reed Holden, *The Strategy and Tactics of Pricing,* 2nd ed. (Upper Saddle River, NJ: Prentice Hall, 1997).

14. Compaq launched a direct channel in 1999.

15. Mark Albion, *Advertising's Hidden Effects: Manufacturers' Advertising and Retail Pricing* (Boston: Auburn House,1983).

16. Lakshman Krishnamurthi and S.P. Raj, "The Effect of Advertising on Price Sensitivity," *Journal of Marketing Research,* vol. 22 (May 1985), pp. 119–129.

17. Lakshman Krishnamurthi and S.P. Raj, "An Empirical Analysis of the Relationship Between Loyalty and Consumer Price Elasticity," *Marketing Science,* vol. 10, no. 2 (1991), pp. 172–183.

18. The legal section of this chapter was written by Eugene Zelek, Adjunct Assistant Professor of Marketing, Kellogg School, Northwestern University, and a Partner in the Marketing Law Group at Freeborn & Peters, a Chicago law firm. The copyright for this section is owned by Eugene Zelek.

CHAPTER 13

VALUING, ANALYZING, AND MANAGING THE MARKETING FUNCTION USING CUSTOMER EQUITY PRINCIPLES

ROBERT C. BLATTBERG and JACQUELYN S. THOMAS

The marketing function is changing rapidly. Over the last 10 years it has become much more customer focused as evidenced by the numerous books and articles written about customer relationship marketing (CRM), retention marketing, and one-to-one marketing.[1] While the 1980s was characterized by concepts such as brand equity, the 1990s and the 2000s were and are focused on the customer. The growth of Internet marketers such as America Online (AOL) and Amazon.com have shown the world that a strong customer-centric focus can generate extremely high market capitalization. While not the only measure of success, the markets are recognizing that firms who understand how to maximize the value of their customer bases have greater long-term value than firms that are simply product focused. This is not to argue that products and services offered by the firm are not important, but the true long-term value of a firm is being driven more and more by its customer base, not its "tangible assets" and products.

Firms that rely only on products without recognizing the importance of the value of its customer may be making a serious error. Dell Computer, one of the great success stories of the last decade, has shown that while product is important, it is more important to understand the customer and the relevant distribution systems. Dell was able to surpass giants like Compaq and IBM who had a greater product focus than Dell. Dell recognized that the product was important, but customers could buy comparable megahertz, internal RAM, and hard drives from a number of competitors. As long as the product met basic standards, Dell could compete on other dimensions such as service and delivery times and at the same time focus on creating a long-term loyal customer. Ultimately the industry giants flinched and began imitating the new breed of PC companies, exemplified by Dell.

In many of the industries in the new economy, we see a similar model. While again products/services are important, it is the focus on the customer that is paramount. Learning to maximize the value of the existing customer base is at the core of this type of marketing.

This chapter recognizes this changing marketing environment and provides a model of the consumer that we will call the *fundamental customer equity equation*. This equation is intended to capture the basis for valuing, analyzing, and managing the marketing activities of the firm. Any firm can use this equation as the basis for its marketing strategy and tactics. But it fits best for those firms that develop integrated and detailed customer databases and who have learned how to utilize these databases to create a model of the customer that is superior.

Examples range from Citicorp, American Express, and America Online to direct marketers who have lived in this environment for the last 30 years. Firms such as Procter and Gamble and Kraft are less likely to use this model because they are far from their end consumer. The historically great marketing companies who generally were in consumer packaged goods are likely to continue to have to rely on mass channels and mass communications in an era that is evolving to detailed customer information and highly targeted communications to the customer. Ironically, their worst nightmare, the retailer/distributor will be better suited to develop these types of marketing programs than will the firms being forced to rely on 1970s marketing technology and approaches.

The remainder of this chapter focuses on what we call the fundamental equation of customer equity and its applications. The first section covers the fundamental equation of customer equity, then we describe the impact of marketing strategy on critical measures derived from the fundamental equation. Next, we explain how to link segmenting, targeting, and the marketing mix with the fundamental equation. We end with a discussion of how to analyze the effectiveness of the marketing mix.

THE FUNDAMENTAL EQUATION OF CUSTOMER EQUITY

The fundamental equation of customer equity captures the major parameters that need to be modeled and linked to marketing activities:

$$CE(t) = \sum_{i=0}^{I} N_{i,t}\, \alpha_{i,t} \left(S_{i,t} - c_{i,t} \right) - N_{i,t}\, B_{i,a,t}$$

$$+ \sum_{k=1}^{\infty} N_{i,t}\, \alpha_{i,t} \left[\left(\prod_{j=1}^{R} \rho_{i,t+j} \right) \rho_{i,y+k} \left(S_{i,t+k} - c_{i,t+k} - B_{i,r,t+k} - B_{i,AO,t+k} \right) \right] \left(\frac{1}{1+d} \right)^{k}$$

$$CE = \sum_{k=0}^{t} CE(t-k)$$

where

$CE(t)$ = Customer equity value for customers acquired at time t

$N_{i,t}$ = Number of potential customers at time t for segment i

$\alpha_{i,t}$ = Acquisition probability at time t for segment i

$\rho_{i,t}$ = Retention probability at time t for a customer for segment i

$B_{i,a,t}$ = Marketing cost per prospect (N) for acquiring customers at time t for segment i

$B_{i,r,t}$ = Marketing costs in time period t for retained customers for segment i

$B_{i,AO,t}$ = Marketing costs in time period t for add-on selling for segment i

d = Discount rate

$S_{i,t}$ = Sales of the product/services offered by the firm at time t for segment i

$c_{i,t}$ = Cost of goods at time t for segment i

I = Number of segments

i = Segment designation

t_o = Initial time period

k = Time since acquisition

This seemingly messy expression, particularly for those who are not comfortable with mathematics, captures many crucial concepts. We will translate it into a verbal description. Customer equity equals:

	The profit from first-time customers which is the number of prospects contacted times the acquisition probability times the sales minus the margin.
Minus	The cost of acquiring the customers which is the number of prospects times the acquisition cost per prospect.

Plus   Profits from future sales to these newly acquired
              customers which is the retention rate in each future
              period times the profit obtained from the customer in
              that period summed across all future periods.

Divided by   The discount rate which transforms the future profits
              into current dollars (or any currency).

Summed   Across all customer segments.

The fundamental customer equity equation can be broken into three components: (1) Acquisition, (2) Retention, and (3) Add-on selling (A-R-A). In each component (A-R-A) of the fundamental equation, there are important subcomponents. These are discussed briefly here and in more detail in the section discussing linking the marketing mix to the fundamental equation.

Acquisition

In the equation, the acquisition rate, α_i, is the probability that a prospect becomes a customer. This variable has a major impact on the firm's investment strategy in acquiring as well as retaining customers. The number of prospects, $N_{i,t}$, is also a very important determinant of the number of customers acquired per period. The other critical acquisition variable is the amount that must be spent per customer for acquisition $B_{i,a,t}$. Clearly, $\alpha_{i,t}$ depends on the spending for acquisition or mathematically, $\alpha_{i,t} = f(B_{i,a,t})$.

Retention

The retention rate, $\rho_{i,t}$, is time specific, partly because the retention rate usually varies by period but more importantly because it varies overtime as the customer duration with the firm increases. Just as in acquisition, the amount spent to retain customers is a critical factor that influences retention rates or $\rho_{i,t} = f(B_{i,r,t}, B_{i,r,t-1}, \ldots)$.

Add-On Selling

This is rarely discussed in most customer relationship management articles or books but is an important element of customer-oriented marketing. It is captured in the model by $S_{i,t}$ which is the sales at time t. Add-on selling is determined by the number of offers made per period ($O_{i,t}$) and the response rate per offer, $r_{i,t}$. The response rate is affected by the quality of the firm's product line as well as the relationship it has developed with its customers. The higher $S_{i,t}$, it is believed, the higher the retention rate or $\rho_{i,t} = f(S_{i,t}, S_{i,t-1} \ldots)$.

Impact of Marketing Strategy on the Critical Measures

As part of the analysis of critical measures (acquisition, retention, and add-on selling rates), it is hypothesized that industries have baseline levels for the critical measures. Prior to Federal Express and other entrants in the air express industry, customer reliability was low. This, no doubt, led to low customer satisfaction levels and low retention rates. Federal Express was able to rethink the logistic strategy through the use of hubs to significantly improve reliability to "absolutely guarantee overnight." This then led to high customer satisfaction levels and likely higher retention rates.

Whether it is Lexus through a superior dealer network which increases customer satisfaction (and hence increased retention rates) or Federal Express increasing reliability (and hence most likely increase retention rates) or it is firms who recognize that if an industry under invests in acquisition marketing, the opportunity exists to determine how the firm's marketing strategy affects one or more of the critical measures in the fundamental equation. This therefore leads to a general principle regarding marketing strategy: Firms who are able to change baseline levels for critical measures greatly increase customer equity relative to competition.

Traditional marketing strategies such as unique products also fit this model. For the firm to be successful with a new product (or service), it must be able to acquire customers at a low enough costs so that future sales will pay for the initial investment. But more importantly, firms are betting on certain retention rates to justify the initial customer acquisition costs. Firms often do not make these assumptions explicit.

The literature on competitive entry can be restated using the fundamental equation. As markets mature, the firm is no longer able to acquire customers ($B_{i,a,t}$ increases) at the same cost it once did (more competitors targeting the same customers) or at the same rate ($\alpha_{i,t}$ decreases). If there are repeat purchases associated with the product/service, similar products/services may steal the firm's current customers resulting in declining retention rates ($\rho_{i,t}$). If the strategy is to sell more to the customers, competitors will be able to target these same customers, often with a lower priced product. The result is that add-on sales (S_{it}) may be below projections causing lower customer value.

By framing marketing strategy in terms of the parameters used in the fundamental equation of customer equity, we force firms to assess how sustainable their strategy is and where it is vulnerable. If the acquisition costs double when competitors enter, can the firm sustain a positive customer equity? What happens to retention rates as similar products enter the market? Can the firm develop a strategy that will allow it to compete when new entrants arrive? How will it manifest itself in terms of the customer equity measures? The fundamental equation serves as a framing device to make marketing strategy less qualitative and more rigorous.

LINKING SEGMENTING, TARGETING, AND THE FUNDAMENTAL EQUATION PARAMETERS

One of the primary marketing methods is segmenting and targeting the firm's customer base. How is this related to the fundamental equation? If one looks at the purpose of segmenting and targeting, it is to reduce the universe of potential customers to a smaller number but those that remain are much more likely to respond to the firm's offerings. Thus, segmenting and targeting affect N, the number of prospects, and α, the acquisition probability. By segmenting and targeting, N is reduced but α is increased which then leads to greater efficiency because total spending, NB_a, is reduced and the cost to acquire a customer, $NB_a/N\alpha$, is also reduced. Thus, segmenting and targeting are critical elements of efficient marketing.

Segmenting and targeting can also affect ρ, the retention rate. If the firm effectively segments and targets, it is more likely that the customer will respond favorably in the longer run to the firm's offerings causing retention rates to increase. In some circumstances, the acquisition rate may be lower but the retention rate higher because the target segments have greater expected loyalty.

Segmenting and targeting can also affect the sales level. Determining the market potential of customers and then segmenting and targeting has two effects: (1) higher sales per customer and (2) more efficient marketing. More efficient marketing evolves because if a segment has low sales potential, in order to generate a payout, it is necessary to lower the acquisition spending for the segment, $B_{i,a,t}$.

In summary, segmenting and targeting can easily be linked to the fundamental equation. The fundamental equation makes explicit the impact of segmenting and targeting. The firm can determine which segments are increasing and which are decreasing the customer value of the firm. The firm can then readjust its customer investments.

LINKING THE MARKETING MIX AND THE FUNDAMENTAL EQUATION'S PARAMETERS

One of the goals of this chapter is to show how the fundamental equation of customer equity is relevant to marketers by showing how to link the parameter values (A–R–A) to the marketing mix. This is the main purpose of this section which contains some mathematical equations to show explicitly how some of the links work. In all cases, the equations are translated into words.

Acquisition

In the fundamental equation, there are three variables that affect acquisition: (1) N (the number of prospects), (2) α (the acquisition probability), and (3) B_a (acquisition spending). There is very little research that focuses directly on acquisition but there are studies and conclusions that are applicable. They come primarily from the literature on new durable goods forecasting models and nondurable goods sales.[2] This literature focuses on the size of the market, how marketing mix affects trial, and the rate of product sales diffusion.

Number of Prospects. Generally the size of the market is determined by the type of products/services being offered and the industry of the firm. In some cases, firms try to find new markets for its existing products. Marketing variables also affect the number of prospects available to the firm. These include: the size of the market (industry and firm's products/services), the channel of distribution being used, the firm's targeting strategy and the prospective customers' awareness of the product or service being offered. Most of the marketing variables are controllable by the firm such as the channel being used, awareness which is determined by advertising and the targeting strategy.

Acquisition Probability (α). Marketing can have a significant effect on the acquisition probability[3] which is determined by many well-documented marketing variables. Pricing influences the value offered by the firm. Promotions are used to generate trial (acquisition). Advertising is used to position the product and to create expectations among prospective customers. Word-of-mouth can create awareness and expectations. The channel determines the availability of the product and the types of service outputs offered.[4] Finally the type of targeting and segmenting used affects the acquisition probability if the firm is able to find likely purchasers versus less targeted prospects.

A noncontrollable variable that affects the acquisition probability is the *industry effect*. Some industries have lower response rates than others. Direct marketing insurance historically has a very low response rate in the range of 0.2 percent but typical direct mail has a 1 percent to 2 percent response rate. This baseline acquisition probability can be affected by a change in the strategy of the firm but generally it is more dependent on the type of product/service being offered than the specific marketing being used. This leads to a maximum acquisition probability (k_a) for an industry.

Acquisition Spending per Prospect (B_a). This is an endogenously determined factor based on a number of considerations. This means B_a can be determined mathematically through optimizing the fundamental equation. Certain factors determine the efficiency of acquisition spending per prospect. We can characterize the relationship mathematically as

$$\alpha = k_a \left[1 - \exp(-\lambda B_a) \right]$$

where α = Acquisition probability
k_a = Maximum acquisition probability
B_a = Acquisition expenditure
λ = Rate at which acquisition expenditures affect the acquisition probability

Stated in words, there is a maximum acquisition probability determined for any given industry, k_a. The coefficient λ in the equation in front of B_a determines how great an impact acquisition spending has on the acquisition probability. The large λ, the higher the acquisition probability for a fixed spending level.

Marketing efficiency determines λ or how effective each dollar is in generating a higher acquisition probability. For example, targeting greatly affects the effectiveness per dollar spent per prospect since it will be much higher if the firm can identify high sales potential prospects. The types of communication vehicles also influence the marketing efficiency. Determining λ by expenditure type allows the firm to allocate its marketing budget more efficiently.

Mathematically, we decompose the prior equation into

$$\alpha = k_a \left[1 - \exp\left(-\sum_{j=1}^{J} \lambda_j B_{a,j} \right) \right]$$

where

a = Probability of acquisition
k_a = Maximum acquisition probability
λ_j = Efficiency of marketing category j
$B_{a,j}$ = Acquisition expenditure for category of expenditure j

In some industries, firms track relative effectiveness of different types of marketing vehicles (e.g., magazine publishers such as Time-Life). Internet firms must decide between banner ads and traditional media based on the cost effectiveness of generating customers.

Table 13.1 summarizes the relationships just discussed. It shows how each marketing mix element affects the acquisition probability (α), size of the market (N), and marketing efficiency (λ).

Table 13.1
Link between Acquisition and Marketing Mix

Marketing Mix Variable	Acquisition Probability (α)	Acquisition Efficiency (λ)	Size of Market (N)
Advertising			
Awareness	x		x
Positioning/expectations	x		x
Word of mouth	x		
Segmentation/targeting	x	x	x
Pricing	x		
Promotions	x		
Product quality			
Quality	x		
Type	x		x
Channel of distribution	x	x	x
Sales force	x	x	
Database marketing		x	

Retention

Within retention we will address the determinants of the retention rate, ρ, and the retention spending level, B_r.

Retention Rate.   The only key parameter of the fundamental equation for which there is a large published literature is the retention rate. Even then the literature is highly fragmented and confused. We will describe how different variables affect the retention rate.

Before proceeding, it is important to mention briefly that retention is different from loyalty. One commonly used definition of loyalty implies that a customer makes a significant percentage of his or her purchases from one firm or one brand. Retention does not require loyalty. A customer could make only 20 percent of his or her purchases each period from the same firm but is still retained. Retention focuses on continual purchasing from a given firm.

The primary focus of most of the retention literature is on how service quality (defined many different way) affects retention rates. It is generally believed that the higher the service quality, the higher the retention rate. Zeithemel describes the literature on this topic and concludes her article with the following statement: "While some progress has been made in the past 10 years in investigating service quality, profitability, and the economic worth of customers, much research remains to be done to validate this early evidence and to build a coherent and integrated body of knowledge."[5] Thus, while it is well accepted that service quality and customer satisfaction should be determinants of retention rates, there are many intervening factors that affect the links between retention rates and service quality and customer satisfaction.

Within the marketing mix, pricing is intriguing because it can actually be used to lower the retention rate but may lead to higher profitability. Blattberg and Thomas[6] show that in many cases it is optimal to charge your best customers more. This may seem counterintuitive but best customers often have much greater value for the product or service and hence are willing to pay more. The increased value is based on the knowledge that those firms or consumers that are long-term customers are often "locked-in" to the firm's technology and hence have higher switching costs.[7] Thus, the optimal price path may be to decrease retention rates while increasing profits.

Contrary to a large but confused literature which states promotions adversely affect retention rates,[8] promotional programs can be used to reward long-term customer buying. Frequent user programs can provide incentives to customers to be retained by rewarding continuous purchasing. A typical reward system uses last period's purchasing behavior to offer a reward in this period. If the firm or customer misses one period, it loses the benefits. Hence, it is advantageous to be a "retained" customer.

Advertising is believed to affect attitudes, which in turn affect retention. This link has been difficult to establish in the real-world. The difficulty is linking advertising spending to changes in attitudes to changes in retention. Without a specific relationship, it is difficult to determine if advertising pays out as a vehicle for increasing retention levels. This needs to become a research focus. However, typically advertising agencies do not use the fundamental equation to relate advertising spending to retention. In fairness it is extremely difficult to make this link explicit but it is crucial if one wants to determine the comparative economic payout of marketing mix variables on increasing customer equity.

Acquisition methods also affect retention. The source of the customer, the offer made and the expectations created all influence retention. If the firm over promises through its advertising to acquire a customer, then when the customer uses the product/service it is more likely to be disappointed. This then leads to lower retention rates.

Another common acquisition tactic is to use aggressive promotional pricing to acquire a customer. The lower the promoted price, the more "price shoppers" that are acquired. This then leads to lower retention rates. While this may bother those that believe high retention rates are good, it may be optimal for the firm to acquire more "triers" and then let those who do not find the product/service provides enough value at the regular price defect. This leads to an important rule: The firm should not try to maximize retention rates but rather maximize customer equity. High retention rates may not be advantageous without understanding all of the trade-offs.[9]

Two other marketing mix variables need to be mentioned: product quality and channels of distribution. Obviously, product quality is viewed as one of the major determinants of retention. However, it is also important to recognize, price also affects retention and if the firm produces a higher quality product but has to charge a higher price, this may not lead to higher retention. Value is the appropriate metric but it is difficult to link the quality of the product to its value. Techniques such as conjoint analysis may help us understand this trade-off and then be linked to retention rates.

Channels of distribution also affect retention rates because they provide availability of the product and service outputs which assist customers/

end-users. These service outputs (e.g., customer service, supplying efficient quantities of the product) as mentioned earlier are very important and if a poor channel partner is chosen, it can negatively affect retention rates. Little research exists linking channel decisions to retention rates, yet it is very important to develop these links.

The final factor affecting retention rates which is emerging as very important is customer knowledge. Customer knowledge, called by some customer intimacy,[10] can greatly affect retention rates as well as add-on selling. By having an understanding of the customer's buying patterns, needs, and problems, the firm can better service the customer and provide the "right product/service to the right customer." Customer databases improve the firm's ability to match customer needs.

Retention Spending per Customer.   Generally, the amount spent on retention is determined by similar variables to those computed for acquisition spending. It is an endogenously determined variable which means that given retention rates and other variables, one can determine the optimal retention spending.[11]

One can represent the impact of customer spending on retention rates by the following equation:

$$\rho_{i,t} = k_r \left[1 - \exp\left(-\gamma B_{i,r,t} \right) \right]$$

where

$\quad$ exp $=$ Universal constant 2.7
$\quad \rho_{i,t}$ $=$ Retention probability
$\quad k_r$ $=$ Maximum retention reached
$\quad B_{i,r,t}$ $=$ Retention spending level for segment i at time t
$\quad \gamma$ $=$ Rate at which retention spending affects the retention rate

Gamma (γ) represents the effectiveness of the retention expenditure level $B_{i,r,t}$ on the retention rate. The higher the value of γ, the faster ρ reaches the value of k_r. Much of what is written about in database marketing is designed to increase the value of γ. For example, the efficiency of the marketing system, the efficiency to service customers, advertising effectiveness and the ability to reach customers efficiently through the use of databases all affect the magnitude of γ.

The maximum retention, k_r, can be industry specific and represents the maximum retention rate the firm can reach. For certain industries, the

Table 13.2
Link between Retention and Marketing Mix

Marketing Mix Variable	Retention Rate (ρ)	Retention Spending (B_r)	Retention Efficiency (γ)
Advertising			
Awareness		x	
Positioning	x		
Word of mouth	x	x	x
Segmentation/targeting	x	x	x
Pricing/value	x		
Promotions	x		
Product quality			
Quality vs. expectations	x		
Type		x	
Channel of distribution		x	x
Sales force		x	x
Database marketing	x	x	x

maximum may be relatively low (e.g., used cars) and for others it can be very high (e.g., traditional banking).

Table 13.2 shows the relationship between elements of the marketing mix and the retention rate (ρ) and the efficiency of retention marketing (γ). These links are based on the existing literature where possible. However, there is little quantification of these links as has been discussed.

Add-On Selling

Very little has been written in marketing about add-on selling but many of the concepts are well known. We will divide add-on selling into three parts: (1) efficiency of add-on selling, (2) number of add-on selling offers given to existing customers, and (3) the response rate to new offers. Mathematically,

$$S_{i,t} = \sum_{j=1}^{J_{i,t}} O_{i,j,t}\, r_{i,j,t}$$

$$B_{i,AO,t} = \sum_{j=1}^{J_{i,t}} O_{i,j,t}\, C_{i,j,t}$$

where

$B_{i,AO,t}$ = Total expenditure on add-on selling to segment i at time t

$O_{i,j,t}$ = Offer j made to segment i at time t

$r_{i,j,t}$ = Response rate to offer j made to segment i at time t

$C_{i,j,t}$ = Cost of making offer j to segment i at time t

$J_{i,t}$ = Total number of offers made at time t to segment i

Add-On Selling Expenditures ($B_{AO,i,t}$). The efficiency of add-on selling is based on how efficiently the firm can make offers to its customers. The easier it is to make add-on selling offers, the greater the number of offers. Credit card companies use their monthly statement mailings to customers to make offers. The incremental cost of making an offer is very low. Firms with regular communications with customers generally have low incremental cost of add-on selling. Other firms who may not communicate often with the customer (e.g., a durable good manufacturer who does not provide service) may have infrequent communications. This increases the cost of communicating add-on selling offers.

Number of Add-On Selling Offers ($J_{i,t}$). The other factor that affects the number of offers is the breadth of the firm's product/service offerings. Those firms with a broad product line or who have the capability of adding to the product line can make more offers to customers. For those firms that have a low cost of communicating offers to customers, broadening the product line becomes very appealing, even if the firm does not own the product or service. Sears is an ideal example because they have "lease" departments which may even be named Sears "something" (e.g., driving school) to sell to their installed customer base.

Response Rate to Offers ($r_{i,j,t}$). The response rate to an offer is an important element of the add-on selling parameter. Factors that affect the response rate include price of the item or service, overall satisfaction with the firm, promotion, advertising, affinity with the firm, and number of prior purchases. Most are obvious, but affinity with the firm needs some discussion.

Affinity is a combination of the relationship the customer has with the firm and the expertise the customer believes the firm possesses. Can a clothing cataloguer sell Jaguar cars? The customer may have a strong relationship with the cataloguer but does not believe the firm has any expertise in car sales or maintenance. Relationship is also important because if

Table 13.3
Linking Add-On Selling and Marketing Mix

Marketing Mix Variable	Add-On Selling Expenditure (B)	Number of Offers (J)	Response Rate per Offer (r)
Advertising			
Awareness			
Affinity		x	x
Word of mouth			x
Segmentation/targeting	x	x	x
Pricing			x
Promotions			x
Product quality			x
Quality			x
Type	x	x	
Channel of distribution	x		x
Sales force			x
Database marketing	x	x	x

the customer does not have a relationship, he or she is less interested in purchasing from the firm and has a lower affinity with the firm.

Number of prior purchases is also an important indicator of future behavior. If the customer has purchased several times from the firm, it is more likely that the customer will make another purchase. This follows from discussions of RFM which shows that customers who have made more past purchases are more likely to make another purchase.[12]

Table 13.3 summarizes the effect of the marketing mix on add-on selling variables, total expenditures (B_{AO}), the number of offers (J) and the response rate (r). Because of the lack of literature in this area, we have relied upon direct marketing experience to assess how different marketing mix elements affect add-on selling.

ANALYZING THE EFFECTIVENESS OF THE MARKETING MIX

Historically, the primary metrics used to assess the firm's position were sales and profits. By using the fundamental equation to maximize customer equity, it forces the firm to measure and analyze other metrics at the segment level. Based on the prior section, it becomes fairly clear what types of metrics need to be developed. We will divide these into two types: (1) statistics computed from traditional measurement and (2) statistical model parameter estimates.

The obvious measures are acquisition probabilities and retention rates by segment and response rates to add-on selling offers. Other measures include the cost of acquiring a customer, the size of the market and market potential by segment, and customer satisfaction by segment. These and other measures are summarized in Table 13.4.

The statistical model measures are more complex but not necessarily less important. The two that are critical in understanding the relationship between acquisition spending and acquisition probability as well as retention spending and retention rates are based on statistical models. These are acquisition efficiency (λ) and retention spending efficiency (γ). To estimate these parameters one needs to use a statistical model based on the two equations given earlier that relate spending to acquisition and retention.

$$\alpha_{i,t} = k_a\left[1 - \exp\left(-\sum_{j=1}^{J}\lambda_j B_{a,i,j,t}\right)\right]$$

$$\rho_{i,t} = k_r\left[1 - \exp\left(-\gamma B_{i,r,t}\right)\right]$$

Table 13.4
Sample of Metrics Generated by Fundamental Equation

Acquisition	Retention	Add-On Selling
Acquisition probability (α)	Retention rate (ρ)	Response to offers (r)
Acquisition marketing efficiency (λ)	Retention marketing efficiency (γ)	Promotional responsiveness
Response to pricing	Customer expectations versus product/service delivery	Affinity with the firm
Response to promotions	Advertising effectiveness in maintaining retention	Cross-buying behavior
Awareness	Customer service scores	Profitability of offers
Consumer expectations regarding product/service quality	Price elasticities	Total add-on selling per customer
Cost of acquiring a customer	Promotional effectiveness	
	Profit of retained customer	
	Cost of retention marketing	

By determining λ and γ, the firm is able to evaluate the efficiency of their marketing spending. While many academics and practitioners discuss the need for this, it is unlikely that anyone has related marketing efficiency to retention rates and acquisition probabilities. We believe that this will become an important part of marketing academic research in the next several years.

SUMMARY

This chapter provides a model-based approach to valuing, analyzing and managing the marketing function using customer equity principles. Its purpose is to provide what we called the fundamental equation of customer equity and then show how the fundamental equation focuses marketers on how the elements of the marketing mix affect the long-term value of the firm's customer base (customer equity). By doing so, we believe this will shift the goals of marketing from sales and short-term output measures to new measures related to acquisition, retention and add-on selling.

Many of the elements of marketing can be linked through the fundamental equation. Specifically, marketing strategy affects the levels of key parameters such as the maximum acquisition probability and the maximum retention rate for an industry. Segmenting and targeting are designed to increase response rates and to improve marketing efficiency, both captured in the equation. In addition, several hypothesized relationships are given demonstrating how the marketing mix affects the critical parameters of the fundamental equation. This paper also identifies the links between marketing mix variables and the model parameters. Additionally, it specifies measures that can be used to evaluate marketing efficiency and effectiveness.

By having a quantitative model, which serves as the basis for customer marketing, some of the qualitative and often incorrect concepts offered into customer relationship marketing can be assessed to determine their validity. Concepts such as maximizing customer retention which seems to be commonly believed but does not meet the standards of economic theory need to be analyzed through a more rigorous filter. The fundamental equation of customer equity provides that more rigorous filter which allows marketing academics and practitioners to develop a greater understanding of how customer equity can be maximized.

Notes

1. Frederick E. Reichheld, *The Loyalty Effect* (Boston: Harvard Business Press, 1996); and Don Peppers and Martha Rodgers, *The One to One Future: Building Relationships One Customer at a Time* (New York: Doubleday, 1993).

2. Robert C. Blattberg and John Golanty, "TRACKER: An Early Test Market Forecasting and Diagnostic Model for New Product Planning," *Journal of Marketing Research* (May 1978); and Gary L. Lilien, Philip Kotler, and K. Sridhar Moorthy, *Marketing Models* (Englewood Cliffs, NJ: Prentice Hall, 1992); and Vijan Mahajan, Eitan Muller, and Frank Bass, "New Product Diffusion Models," in *Handbooks in Operations Research and Management Science—Marketing,* Vol. 5, eds. J. Eliashberg and G.L. Lilien (Amsterdam: North-Holland, 1993), pp. 349–408.

3. See note 2, Mahajan, Muller, and Bass.

4. Louis W. Stern, Adel I. El-Ansary, and Anne T. Coughlan, *Marketing Channels,* 5th ed. (Englewood Cliff, NJ: Prentice Hall, 1996), pp. 16–19.

5. Valerie Zeithaml, "Service Quality, Profitability and the Economic Worth of Customers: What We Know and What We Need to Learn," *Academy of Marketing Science* (winter 2000), pp. 67–85.

6. Robert C. Blattberg and Jacquelyn Thomas, "Pricing Based on Customer Relationships," working paper (1999).

7. Carl Shapiro and Hal R. Varian, *Information Rules* (Boston: Harvard Business School Press, 1999).

8. Robert C. Blattberg and Scott Neslin, *Sales Promotions* (Englewood-Cliffs, NJ: Prentice Hall, 1990).

9. Robert C. Blattberg and John Deighton, "Manage Marketing by the Customer Equity Test," *Harvard Business Review* (July/August 1996), pp. 136–144.

10. Michael Treacy and Frederik D. Wiersema, *The Discipline of Market Leaders: Choose Your Customers, Narrow Your Focus, Dominate Your Market* (New York: Perseus, 1997).

11. See note 9.

12. Arthur M. Hughes, *The Complete Database Marketer* (Chicago: Probus Publishing Company, 1991).

CHAPTER 14

SERVICES MARKETING AND CUSTOMER SERVICE

DAWN IACOBUCCI

The premises of this chapter are simple: (1) services are important, and (2) services differ from goods, and these differences have implications for the marketing and management of services. Occasionally, you may find a marketing manager who still protests that "marketing is marketing," that is, the marketing concepts applicable in manufactured goods arenas (e.g., consumer packaged goods, durables, and automobiles) are directly transferable to service sectors. At a sufficiently high level of abstraction, perhaps this is so; if one defines marketing as "understanding the needs of one's customers and trying to deliver on those needs," then certainly marketers of goods and services seek the same goals. Nevertheless, in this chapter, we shall see that services are conceptually different from goods along several key dimensions. Furthermore, even if there were few conceptual differences, the tactical differences between goods and services in executing sound marketing practices are immense. The literature in marketing on services has become extensive, as scholars delineate more finely these strategic and tactical distinctions.[1]

The term *service* is used broadly in this chapter, to cover service industries (e.g., from health care and consulting to fast-food restaurants), as well as in the colloquial use of the term, for example, "I got good service," which reflects the quality of the interactions between customers and an organization's frontline service personnel—the so-called "moments of truth." (The contexts will make the uses of the term clear.) A wide net is also cast to include many industries: those that might be said to be the "purer" service sectors (e.g., hotels, lawyers, investments counselors), as well as those "mixed" industries in which the core transaction may be the purchase of a good in conjunction with a large service component (e.g., retail outlets, restaurants, automobile dealerships, realtors or mortgage brokers).

Let us begin. Remember: Services are important, and services are different.

SERVICES ARE IMPORTANT

Economic statistics attribute at least two-thirds of the global economy to services sectors.[2] Moreover, service sectors thrive in exporting,[3] moderate inflation,[4] and provide vast employment.[5] That our economy is comprised increasingly of services is being reflected in current efforts to modify Standard Industrial Classification (SIC) codes.[6] For example, new categories include those for information processing (publishing, software, motion pictures, broadcasting, telecommunications); arts, entertainment, and recreation (performing arts, spectator sports, producers and agents, museums, amusement parks, casinos); professional, scientific, and technical services (legal, accounting, management consulting, computer-system design, advertising, marketing research, polling); and health care and social assistance (health care, nursing homes, individual and family assistance, child care).

Competition is intensifying in many industries due to factors such as deregulation (e.g., in the domestic transportation or telecommunications markets, and in many markets abroad), industrial restructuring (e.g., in the pharmaceuticals industry), or technology (e.g., the creation of consumer databases or the provision of interactivity or self-service automation).[7] Accordingly, in an attempt to create distinct advantage, managers often seek to provide added value to customers and enhance their corporate competitive advantage by offering better customer service. The enhancement of customer service is perpetual, because initial competitive advantages are often easily met, turning the previous distinction into a commodity-like attribute of the service encounter, thereby also raising the expectations of the ever-demanding customer. Thus, services comprise a substantial market presence and are likely to continue to do so.

SERVICES ARE DIFFERENT

To try to understand how to execute superior customer service, we can begin by examining some of the fundamental characteristics of services. Services and goods have some conceptual differences and numerous tactical differences that must be considered in designing their optimal marketing and management. Services tend to be (1) intangible, (2) produced and consumed simultaneously, and (3) heterogeneous. Each of these qualities has implications for the marketing and management of customer service.

Services Are Intangible

The service encounter is often described as an interactive performance: A corporate service provider produces an experiential process in which the consumer and frontline service personnel engage in a communicative exchange through which each party obtains from the other some essence of value. The customer exits the exchange having been processed in some manner that may be tangibly detectable (e.g., having one's hair cut) or not (e.g., having one's taxes figured). The performance element of services has been elaborated in a drama metaphor (e.g., the frontline service providers considered as cast members, the customers as audience, the physical environment as scenery and props).[8] The metaphor is used to pose questions such as, "does the customer observe a smooth performance on stage" and "what elements in the service operations must be in place behind-the-scenes to provide a smooth on-stage performance."

Advertising. The intangibility of services has a number of managerial implications. For example, it has been suggested that advertisements for services should provide symbols, or tangible cues, as concrete signals of the service's abstract attributes. The insurance industry has long excelled at invoking imagery through its use of tangible symbols in its advertising, surely in part due to the fact that they provide one of the more intangible services around. For example, symbols suggest that customers imagine the comfort of being in All State's hands, there is solidity on Prudential's rock, State Farm is neighborly, and Travelers' umbrella protects us from the elements. Without the helpful imagery, our only concrete thought about our insurance agent is that they send us bills and we send them checks. The advertisements remind us why we engage in this transaction—that the party with whom we interact minimizes our risks.

Customer Satisfaction. In addition to implications for advertising, the subjectivity and intangibility of services also has an effect on customers' evaluative judgments. Whereas many aspects of the quality of a produced good can be measured somewhat objectively, service quality and customer satisfaction in services are defined by consumers through their subjective, evaluative assessment of the service experience. These models posit the customer evaluations as a comparison of the encounter experience to one's prior expectations. Specifically, if one's experience exceeds one's expectations, the models predict satisfaction. These models are the source of the industry movements toward such claims as "we want to exceed our customers' expectations," or even the over-puffed exclamations like "we don't want to just satisfy our customers, we want to delight them." Expectations are thought to be developed through the communications of the firm (e.g., advertisements, other customers via word-of-mouth, or the customer's own past experience with the focal or competitor firms). Expectations are highly dynamic, monotonically increasing, usually rapidly, as the ever-demanding customer questions the firm, "What have you done for me lately?"

Satisfaction and quality are judged in both a gestalt, overall sense, as well as in an attribute-by-attribute analytical sense. While an overall satisfaction measure gives a crude index of customer perception, the attribute-level quality indicators are those that can provide useful diagnostics. The detail allows for a pragmatic utility in assessing the financial effectiveness of corporate initiatives intended to enhance customer service and satisfaction. Certain actions or modifications of the service delivery system will please customers more than others, so the challenge becomes one of identifying those valued qualities—those that drive repeat purchase most directly and therefore of greatest priority. Furthermore, it is important to tie indicators of satisfaction to firm-level financial performance measures,[9] to demonstrate that the seemingly simple and mundane human interaction involved in service encounters (the frontline's competence and empathy) indeed impacts the corporate bottom line, albeit somewhat indirectly.

Core versus Supplementals.   An organization that provides service, either as its central provision or in a value-added capacity in a bundle of attributes included in a customer's purchase of some good, may find it useful to distinguish those elements of the service purchase experience that are "core" from those that are "supplemental." The core of a purchase is that which forms the business identity ("we do brakes on cars," "we're a photocopy shop," etc.). The supplemental services are the components of the service delivery system that are intended to facilitate and enhance the customer's experience ("we'll also check the status of your automotive fluids;" "we also fax, send overnight express packages, and can make overhead slides"). Initially the supplemental services are introduced as competitive advantages, distinct features that the competition does not offer. Often, as with these examples, the supplemental services are easily met, so that soon all competitors have enriched their offerings to meet the requirements in the marketplace. The new array of services becomes commoditylike, and each firm must seek additional unique, supplemental services to begin the distinguishing process again. Continual improvement efforts like these also contribute to the customer's ever-increasing expectations.

The core-supplemental distinction also has implications for customer satisfaction. The core service of an airline is transportation from one city to another, and supplemental services include features such as: frequent flyer accounts, conveniently located hubs, movies and meals on board, and so on. Rarely will customers state explicitly that they seek "safety," though presumably of course they do. Safe arrival is a critical attribute of the core, and one that is assumed to be true. There should not be variance among competitors on core attributes. Competitive distinctions can occur on the value-added services. Hence, achieving good quality on the core service does not enhance customer satisfaction—good quality on attributes like safety is a "given." Poor service on core attributes can certainly drive customer dissatisfaction however (as reactions to extended delays or near-miss accidents can attest). In contrast, variability on supplemental services can drive customer satisfaction or dissatisfaction (hence positive customer affect to flight attendants' humor on Southwest, for example).

As another example of the core-supplemental distinction on satisfaction, consider hospitals in the health care system, an industry beginning to discover customer satisfaction surveys. Summary statistics on such surveys can be grim, and also eye-opening. More than one hospital administrator has bemoaned, "They judge us on the little things!" That is, a hospital may pride itself on recruiting the best medical talent and investing huge expenditures into current technological equipment, yet the patient is not equipped to judge such things, and further, would expect such core elements to be strong. Instead, the patient complains that the hospital room's television is too loud, or that the dinner included green jello again. These reactions make sense, if customer competencies allow for the evaluation of the supplementals and not the core, and given the usual lack of variability on the core quality with greater variability on the quality of the supplementals, which in turn should give the manager some license in taking customer satisfaction survey results with a grain of salt.

Value.   Finally, academics are finding it increasingly apparent that neither evaluations of quality nor satisfaction impact repeat purchasing and loyalty as much as customer perceptions of value. Value is typically defined as some trade-off comparison between quality or satisfaction against price, including both economic and psychological prices, such as search and purchase efforts. Stronger customer service is expected when paying higher prices, and poorer customer service may be tolerated when paying lower rates: customers value value!

Services Are Simultaneously Produced and Consumed

Goods are largely produced out of the line of vision of the customer. The manufacturing plant and its workers and distributors have no immediate impact on customer satisfaction. The goods are stored, shipped, priced, and shelved. By comparison, the consumer is often involved in the co-creation of a service, so the production and consumption of services usually requires the customer's presence. As a result, the services marketing manager must consider the physical environment of the service shop (that "front stage" in the drama metaphor), as well as the frontline employees who help create the string of moments-of-truth, each of which plays a small but potentially significant role in the customer's formation of an evaluative judgment. One's office provides tangible cues about the quality of service provision (e.g., an attorney's office can imply that the legal mind is messy and disorganized or that the lawyer is highly successful and enjoys the luxury of much overhead). Aesthetics serve as important cues.

Perishability.   The simultaneity of production and consumption also drives the aspect of services that they are perishable: the flight that lifts off with empty seats can never retrieve those seats for future use; the professional's time spent on seasonal projects must also manage supply and demand imbalances. The closest approximation services managers have to inventories is queuing, but this solution is not often desirable to customers. Laundry detergent, athletic shoes, and cars don't seem to mind being stored in inventory warehouses, but people do.

In some service sectors, technology is assisting in yield management. The old retail adage that "location, location, location" is important, spoke most directly to site access, and indeed for services beyond retail, access is important. However, access also implies convenience of hours open for conducting business. Some consumer services, such as banking, are facilitating access through electronic means that can help resolve issues of both physical access (one's personal computer) and time availability (2 A.M.). Even so, such vehicles must also be considered for the impression they offer; most software and Web pages stand room for improvement for both ease of use and aesthetic quality.

Employees. Another management challenge resulting from the customer being involved in co-creation of the service is the interaction between the customer and members of the frontline staff. A surly overseer of a manufacturing chemical vat is irrelevant to the ultimate customer's experience, but a surly physician prescribing, or pharmacist filling, or cashier charging for medications impacts the customer experience directly.

Services is perhaps the key opportunity in marketing to discuss the importance of employees and their empowerment. Increasingly researchers are finding empirical support for the concept that employee satisfaction and customer satisfaction are interrelated.[10] Thus, a key to customer retention is keeping one's employees satisfied. Specifically, if the frontline jobs are well-designed, and management is selective in hiring, and generous in training and compensation, their employees will be capable and loyal. Their lower turnover contributes to profitability (lesser resources need be devoted to additional hiring and training) and to customer satisfaction, due to their extended experience and true behaviors of empowerment. In turn, with more knowledgeable frontline personnel, customer satisfaction should rise. There should be reduced service failures and enhanced opportunities for customization. Customer retention also clearly contributes to profitability, through repeat purchasing, positive word-of-mouth, lesser marketing resources directed toward new customer acquisition. In addition, customer satisfaction reciprocally contributes to employee satisfaction—working with happy customers is a happier employment experience. Thus, satisfaction begins in-house.

The fact that a large component of services is interpersonal, between the customer and service provider, contributes to the challenge of managing and marketing services. Even competent, well-intended frontline employees can have moments of poor judgment. The frontline serves as an intermediary in the relationship that the company wishes to forge with its customers. Indeed, a large complaint and source of "burn-out" of frontline employees is the role conflict they frequently experience—wishing to please the customer but having to follow bureaucratic rules, or wishing to do a good job but wanting the customers to go away.

Part of a frontline person being "professional" is to play the role of the helpful service provider, regardless of that person's momentary state. The frontline is expected to function in the "role" of a caring, competent service provider—doing so can involve immense emotional labor, given that the human functioning in the role can be experiencing conflict or exhaustion or limited ability to respond, given poor training or constrained (un)empowerment.

Service Encounters Are Heterogeneous

The fact that services are co-created by two dynamic and fallible humans also leads to services being described as heterogeneous. Service provision varies across customers and across frontline employees at multisite or even the same-site location. Different employees have different skills and attitudes, and different customers have different needs. Like cholesterol, there is good and bad heterogeneity. Good heterogeneity is the opportunity in the interactive service encounter to tailor the service provided to suit a customer's unique needs. Bad heterogeneity is error.

Just as heterogeneity, or variance, in the market is considered financial risk, variability known to be inherent in services also makes them perceived as riskier purchases. One's computer may be manufactured with Six-Sigma precision, but one's sushi will never be prepared identically.

Another source of variability in services is attempts to offer one's services at multiple site locations. Franchising is the typical format of distributing service delivery systems, and some franchise systems excel at maintaining consistency across their multisite operations. However, even with the same basic service operations in place, much of the execution is fundamentally driven by the frontline service providers, their immediate supervisors, and the leadership overseeing the entire service shop—all of these key components involve personnel, and heterogeneity in the service experience can result.

Service Guarantees. A marketing tool gaining some momentum among the better providers in many industries is the service guarantee. This marketing instrument serves to reduce the perceptions of the riskiness of the purchase, and it serves as a cue to the quality of the service to be expected. After all, the customer reasons, how could a firm offer a guarantee unless they are good enough and confident that they will not require frequent redemption. It also serves as a very clear tool for the frontline employees regarding what errors are intolerable, and what redress is expected by disgruntled customers—the guarantee provides explicit empowerment.

As we saw in the core-supplemental discussion, many value-added aspects of customer service are easily met by competitors, and as these additional services diffuse throughout the industry, they no longer serve as points of competitive distinction, but rather customers see them as commodities. The expectation bars raise, and customers will demand even more. On the surface, service guarantees would seem to be easily met as well. The point of distinction, however, is that they are less easily sustained. A "me-too" provider whose quality does not match the leader cannot afford to offer a competitive guarantee.

Guarantees also provide a clear means of feedback to the company. In the vast majority of instances, a customer receiving poor service simply complains to friends, family, and co-workers, but corporate headquarters will never learn of the problem, nor pursue the opportunity for design modifications that will prevent future errors. But a service guarantee can become a very useful diagnostic tool in identifying the kinks in the service delivery flow.

Service Recovery.   Occasionally, despite a provider's best efforts, the service exchange can go truly wrong—heterogeneity of the worst sort, and effective service recovery is mandatory. "Be empathetic, Compensate, Plus One," currently seems to be the collective wisdom regarding service recovery, meaning: (1) be sure to have a caring and understanding attitude that validates the customer's complaint and ensuing situation; (2) fix the problem; and (3) (over)compensate for the mistake by doing one thing beyond what the customer paid for. It is somewhat embarrassing to admit that we marketing academics cannot offer more substantial advice on the topic of service recovery. This "wisdom" seems to reduce to the universal moral exhortation: do unto others . . . still, if observed, customer service would indeed improve given that the majority of customer complaints in services industries do not address the failure of the core service, nor its price, but rather the complaints focus on the (in)competence and (poor) attitude of the frontline personality.

CONCLUSION

The key principle in services marketing and management is to remember that "people," both the customers and the service providers, are much more intricately involved in the marketplace exchange than for the relatively simpler purchase of most goods. Keeping in mind this customer-service provider dyad helps the marketing manager gain empathy for the customer experience, hopefully with the goal of designing service delivery systems that provide opportunities for inherently high-quality interactions, and that accommodate modifications, either for still higher quality customization requests, or in recovery to reattain high-quality provision.

Services are more interesting and more challenging than goods in large part due to the interpersonal element of the encounter. I frequently hear marketing managers exclaim that they think marketing services is more difficult than marketing goods. It seems to be of some consolation to them when I confirm: It is! But we services marketers are not fainthearted.

Notes

1. Dawn Iacobucci, "Services: What Do We Know and Where Shall We Go? A View from Marketing," in *Advances in Services Marketing and Management: Research and Practice,* vol. 7, eds. Teresa A. Swartz, David E. Bowen, and Stephen W. Brown (Greenwich, CT: JAI Press, 1998), pp. 1–96; and Teresa A. Swartz and Dawn Iacobucci, eds., *Handbook of Services Marketing and Management* (Thousand Oaks, CA: Sage, 2000).

2. Ronald Henkoff, "Service is Everybody's Business," *Fortune* (June 27, 1994), p. 48; Myron Magnet, "Good News for the Service Economy," *Fortune* (May 3, 1993), p. 46; and Michael J. Mandel, "Financial Services: The Silent Engine," *Business Week* (December 21, 1998), pp. 76–77.

3. Ralph T. King, Jr., "U.S. Service Exports Growing Rapidly," *Wall Street Journal* (April 21, 1993), p. 1.

4. Michael J. Mandel, "Whodunnit to Inflation," *Business Week* (May 12, 1997), pp. 36–38.

5. Mike McNamee and Joann Muller, "A Tale of Two Job Markets," *Business Week* (December 21, 1998), pp. 38–39.

6. The SIC codes are being replaced with the North American Industrial Classification System (NAICS) codes. See Michael J. Mandel, "Vital Statistics for the Real-Life Economy," *Business Week* (December 29, 1997), p. 42.

7. Christopher H. Lovelock, *Services Marketing* 3rd ed. (Upper Saddle River, NJ: Prentice Hall, 1996).

8. John F. Sherry, Jr., ed., *Servicescapes: The Concept of Place in Contemporary Markets* (Lincolnwood, IL: NTC Business Books, 1998).

9. Roland T. Rust, Anthony J. Zahorik, and Timothy L. Keiningham, *Service Marketing* (New York: Harper Collins, 1996).

10. Leonard A. Schlesinger and James L. Heskett, "Breaking the Cycle of Failure in Services," *Sloan Management Review,* vol. 32 (spring 1991), pp. 17–28.

CHAPTER 15

MANAGING MARKET OFFERINGS IN BUSINESS MARKETS

JAMES C. ANDERSON, GREGORY S. CARPENTER,
and JAMES A. NARUS

Managing market offerings is the process of putting products, services, programs, and systems together in ways that create the greatest value for targeted market segments and customer firms. The challenge for business market managers is to construct offerings that uniquely leverage a business' resources to provide this value. The process involves both responsively meeting targeted segment and customer requirements, and managing their expectations of a supplier.

What exactly do we mean by market offering? To better understand this, we begin by unraveling what in the past has been called a product offering, viewing it in several layers.[1] The *core product* is simply the fundamental, functional performance a generic product provides that solves a customer's basic problem. For example, the core product for an agricultural herbicide would be a specific chemical compound that has the ability to control particular broadleaf and grassy weeds. The *minimally augmented product* adds to this core product the least amount or number of services, programs, or systems that customers consider absolutely essential for doing business with *any* supplier. Examples of these might include payment terms, delivery, and customer service for problems with the core product.

The *augmented product* adds to the core product those services, programs, and systems a supplier offers to meet a broader set of customer requirements and preferences, or to exceed the customer's expectations in ways that add value to or reduce cost in what the customer does. Examples of augmenting services, programs, and systems offered in business markets appear in Table 15.1. Finally, a *potential product* goes beyond the augmented product to encompass any imaginable product change or

Table 15.1
Examples of Augmenting Services, Programs, and Systems

Services	
Corrective/remedial:	Problem solving, trouble shooting, operations assistance
Fulfillment:	Availability assurance, order quantity, logistics, delivery, installation, maintenance, training, returns, warranty
Programs	
Economic:	Deals, terms, conditions, freight, co-op allowances, rebates/bonuses, risk-sharing agreements, gain-sharing agreements
Relationship:	Advice and consulting, specification, co-design, and co-development, process engineering, process redesign, cost reduction, responsiveness to information requests, joint marketing research, co-promotions, communication, partnering, and participation in other customer programs
Systems	
Linking:	Online customer support, shared material resource planning (MRP), information exchange (EDI)
Efficacy:	Internet and Extranet ordering and payment, online product technical support and expert systems, logistics management systems

service, program, or system a supplier might create to add value or reduce cost in ways that sets the product apart from others. As these potential additions are realized, they become a part of the augmented product. For example, an agrichemical supplier and dealer might consider offering jointly a "rain guarantee," whereby if the dealer applies the supplier's herbicide to the grower's fields and unexpected rain washes it away, the dealer will reapply the herbicide at no charge.

We prefer *market offering* to the more often used *product offering* as a way to capture these layers of meaning for three reasons. First, the core product may not be a concrete, palpable "thing" but instead may be a service, such as management consulting or building maintenance. "Market" accommodates either equally well. Second, even when the core product *is* a concrete and tangible "thing," use of market offering emphasizes that what a supplier brings to the market is a package comprised of a core product or service *and* a set of augmenting services, programs, and systems. The package as a whole, not simply the core product, must create value for the customer, and in a number of instances, the augmenting services, programs, and systems provide the predominant part of the value over competitors' offerings. Finally, "market" reinforces an outward-focused perspective on what the supplier is trying to accomplish in the marketplace, as contrasted with "product," which can promote an inward-looking or technology-driven perspective.

In this chapter, we discuss constructing and managing market offerings. We first consider how firms can gain an accurate understanding of the extent to which their market offerings have become commodities, and then suggest some ways for rebuilding differentiation into these offerings. After this, we present our approach to managing market offerings, which we call *flexible market offerings*. We conclude with implementation considerations for putting flexible market offerings into practice.[2]

REBUILDING COMMODITY OFFERINGS INTO DIFFERENTIATED OFFERINGS

The widespread implementation of quality management in production and the greater availability of comparable alternatives from international sources have resulted in a narrowing of perceived differences among suppliers' offerings in the minds of customers. In many business markets, customers make their purchase decisions for an increasing amount of business based solely on price—the definition of a commodity. These customers pressure suppliers to reduce their prices and provide additional price discounts.[3] As a result, suppliers in industry after industry find that although their sales revenues are growing, it is often at the expense of profitability.

What can suppliers do to forestall or reverse this trend toward commoditization? In this section, we discuss ways for suppliers to rebuild their market offerings into differentiated offerings that customers value more than those of competitors. We then discuss what suppliers might seek as an equitable return for providing this superior value. The initial step for suppliers to take is to understand the true extent of commoditization for their offerings, which also uncovers some possibilities for differentiation.

Understanding the True Extent of Commoditization

Often, suppliers conclude, "We're in a commodity business," because they are thinking narrowly about the core product or service. That is, the personal computer, hospital supplies, or letter-of-credit that the customer purchases may be nearly or exactly the same across suppliers. But the market offerings that customers purchase typically are more than simply the core product or service. These market offerings contain supplementary services, programs, and systems that enhance the value of the core product (or service) and that provide additional value to customers.

Thus, before concluding they are in a commodity business, suppliers need to carefully examine exactly what differences there are between their offerings and those of competitors, drawing on market and internal data. Specifically, they should gain estimates of the value that customers receive, validate their market pricing, and gain estimates of their firm's share of their customers' business.

Gain Estimates of the Value Customers Receive.   Although much attention in recent years has been given to value and its provision to customers, remarkably few firms have the knowledge and capability to assess value in practice. What exactly do we mean by value? *Value* is the worth in monetary terms of the technical, economic, service, and social benefits a customer firm receives in exchange for the price it pays. Considerations of value take place within some context. Typically, this is a comparison of the value of one supplier's offering relative to what the customer is using presently or the next-best-alternative supplier's offering.[4]

Thus, value is the worth in monetary terms of all that a market offering provides to a customer firm. To gain an estimate of the value that a customer receives, the supplier gathers comprehensive and elemental data on how its offering adds value or reduces costs in the customer's application. At the same time, suppliers should investigate what potential changes in their market offerings would be worth to customers. Although suppliers are more conversant with the technical and economic benefits of their offerings, they should not neglect service and social benefits, which can be significant sources of value.

Consider, for example, safety glasses (protective eyewear). Safety glasses provide the technical benefit of protecting workers' eyes from infrared and ultraviolet light, and foreign substances such as chemicals. They provide the economic benefit of fewer lost days due to on-the-job injuries and lower insurance premiums. But, to obtain these technical and economic benefits, the worker must wear the safety glasses. Younger workers more concerned about how they look than about safety often do not wear them when they should. Taking a more comprehensive view of value, Dalloz Safety Products designed a line of protective eyewear that looks like designer sunglasses. The glasses have contoured wraparound frames that come in a variety of colors, with the lens in a selection of tints and colors. Workers actually like wearing their stylish Dalloz protective eyewear, making workplace compliance no longer a problem.

Validate Market Pricing.   Gaining an accurate understanding of competitors' prices often is difficult in business markets because of problems in determining comparability. A supplier should investigate what supplementary services are and are not included in a competitor's quoted price for a market offering. In pursuit of their own interests, customers may dissemble about a competitor's pricing and offering comparability. Further adding to the difficulty of accurately understanding a competitor's pricing is the increasing use of a variety of off-invoice discounts, such as year-end rebates.

Suppliers must gather data from the field on the range of prices that customers are paying for market offerings. Suppliers also should seek out disconfirming as well as confirming evidence on competitor pricing moves. For instance, a salesperson might report that a competitor has cut the price of its market offering. In addition to seeking out other instances of price-cutting to confirm this report, a supplier also should seek out disconfirming instances where the competitor did not cut the price of its offering. Gathering this data will give the supplier a finer-grained understanding of variations in competitor pricing in the marketplace.

A supplier must also gather data about its own prices. Use of off-invoice rebates or allowances, whose percentages may depend on the amount of business that the customer has done with the supplier during the quarter or year, make it difficult for a supplier to know at the time exactly what price it is realizing from a given transaction.[5] Monitoring transaction prices enables a supplier to learn the extent to which exceptions are being made from set pricing strategy and tactics. One supplier discovered that 67 percent of its business was done on the basis of out-of-policy requests—transaction pricing that deviated significantly from established pricing policy.

Gain Estimates of Share of Customer's Business.   What percent of a customer's total purchase requirements for some product or service does a supplier obtain? Although most firms in business markets have some estimate of their market share, fewer have estimates of their shares of each customer's business in the markets they serve. Yet, share of customer's business is much more diagnostic in that it pinpoints customer accounts that perceive the supplier's offering as superior to those of competitors and suggest sources of differentiation.

Suppose that a supplier has a 20 percent market share. It is unlikely that each customer in the market is purchasing 20 percent of its requirement from the supplier. Rather, some customers purchase nothing from the supplier and others are purchasing more than 20 percent of their requirements from the supplier. What differentiates large-share customers from minor-share customers and what sources of differentiation are possible if the customer were to give the supplier 100 percent share?

Sources of Differentiation

In business markets where the core product or service is seen as a commodity, it may be extremely costly or difficult to achieve a difference in the core product or service that customers would perceive as significant. By considering more broadly how they might deliver value to customers, suppliers can identify significant sources of differentiation. Supplementary services, programs, and systems most often are more profitable sources of differentiation that can significantly change the way customers value market offerings.

Create Knowledge Banks.   Suppliers can search for knowledge that would be valuable for customers to have, yet difficult for them to gain by themselves. One sort of knowledge is how the customer operations and ways of doing things compare with those of competitors. Allegiance Healthcare, a leading distributor of hospital supplies, has built a best-practice database from the experiences of 100 leading hospitals for the 30 surgical procedures that drive 80 percent of a hospital's volume. This database details the activities performed and resources consumed for each of these surgical procedures. Armed with the knowledge this database provides, Allegiance clinician consultants work with hospital customers to identify where the hospitals deviate from best practice and assist in efforts to reduce costs and improve productivity.

Build Leveraging Expertise.   Suppliers can search for problems or nuisances that a number of customers each experience, where the supplier could invest in expertise that could be shared across customers to solve or alleviate the problems. In doing so, the suppliers are able to provide superior solutions to customer problems, often at lower costs, and differentiate themselves from competitors.

GLS Inc., a leading distributor of composite materials and elastomers, recognized that it could leverage its superior expertise in environmental, health, and safety regulatory compliance as a value-adding service for its customers, which mostly are medium and small firms. GLS monitors the *Federal Register* and writes bulletins alerting customers on regulatory changes, as well as reminding them of existing standards. It provides customers with a regulatory compliance manual, performs audits of Environmental Protection Agency (EPA) and Occupational Safety and Health

Administration (OSHA) regulatory compliance at customer locations, and assists smaller customers in preparing their annual toxic chemical release inventories and air emissions statements. Without GLS's assistance, these customers would find it difficult and costly to keep appraised of regulatory changes, and what they need to do to comply. Senior management at these customers greatly appreciates GLS's support, because failure to comply can lead to criminal prosecution.

When corporate customers purchase personal computers (PCs), they often want to install software that is specific to their firms, in addition to software licensed from firms such as Microsoft. To do this, though, typically takes an hour or two, costs between $200 and $300, and is a bother to both the user and the firm's PC support staff. Dell Computer Corporation recognized that it could build some leveraging expertise that would enable it to solve this costly nuisance for its major customers. It created a high-speed, 100-megabit Ethernet at its factory that can instantly download a tailored mix of software onto it major customers' PCs.[6]

Change the Customer's Frame of Reference. Customers that focus on the core product or service tend to see only lowering price, not total cost, as a way of suppliers setting themselves apart from one another. Yet, suppliers that change the customer's frame of reference to total cost have much greater opportunities to add value, reduce costs, and differentiate themselves from competitors. As an example, Boeing has 100,000 Dell PCs. Dell Computer has 30 employees onsite at Boeing, who work closely with Boeing managers in planning their requirements and configuring their network. Because of this, the Dell personnel are regarded more like Boeings' PC department than a PC vendor.[7]

In exchange for 100 percent share of a customer's business, suppliers sometimes are able to change how they do business with the customer. As an example, a coatings supplier was willing to put a technician onsite to oversee the painting process and to quote a price per coated object rather than the customary price per liter of coating. And, after all, isn't price per coated object what the customer should really care about?

Selectively Partner in Ways That Align Business Interests and Goals. Often, the customer and supplier have to work together to produce superior outcomes. *Collaborative risk-sharing, gaining-sharing agreements* refer to arrangements where a customer and supplier work together with the intent of improving the customer's performance, and in doing so, the supplier exposes itself to potential losses, yet also receives a prespecified portion of any success. Allegiance Healthcare provides an example of such an agreement.[8]

Allegiance managers believe that their experienced clinicians, acting as consultants, can assist the typical hospital in lowering its total operating costs by about 20 percent. Often, these savings come in the form of improved supply management processes, product standardization, and more efficient product utilization. Yet, the more productive and efficient a hospital becomes in its use of supplies, the fewer the products and services it purchases from Allegiance. Rather than promote the wasteful use of supplies by hospitals, Allegiance is willing to trade its expertise for an equitable share of realized cost savings. Thus, Allegiance proposes a gain–sharing agreement with its strategic hospital customers.

Once an agreement is signed, Allegiance places its clinician consultant onsite to go to work on improving the customer's whole supply management process. At the end of the first year, cost savings are audited. The hospital and Allegiance split the savings 50–50. Each year thereafter, the hospital gains a greater portion of the savings. On the risk side, Allegiance must not only keep the hospital's costs from rising above the baseline established from the previous year, it also needs to discover incremental cost savings such that its portion covers its costs of participation, which are substantial.

Construct Flexible Market Offerings.   No matter how precisely a supplier segments a market, some residual variation in the product and service requirements of segment members will remain. That is, even though customers within a segment may be essentially the same in many of their requirements, they remain different in some. Rather than ignore this remaining variation, perceptive suppliers take advantage of it by building flexibility into their market offerings. Later in this chapter, we discuss at length constructing and managing flexible market offerings. Here, we simply mention that flexible market offerings do set a supplier apart from its competitors, which continue to offer a "standard" offering constructed for the "average" customer that "defines" each segment.

Seek an Equitable Return for Differential Value Provided

Rebuilding differentiation in a commodity offering does suppliers no good if they cannot obtain an equitable return on the value provided. Getting an equitable return, though, does not necessarily mean that suppliers have to charge customers a higher price. Gaining a greater share of customer's business and "cooperative pricing" provide greater profitability through lowering a supplier's costs. Slight price premiums or "pocket price" improvements and for fee, value-adding services allow suppliers to realize a higher price on the business they do with customers.

Greater Share of Customer's Business. Suppliers might seek to have customers reward them for providing superior value through giving them a greater share of their business. After all, the customer must purchase its requirements from someone, so why not concentrate its purchases with few suppliers or even a single supplier? This is especially effective when the supplier can offer some compelling advantage to having a larger share of the customer's business, as in the previous coatings example, and can alleviate customers' concerns about continuity of supply and single sourcing. Suppliers also must have an accurate understanding of their own costs associated with providing a large share or 100 percent of the customers' business to be certain that they are indeed getting something in return.

Cooperative Pricing. When customers simply demand lower price, a supplier that wants to do business with them needs to work with them to find ways to reduce it. With cooperative pricing, the supplier and customer work together to detect "minimum" performance specifications that are unnecessarily restrictive in the customer's application and that can be relaxed in exchange for lower price. As an example, the two firms might trade longer lead times, fewer product variations, fewer delivery locations, or less technical support for reduced prices. In each case, the supplier may retain a portion of the cost savings as incremental profit, and pass on the remainder to the customer as incentive to change.[9]

Slight Price Premiums or "Pocket Price" Improvements. On occasion, suppliers can realize slight price premiums for differentiation initiatives. A pigment supplier, for example, was able to get a half a cent per pound price premium for providing its pigment in slurry form rather than in 50-pound dry bags. This change in product form facilitated handling of the pigment for coatings customers in that it arrived in a liquid form, it did not expose workers to the hazards of pigment dust in tearing open the bags, and it eliminated disposal of the bags, which had become difficult and costly.

Suppliers also can improve profitability through monitoring *transaction pricing,* which focuses on realizing the greatest net price for each individual order. To monitor transaction prices, supplier managers first construct a *pocket price waterfall,* which refers to all terms, discounts, rebates, incentives, allowance, and bonuses that a customer firm receives for a given transaction. Managers then subtract these waterfall elements from list price to produce a *pocket price,* which refers to the revenue a supplier firm actually realizes from that transaction. Analysis of pocket prices reveals such things as which customer segments receive the greatest discounts, customers' willingness-to-pay, and how appropriately field salespersons are exercising their pricing authority. Reducing the number of pricing exceptions can dramatically affect profitability. Marn and Rosiello contend that a 1 percent improvement in price, assuming no volume loss, increases a supplier firm's operating profits by 11 percent.[10]

For Fee, Value–Adding Services That Differentiate.   Many supplier managers believe that to differentiate themselves from competitors, they must give away value-adding services for free to customers. This is not necessarily the case, provided that they can persuasively demonstrate the value of the service that they provide compared with what competitors provide, and that this value difference is substantial. For example, although Dell Computer estimates that loading a tailored mix of customer software at the factory saves the customer $200 to $300 per PC, it charges only $15 to $20 for this service.[11]

Rebuilding Differentiation over Time

Just as differentiated offerings did not become commodities overnight, so too, the supplier cannot rebuild commodity offerings into differentiated offerings overnight. So, our emphasis has been on changes that the supplier might make that over time will reduce the amount of their business that is done solely on the basis of price. We recognize that price likely will still be important to customers, but the sources of differentiation we have discussed can decrease the relative emphasis customers place on it.

Value assessment provides a deep understanding of customer requirements and preferences, and what it is worth for suppliers to fulfill them. Superior knowledge of value also provides suppliers with a means to get an equitable return for their efforts as well as to judge how well the supplier has succeeded in this. Motivation for supplier managers to embark on a value-based rebuilding of differentiation is perhaps best captured by an observation that a senior manager at one firm that does business based on value made: "Selling only on price. Where is the fun in it?" He recognized that when there is market pressure on price, his business unit needs to respond by demonstrating that it has something different it can offer, something that provides superior value to its customers compared to the offerings of its competitiors. Why not have some profitable fun?

CONSTRUCTING FLEXIBLE MARKET OFFERINGS

Firms in business markets are learning that success depends on adroitly balancing three pervasive, but often conflicting, marketplace requirements. First, markets are becoming highly fragmented and customers are requesting, and getting, more customized offerings.[12] Second, customers are uncompromising in their demands that market offerings be sold for either the lowest price or the lowest total cost. Third, due to the success of the total quality management movement, many purchasers now take quality as a given and believe there are few meaningful differences between competing products. Customer firms increasingly expect suppliers to deliver added-value and differentiation in the form of an augmenting bundle of services, programs, and systems such as those listed earlier in Table 15.1.[13] Hereafter, for simplicity, we most often refer to these inclusively as "services."

Yet, few firms have discovered all the implications of these requirements. Instead, most choose to add layer upon layer of services to their market offerings at prices that reflect neither customer value nor their own costs, in the hope of keeping customers satisfied and gaining some competitive advantage. As the anecdotes on page 341 reveal, such efforts often produce unintended results.

How can business market managers avoid such nightmares and confront seemingly paradoxical pressures to differentiate themselves from competitors, yet keep their own costs, and prices to customers, down? On the product side of the market offering, flexible manufacturing, modularization, and product platform design have each been part of a paradigm shift that has challenged conventional thinking that it is impossible to provide product variety and low cost.[14] On the services side of the market offering, a counterpart paradigm shift is occurring. The firms leading the way have begun to provide what we call *flexible market offerings,* consisting of naked solutions, with options.[15]

The Concept of Flexible Market Offerings

Business market managers start with the realization that no matter how precisely a firm segments a market, some variation in the product and service

Market Offering Practice Runs Amok

A supplier of closures and terminals for copper and fiber optic cables lost a multimillion dollar contract to a renegade, "bare bones" competitor. The customer had been an account for over 15 years, and the supplier felt that it completely understood its requirements. At contract renewal time, its sales personnel had visited the customer's plant site and come away with a list of detailed product specifications and service requests. In response, the supplier had developed a premium-priced, full-service package that completely met the customer's stated requirements.

Supplier managers were shocked when they learned they had lost the account to a new competitor offering a low-priced, no frills package. Not only did this competitive offer contain no support services, but the products included also fell slightly below the customer's stated specifications. When asked why they had switched to the new vendor, customer managers replied that the competitor's quote was so low that even if the products failed, the firm would have enough funds available from the price difference to readily pay for a consulting engineering company to correct the problems. In retrospect, supplier management concluded that if its sales force had spent more time understanding what the customer actually valued and was willing to pay for, it might have avoided this sizable loss in sales.

In an attempt to grab market share in a stagnant, commodity marketplace, a textile producer volunteered to store its products "on consignment" at the plants of a major, apparel-producing customer. In addition to keeping the inventory on its books until the customer firm used it, the textile producer agreed to: lease warehouse space in the customer's plant to store the inventory; furnish an optical scanner and computer system to monitor textile consumption; and pay for insurance against inventory damage, theft, or loss. Not surprisingly, the customer immediately jumped at the opportunity to implement this innovative program.

What came as a shock to the textile producer, though, was that within one week, all three of its major competitors had duplicated that program for the apparel producer. Moreover, after a short-term increase in its share of the customer's business, the textile producer saw its share and those of its competitors return to their preprogram levels. And, other apparel producers began to demand the same service. Taking stock at the end of the year, the textile producer discovered that the consignment program had resulted in an overall loss of several million dollars in operating profits. Its managers assumed the same was the case for its competitors. The textile producer took little solace in the fact that its customer satisfaction ratings from the apparel producer had soared to an all-time high.

requirements of segment members will remain. That is, even though customers within a segment may be essentially the same in many of their requirements, they remain different in others. In the past, suppliers either ignored or were unable to deal with this variation, choosing instead to provide market offerings comprised of "standard" bundles or packages of products and services designed to meet the needs of the "average" customer within each segment. Even worse, in many instances, suppliers have provided what is essentially the same "vanilla" offering across all segments. As a result, some customers felt that they were forced to pay for services they did not need, while others did not get the depth of service they required, even if they were willing to pay extra.

Rather than ignore residual variation, perceptive business market managers take advantage of it by building flexibility into their market offerings. They do so by first constructing naked solutions for each market segment— the bare minimum of products and services that all segment members uniformly value. Importantly, naked solutions are sold at the lowest profitable price. In turn, naked solutions are wrapped with options that are offered separately for those segment members that value them.

Table 15.2 contains simplified examples of flexible market offerings from Siemens Electrical Apparatus Division for the small manufacturing firm segment, and from Mitsubishi Electric Industrial Controls for the machining center segment. One dimension differentiates between the product component and the service component of a market offering.[16] On the other, we distinguish between standard elements that everyone gets at no charge and options the firm offers for additional charges. Although flexible market offerings comprise both product components and services components, hereafter in this chapter, we focus primarily on the services part of the market offerings. In many industries, business market managers find that services are the predominant means of creating value to differentiate their offerings from those of competitors.

How can suppliers move to flexible market offerings? In the following sections, we discuss how this approach is put into practice. In the process, we consider the difficulties business market managers can expect to encounter, and suggest solutions.

Articulate the Present Market Offering for Each Market Segment

To start, business market managers need to take stock of how their firm is doing business by summarizing their current market offerings for each

Table 15.2
Two Simplified Examples of Flexible Market Offerings

	Product(s)	Service(s)
Siemens Electrical Apparatus Division **Small Manufacturer Market Segment**		
Standard	Metal clad boxes	Product availability Delivery Product reliability warranties
Options	Electromechanical or electronic instrument controls Enhancements Communications peripherals	Installation Maintenance contracts Tests, inspections Drawings Retrofit designs
Mitsubishi Electric Industrial Controls, Inc. **Machining Center Segment**		
Standard	Computerized numerical controls CRT terminal Program panel Axle and drive motors Spindle drives and motors Basic software	Product availability Delivery Installation Set-up Training Field engineering
Options	High-performance hardware Interactive screens Advanced drives and motors	Customized software Two-year guarantee on parts, labor, repair Retrofitting Customized PLC design

segment. As an illustration, consider the service portion of Baxter Healthcare Corporation's market offering to two segments of interest: transactional hospital customers who do business with Baxter on an order-by-order basis; and strategic customers, which are hospitals that have made a commitment to a closer relationship with Baxter (see Table 15.3).[17] Baxter constructed these offerings to provide ordinary and extraordinary levels of service, programs and systems that reinforce their commitment to fulfilling strategic customers' requirements and enhancing their medical services and financial performance. Even programs that are options and that it charges for separately, such as Baxter Corporate Consulting, reflect this commitment because they provide value or savings that far exceed their cost to the strategic customer.

Table 15.3
Baxter Healthcare's Market Offerings to Two Segments:
Transactional and Strategic Hospital Customers

	Segment	
Market Offering Element	Transactional Customer	Strategic Customer
Services		
Product returns	Standard	Standard
Technical assistance	Standard	Standard
Single point-of-contact	Not offered	Standard
Future disease incidence forecast	Not offered	Option
⋮		
Programs		
Price deals	Standard	Standard
Corporate customer bonus (financial incentive)	Not offered	Standard
Executive perspectives	Not offered	Standard
Consolidated purchasing report summary	Not offered	Standard
ACCESS program	Not offered	Option
Baxter corporate consulting	Not offered	Option
⋮		
Systems		
ASAP order-entry system	Standard	Standard
COMDISCO technology assessment	Not offered	Standard
ValueLink stockless inventory program	Option	Option
COMDISCO asset management system	Option	Option
⋮		

Businesses that have market offerings as well-articulated and well-managed as Baxter's are rare. More often, managers' understanding of the services, programs, and systems their firm offers within and across market segments is piecemeal, uneven, and inaccurate. For this reason, managers from all functional areas that "touch" the customers in some way should take part in a structured process to elicit the present market offerings for each segment. Meeting as a group, a facilitator systematically takes these managers through the various kinds of services, programs, and systems a business might offer. For each one, the managers are asked, "Are you doing something like this?" As a follow-up question, the managers are asked, "Are you doing this sometimes, for some customers?"

Supplier managers can gain at least three different kinds of insights from this process: the true breadth of the market offering, the arbitrary nature of charges, and lack of variation across segments.

The True Breadth of the Market Offering.   Managers invariably spend more time, and have less difficulty, thinking about the product portions of their market offerings. On the other hand, most have trouble identifying the services their firms provide. Inevitably, the services portions of market offerings are found to be more extensive than any one manager realizes.

The Arbitrary Nature of Charges.   Another revelation is the lack of discipline in what is offered as standard at the package price, and what is marketed as an "option" for which customers pay separately. All too often, suppliers find that their sales forces are guilty of "fourth-quarter habits"— that is, the practice of giving away service options "for free" at the end of the year in order to meet their sales quotas. In doing so, they cloud customer expectations of what services are standard and what are optional. Suppliers sometimes discover that certain customers are adept in circumventing charges, perhaps through knowing whom to call for a favor or special treatment.

Lack of Variation across Segments.   A final insight that many suppliers gain from the examination of market offerings is the "vanilla" nature of their offerings across segments. In business markets, a number of firms still segment the market and then proceed to provide much the same, if not exactly the same, offering to each segment. As the marketing manager for a large chemical company related, "For 90 percent of our customers, we offer the identical mix of support services."

Assess Customer Value and Supplier Cost

Before supplier managers can formulate flexible market offerings for each segment, they need to gain an estimate of the value of each service, and the cost to provide it. Having this knowledge would seem to be fundamental in managing market offerings. Yet, few businesses have undertaken any formal value or cost assessments.

Measuring Customer Value.   Many business market managers seem content to rely solely on measures of customer satisfaction. As one manager observed, "Our research exclusively takes the form of 'how-are-we-doing' surveys (i.e., customer satisfaction) rather than 'how much are they worth to you' studies (i.e., value assessment)." Customer satisfaction studies capture a supplier's performance against expectations about services that have been shaped by customers' past experiences with a supplier as well as with its competitors. They also capture what the customer perceives to be "fair and appropriate" in a market offering's content and price.

Because they delineate customer expectations and measure supplier performance against them, customer satisfaction measurement studies are worthwhile, but sole reliance on them can lead to serious errors in judgment. Naturally, customers will be more satisfied when they receive services for free than when they have to pay for them. After all, the supplier is giving value away. Suppliers can easily overcommit resources and overspend budgets by blindly pursuing incremental improvements in customer satisfaction.[18] Finally, if they do not assess the worth of services, marketers are ill-equipped to set market offering prices at fair levels.

How do leading-edge firms measure the value of their augmenting services? Greif Brothers Corporation, which manufactures fiber and plastic drums, routinely conducts what it calls cost-in-use studies to document the incremental cost savings, and thus the superior value, that a customer gains by using Greif products and services in place of those of a competitor. To add credibility to the results, one of Greif's technical service managers works together with customer managers to complete the research. In addition to examining manufacturing, the team undertakes a series of process flow analyses in which it diagrams the customer's business operations and estimate their current costs. From these estimates, Greif managers brainstorm system solutions for the customer. For example, they might envision a complete materials handling system including just-in-time deliveries, utilized delivery systems (e.g., placing rollers on trucks to facilitate unloading), and drum recycling. Importantly, Greif gives the customer a variety of service alternatives along with estimates of cost savings. In this way, customers can make informed purchase decisions based upon the worth of proposed system solutions to them.

Coming to Grips with Service Costs.   As for costs, recent strides in the development and implementation of activity-based costing (ABC) techniques would seem to facilitate the assessment of costs on a customer-by-customer basis.[19] However, few companies appear to be using ABC in the management of their market offerings. Why? For starters, existing ABC techniques are best suited for the measurement of manufacturing and product-related costs. Little work has been done to apply ABC techniques to service, program, or system costs.[20] Thus, many firms simply don't know how to apply ABC to services. We find three specific factors inhibiting the application of ABC techniques in managing the services portion of the market offering: services definitions are often "fuzzy"; service costs are often buried in the fixed costs of staff departments; and many companies remain organized around the products they sell rather than around market segments or customers.

Overcoming inertia and systems impediments are essential, because more fully and more accurately allocated costs can provide quite a different picture of how costly some services actually are. In an activity-based costing study, drug wholesalers found that the returned goods service they provided to customers cost approximately 3.7 percent of the average wholesaler's gross sales, not the 1 or 2 percent that was commonly thought. This substantial disparity was due to reliance on credited dollars as a percent of sales as a measure of service cost, which did not recognize a number of "hidden" transaction costs for wholesalers.[21]

How do progressive companies understand the services costs associated with their market offerings? To eliminate the problems associated with fuzzy services and the tendency of sales reps to bury service costs, Van Den Bergh Foods, a manufacturer of food additives and seasonings, revamped its service delivery and planning systems. For starters, the company defined more precisely its services and the levels of each it offered. Its sales force, which is composed of highly trained technical representatives, now is required to handle all minor services, such as basic problem solving. Charges for such services account for a portion of the total yearly budget allotted to each sales representative. All major services, such as detailed technical problem solving, are now offered on a project basis and delivered by technical experts from departments such as customer service. Either the customer directly pays for the project, which is preferred, or a charge is placed against the allotted, discretionary budget of its sales representative. At the beginning of each year, Van Den Bergh managers construct an Annual Operational Plan for each major customer account that defines financial and volume targets and specifies the levels of services Van Den Bergh will provide. At the end of the year, the managers review these plans, examine service costs and account profitability, and recommend changes in level of account services for the next year.

Arthur D. Little, Inc. (ADL) provides another outstanding example. ADL knows the profitability of each account. It scrupulously tracks the amount of resources and billable hours of consultant time devoted to each account. In addition, it monitors specific services it provides to each customer. Because costs and revenues are largely a function of the billable hours and services ADL provides, calculating profit per account becomes a relatively straightforward task. ADL has created a measurement system that determines whether or not its market offerings are successful and how productive its consultants are at billing clients. With this system, ADL management can tell whether a service is not in demand or unprofitable, and shed it quickly.

The Payoff from Value and Cost Assessments.   What results can supplier managers expect when they perform value assessments in conjunction with cost assessments, as we advocate? On page 349, we detail the experience of AKZO Industrial Coatings (now AKZO NOBEL), which demonstrates that the payoff can be substantial.

An understanding of the value of services to customers and the cost to perform them enables business market managers to identify value drains, which are services that cost the supplier more to provide than they are worth to customers receiving them and have no strategic significance. A producer of chemicals for use in extracting oil from wells routinely performed a field analytic monitoring service for each of its customers to determine when, and in what amounts, they should apply its products. A salesperson visiting one of the firm's smaller, less-sophisticated customers noticed the analysis reports stacked in a corner of the production shed. When asked about their usefulness, the customer replied that he was not using the information at all, and instead just had the producer's truck driver pump a few gallons into each well whenever the truck came by. Learning this, the producer offered to discontinue the field testing, and in exchange, give the customer a 7 percent per gallon price reduction. The customer readily agreed, and significantly, account profitability went from −6 percent to +32 percent! Rather than finding value drains by chance, as in this example, suppliers proactively can use value assessment in conjunction with activity-based-costing analysis to detect them.

Gaining an estimate of the value of market offering elements is not always easy; having one, though, is essential. With an understanding of value, discussions with customers focus on performance and meeting customer requirements. Without this knowledge, discussions center on price. Yet, fine-grained estimates of each element are not required. Instead, managers are seeking to make a basic, categorical judgment about the value of each element. That is, what supplier managers are trying to do is to isolate those elements that are uniformly highly valued within a segment from those that are highly valued by some but not others within the segment, and those that are not highly valued by any customers in the segment.

Putting Measures of Expectations, Value, and Costs to Use

About 10 years ago, spurred on by unacceptable profitability, managers at the Netherlands-based AKZO Industrial Coatings (IC) asked themselves the question, "Are we not giving more service than the customer is paying for?" To answer this, AKZO managers first developed a method based on ABC costing and then undertook an analysis of the contribution to profit (CTP) of each customer. Next, relying on a field value assessment, they determined the value of each service that they provided. So, for example, when an investigating engineer was dispatched to analyze dust in a customer's paint line and identify where the dust came from, the value of this service would be quantified in terms of the effects of this problem on customer cost (e.g., downtime and scrap parts) and other performance parameters, such as the first-run OK percentage and the percentage of defects.

AKZO managers discovered that they were in fact giving away more service than many customers were paying for. Furthermore, they learned that some of their services provided little value to customers. Although many of these services were offered by competing firms "for free" and customers expected to get them, even though they didn't place much value on some, AKZO managers decided to take unprecedented strategic action. First, embracing a philosophy of "growth in selected areas," they targeted those industries and market segments where AKZO products furnished the greatest customer value and thus had the greatest profit potential. Second, utilizing CTP measures, they revamped their market offerings and pricing. Price discussions were held with selected customers, where AKZO was determined to get an equitable return on the services it provided. Although AKZO IC lost some customers because they no longer got a variety of services for free, overall, its perseverance resulted in stable sale volume at significantly better profitability, even during the last recession.

Much the same can be said about trade-offs between precision and cost in activity-based-costing analyses. AKZO managers caution against pursuing too fine a level of allocation. The goal of a realistic assessment of each business activity needs to be acceptably met. Beyond this, resources are better directed elsewhere. As a useful start, if supplier managers have not already done so, they should establish baselines of services usage by customers within segments.

Formulate Flexible Market Offerings by Market Segment

When formulating flexible market offerings for each market segment, business market managers can choose from three strategic alternatives for each service element: Do not market the service, market it as standard for which there is no charge, or market it as an option for which there is a charge. Each service itself has one of three statuses: The service is a new one (meaning that it has not been previously marketed by the supplier although it may have been offered by some competitor), it is an existing standard service, or it is an existing optional service. We cross service status with service strategic alternative to provide nine unique combinations. A useful way of organizing these nine resulting strategies is a flexible market offering strategy matrix, which we show in Table 15.4. By arranging the services in their appropriate cells, this matrix can provide a systematic picture of the nature and balance of a supplier's market offering. It also can promote further inquiry and offering strategy development, as when, for example, managers find one or more cells empty of elements. We consider below, in turn, the rows of this matrix. We then discuss the pricing implications of flexible market offerings.

Reevaluating Existing Standard Services.   Because the overriding philosophy is to keep the standard offering as "naked" as possible, only those service, program, and system elements that *all* firms within a segment highly value should be standard. The first place to start putting this philosophy

Table 15.4
Flexible Market Offering Strategy Matrix for
Services, Programs, and Systems

	Service Element Deployment		
Service Element Status	*Do Not Market*	*Market as Standard*	*Market as Option*
Existing standard service	Prune from standard offering	Retain in standard offering	Recast as surcharge option
Existing optional service	Discontinue option	Enhance standard offering	Retain as value-added option
New service	Keep on shelf	Augment standard offering	Introduce as value-added option

into practice is by reevaluating the existing standard services. By discontinuing, or "pruning," some of these, and recasting others as options, business market managers retain just the subset of standard services that will serve as the base of an updated standard offering.

Suppliers are often far more reluctant to discontinue existing services than they are to add services. Nonetheless, managers need to scrutinize existing elements for pruning candidates. One source is those services that most segment members rarely use. The customers that still value the service are so few that it is not worthwhile for the supplier to continue to offer it. In the interest of these customers, though, the supplier sometimes can outsource the service, or suggest another firm that provides it.

Certain services are readily pruned. For example, those value drains that provide low customer value yet incur high costs for the supplier are ideal candidates. Following detailed investigations, a chemical manufacturer learned to its chagrin that while each of its 186 services continued to incur annual fixed costs, some had not been used in the past year! Its managers responded by pruning a large number of these services. Many customers didn't even realize it had discontinued the services.

Beyond those services that all firms within a segment highly value, there are some circumstances where a supplier retains additional services in the standard offering. The success of certain services, in terms of their value or cost, depends upon their widespread usage by customers. Electronic data interchange (EDI), and logistics management systems are examples.

Service elements that a supplier cannot readily differentiate from those of competitors are candidates for matching, and most likely, for inclusion in the standard offering. Such elements, often regarded as standard in industry market offerings, can often make up a substantial part of the naked offering. The challenge in offering these parity services is to have customers perceive their value as not significantly less than competitors' comparable services, but at the same time manage their costs down below those of the competitors. The rationale is that because customers typically do not place much value on these services, they do not factor into customers' decisions about changing suppliers as long as they are minimally acceptable.

Supplier managers universally report that recasting a standard service as a surcharge option is the most difficult of the nine strategies to implement. Customers may react angrily when told they must now pay for something they had expected to get for free. It is even more difficult when competitors continue to market the service for free as part of a standard offering. Nowhere is this more of a problem than in industries characterized by high levels of fixed costs, such as commodity industrial chemicals and fully integrated steel mills. In such industries, managers are hesitant to implement any scheme that may result in reduced sales volume because it may jeopardize their ability to reach profitable capacity-utilization levels. As a result, they routinely add services to retain volume and rarely drop any.

Infrequently performed services that deliver value at specific points in time, such as training, installation, and retrofitting, are perhaps the best candidates for redeployment as surcharge options. By marketing these services as value-added options, suppliers retain the business of those customers that still derive value from them and are willing to pay for them. Often, this provides a "litmus test" for services that customers claim have no value for them (or are said to be the same as those obtainable for free from other suppliers), but that suppliers believe are worth something to customers. Depending on the market response, in the next period suppliers can either continue them as value-added options or discontinue them.

Leading supplier firms use a variety of approaches to recast services as value-added options. To make the overhaul of its standard service package more palatable to its customers, one specialty chemical company implemented a variation of this strategy. Along with specialty organic chemicals, the company offers a variety of services including laboratory support, field consulting, on-site testing, and educational seminars, all of which are costly. Realizing that its customers value and use these services differently, the company offers customers a variety of levels for each service. If a customer purchases a minimum amount of products each year, it receives "basic" levels of services along with the standard offering. If that same customer wants to receive a higher level of service, it can either increase its annual purchases to a prespecified amount or pay extra. Thus, some level of each service that customers expect is available with each standard offering. Customers that place greater value on the service have the option to buy more.

As a prelude to making some previously standard package services value-added options, a large computer company began listing a charge for the provided services, which was then subtracted with the notation "Do not pay this." An accompanying letter explained that the company was pleased to have been able to provide the field service and stated what it estimated this service was worth to the customer, using market-based rates for independent industry consultants. In doing so, the company established the value of its services in the minds of its customers and positioned the services as not necessarily being performed at no charge in the future. Thus, a sharp distinction can be drawn between offering an element separately, even as an invoice reduction "No charge," and simply burying it within the standard package.

Another alternative is to have the customer pay, in full or in part, for whatever options they value with bonus dollars, earned from doing business with the supplier. Strategic customers accrued "Baxter dollars" based on the amount of and growth in their purchases from Baxter Healthcare, which they then applied to any of a number of optional services, programs, and systems. In this way, strategic hospital customers used a common Baxter dollars resource to tailor Baxter's market offering to their own, individual requirements.

Reexamining Optional Services.   Next, supplier managers should reexamine existing optional services to determine whether they should be discontinued, used to enhance the standard offering, or continued as options.

As is the case with the standard package, evaluation and construction of options menus should begin with a deliberate attempt to prune existing optional services. Optional services that were once good sources of revenue for the supplier but are no longer used enough to justify their fully allocated costs are pruning candidates. Similarly, services whose cost has outstripped customers' willingness to pay for them (due to changes in technology, necessary expertise, or insurance risk) are also candidates. For example, because of insurance risk, most manufacturers are unwilling to provide transportation for drums of solvents, even for an additional delivery fee. As with pruning standard services, suppliers sometimes can help customers that still need these services to outsource them from other firms.

At times, supplier may fold into standard offerings services that they have marketed as options. Where the core product of the market offering is regarded as a "commodity," suppliers look to enhance the standard offering as a means of differentiating themselves in the marketplace. Their underlying belief is that customers do business on the basis of which supplier has the best or most extensive set of services. But, because customers within segments will vary in how they value these services, the supplier is often driven to offer more elements in the standard offering.

Instead, suppliers should consider trimming the standard offering to the naked solution, offering a set of options, and letting customers pay, in full or in part, for whatever options they value with bonus dollars. The more customers concentrate their purchases with the supplier, the more bonus dollars they earn, and the more services they can purchase. Not only does this allow customers to tailor the supplier's market offering to their own particular requirements, it reinforces to them that they do not have to pay for services they do not want, as is the case with the totally bundled offering. And, to underscore the value of the services it offers, a supplier can promise to give customers cash for any unused bonus dollars at the end of the agreement, as did Baxter Healthcare.

Building Flexibility with New Services.   What are the sources of new services? Some suppliers rely on their own strengths and capabilities to identify new services to offer. Another source of ideas is to focus on the cost structures and strategic imperatives of targeted key customers. What new services can the supplier innovate that will assist these customers in their own initiatives to lower costs or improve performance?

Because they have not been offered in the past, new services do not carry the baggage of customer expectations about how a supplier should provide them ("Now you want us to pay extra for something we used to get for free?"). Thus, new services provide the best means to build flexibility into market offerings. So, while they should try to preserve new services as stand-alone options, at times, suppliers may elect not to offer them or use them to enhance the standard offering.

Suppliers may decide not to offer a new element because of a variety of market timing issues. It may be that customers have not yet recognized an element's value, the cost of providing it is still too high, or the present element that it would replace is still deemed adequate. AKZO Industrial Coatings (IC) provides an example. Anticipating greater environmental concerns about current painting technologies, AKZO IC invested substantial time and resources in the technological development of a process for water-borne paint application. As a service to its customers, AKZO would consult with them on changing to this more environmentally benign technology. Unfortunately, although many customers were interested to learn that AKZO possessed this capability, no one was willing to pay extra for it. AKZO managers believed that customers would not value the process until environmental protection laws required a significant reduction in solvent emissions. As a result, they decided to keep the technology on the shelf until customer value increased.

Suppliers sometimes enhance the standard offerings with new services. Where suppliers segment the market by relationships, managers look for new elements that will sustain and invigorate the collaborative relationships. One way is to add new services that anticipate and are responsive to customers' changing requirements. Okuma, a Japanese builder of computer numerical control (CNC) machine tools, provides an example. In one year, it introduced a 24-hour parts shipment guarantee, while in the next, it began to sell a guaranteed trade-in program. Okuma management believed that in addition to being responsive to a changing marketplace, the practice forced its distributors and employees to be more efficient—they must learn how to ship parts anywhere in the United States in 24-hours. It also gave the sales force something new and interesting to discuss during sales presentations.

Shrewd suppliers also add new services to standard offerings to thwart or stymie competitors. Baxter Scientific Products' Industrial Division, for example, deliberately seeks out new services that customers value and that Baxter can perform better than the competition or at lower costs. By bundling them in with the standard offering, Baxter forces competitors to choose from a series of unpleasant alternatives. If competitors decline to offer the service altogether, Baxter can tout its unique service to customers as an extra benefit of doing business with Baxter. If competitors attempt to match Baxter and offer the service, they must incur both added costs and time delays associated with learning how to deliver the new service.

New elements that also are likely candidates for inclusion in the standard offering are those for which: most of the costs are incurred in their initial development or deployment; continuing costs are relatively invariant over the number of customers actually using the element; or usage of the element in some way reduces the supplier's own costs. ABB's Low Voltage Apparatus business has developed competence in electronic data interchange (EDI) for an order management system. Because it reduces the costs of ordering for both parties, ABB would like to have all of its customers use this system. To start, though, ABB built a priority list of customers to approach, focusing on those with the largest business potential and the most frequent orders. In time, ABB worked down to the smaller customers to get them on the system.

Offering new elements separately provides value-added options for customers that seek them and allows suppliers to readily gauge interest in new services, programs, and systems. For example, although R.R. Donnelly Company's traditional business has focused on printing, binding, film preparation, and prepress work, its management believes that future growth and profits will come from innovative services, such as database management, consulting and training, dimensional and talking ads, direct marketing, layout systems, and mapping services. To test their viability in the marketplace, Donnelley has offered these services as value-added options.

"New" elements that a supplier can offer separately as value-added options can emerge from reconsidering services in the standard offering. For each service that is offered at a constant level, supplier managers should ask whether they can define alternate levels that would have different value for different customers. In one electrical wholesaler, an overworked inside sales force used overnight air freight to cover mistakes in orders or delivery dates. It regarded this as standard (i.e., the sole service recovery element) when, in many instances, second-day United Parcel Service (UPS) and third-day common carrier would have been viable options.

ABB's Power Transformers business has recognized that not all customers want the same level of maintenance service, nor do they value it the same. Traditionally, utilities have had equipment maintenance. Instead of simply offering equipment maintenance service, as in the past, ABB now offers different levels of maintenance service as part of a service agreement. ABB draws on its experience in providing the different levels of service to customers to price these service agreements. Rather than having service on all their transformers, some customers even tell ABB what transformers to check and then ask how much ABB will charge for providing just that service.

Finally, in some situations, suppliers may not want customers to know what the charge is for an individual service. This occurs, for instance, when suppliers are concerned that customers might impute the value of a service from its charge. When this is the case, suppliers can group elements in one or more option packages that they offer separately, as auto manufacturers have long done.

Pricing Implications.   It is crucial to recognize that constructing flexible market offerings says little, if anything, about their pricing. This must come from consideration of the supplier's strategy for each market segment. For example, suppliers that pursue enhancing the standard offering with additional services may alternately decide to raise the price, keep it the same, or even lower it. The market offering's price might be raised commensurate with the greater value provided, or raised less than the added value to "soften" the effects of a needed price increase due to rising costs. A supplier might keep the price the same in a stable marketplace to gain new or incremental business through superior value, or in a price-declining marketplace, simply to hold price. The price might even be lowered in support of an aggressive market development or market share growth strategy.

Further, customers may value certain services offered as standard, but the only way they are affordable to a supplier is if it has all the customer's business. With single sourcing, a supplier can take responsibility for the customer process in which its products play a principal role, such as a coatings supplier taking responsibility for the whole painting process in a customer's paint shop. These single-source service arrangements can lead to innovative pricing, such as the customer paying for the number of coated objects, rather than liters of paint. The supplier may even be paid more for lower rejects and rework on the coated objects.

Similarly, pruning offering elements has no inherent pricing implications, but again the effect depends on the segment market strategy. A supplier might lower its price equal to the cost of the discontinued services, thereby maintaining the competitive status quo. Alternatively, to improve contribution margins, a supplier might not lower the price at all, or lower the price less than the cost of providing the service. This latter tactic has the dual advantage of improving the value of the offering to customers that did not value the pruned service, while providing an incentive for competitors that are similarly looking to improve their profitability to match the supplier's action. Suppliers might even raise prices in situations where they are pursuing a harvest strategy, taking as much profit out of the business as possible while letting it decline.[22]

Offering services separately provides flexibility not only to the customers within a segment, but to the supplier, too, in terms of pricing. One alternative is to show the service charge on an invoice and then "net out" the charge for a specific reason (e.g., initial use discount). This has at least three advantages. It provides a readily captured way of tracking service "give-aways." Suppliers employ it in a selective, transitory way, such as to close a deal, to blunt a competitive inroad, or to attract business in targeted new segments. For example, Mitsubishi Electric Industrial Controls offers as an option a proprietary software development tool, but to win targeted new accounts, it may provide the tool at no charge. Consulting on usage of this software tool, which it also offers separately, may initially be provided at no charge, but subsequent consulting is not. Finally, showing a charge establishes and reinforces the value of services to customers and the supplier's salespeople. On page 358, we provide examples of flexible market offerings from Okuma and Microsoft.

Prepare to Implement Flexible Market Offerings

Next, suppliers need to decide how they will present flexible market offerings to the marketplace. In the process, they must anticipate implementation problems with customers and breaking away from the pack of competitors' market offerings.

Two Examples of Flexible Market Offerings

In the past, Okuma sold only state-of-the-art computer numerical control (CNC) lathes that performed universal turning functions including milling, drilling, and boring. All these machines were high performance, but they also tended to be high priced. This prevented smaller manufacturers that bought on price or that did not own computer-controlled equipment from purchasing Okuma machines. Realizing that small-job shops would be a primary source of growth in the future, Okuma Charlotte championed the development of an affordable line of CADET horizontal lathes. The CADET line, which performs basic horizontal turning operations and is offered in five different versions, is responsive to a large and competitive market niche. It comes with rudimentary computerized controls and sells for a low price. Once a CADET is sold to a small manufacturer, Okuma and its distributor demonstrate the value of computer-controlled machines to the customer. After six months, the customer is usually ready to invest in a higher performance, vertical CNC machine.

Most Okuma services offered with the CADET are optional. However, because the CADET is a narrow use product, the extent and nature of technical assistance, engineering, and training are more focused. Management recognizes that because the product competes in a highly price-sensitive market, a naked solution at an attractive low price is a necessity for success. Interestingly, though, management has discovered its broad set of separate service options are often the deciding factor in product acquisition decisions, simply because most competitors offer little service, even as options.

Spurred on by customer requests for greater choice and by its own rising costs, the Microsoft Corporation has implemented flexible market offerings for its support services. Now, customers can select among four basic types of increasingly sophisticated, technical support, ranging from "Fast Tips & Electronic Services" (a 24-hour automated system) to "Premier Support" (custom consulting on highly specialized applications). Depending on the type of software purchased, which ranges from "Desktop Applications" (e.g., Word or Excel) to "Advanced Systems" (e.g., Windows NT), these services are either not offered, marketed as standard, or marketed as optional for fee. In addition, for each optional service, Microsoft gives customers a choice of payment plans. They can buy an annual contract, they can purchase "incident packs" for selected numbers of technical-support episodes, they can pay by the incident, or they even can choose to be billed by the minute!

The response to Microsoft's flexible offering of support services has been positive. There was no backlash from customers over the fee structures, and corporate and developer accounts were delighted with the new high-end service options. Within two years, most software companies followed Microsoft's lead and introduced their own flexible support service offerings.

Option Menu versus Tailored-Value Package.   What will the customer see in making its decision: an option menu or a tailored-value package? The option menu approach makes the flexible market offering transparent to the customer, listing all optional elements. Although the salesperson provides consultation, the customer has the primary responsibility for tailoring the market offering to its perceived requirements. Apple Computing and Microsoft each provide detailed, multiple-page menus of technical support services with pricing options, and let customers decide.

Rather than treating all elements as options, suppliers most often provide a standard package with a menu of options, and let the customers craft their own market offering. Certainly, in negotiated bid situations, a preferred strategy is to start with a naked offering at the lowest possible bid price, so as to be selected for further negotiations. The supplier then uses consultative selling efforts to "trade-up" the customer to select options that will provide value. Astute suppliers realize that if they do not have a competitively low bid price, they have no opportunity to do business, and so they develop a two-part negotiations strategy.

In contrast, the tailored-value package approach keeps the flexible market offerings opaque to customers. Working with the customer, the salesperson develops a list of specifications and then crafts an offering based on a menu of options that only the salesperson sees. This places greater responsibility on the salesperson to accurately comprehend and respond to stated customer requirements. In practice, salespeople would most often respond with several packages and let the customer choose amongst them. Purchasing managers may request several packages in an attempt to gain an understanding of the trade-offs the supplier is implicitly offering.

Sonoco's Industrial Products Division uses both approaches. The division manufactures fiber cores around which products such as newsprint, commercial printing paper, textiles, yarns, plastic films, and aluminum foil are wrapped. Its customers select from several market offerings. For customers that want the lowest possible price, it markets a naked solution comprised of parent cores (uncut cores in standard lengths ranging from 8 to 30 feet) plus a minimum of support services. Sonoco will also sell these customers trimming equipment to cut the parent cores into usable sizes. For those customers that don't want to be bothered with the tasks and investments associated with cutting cores, Sonoco markets fiber cores that match customer specifications. Along with fiber cores, Sonoco offers a variety of optional services such as process redesign of customer packaging systems. Finally, for customers located great distances from Sonoco plants and concerned that deliveries won't arrive on time, Sonoco will even set up a satellite plant near the customer's location (often in space leased in an industrial park). There, Sonoco employees will cut the cores to customer specifications. Sonoco also offers these customers the optional services.

As mentioned, Sonoco sales representatives sell these market offerings in two ways. If the customer desires it, representatives will provide a detailed menu of all Sonoco products and services along with their respective prices. The customer can pick and choose the products and services it desires. Alternatively, Sonoco sales representatives can use their expertise to assemble several tailored packages of products and services. Along with the price of each proposed package, Sonoco sales representatives provide a summary of the cost savings the customer can expect to gain if they buy the package. In this way, the customer can choose an appropriate package based not only on its price, but also on its value. Sonoco managers report that since they began offering customers such extensive choices, both division sales volume and market share have increased.

Anticipating Implementation Problems with Customers. Suppliers can minimize implementation problems by understanding customer requirements and shaping customer expectations through education and persuasion about the superior value of the flexible market offerings. Suppliers need to manage service and pricing expectations to avoid acquiring a "nickel and diming" reputation. They can do this by developing collateral materials and case histories that convey less is more, and that combat the "we used to get it for free" gripes. These messages portray flexible market offerings from the perspective, "You don't have to pay for what you don't want."

Suppliers need to be relentless in communicating the value story to customers. As mentioned earlier, new services provide perhaps the best opportunity to implement flexibility in market offerings. As a rollout or phase-in, suppliers also might consider implementing flexible market offerings at the same time as they make product changes or introductions.

Ross Controls, a maker of pneumatic valves, had to educate its customers about the value its new customized service offering provided. Ross' customers were used to making purchasing decisions based on price, and did not see the benefit of spending a lengthy amount of time working with Ross to design valves for their specific applications. Because of its investment in computer-aided design tools and equipment automation, however, Ross could design and produce custom parts in several days, which in the past could have taken up to 16 weeks. To demonstrate this new service capability to design and produce custom valves quickly, Ross asked its customers to provide prototype specifications. Then, within a few days, Ross provided them an actual prototype valve for free, which could cost as much as $20,000. Customers were delighted with Ross' responsiveness to their prototype specifications, and were even willing to pay a premium for it. As a result, Ross has experienced growth in an otherwise stagnant-to-declining industry.[23]

Breaking Away from the Pack.   In our field research, a number of managers wistfully expressed a desire for change, but were concerned about what competitors would do. These managers believed that their competitors similarly were looking to improve profitability, but what if their competitors didn't match the move to flexible market offerings? In addition, there are timing and discipline concerns. Before discussing these, we first consider breaking away as a means of countering competitors' dubious parity claims.

One way to break away (which also works for services included in the standard offering) is to guarantee outcomes based on the service. The larger and more complicated the list of services a firm markets becomes, the more likely that its competitors will promise, "We can do that." When this occurs, savvy marketers respond by transforming service claims into guarantees. For instance, when Okuma's competitors began to promise rapid delivery, Okuma announced its 24-hour shipment guarantee. If a customer orders a part and it is not shipped in 24 hours, the customer gets the part for free. Greif Brothers Corporation takes the guarantee one step farther. In the past few years, Greif introduced a guaranteed cost savings program. If a customer requests that they be given a 5 percent price cut, Greif guarantees to find at least a 5 percent cost savings. This is formalized into a written contract. If the customer doesn't realize the 5 percent savings, Greif agrees to pay the difference. If more than 5 percent of savings are found, the customer gets to keep it all. To date, Greif has had no problem delivering as guaranteed. Furthermore, managers find that it's a great way to turn discussions away from price.

Knowing when to break away and unbundle is difficult. Is there an advantage to being the first, or is it better to be a rapid follower? To be an industry paradigm-breaker, the first supplier must have tough resolve and be willing to "take the heat." An intermediate strategy is to pilot test flexible market offerings in one of two ways: either add two new services but offer them as options, or pick two services from the present industry "standard" package and unbundle them, making them surcharge options. Going against industry standards can be the first step toward an industry paradigm shift and changing the rules about market offerings.

Many companies refrain from implementing flexible market offerings because they fear that they will lose certain customers by requiring customers to pay extra for optional services. Instead, managers might adopt the philosophy of MCI. Rather than worrying about accounts that it might lose, MCI focuses on all of the new business it will pick up because its market offerings more closely meet customer requirements at reasonable prices. Other suppliers that have implemented flexible market offerings have found that they now get a better return on their resources by focusing them on the segments and customers that value them.

Timing is always a concern. AKZO IC initiated its customer contribution to profitability approach in Europe about ten years ago. Because revamping service offerings and pricing them to get an equitable return on the value provided was new to the industry, and internally controversial, AKZO IC decided to implement it first in the Netherlands and Germany, "home" markets where AKZO was strongest. It then rolled out the approach to Northern Europe. Southern Europe, the last to be converted, proved to be the most difficult markets to bring around due to sales force resistance (because of anticipated decreases in their commission incomes). Although AKZO IC lost some customers, because they no longer got a variety of services for free, overall, its perseverance resulted in stable sales volume at significantly better profitability.

A Final Practical Consideration

A final, practical consideration that is paramount in implementing flexible market offerings is to be disciplined, operating within the defined flexible ways of doing business with customers. To maintain this discipline requires development of a most difficult to acquire customer skill: adroitly saying "no" to some customers. Flexible market offerings provide customers with choices from which they choose, but suppliers must be willing to say no to those customers that want full-service packages at no-frills prices.[24] Without this skill, flexible market offerings devolve to business as usual, "giving it away." Practiced deftly, it builds a reputation for the supplier within the industry as firm, consistent, and fair.

CONCLUSIONS

Managing market offerings is the process of putting products, services, programs, and systems together in ways that create the greatest value for targeted segments and customers. We began by discussing how suppliers can forestall or reverse the trend toward commoditization by rebuilding their market offerings into differentiated offerings customers value more than those of competitors. To understand the true extent of commoditization for their offerings, suppliers first should gain estimates of the value that customers receive, validate their own and competitors' market pricing, and gain estimates of their share of their customers' business. Suppliers should then consider supplementary services, programs, and systems as profitable sources of differentiation that can significantly change the way customers value market offerings. Creating knowledge banks and building leveraging expertise were some of the specific, promising means of building differentiation we covered. A greater share of the customer's business, "cooperative pricing," slight price premiums, and fees for value-adding services are each ways in which suppliers can get an equitable return on the value that their rebuilt, differentiated offerings deliver.

Recognizing the variation in customer requirements that remains no matter how finely a market is segmented, *flexible market offerings* provide naked solutions consisting of offering elements that all segment members highly value, augmented with optional offering elements that some, but not all, segment members value. We advocate flexible market offerings as an approach for managing market offerings. Business market managers begin by articulating the present market offering for each market segment, which most often turns out to be far greater than any manager realizes. Business market managers next assess customer value and supplier cost for each service. Armed with this knowledge, they construct flexible market offerings for each market segment, specifying which service elements will be standard, which will be options, and which services they will not offer (but which perhaps a third party will provide). We considered some implementation issues, such as whether a supplier should provide flexible market offerings as naked solutions with option menus or as tailored-value packages; how suppliers should communicate about flexible market offerings to the marketplace; and how to break away from the pack to move to flexible market offerings.

Notes

1. Theodore Levitt, "Marketing Success through Differentiation—of Anything," *Harvard Business Review,* vol. 58 (January/February 1980), pp. 83–91.

2. The section, "Rebuilding Commodity Offerings into differentiated Offerings," draws from James C. Anderson and Gregory S. Carpenter, "Escaping the Commodity Trap in Business Markets," *Financial Times,* Mastering Marketing Supplement (November 2, 1998), pp. 4–6. The remainder of the chapter draws heavily

from Chapter 5 of James C. Anderson and James A. Narus, *Business Market Management: Understanding, Creating, and Delivering Value* (Upper Saddle River, NJ: Prentice Hall, 1999).

3. Howard Gleckman with Gary McWilliams, "Ask and It Shall Be Discounted," *Business Week* (October 6, 1997), pp. 116, 118.

4. For a more thorough discussion of value and its assessment, see James C. Anderson and James A. Narus, "Business Marketing: Understand What Customers Value," *Harvard Business Review*, vol. 76 (November/December 1998), pp. 53–65; and Chapter 2 of James C. Anderson and James A. Narus, *Business Market Management: Understanding, Creating, and Delivering Value* (Upper Saddle River, NJ: Prentice Hall, 1999).

5. Michael V. Marn and Robert L. Rosiello, "Managing Price, Gaining Profit," *Harvard Business Review*, vol. 70 (September/October 1992), pp. 84–94.

6. Joan Magretta, "The Power of Virtual Integration: An Interview with Dell Computer's Michael Dell," *Harvard Business Review*, vol. 76 (March/April 1998), pp. 72–84.

7. Ibid.

8. See note 1, Anderson and Narus.

9. James C. Anderson and James A. Narus, "Partnering as a Focused Market Strategy," *California Management Review*, vol. 34 (spring 1991), pp. 95–113.

10. See note 5.

11. See note 6.

12. "The Secrets of the Production Line," *The Economist* (October 17, 1992), pp. 5–6.

13. Rahul Jacob, "Beyond Quality and Value," *Fortune* (October 31, 1993), pp. 8–11; and Fay Rice, "The New Rules of Superlative Service," *Fortune* (October 31, 1993), pp. 50–53.

14. B. Joseph Pine II, Bart Victor, and Andrew Boynton, "Making Mass Customization Work," *Harvard Business Review*, vol. 71 (September/October 1993), pp. 108–119; and Steven C. Wheelwright and Kim C. Clark, *Revolutionizing Product Development* (New York: The Free Press, 1992).

15. This section draws heavily from the same research project as James C. Anderson and James A. Narus, "Capturing the Value of Supplementary Services," *Harvard Business Review*, vol. 73 (January/February 1995), pp. 75–83.

16. In service industries, business market managers would use cores services and augmenting services as the rows.

17. Baxter International Inc., based in the United States, has split into two, separate entities. Baxter Healthcare in this example and those following is now Allegiance Healthcare Corporation.

18. Joseph Lampel and Henry Mintzberg, "Customizing Customization," *Sloan Management Review*, vol. 37 (fall 1996), pp. 21–30.

19. Robin Cooper and Robert S. Kaplan, "Profit Priorities from Activity-Based Costing," *Harvard Business Review*, vol. 69 (May/June 1991), pp. 130–137.

20. Barry J. Brinker, ed., *Emerging Practices in Cost Management* (Boston: Warren, Gorham & Lamont, 1992); and William Rotch, "Activity-Based Costing in Service Industries," *Cost Management,* vol. 13 (summer 1990), pp. 4–14.

21. William R. Benfield and Dale B. Christensen, *Keeping the Wholesaler's House in Order: How Attention to Returned Goods Processing Can Improve the Bottom Line* (Reston, VA: National Wholesale Druggists' Association, 1993).

22. Philip Kotler, *Marketing Management: Analysis, Planning, Implementation, and Control,* 10th ed. (Upper Saddle River, NJ: Prentice Hall, 2000).

23. Mark Ingebretsen, "Mass Appeal: Ross Controls Builds Customers for Life with Mass Customization," *Business Marketing,* vol. 13 (March 1997), pp. 1, 14, 52.

24. V. Kasturi Rangan, Rowland T. Moriarty, and Gordon S. Swartz, "Segmenting Customers in Mature Markets," *Journal of Marketing,* vol. 56 (October 1992), pp. 72–82.

CHAPTER 16

THE SUCCESSFUL SELLING ORGANIZATION

ANDRIS A. ZOLTNERS, PRABHAKANT K. SINHA,
and GREG A. ZOLTNERS

Sales forces represent a major investment for most firms. In the United States alone there were approximately fifteen million people involved in direct and retail selling in 1998. This represents about 9 percent of all people who are employed full-time. With approximately $500 billion spent on sales forces and sales force materials, field selling is an important factor in the U.S. economy. Sales forces cost companies anywhere from 5 percent to 40 percent of sales. The significance of the sales force goes beyond its cost. Sales forces are possibly the most empowered organization within the firm. They represent the company publicly, and they are entrusted with the most important corporate asset: *the customer.*

The sales force is empowered to create sales. It drives the top line and not just expenses. More salespeople will create higher sales than fewer salespeople. A motivated sales force will sell more than an unmotivated sales force. A well-trained, well-coached sales force will sell more than its undisciplined counterpart. The ingenuity of the selling organization has a direct effect on the company's sales and profitability.

The sales force is a *force.* There is not a sales force anywhere that could not seriously hurt its company's performance. At the same time, there is not a sales force anywhere that could not significantly enhance a company's position.

Because of its importance, corporate managements typically pay careful attention to their selling organizations. Several questions get asked repeatedly:

- Is our investment appropriate? Are we sized correctly? Are we structured correctly?
- Are we getting the right coverage? Do the field salespeople provide us with strategic advantage?

- How good are our people? How do we compare with the best selling organizations?
- Are we meeting customer needs? How high are we scoring on customer satisfaction?
- Why are sales growing so slowly? How do we increase new business?
- Is the sales force too expensive for the results they are producing? Can we be more productive?

All of these questions can be answered. The best way to assess the productivity of a sales force is by first developing a framework for viewing sales forces and then by assessing the sales force in terms of this framework. We present a framework for evaluating selling organizations in the next section.

THE COMPONENTS OF A SELLING ORGANIZATION

The components of a selling organization represent a good starting point for examining your sales force productivity opportunity. As we depict in Figure 16.1, every selling organization can be viewed in terms of three basic components.

First, there is sales force investment in salespeople and sales support. People costs can include salesperson compensation, sales manager compensation, and benefits. Sales support costs can include such cost items as hiring, training, sales meetings, sales data, sales systems, and laptop computers. Total annual cost can be as little as several hundred thousand dollars for a

Figure 16.1
The Components of a Selling Organization

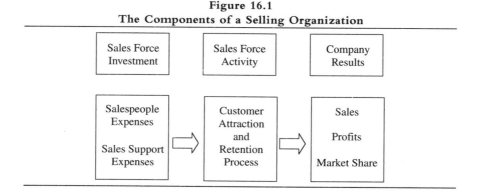

Sales Force Investment	Sales Force Activity	Company Results
Salespeople Expenses Sales Support Expenses	Customer Attraction and Retention Process	Sales Profits Market Share

small selling organization comprised of just a few salespeople, to several billion dollars for a large, multilevel sales force.

The sales force investment buys the company headcount that delivers sales force activity. This activity is directed at a marketplace that responds to the sales force activity and creates sales and profit results for the company. Sales force activity usually manifests itself as a company-adopted selling process. The selling process can include such activities as lead generation, prospecting, needs analysis, solution development, proposal presentation, negotiation, installation, account maintenance, and account expansion. We will refer to the selling process as the customer attraction and retention process.

The company results that the sales force generates are usually expressed in terms of sales, profits, and market share. They can be measured in terms of absolute levels, percent of objective attainment, or growth over last year. It is useful to evaluate these statistics from a short-term as well as long-term perspective, because sales force decisions impact both time frames. A successful selling organization is able to efficiently convert selling costs into effective selling activity that drives noteworthy company results. Each of these three components is usually measurable so that sales force efficiency and effectiveness can be established.

Two components need to be added to complete our conceptualization of the sales force. These new components are *people* and *culture* and the *customer* (see Figure 16.2).

An organization's ability to convert its sales force investment into effective sales force activity is directly related to its people and its sales force culture. Competent, highly motivated people working in a "success" culture will engage in the right activities. The sales force activity is acknowledged

Figure 16.2
The Components of a Selling Organization

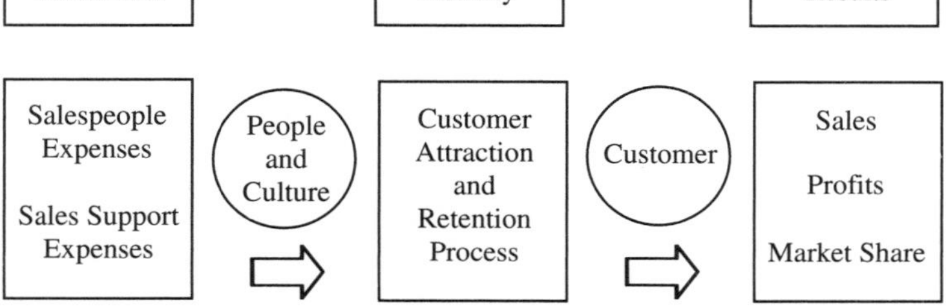

by one's customers in either a positive or negative way to generate company results. These two components are more ambiguous than the prior three components, and their measurement is more problematic.

There has been considerable effort directed at measuring customer satisfaction recently. In addition to measuring product satisfaction, a number of companies measure the extent to which the selling organization affects customer satisfaction. But sales force people and culture measurement is in its infancy.

How do we use this conceptualization to develop a successful selling organization? Certainly our components describe pieces of the answer. A selling organization is successful if it has low costs, significant sales and profits, appropriate selling activities, returns per unit of activity are high or activity levels are high relative to costs. The organization is successful if it has high customer satisfaction. And, success is more likely with highly motivated salespeople and a positive sales force culture.

Sales force productivity is not a static condition. Good productivity cannot be achieved once and kept forever, because productivity fluctuates over time. Market, competitive and other environmental changes can affect the productivity of a selling organization. Markets shift as customers consolidate their buying processes and become more sophisticated. New products, frequently predicated on new technologies, make existing selling approaches obsolete. Boundaryless supplier relationships require a revision of the traditional approach to selling.

Companies look to their sales forces for productivity gains when they attempt to increase profitability through cost reduction programs. Alternative ways to go to market, such as telemarketing, direct mail, part-time selling organizations, and rental selling organizations are explored.

Sales forces are also mindful of competitive actions. They may need to constantly adapt to competitive marketing strategies, product launches, and pricing changes. Finally, federal and local governments can impact markets and their sales forces. Even regulated utilities are reengineering their sales forces for the first time in decades because of imminent deregulation.

The successful selling organization is an evaluative organization. It is paranoid. "Only the paranoid survive," suggests Andrew Groves of Intel. The successful selling organization evaluates constantly, when markets are changing dramatically or just simmering. Our framework provides a sales force diagnostic. It organizes the questions that need to be asked:

Sales force investment: Are our costs too high? Is the sales force sized correctly?

People and culture: How good are our people? Is turnover too high or too low? Do we have a "success" culture?

Sales force activity: Is our coverage adequate? Are we getting enough calls?

Customer: Are customer needs getting met?

Company results: Can we increase sales, market share, profits? How do we increase new business?

These are all valid questions, and they all represent concerns about the five components that describe selling organizations. However, these five components are only descriptive. They allow us to assess the productivity level of a selling organization, but they are unable to help us determine how to increase sales force productivity. For improving productivity, we need to introduce the concept of sales force productivity drivers, a sixth dimension in our sales force model.

THE SALES FORCE PRODUCTIVITY DRIVERS

The sales force productivity drivers are the basic decisions that sales managers make that directly affect all five components of the selling organization. They fall into four categories.

1. *Research,* including the data that are gathered and analyses that are performed to enable the selling organization to segment its markets and understand the buying behavior in each market segment.
2. *Sales force strategy,* including decisions on the appropriate size for the sales force, the best sales force organizational structure, and a definition of the customer attraction and retention process. These tend to be the decisions of most interest to top management.
3. *Customer interactions,* decisions which have the biggest impact on the interaction with the customer. These include who is hired, how these employees are educated to be successful, and the selection of sales team leaders. The persona that the customer sees is the result of these decisions on hiring, training, and the "success" atmosphere that the sales manager creates and fosters. Most regional and district sales managers view these decisions as having the highest impact on sales success.

4. *Sales systems,* or management decisions that affect the five sales force components, but affect customers indirectly. Compensation, sales territory alignment, sales force data, tools, and processes, and other productivity enhancement programs are all decision areas that fall into this category (Figure 16.3).

The sales force productivity drivers represent the root of sales force productivity enhancement. They are the decisions that, if made correctly, keep costs in line, create a successful culture, establish the right activity to create a satisfied customer, and thereby drive positive company results.

Any sales force effectiveness assessment should focus on these drivers because they ultimately determine the success of a selling organization. We know that we have a successful selling organization if we know that the

Figure 16.3
The Components of a Selling Organization

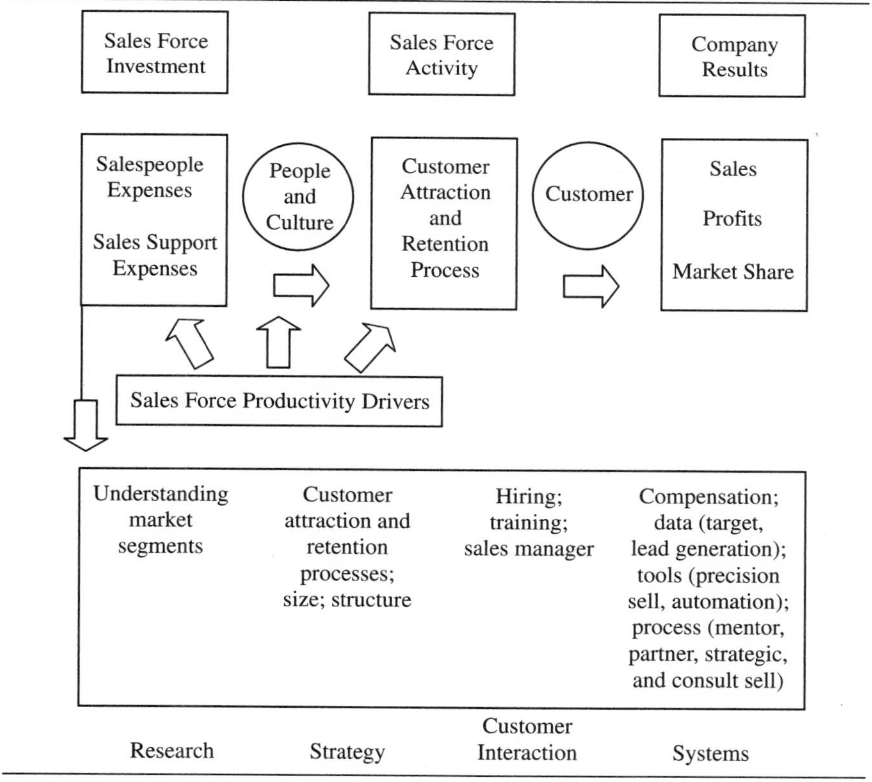

people we have recruited this year are exceptional (better than the ones we hired last year), our training program is of high quality, our sales management team is professional and competent, our sales force is right-sized and structured properly, our customer attraction and retention process is well conceived, and our compensation plan is truly motivational and encourages the right sales force activity and results.

We need to examine the sales force productivity drivers to assess and improve the effectiveness of a selling organization. However, the measurement of the sales force drivers is difficult to do. How do we measure a compensation plan? How do we measure a recruitment program? The best way to assess how well your sales force is performing is by comparing your sales forces driver decision processes with best practice approaches. Later in this chapter we will provide a summary of some of our experience-based insights that will be useful for making these critical sales force decisions. (You can constantly improve, but you still need some benchmarks, some "shoulds" and we will provide these.)

The successful selling organization is an evaluative organization. So, let's first discuss the measurement of the six components of our sales force model. This is a good place to start, since you "can't manage what you can't measure," as suggested by William Hewlett.

Sales Force Measurement

Each of the components of a selling organization is measurable to some extent. Sales force investment, sales force activity, and company results are usually the easiest to measure. Cost and result data are maintained in the corporate accounting system. Activity data can be obtained through self-reporting mechanisms or from sales managers who travel with the sales force. The productivity drivers, people, culture, and customer components are more difficult to measure. Figure 16.4 describes several measures that can be used to understand how well a sales force is performing.

Measurement lets us assess the current situation so that improvement programs can be developed. Each of the six areas of sales force productivity *can* be measured, but most companies do not attempt to measure all of these areas, because extensive measurement requires data and costs money.

Measuring Sales Force Productivity Drivers

Measuring sales force productivity drivers involves looking at sales management decisions. To do so, one can benchmark against best practices.

Figure 16.4
Sales Force Measurement

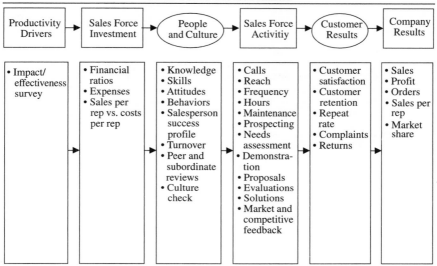

Table 16.1 presents a sales force productivity assessment test that will enable the detection of those productivity areas that may need immediate attention. Too many "C" grades indicate that a major overhaul is required. This questionnaire is a quick way to evaluate one's sales force.

Another insightful way to determine where to concentrate efforts is to evaluate the current importance of various drivers and the capacity to improve these drivers. First, develop or understand best practices. Then determine one's own current practices, and assess the gap between actual and ideal. This will help to establish the current state of effectiveness relative to this driver, and the degree to which improvement is possible. Then estimate the importance of the driver. What is its impact on the ability to generate customer satisfaction and sales success? Work to improve those drivers that have the largest gaps and are important to success. In the example depicted in Figure 16.5, the most important drivers might be hiring, compensation, or sales force structure.

We will present numerous ideas that lead to best practices later in this chapter. Any well-functioning selling organization is susceptible to forces that can diminish its productivity. Continuous attention to the environment and continuous improvement are the hallmarks of good management.

Table 16.1
The Effectiveness-Impact Inventory

Productivity Driver	C	B	A	Your Grade
Customer needs, buying process definition	Customer needs and buying process are understood at an intuitive level.	Customer needs are researched periodically and understood.	Customer partnerships enable a continual assessment of customer needs and definition of the best way to meet them.	
Market segmentation	No formal market segmentation has been done.	A general segmentation is specified but it is not research based.	A precise, well-researched market segmentation has been developed.	
Channel design	The current channel strategy may have been appropriate in the past, but it is no longer appropriate for the current environment.	There is a recognized need to develop a channel strategy that meets market segment needs; work is in progress.	A clear and appropriate channel strategy for each market segment has been developed.	
Sales force strategy	Strategy is imprecise; sales force is on its own to sell however it can.	Sales strategies are defined but their effectiveness is not fully understood or universally applied.	Effective and tested customer attraction and retention strategies are in place and universally applied.	
Sales force organizational structure	The current sales force structure may have been appropriate in the past, but it is no longer appropriate for the current environment.	There is a recognized need to develop a new sales force structure that better meets customer needs and is consistent with sales force strategy; work is in progress.	The sales force structure clearly and appropriately meets market and corporate requirements.	
Sales force size	Company management is not aware that the sales force is not sized correctly to meet market opportunities in a cost effective fashion.	Upsizing or downsizing is anticipated.	The sales force is right sized; a profitability and coverage analysis has demonstrated the need for the current size.	
Hiring	The hiring process is based exclusively on ad hoc interviews with the first-line sales manager and the national sales manager.	The hiring process incorporates several effectiveness enhancing approaches such as behavioral interviewing or candidate testing.	The hiring process uses a formalized well-founded process including candidate profile definition, appropriate applicant pools, effective candidate selection processes, and effective attraction schemes.	

Table 16.1 (*Continued*)

Productivity Driver	C	B	A	Your Grade
Training	Training mostly consists of ad hoc approaches implemented by field sales managers.	Some good training programs exist but they are not consistently applied.	Professional programs are in place and are applied consistently; training needs are continually reassessed and program content and methods are adapted appropriately.	
Sales manager	Sales managers are either war horses or comets that have been selected using an ad hoc process; managers receive little or no professional development training.	A sales manager selection process incorporates several effective concepts such as candidate testing; some professional development exists but it is not consistently applied.	A well-developed selection process produces successful managers; managers continue to learn and grow professionally; the role of the sales manager evolves with changing market conditions.	
Compensation	The plan is complex and leads to unanticipated behavior, rewarding the territory and not the salesperson.	The plan meets some company, customer, or salesperson criteria but some improvement is required; improvement plans are underway.	The plan is simple, consistent with marketing strategy, ensures that the customer will be treated appropriately, is fair and rewards the high performers.	
Sales force tools and data	Not much data is available, most progressive salespeople use their own computers, and the sales force is on its own to sell however it can.	Databases are under development; the sales force is testing a few automation tools with some success. Customer information is passed on when a new salesperson takes the job.	Cost-effective database-based tools are available for such tasks as identifying customer needs, targeting, effective time management, performance evaluation, and for providing value-added services for customers.	
Total sales force productivity	Reactive studies of the productivity drivers are initiated when sales results are below expectation.	Ongoing program development in several productivity driver areas, but mostly due to "putting out fires" and "pet projects."	The productivity drivers are evaluated on an ongoing basis; areas of improvement are identified; best practices are researched and communicated; and a continuous improvement program has become part of the culture.	

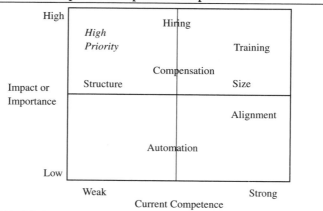

Figure 16.5
Example of Competence/Impact Matrix

Sales Force Investment

Sales force investment is one of the easier measures to obtain. Measurement is usually done by the finance and accounting functions. Sales management needs to keep a close eye on expenses as well, because sales management often has a better understanding of what the sales force expenses are buying.

People and Culture

For a company to thrive, it must have good people and an appropriate culture. A culture consists of attitudes, values, and actions that help the company do its work effectively. There are as many sales force cultures as there are selling organizations. Some are empowering and others are controlling; some are focused on short-term results, others on long-term results. Different cultures can succeed in the same industry. The pharmaceutical industry has over 30 worldwide competitors with selling organizations. Their sales force cultures differ across companies and across countries. Some are 100 percent salary and "home spun," whereas others have highly leveraged compensation plans and are aggressive. In spite of their cultural differences, many selling organizations have had success in this industry.

While it is true that different selling cultures can coexist in the same industry, it is likely that some cultures will be more successful than others and that some cultures might be better suited for some industries; for example, it is difficult to envision a "salary-only" life insurance sales culture. The marketplace and competitive environment strongly influence the cultures that survive.

A culture check can be employed to measure a culture. The culture check asks the following questions and assesses the answers in terms of the market and competitive environment:

What are the sales force values?

Customer first or income first?

Empowerment or control?

Short-term or long-term?

Who are the heroes?

What are the legends?

How does the organization communicate?

The first level sales manager is an important part of the sales force culture because managers provide the link between headquarters and the field. How often do sales forces assess their sales management teams? Not very frequently! Usually companies rely on sales results to evaluate sales management. However, it would also be useful to determine how managers are contributing to salesperson growth, culture formation, and customer satisfaction. Peer and subordinate reviews (sometimes called 360-degree reviews) are a good measurement tool for this purpose. The most progressive selling organizations use them.

Activity

It is expected that salespeople will do the right things in order to get the sale. Depending on the business they're in, they will influence customers and prospects in a variety of ways. What will they do? They will generate leads, calling on customers or prospects, by phone or in person. They will bid on business, write proposals and letters, take orders and service customers. They will demonstrate the product or leave selling aids and they will target accounts and call on the appropriate level in the customer's organization. Any sales force activity can be tracked to see if the sales force is doing the "right stuff."

Sales activity measurement is a debated area. The results of a sales force activity report can easily be understood by all levels of the sales organization. It states clearly what the salesperson has accomplished during the report period. Some sales force managers feel that they would like to know (and even control) what the field force does. Managers with strong beliefs about what the salespeople should be doing frequently design elaborate call reporting systems. In contrast, many sales managers believe that the sales force should be completely empowered. They feel that the sales force needs to drive sales results, and that measuring sales activities is only a distraction.

Even in the case of the totally self-managed selling organization, activity measures can be obtained. When internal reporting mechanisms are not available, simple sales force activity questionnaires can be administered without much intrusion.

Sales activity measures do have drawbacks. The most important are the assumptions about what causes sales success. Which particular sales force activity causes sales to occur? Do high call frequencies really cause sales? Do frequent demonstrations drive sales? The activities that are easy to count and measure might not be the activities that most affect sales results. A simple call count gives no indication as to the quality and effectiveness of a sales presentation. One really good presentation is better than 10 half-hearted ones.

In addition, these measures are generally self-reported, and therefore subject to the vagaries of human honesty and memory. Did the sales representative really mention a particular product during the sales call? Even the salesperson might not be sure. Moreover, the company may give account level required calling frequencies. A salesperson who knows the frequency isn't right for a particular account will call that often only because it will show up on a report.

These drawbacks are largely overcome in most organizations. The activities that matter most for sales success can be determined by careful study of the best salespeople, and a culture of professionalism and honesty, with good field to management communication, will keep activity goals meaningful and reports accurate.

Customer Results

Customer results are a good measure of sales success. As illustrated in Figure 16.6, through successful interaction with customers, the sales force can

Figure 16.6
Value-Added Chain

| Needs | → | Solutions | → | Satisfaction | → | Delight | → | Trust | → | Relationships | → | Partnering assessment |

create customer solutions, customer satisfaction and delight, and sustainable profitable relationships. Customer retention rates, repeat rates, and complaints have been used to evaluate customer relationships, but improved results in these areas can take time in comparison to the more immediate measure of customer satisfaction, which has become popular among U.S. companies. Questionnaires are frequently used to measure customer satisfaction. It is important when evaluating the results of the surveys to distinguish between salesperson and product effectiveness. When designed and administered properly, these questionnaires can help to determine if one's sales force is adding value for customers.

Customer measurement has several levels. The basic level is a sale—a solution to the customer's problem. Customer satisfaction comes from a solution—a filled need. Delighted customers are harder to lose, and relationships are formed when steady customers buy at profitable prices and intend to be customers in the future. Partnering involves the further steps of data sharing and business integration. Table 16.2 demonstrates how we can attempt to measure any of these customer results using a simple assessment form.

Table 16.2
Customer Measurement

How would you assess your interaction with John Smith? Please rate the following statements from 1 to 7.

	Strongly Disagree 1	2	3	4	5	Strongly Agree 6	7
He presents himself in a professional manner.							
He understands my needs.							
He knows his products well.							
He meets all of my deadlines.							
He maintains contact throughout the year.							

These items may be specially formulated to deal with product and industry specifics. For instance:

He recommends mail processing machines with capacity appropriate for my current and future payroll check volume.							

Company Results

The sales force creates sales, so it would be useful to measure its effectiveness based on company results as well. Some measures to be used include ales, profits, and market share, often considered to be overall company measures of success. These are good initial measures, though adjustments may be necessary. Sales lag orders, so it might be better to track results as soon as orders are written, not the moment defined by strict accounting methods. Market share measures also can be useful since they reflect the competition and market potential. Percentage of objective achieved is often used as a company results measure. Well-set objectives usually incorporate market, competitive, and environmental factors.

Frequently, the relevant sales force results are derived from the company strategy. If the company goals include growing sales, orders, or market share, then the sales force results will be specified in terms of these measures as well. However, as we illustrate with Figure 16.7, the sales force is not the only factor creating sales. In fact, there are many more. Our statistical studies with several hundred selling organizations suggest that the sales force effect at the territory level is anywhere from 5 percent to 80 percent of one-year territory sales. The rest is due to the cumulative product/service strength (sales carryover from prior years' activity) and the factors in the following figure. The sales force drives the top line but is only one factor.

Figure 16.7
Impacts on Company Results

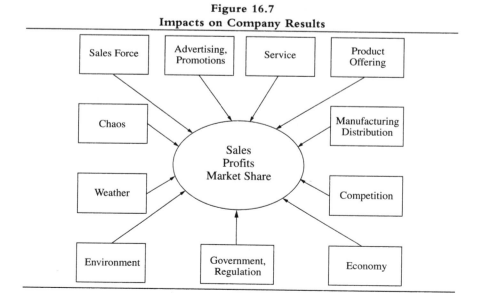

Measurement Spotlight: Sales per Person

Be careful using only a single measure for sales force productivity. Sales-per-salesperson is an example of a typical productivity measure that combines results with activity measures to make an insightful ratio. Average sales per call is another common performance measure that is designed this way. Unfortunately, these types of productivity measures often make for good reading, but not good management.

It is easy to think that if sales-per-person are up then productivity is up, but this ratio has a numerator and a denominator. Tremendous sales-per-salesperson can result if you fire all of the salespeople except one. Further, smart businesspeople should disagree with the intuition that a high sales-per-salesperson ratio is good; if incremental sales-per-person are higher than the full cost of a salesperson, then adding salespeople will lower the sales-per-person ratio and increase the profits of the firm at the same time.

Thus, one should not diminish its impact, but neither should one overstate its impact when using sales results to assess a selling organization.

Use Several Measures

The sales force is complex, and it needs to be evaluated with multiple measures. A single measurement cannot capture all of the dimensions of a selling organization. Our six component model provides a framework for measuring the critical aspects of a selling organization. Some useful measures will be qualitative, others quantitative. The qualitative measures suffer from the vagaries of subjective measurement, but they are likely to provide more insight into sales force effectiveness. Measurement of people and culture, customer satisfaction, and the sales force drivers is difficult to do objectively, but understanding these areas is crucial for developing a successful sales force. Collectively, the best measurements of these areas can provide a comprehensive understanding of the sales force and lead to the answers to the sales force productivity questions that most managements raise.

NATURAL CHANGE SEQUENCE

Our sales force measurement can reveal problem areas, but the correction is not always obvious. For example, suppose that a selling organization is not generating enough new business. This issue can be addressed in several ways: different kinds of people can be hired, salespeople can be trained to "hunt" more effectively, a well-crafted incentive program can be created to encourage salespeople to develop new accounts, or the sales force can be reorganized into "hunting" and "farming" teams.

An analysis is usually required to determine the appropriate set of decisions to address the problem area. However, if a sales force change is anticipated, there is a natural hierarchical sequence that should be followed. Some decisions about the productivity drivers naturally precede others. In fact, the sales force productivity driver decisions fall into three categories. We have called these decisions Level 1, 2, and 3 decisions in Figure 16.8.

Level 2 decisions need to be consistent with Level 1 strategies. If the sales force is undergoing change it is best to articulate the corporate and marketing strategies before finalizing the channel structure, the customer attraction and retention process, and the size and structure of the selling organization. Similarly, Level 2 decisions need to precede Level 3 decisions. As an illustration, a major compensation overhaul prior to a sales force reorganization that will create a new team-selling environment will probably

Figure 16.8
The Natural Sales Force Decision Sequence

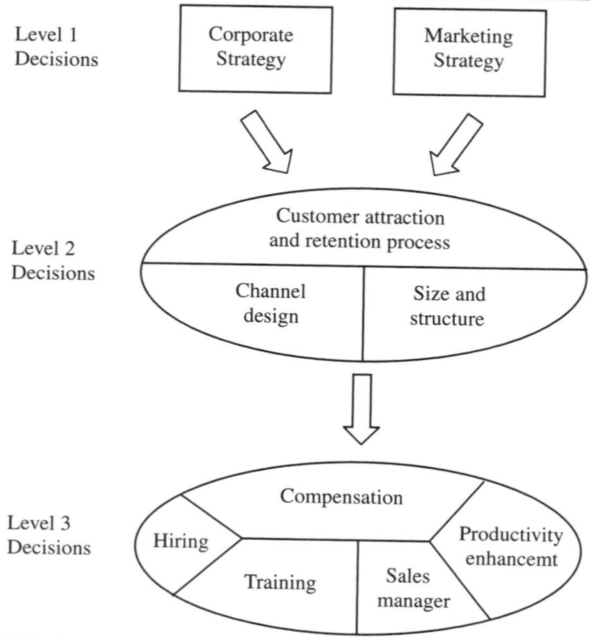

require a reexamination after the reorganization. It would be best to accelerate the reorganization and implement a single compensation change. In addition, the recruiting profile, training requirements, and sales information systems may also need to be updated because of the reorganization.

To summarize, sales force measurement enables the diagnostic that change may be required. The requisite change may not be obvious; as the sales force driver hierarchy suggests, there are interdependencies among the sales force productivity decisions. However, one principle is clear: if the sales force productivity decisions are made successfully, the sales force organization will be successful.

TIME FRAME FOR IMPROVEMENT

Some productivity changes can have an immediate impact while others will have a significant impact over longer periods of time. Table 16.3 predicts the

Table 16.3
Time Frame and Requisite Coordination for Productivity Drivers

Productivity Area	Time Frame	Who Is Involved
Hiring	Long-term, unless there is high turnover	Sales management, HR
Training	Short-term/intermediate	Sales management, HR
Sales manager	Intermediate/short-term	VP sales
Sales force strategy		
Size	Intermediate	President, VP sales
Structure	Intermediate	President, VP sales
Account targeting	Short-term	Sales management, sales force
Compensation	Short-term	Sales management, sales force, HR
Territory alignment	Short-term	VP sales, sale management
Innovative programs	Short-term/intermediate	
Automation		Sales force, IS
Telemarketing		Sales management, sales force, customers
Partnering		Sales management,
Consultative selling		sales force,
Team selling		customers
Networking		Sales management,
Mentoring		sales force

time frame for the impact of each of the drivers, as well as a recommendation of who within the organization should participate in the improvement of the productivity area.

Implementation

Once changes are prioritized, implementation may proceed. A characteristic of a successful selling organization is that it implements vigorously. Further, implementation is the step that keeps the improvement cycle going. We cannot state too strongly that implementation may be the most important step of the improvement process: *Sales success is 10 percent inspiration and 90 percent implementation.*

Process reengineering and kaizen are two forms of implementation. Reengineering reinvents the sales process, whereas kaizen is an incremental approach that requires small but constant improvement by everyone. Sales force kaizen is preferred but sometimes reengineering is required.

CONCLUSIONS

Productivity is about results and output. It is about sales, market share and profits, contracts, orders, and equipment evaluations. Productivity is up when costs are down, orders are up, sales are up, and profits are up.

The ultimate measure of success is company results. Sales, profits, market share, and orders are all measures of company results. However, the sales team can be successful even with average company results. Remember that company success is not entirely in the hands of the sales force. If it were, there would be no other departments at all.

Productivity is about *customers;* how they are treated and helped. It is about customer solutions, partnerships, and relationships. It is about delighting customers, profitably. Productivity is up when our customers are satisfied with performance.

Productivity is about *activities.* It is about calls and presentations, telephoning, letter writing, lead generation, and follow-up. It is about better targeting, increased frequency against the most important accounts, increased face time, and sales cycle reduction. Productivity is up when calls are up, especially high-quality calls.

Productivity is about *people.* It is about the salespeople who interact with the customers and prospects, making calls, generating results by delighting customers within a "success" environment created by our management team. Productivity is up when there is low turnover among the high performers because they feel that they are part of a vital, progressive, successful organization. Productivity is up when salespeople are motivated and satisfied.

Finally, productivity is about *sales management*. It is about a management team that structures the sales force appropriately; determines the right size, hires the right people, prepares them well with training, selects a first-line management team that creates an atmosphere and culture for success, and establishes a compensation plan that is fair and rewards for accomplishment. It is about management that deals with career plateaus and finds ways to get the job done with fewer people. Productivity is up when sales management is doing their job well.

Improving productivity means improving one's ability to make the appropriate sales decisions that create a successful culture with people who perform the best activities to yield positive customer results and contribute to overall company success.

CHAPTER 17

MARKETING IN THE AGE OF INFORMATION DEMOCRACY

MOHANBIR SAWHNEY and PHILIP KOTLER

We are rapidly moving into the Information Age, yet our thought processes are stuck in the Industrial Age. Business and marketing in the Information Age will be conducted on vastly different principles. Companies that continue their Industrial Age thinking will lose the race for market leadership.

The Industrial Age was the age of *information asymmetry*. Information exchange between firms and their customers was one-sided, expensive, and inefficient. As a result, customers were ill-informed, information was marketer-controlled, and exchanges marketer-initiated. But the Information Age is the age of *information democracy*. Information is becoming ubiquitous and cheap. Customers are being empowered with far better information about marketers as well as their competitors.

The leveling of the information playing field has tilted the balance of power in favor of customers. This shift in the balance of power demands radical changes in the thought and practice of marketing. It requires reversing conventional wisdom on the marketing concept, the marketing process, and the marketing organization. It requires marketers to come to terms with customer-initiated marketing.

To understand the implications of information democracy on marketing, we will:

- Examine the assumptions and metaphors underlying industrial-age marketing thinking.
- Show how the new capabilities of buyers are reshaping their role in marketing exchanges.

386

- Propose the new assumptions and a new metaphor that will characterize marketing in the Age of Information Democracy.
- Outline how marketing processes and marketing organizations will need to evolve to take advantage of the changed information regime.
- Identify the new mediators that will facilitate customer-initiated marketing.
- Show how marketing organizations will change.
- Offer a diagnostic tool to help companies determine where they stand in this change process, and how they can improve to capture or retain market leadership.

ASSUMPTIONS OF INDUSTRIAL-AGE MARKETING

Industrial-Age marketing thinking is rooted in the metaphor of *marketing as hunting*. The marketplace is seen as a jungle. Marketers have to scope out the jungle (*market research*) and define the prey that they want to capture (*target marketing*). Marketers must study the prey's habits and habitats (*consumer behavior*). Marketers have to build a better mousetrap (*product differentiation*), lay traps and bait (*advertising, direct mail, sales promotions*), and secure the prey and prevent it from escaping (*customer retention, relationship marketing*).

The hunters/marketers assume that the prey is not as smart or well-informed as they are. The prey acts on emotion (*positioning*), is easily seduced by trinkets (*promotions*), and wanders unwittingly into the danger zone (*retail stores, salespeople*). The hunter has extensive information about the whereabouts of the prey, and knows how to aim the rifle (*value proposition*) at the prey's soft spot.

In the age of information democracy, these assumptions are being turned on their head. Customers are arming themselves with information, and the hunters have become the hunted. Buyers can now seek out the best sellers, and can initiate relationships with sellers of their choice. The implication is devastating for Industrial-Age marketing. It means that buyers do not need to see advertisements, receive salespeople, or visit retail stores to obtain what they want. They do not need to overpay out of price ignorance. They do not need to exert physical effort to consummate a purchase. They can dictate whom they will do business with, and the terms that they will do business on. The information-rich regime empowers customers with a new set of capabilities.

The New Capabilities
of Customers

As illustrations of the new capabilities, consider how consumers can use the Internet today to buy an automobile through www.edmunds.com or to secure a home mortgage loan through www.homeowners.com.

The Edmunds site provides unbiased, third-party information and advice on automobiles. Using the Edmunds site, auto buyers can:

- Begin their search and evaluation process by comparing features, quality, and dealer costs/margins for any automobile on Edmunds' site. They can narrow their search to a few makes and models, and conduct side-by-side comparisons. They can request Edmunds, in collaboration with the manufacturers, to mail them customized brochures with information on their selected makes and models.
- They can seek advice from customers by entering the Edmunds Town Hall discussion area to interact with other consumers who have bought or own these autos. They may even visit Web sites that present complaints of customers who have had negative experiences with a particular seller (e.g., www.bmwlemon.com).
- In the near future, buyers will be able to sign up for appointments to test drive multiple brands and models at a predefined place and time, sponsored by Edmunds and partners like CarMax or AutoNation. They will be able to "kick the tires" for their favorite brands side-by-side, with no sales pressure from dealers, and without ever visiting a brand-specific dealer. The appointments will be pre-arranged, so that buyers will have exactly the models they want ready for test drives.
- When buyers decide on a brand and make, they can define the features and options they want, and ask Edmunds' partner AutoByTel (www.autobytel.com) to act as their buying agent. AutoByTel informs several local car dealers that there is a "hot" prospect for the particular auto, and invites them to bid for the business.
- Buyers can round out their transaction by using other Edmunds business partners. They can prequalify for financing from Nations Bank; get extended warranties from Warranty Gold; buy auto insurance from GEICO; and accessorize their auto with spares from J.C. Whitney.

Visiting the Homeowner site enables prospective home buyers to research home mortgage rates, interest rate trends, use financial tools to analyze loans, and sign up for an e-mail service that keeps buyers informed of trends in loan rates. They can also apply online for home mortgages from a variety of home mortgage providers, and obtain responses within one business day. In addition, they can connect with realtors in specific locations and neighborhoods for buying and selling homes.

Thus, it should be clear that with the assistance of this variety of intermediaries and agents, buyers have gained enormous capabilities in this new information-rich age. Through the use of the Internet, they are now able to:

- Get objective information for multiple brands, including costs, prices, features, and quality without relying on the manufacturer or retailers;
- Initiate requests for advertising and information from manufacturers;
- Design the offerings that they want;
- Hire buying agents and invite offers from multiple sellers; and
- Buy ancillary products and services from specialized third-party sellers.

HOW MARKETING ASSUMPTIONS MUST CHANGE

With power in the marketplace shifting from sellers to buyers, enlightened sellers will need to adopt a new set of assumptions about what constitutes effective marketing. Effective marketing in the Information Age will require a reversal of three key marketing assumptions.

First, marketers will need to change their role in exchanges from *controlling exchanges* to *facilitating exchanges*. Marketers traditionally have initiated exchange transactions, and have been in control of the exchange process. But in the information-rich regime, exchanges are increasingly being initiated and controlled by customers. Marketers and their representatives are held at bay till customers invite them to participate in the exchange. Even after they enter the exchange process, customers define the rules of engagement, and insulate themselves from marketers with the help of agents and intermediaries. Customers define what information they need, what offerings they are interested in, and what prices they are willing to pay. This customer-controlled exchange process reverses many time-honored marketing practices (see pages 390–391).

Second, marketers will need to change their information policies in dealing with customers from *opaqueness* to *transparency*. Industrial-Age marketers have thrived by making it difficult for customers to compare their offerings with competitors, and by not fully disclosing information that customers need in order to make better choices. Mattress manufacturers, for instance, create different brand names for the same products for different

The Rise of Reverse Marketing

Traditionally, marketing activities have been initiated by marketers. In the Information Age, this logic is being reversed this logic, and we are seeing the rise of *reverse marketing,* where customers initiate exchanges and pull the information they need. Here are some examples of reverse marketing activities:

- *Reverse promotions:* Customers reverse the flow of consumer promotions by either soliciting promotions directly from marketers through intermediaries like Yoyodyne, NetCentives and mySimon, or by requesting specific offers through third parties like BonusMail, FreeRide, and Internet Service Providers. These intermediaries block unwanted offers and relay consumer requests to marketers without divulging personal information.
- *Reverse advertising:* Conventional advertising has been traditionally pushed to consumers by marketers. But customers can now click on advertisements that interest them, and request promotional information from manufacturers. Advertising is pulled by customers and is customer-initiated. Interestingly, services like PointCast that used the Internet to push content and advertisements have fallen out of favor.
- *Reverse pricing:* Priceline.com allows customers to set the prices for automobiles, and to put out their offer for bidding. Buyers specify the price, model, options, pickup date, and the distance they are willing to drive to complete the sale. Customers provide their own financing and guarantee offers with a $200 security deposit charged to a major credit card. Priceline faxes bids to dealers. Priceline removes contact information from the offer and faxes it to all relevant dealers. Priceline makes its money on completed deals only. Buyers pay $25; dealers pay $75. It plans to offer financing and insurance next, allowing consumers to shop using a similar bidding model.
- *Reverse product design:* Customers can design and configure their own products, using their imagination and tools provided by marketers. Garden.com offers a garden planner that lets visitors create and save their own ideal garden designs. At the same time, it cues them up to purchase the plants and implements they will need to realize their dreams. The site's notepad lets would-be buyers scribble and save ideas about products as they browse.
- *Reverse segmentation:* Marketers have traditionally used customer purchase histories to create customized offers. But now, customers are self-selecting and co-customizing offers with marketers. BroadVision offers Business-to-Business personalization software that combines marketer-controlled

---

The Rise of Reverse Marketing *(Continued)*

customer behavior information with customer-specified preferences to create tailored commission structures, tailored pricing information, educational programs, profile-accelerated transactions, and activity reports.
- *Reverse distribution channels:* Public Technologies Multimedia (PTM) offers "Your Personal Model" on the Lands' End site. It asks shoppers to describe their body type—for example broad shoulders and wide hips—then generates a 3-D representation. Shoppers view the model on-line in outfits recommended for their body types. Instead of having to go to the store to try out apparel, customers can try out a variety of outfits in the comfort of their home. The showroom comes to the customer, instead of the customer going to the showroom.

---

retail chains, which in turn offer to match the lowest competing price for the same *brand*. Cellular phone companies excel in creating pricing plans that deliberately make it difficult for customers to make price comparisons across service providers. Even when manufacturers do compare their product with competitors, such comparative advertising is generally biased and portrays competitors in a poor light.

In the new information regime, buyers will demand objective and unbiased information from manufacturers. Or else they will turn to third-party intermediaries for comparative assessments and prices. For instance, the Comparison Shopping network (www.comparisonshopping.net) allows consumers to do comparison shopping for a number of product categories, and Energy Market (www.energymarket.com) offers businesses price comparisons for natural gas providers. Even service and quality ratings of marketers are available from third parties like BizRate (www.bizrate.com).

In the age of information democracy, there is no place to hide, and profiting from customer ignorance is a dangerous way to make a living. Enlightened marketers may even decide to post the competitors' prices along with their own as a show of good faith. For instance, the online bookseller Books.com (www.books.com) allows customers to compare its prices with competitors on its own site. This is an advantage, of course, if the marketer is the price leader. But it can also be used when the marketer charges a higher price and shows why his offering provides better value.

Third, marketers will need to shift their energy from *acquiring new customers* to *serving their current customers* more fully. While customer acquisition will always be required, it will be less important because buyers will seek out the best sellers. Marketers historically have been primarily interested in creating one-time *exchange value,* namely making a sale. Information-Age marketers will need to build *relationship value* with their clients. This requires understanding each customer more intimately through customer knowledge management, learning how to cross-sell and up-sell to their customers, and building relationship capital that makes it more profitable for customers to do business with them. The emphasis in the Information Age will shift from customer acquisition to customer retention, and from transactional value to lifetime customer value.

TOWARD A NEW METAPHOR FOR MARKETING

These changed assumptions suggest a new metaphor for the marketer, from a *hunter* to a *gardener.* Instead of thinking of marketing as hunting for customers, we need to think of marketing as cultivating relationships with customers and complementors. This evolutionary shift parallels human evolution from a hunter-gatherer to a settler-gardener. As humans invented the plow and became more skilled at farming, they realized that they could live better lives by cultivating farms and tending to their gardens. Similarly, as marketers become better at creating and sustaining relationships with customers and partners, they will create greater value by serving customers more fully. Just as gardeners create the right environment and provide the right ingredients for plants to grow, marketers need to become skilled at seeding, feeding, and weeding customer relationships. And just as a garden is an ecosystem where every form of plant and animal life is connected, customers and complementors constitute a densely interconnected ecosystem.

But perhaps the most important insight from the gardening metaphor is the fact that a gardener can never fully control what plants will grow, and what flowers will bloom. Unlike the hunter who seeks out and selects his prey, gardeners can sow good seeds and nurture their plants, but they then need to let their garden evolve organically. Information-age marketers will need to let customers lead the way, and go with the flow.

HOW MARKETING ACTIVITIES MUST EVOLVE

As the growing availability of information shifts power from sellers to buyers, marketing activities must evolve to keep pace with the change. The evolution will occur on all value-creating activities. And the evolution will not happen in one step. Rather, there will be a transition phase between Industrial-Age marketing activities and Information-Age marketing activities. This evolution path is shown in Figure 17.1.

Designing the Offering

In traditional industrial firms, the new offerings often originated in the engineering department, and marketing would be given the task of selling the offerings after the design had been completed. More progressive firms have reversed this process, and the marketing department transmits the "voice of the customer" to the organization before the development begins. However, this marketing-led process still assumes a sequential process for designing offers and messages. Marketers first survey customers, and then use this information to create offers and messages.

In the new information-rich regime, the sensing and responding processes are becoming simultaneous, not sequential. Instead of playing a role at the beginning and at the end of the design process, persistent connectivity with

Figure 17.1
The Evolution of Marketing Activities

	Industrial-Age Marketing	Transitional Marketing	Information-Age Marketing
Designing the offering	Engineering-led	Marketing-led	Customer-led
Customizing the offering	Segmentation	Mass-customization	Customer-configured
Pricing the offering	Cost-based pricing	Value pricing	Lifetime pricing
Communicating the offering	Persuasion-based	Information-based	Permission-based
Delivering the offering	Physical channels	Multiple channels	Seamless channels
Augmenting the offering	Vertical partners	Horizontal partners	Business network
Supporting customers	People access	Information access	Process access

customers allows them to play an active role in designing, creating, and adapting new offerings. Consider the popular Internet-based auction service eBay. The eBay site conducts person-to-person auctions in over 1,000 categories, including collectibles, antiques, sports memorabilia, computers, toys, beanie babies, dolls, figures, coins, stamps, books, magazines, music, and pottery. Unlike traditional auction houses that specialize in a few categories, eBay's categories are adapted on an ongoing basis, based on what customers want to buy and sell. Customers provide the merchandise, and customers keep sellers honest by rating them on an open forum. The eBay site acts as a facilitator of exchanges. It does not control the exchange, and it does not participate directly in the exchange. The offers are created, adapted, and consumed by customers.

Another information-age firm that is changing the rules is *Silicon India Magazine* (www.siliconindia.com). This magazine serves the community of information technology professionals of Asian origin in the United States. When it was founded in 1997, its founders had no prior publishing experience. So they turned to their customers for advice and created an online prototype of the magazine six months before the print version was created. The online prototype was refined with the input from a 6,000-member community, who engaged in a dialog with the publishers to design the layout, the content, and the editorial atmosphere of the magazine. When the magazine was launched, most of these founding members signed up as subscribers for the print magazine. Within a year, Silicon India's subscriber base has grown to over 40,000 subscribers. The online magazine continues to act as a test bed for new features, and a feedback channel for customer input into the evolution of the magazine.

Customizing the Offering

Marketers have long understood the value of target marketing—the process of customizing offerings to match the preferences of different groups of customers. Like other marketing activities, customization has been marketer-controlled. Marketers configure a set of offerings, and target these at specific customer groups. With the availability of flexible manufacturing techniques, the segmentation logic has been pushed to the extreme of mass customization, where marketers create customized offerings for each customer. But marketers can never know customer preferences as well as customers know themselves. In the information-rich regime, marketers need to evolve further towards customer-configured offerings, where the customization is done by customers, and not by marketers. The role of marketers shifts to assisting customers in defining their preferences, and creating their own offers.

Marketers of computer hardware and web-based information services are moving towards the customer-configuration model. Gateway 2000, a PC maker, has trademarked the term "YourWare," and the search engine companies (e.g., Yahoo!, Excite) allow a high degree of personalization of their offerings.

But customer-defined offerings are reaching into other industries too. Garden Escape (www.garden.com) offers a Garden Planner application on its Web site that customers can use to design their garden. Customers can select plants, customize the layout of the plants and flowers, and choose from a set of predefined garden templates. The application uses information on the geographical location of the customer to determine the temperature and soil conditions, and to select appropriate flowers and plants. When customers have completed their design, they can save it, and they can order all the plants, flowers, and implements that they would need for their dream garden. Garden Escape puts customers in control of customizing its offering to suit their needs.

Pricing the Offering

In Industrial-Age marketing thinking, pricing strategies were designed to maximize profits from a one-time exchange transaction, based on costs. But persistent connectivity with customers requires firms to shift their focus to pricing for maximizing lifetime revenues from a customer relationship. The lifetime pricing approach may even dictate giving away the initial offering as an incentive for customers to initiate a relationship. As the relationship grows, the initial expenditure on customer acquisition can be recovered over time, by selling follow-ons, add-ons, and services.

Even manufacturers of traditional products like automobiles are realizing that lifetime revenues from information services like navigation devices, roadside assistance and wireless Internet access may far exceed the profits from selling the automobile itself. Personal computer manufacturers like Compaq believe that computers, like cellular phones, may be given away almost free in the near future, in return for signing lucrative long-term service contracts for Internet services. In the Information Age, every product can be enhanced with digital services. And some software products can be replaced entirely by digital services that can be rented rather than bought. The cash flows from these service revenues and complementary products will in many cases outweigh the prices of the products.

Communicating the Offering

Traditional marketing communication follows the persuasion model. But Information-Age marketers will have to replace persuasion with permission, and push with pull when they communicate with prospects. They will ask prospects and customers about whether and how they prefer to be reached with marketer messages and offerings. Buyers are irritated by the ceaseless barrage of intrusive print and broadcast messages that have no relation to their needs or interests, not to mention the phone calls that interrupt their dinnertime meal or the several pounds of catalogs mailed to their homes daily. They want to move to a "permissions-oriented" social contract with marketers. For instance, IBM will ask customers how they prefer to be informed about a new piece of information or an offering. IBM calls this "consensual communication."

Marketers can also take advantage of the interactivity that the Internet allows to engage in "suggestive marketing." They can use premiums and incentives to cross-sell and up-sell to customers *during* the purchase experience, and based on the items purchased. Gap uses suggestive marketing to cross-sell complementary products on its site. When a customer drops a pair of Gap khakis into a shopping basket, Gap suggests that the shopper add a matching sweater. It can make the incremental sale compelling by tossing in an immediate, low-value, effortless incentive—half-off shipping if the customer takes the sweater or a free pair of crew socks to go with the combination.

Delivering the Offering

Marketers have traditionally delivered their offerings to customers through physical channels. These vertically integrated intermediaries bundled products, information, and complementary products and services. In the information-rich regime, the Internet is emerging as a new channel for delivering information to customers. In the case of information products, the Internet can be a channel for physical product or service distribution as well. Marketers are exploiting the power of the Internet by creating Web-based mechanisms for delivering information about their offerings, or in some case delivering the offerings themselves. Customers can now access multiple delivery channels: personal channels, reseller channels, or Internet-based direct channels. But these channels are often poorly coordinated, and there are jarring discontinuities among different delivery channels.

In the information-rich regime, marketers will need to go beyond offering a separate web-based delivery mechanism for products and information.

They will need to integrate all their delivery platforms into a seamless composite channel. Customers will expect to access any and all delivery channels, and they will expect consistency across channels in prices, product information, and service. Forcing customers to use a specific delivery channel will not be an option. Neither will it be possible to offer inconsistent services or pricing across channels, hoping that customers will not discover the differences.

Charles Schwab found this out the hard way when it launched its online brokerage service eSchwab. Schwab tried to prevent its online customers from using the support and services it provides to its regular customers who pay more to interact with brokers. This discrimination provoked a violent reaction from Schwab's online customers, forcing it to offer the same services to all its customers. Other full-service financial service firms are also finding that their customers demand availability of an online trading option, while also being able to access brokers to place trades.

Augmenting the Offering

The value chain concept has anchored conventional thinking on partners who augment the firm's offering. Vertical partners, including "upstream" suppliers and "downstream" resellers, have been viewed as the traditional set of partners that the firm needs to work with. More recently, this view has been extended by including horizontal partners who augment the firm's offering with complementary products and services.

But in the Information Age, value will no longer live in chains. Every firm will exist at the center of a network of partners that it will create around itself. The firm will evolve from being a coordinator of the supply chain, to the manager of its business network. In this network manager role, marketers will need to augment their skills in business development and negotiation. Instead of developing winning products, marketers will need to create, sustain, and defend winning relationships with business partners. As firms strive to focus on performing a small set of functions in-house while outsourcing the rest to best-of-breed partners, a key activity of marketers will be to manage this network of relationships. Leading-edge firms like Yahoo! are honing their capabilities in network management by outsourcing production of content, services, and infrastructure, and confining themselves to an aggregator role. By creating a web of relationships with suppliers of software, services, and content, network managers like Yahoo! are able to configure a far more comprehensive offering far more quickly than they could have created on their own.

Supporting Customers

Customer support has traditionally been a people-driven function, with customers calling into a call center staffed by representatives who knew nothing about the customer or their problem. Firms are progressing beyond to the next generation of support, where customers can access information that is customized to their needs. Through Frequently Asked Questions (FAQ) databases and natural language queries, customers can search knowledge bases for information.

But Information-Age marketers are evolving to a much more sophisticated model of customer support, where customers serve themselves, and the information they access is linked directly to the firm's business processes. Consider the new customer-focused e-commerce site launched by Intel in July 1998 to support over 200 business customers in 30 countries. The site puts customers in control of the ordering process. Customers can buy any Intel products on the spot. They can also check pricing, availability, backlog status, and committed delivery dates. Large customers can even load their manufacturing plan data directly into Intel's systems to facilitate collaborative inventory planning. Customers can create personalized Web sites, so that different customer types—engineers or purchasing managers—only see the content and transactions that matter to them. Doing so makes it easy and efficient for every customer not only to do research but also to take appropriate action. In addition, Intel directly and securely transmits confidential design information. The result is over $1 billion of bookings per month on the Web, dramatic reductions in expenses, and improved delivery cycle time.

CUSTOMER-CENTERED MEDIATORS

Traditionally, mediators who have facilitated marketing exchanges have owed allegiance to marketers. This was a logical arrangement, because marketers controlled the exchange process, and they controlled the information in the exchange. However, the rise of customer-controlled exchanges will require a reversal in how we think about mediation, and will spawn a number of *customer-centered mediators*. These customer-centered mediators will work for customers, and will facilitate various activities in the customer-initiated exchange process.

To approach mediation from the customer's perspective, marketers need very different lenses. The activities of marketing channels have traditionally been viewed through the lenses of *products* that were sold by the channel, and the *channel flows* that were involved in moving products from the marketer to the customer. But customers don't think in terms of products. Customers think in terms of *activities* that they perform. Products and services are the *means* by which these activities are performed and supported. They are not ends in themselves. The traditional view of mediators as providers of information and product flows focuses on marketer activities, and ignores the activities that customers perform when they engage in marketing exchanges. As customers initiate and drive the exchange process, it is logical to see the exchange process from their viewpoint.

Customer activity clusters can be characterized along two dimensions: *activity breadth* and *activity depth*. Activity breadth refers to the diversity of the activities that constitute a specific activity cluster. The greater the activity breadth, the larger is the set of complementary products and services that consumers will need to perform the desired activities. Consider home ownership. Home ownership is an activity cluster that is very broad. It includes home buying, home financing, home repair, home remodeling, home refinancing, home insurance, and a whole host of other activities.

Activity depth refers to the number and the complexity of steps in the consumer decision process for an activity cluster. The greater the activity depth, the more complex the consumer decision process, and the more the assistance they will need in the decision process. Consider home buying. Home buying is an activity that is very deep, because the steps involved in the decision process to buy a home are numerous and complex.

Horizontal Mediation Opportunities: Metamediaries

Activity clusters that are broad create *horizontal* mediation opportunities for customer-centered mediators. New mediators can emerge to create virtual *metamarkets,* which we define as markets that represent the diverse set of products and services needed to service a broad activity cluster. While the activities that constitute a metamarket are logically related from the consumer's perspective, the products and services that they map into may be quite unrelated from the producer perspective. For instance, activities like home financing and home repair may be logically related in the minds of consumers as being part of the home metamarket, but home financing firms are in a completely different industry from the producer perspective.

The disconnect between how consumers think of markets (in terms of activities) and how marketers think of markets (in terms of products) presents opportunities for mediating between customers and marketers in broad activity clusters. We call such mediators *metamediaries*. Metamediaries work for consumers, and create enormous efficiencies by providing them consumers with a single point of contact between consumers and a diverse set of marketers in a metamarket (see Figure 17.2). Metamediaries can organize metamarkets around activity clusters corresponding to important events

Figure 17.2
Horizontal Mediation in an Activity Cluster:
The Automobile Metamarket

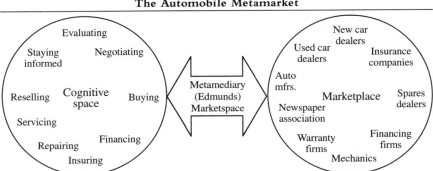

(e.g., weddings, childbirth, college education), or important assets (e.g., home ownership, auto ownership). By being the one-stop shop within an activity cluster, metamediaries can control valuable cognitive real estate.

Vertical Mediation Opportunities: Facilitators

Activity clusters that are deep place an enormous burden on consumers in searching, evaluating, and negotiating directly with marketers. This increased burden in turn creates opportunities for *facilitators* who assist consumers in various steps of the decision process in the decision process (see Figure 17.3). These facilitators will include:

- *Search facilitators:* As consumers begin their search for marketers, they will seek the assistance of search facilitators who will reduce their search costs, and make the search process more efficient and effective. The earliest search facilitators were the Internet-based search engines like Yahoo! and Excite. More recently, category-specific aggregators like Insure Market (insurance), E-loan (loans), and Quicken.com (financial services) are emerging to provide information on multiple vendors within a category. And matchmakers like CareerCentral.com (MBA recruiting), PlasticsNet.com (plastics) and FastParts.com (components) are bringing buyers and sellers together in online marketplaces.
- *Evaluation facilitators:* After they have found potential sellers, consumers typically need to narrow down the plethora of available choices by identifying the sellers and offerings that best match their needs.

Figure 17.3
Vertical Mediation Along the Customer Activity Sequence

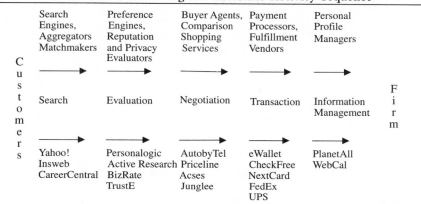

The evaluation process will be facilitated by preference engines from firms like PersonaLogic (www.personalogic.com) and Active Research (www.activeresearch.com), who help customers in calibrating their preferences, and rating providers on these customer-defined preferences. Evaluation will also be assisted by firms who will rate historical performance of sellers, (e.g., Bizrate.com and Better Business Bureau Online); and firms that rate the compliance with sellers on privacy issues (e.g., Truste.com).

- *Negotiation facilitators:* Even after consumers decide which products they want to buy and which vendors they want to deal with, they still need help in negotiating with alternative vendors to get the best possible terms. Customers will enlist buying agents to assist them in the negotiation process. Mediators like AutobyTel (www.autobytel.com) and PriceLine (www.priceline.com) will help customers in placing bids with sellers, and negotiating terms.

- *Transaction facilitators:* Once the terms of the transaction have been defined, another set of mediators will assist consumers in consummating the exchanges. One set of transaction facilitators will ensure the safe, speedy, and secure completion of transactions using cash or credit cards, as well as bill payment and bill presentation. Examples of these payment facilitators include NextCard, Cybercash, CheckFree, First Data, and VeriSign. Another set of transaction facilitators will assist in inventorying, shipping, and delivering the goods to customers. These fulfillment providers include logistics firms like UPS, FedEx, and Ryder who deal directly with customers.

- *Information Safekeepers:* As consumes take control of exchange relationships, they will need to provide sellers with personal profile information. Traditionally, marketers have managed and controlled this information. But in customer-controlled exchanges, customers will want to control this information, and to release it selectively to authorized sellers. This will give rise to another category of customer-centered mediators that will act as safekeepers of personal profile information. These mediators may keep information like personal measurements, medical records, credit card information, passwords, and other sensitive profile information.

A key challenge for customer-centered mediators is to decide their *locus* in the customer activity sequence, and the *scope* of activities that they will facilitate. The locus decision is important, because some activities may create more value for customers and may be more profitable than other activities. For instance, eBay.com, an Internet-based auction firm, facilitates search and negotiation, but does not take possession of the inventory or participate in the transaction. But Onsale.com, another auction firm, sources its own products and participates in fulfillment. As a result, Onsale is far more limited in terms of how much and what it can sell, and its profit margins are lower because of inventory carrying costs. eBay is quite profitable, but Onsale is not.

On the scope dimension, metamediaries would ideally like to support as broad a set of related customer activities as possible, in order to create more valuable franchises. However, there are logical boundaries that constrain the scope of a metamarket. While every activity that consumers perform is potentially related to all other activities, there are logical activity clusters that most consumers identify and relate to. If the metamediary provides an offering that is too narrow, consumers may perceive it as incomplete. But if the offering is too broad, it may lose focus and clarity.

HOW MARKETING ORGANIZATIONS WILL CHANGE

Traditional marketing organizations consist of sales forces, product and brand managers, marketing researchers, various communication specialists, and customer service representatives. Many of these positions will remain in the Information Society but there will be some realignment of roles and responsibilities. We foresee that a larger proportion of marketing work will be done outside of the marketing department. Companies today are trying to eliminate functional boundaries by building multidisciplinary teams around basic processes. Marketing and salespeople are likely to be assigned to many of these teams. Companies form further teams to deal with external partners and some team members will end up as "implants," living and working with the external partners. In general, there will be an increasing dispersion of marketing activity.

The role of marketing in the organization will also have to change. The marketing organization will need to redefine its roles from being a *mediator* of firm-customer interactions to an *integrator* of customer-facing processes. Traditionally, marketers have played the role of middlemen, charged with understanding customer needs, and transmitting the voice of the customer to various functional areas in the organization, who then acted upon these needs. Underlying this definition of the marketing function was the assumption that customers were hard to reach, and that customers could not interact directly with other functional areas. But in a networked enterprise, every functional area can potentially interact directly with customers. Operations can allow customers to configure and order products online. Information technology can create a front-end Web presence and the back-end information infrastructure that allows customers to interact electronically with the firm. Customer support can create electronic systems for customer care. Engineering can set up electronic links with key customers and suppliers to get inputs into product development and design. Marketing no longer has sole ownership over customer interactions, and can no longer serve as the sole mediator of firm-customer interactions. Rather, marketing needs to integrate all the customer-facing processes, so that customers see a single face and a single voice when they interact with the firm. This requires marketing to work closely with all functional areas, especially with the information technology function, because the key to functional integration lies in information integration. Without information integration, marketers can never deliver on the promise of seamless and end-to-end transactions that cross functional and business unit boundaries.

More emphasis will be placed on *key account management* because the firm's key accounts will provide a disproportionate share of its revenue and profits. Companies will assign a key account manager to maintain and grow the business with each key account. The key account manager is a gardener, well-aware of the soil conditions, seeds, and fertilizers necessary to produce a rich harvest of mutually beneficial crops. Today we find companies placing more senior managers into key account positions, and even setting up cross-functional teams to add value to the relationship.

Key account management is part of a larger shift of companies from a *product* or *brand focus* to a *customer focus*. Customers vary in their requirements and therefore companies must vary their offerings. Those closest to the customers are salespeople. There will be a shift of resources from product and brand management to the sales organization to enable sales people to build stronger and more adapted relations with specific major accounts. Brand management will still be needed, but more of it will fall under category management and customer management, rather than individual brand management.

In this new marketing regime, marketers will need to upgrade their skills. It is no longer sufficient for marketers to be good at persuasion, negotiation, and brand image-making. As team members, marketers will need a better understanding of the other business functions. They will need a more sophisticated understanding of accounting and financial concepts like activity-based costing and customer account profitability. They will need to master information technology in order to manage customer relationships better. They will need more skill in presenting their views to their teammates as well as presenting stronger arguments to senior management for additional resources needed by key accounts.

Companies will have to improve their measurement and reward systems. Accounting systems measure product profitability poorly and are considerably less effective in measuring the profitability of individual customers or customer groups. This is because costs are typically allocated to products rather than customers. Without knowing the profitability of individual customers or customer groups, it is hard to ascertain performance, and therefore to assign rewards. A major challenge will be determining how to reward key account managers as well as whole teams.

DETERMINING WHERE YOUR COMPANY STANDS

Where does your company stand in the midst of these information sea-changes? We would recommend that you appoint a high-level committee to give transparency to the basic marketing assumptions underlying your current marketing practice. You must begin with an understanding of the changed customer expectations that result from the new capabilities of buyers (see page 405).

Then, you must examine your assumptions about how your buyers will want to obtain your goods and services in the future, how they will want you to communicate with them, how they will want to communicate with you, and how they want value to be delivered. To help you assess where you

A Customer Bill of Rights for the Information Age

As marketers shift their mindset from treating customers as prey to customers as citizens, they will be well-served to acknowledge and respect some fundamental customer rights and expectations. The following *Customer Bill of Rights* summarizes the vastly changed expectations of customers in the age of Information Democracy. Violating these fundamental rights, while tempting and even profitable in the short run, will be disastrous in the long run:

- *Right to know:* Customers will expect full information about the firm's products and services. This will include price, quality, and service information, and will also include comparisons with competitors.
- *Right to expect silence:* Customers will expect marketers to seek permission before they are contacted about an offer. Advertising and direct marketing will be on an invitation–only basis. And conversely, customers will expect to be able to revoke this invitation, and not be bothered in the future.
- *Right to vote:* Customers will expect to have a voice in the creation of products and services, and in the post-sales support policies. They will expect marketers to solicit and act upon customer feedback.
- *Right to anonymity:* Customers will expect marketers to explicitly state the purpose of collecting personal profile information, and the intended uses of the information. And they will expect marketers to respect these privacy rules.
- *Right to be remembered:* Customers will expect marketers to remember all the information they have ever provided to the firm. And they will expect every employee in the firm to have access to this information in all future dealings with customers.
- *Right to share payoffs:* Direct marketers will be expected to offer incentives to customers to share information. They will also be expected to share in the profits that marketers make from reselling customer information.
- *Right to expect accountability:* Customers will expect marketers who own the customer relationship to be accountable for the performance of all their partners and complementors. Handing off customers to a partner will not absolve marketers from being accountable for the actions of their partners.

Table 17.1
Do You Have Information-Age Marketing?

For your company or business unit, answer the following questions by checking the item that most closely characterizes your marketing assumptions, your marketing process, and your marketing organization:

A. Marketing Assumptions

Marketing concepts

_____ 1. The key marketing concepts we use are the 3 Cs (customer, company, competition), the 4 Ps (product, price, promotion, place), and STP (segmentation, targeting, and positioning).

_____ 2. The key marketing concepts we use are the processes by which we understand, create, and deliver value to customers.

_____ 3. The key marketing concepts we use are the business design that drives our assumptions, and the processes by which we maintain fit between our customers, offerings, channels, and complementors.

Profit policy

_____ 1. We aim to maximize profits from products.

_____ 2. We aim to maximize profits from customer accounts.

_____ 3. We aim to maximize profits over the lifetime of customer relationships.

Information policy

_____ 1. We believe that if our customers were fully informed, our profitability would suffer.

_____ 2. We believe that if our customers were fully informed, it would not affect our profitability.

_____ 3. We believe that if our customers were fully informed, our profitability would improve.

B. Marketing Process

Designing the offering

_____ 1. We develop our products internally and then test them with customers.

_____ 2. We research customer requirements in designing our products and turn this information over to product designers and engineers.

_____ 3. We encourage customers to participate in designing new products and services.

Customizing the offering

_____ 1. We create a fairly standard offering for each customer segment.

_____ 2. We design customized offerings for each customer.

_____ 3. We allow customers to customize their own offering.

Table 17.1   *(Continued)*

B. Marketing Process

Pricing the offering

_____   1. We base our prices on our costs.

_____   2. We base our prices on the value we create for our customers.

_____   3. We price our products based on the lifetime revenues from a customer.

Communicating the offering

_____   1. We rely heavily on advertising and sales promotions to sell our products.

_____   2. We make it fairly easy for customers to reach us by phone, fax, or e-mail.

_____   3. We allow customers to choose when and how they want to be contacted by us.

Delivering the offering

_____   1. We do not offer an Internet-based direct channel for selling our products.

_____   2. We sell our products directly over the Internet, but we use separate information systems and supply chains for the Internet channel and our physical channels.

_____   3. We sell our products directly over the Internet, and we use integrated information systems and an integrated supply chain for all channels.

Augmenting the offering

_____   1. We stick to making goods and services that we can supply ourselves.

_____   2. We add complementary products and services to gain a greater share of customer spending.

_____   3. We provide end-to-end customer solutions, and involve a network of partners to manage the solutions.

Supporting customers

_____   1. If our customers contact us on the Internet, they can access product information and FAQ databases.

_____   2. If our customers contact us on the Internet, they can access customer support representatives either in person or through e-mail.

_____   3. If our customers contact us on the Internet, they can access our order processing and customer support systems directly, before they request customer support in person.

C. Marketing Organization

Role of marketing

_____   1. The role of marketing is to promote our offerings in the marketplace.

_____   2. The role of marketing is to act as middleman between customers and the firm.

_____   3. The role of marketing is to facilitate all customer-facing processes in the firm.

(continued)

Table 17.1 *(Continued)*

C. Marketing Organization

Organizational structure

_____ 1. Our marketing organization is based on the products and brands we offer.

_____ 2. Our marketing organization is based on the markets and customers we serve.

_____ 3. Our marketing organization is a hybrid, with a back-end organized around products and a front-end organized around markets and customers.

Servicing of national accounts

_____ 1. Our key customer accounts are served by our regular sales force.

_____ 2. Our key customer accounts are served by a national accounts sales force.

_____ 3. Our key accounts are served by a cross-functional key accounts team.

Information technology and marketing

_____ 1. The CIO is responsible for all strategic information technology decisions involving marketing and sales.

_____ 2. The CIO and CMO share responsibility for strategic information technology decisions involving marketing and sales.

_____ 3. All strategic information technology decisions are the joint responsibility of the CIO, CFO, COO, CMO, and CEO.

Management accounting

_____ 1. Our costs and profits are allocated to individual business units and divisions.

_____ 2. Our costs and profits are allocated to individual products and brands.

_____ 3. Our costs and profits are allocated to individual customer accounts.

Scoring your company: The possible number of points range from a low of 15 (if you checked option 1 in all cases) to a high of 45 (if you checked option 3 in all cases). Generally speaking, a company's marketing style can be classified as follows:

  15–25 points: Industrial-Age Marketing
  26–35 points: Transitional Marketing
  36–45 points: Information-Age Marketing

stand, we offer a diagnostic instrument that should reveal how much progress your firm has made on this journey, and how far it still needs to go (see Table 17.1). Examine carefully how your competitors are responding to the information availability and customer value changes. If you detect a growing value gap between what you are offering and what your customers want, or a growing value gap between your marketing approach and that of your competitors, it is time to act. Customers can be lost overnight to companies that are asleep at the wheel.

ABOUT THE CONTRIBUTORS

James C. Anderson is the William L. Ford Distinguished Professor of Marketing and Wholesale Distribution, and Professor of Behavioral Science in Management, Kellogg Graduate School of Management, Northwestern University. He is also the Irwin Gross Distinguished ISBM Research Fellow at the Institute for the Study of Business Markets (ISBM), located at Penn State University. He teaches business marketing to MBA students and executive development programs at the James L. Allen Center. He has consulted and provided seminars for a number of companies in North America and Europe, such as Asea Brown Boveri, AT&T, Dow Europe, G.E. Capital Services, Johnson & Johnson, Monsanto Canada, and Pharmacia & Upjohn. Professor Anderson's research interests are the working relationships between firms in business markets and measurement techniques for assessing the value of market offerings. He has written more than 30 journal articles and co-authored the book, *The Wholesale Distribution Channel: Building Successful Working Partnerships*. His most recent book is *Business Market Management: Understanding, Creating, and Delivering Value,* published by Prentice Hall. Anderson is the AT&T Research Fellow at the Institute for the Study of Business Markets and is a member of its advisory board. He is also a member of the International Advisory Board of the Department of Business Studies at Uppsala University. He has been vice president of the business marketing division of the American Marketing Association and a member of the board of directors of the AMA.

Robert C. Blattberg came to Kellogg in 1991 after many years at the University of Chicago. He is the Polk Bros. Distinguished Professor of Retailing and director of the Center for Retail Management, Graduate School of Business. He teaches courses on marketing strategy, category management and sales promotions. His career and recent professional awards for teaching include the Robert C. Clarke Award; Direct Marketing Association Educator of the Year, 1990; the John D.C. Little Best Paper Award; and the *Marketing Science* and *Management Science* Best Paper of the Year for

"Price-Induced Patterns of Competition," 1990 co-authored by Kenneth Wisniewski. He has been a Marketing Science Institute Trustee and is the director of the Center for Retail Management. His Research Areas include database marketing, retailing, customer equity, and sales promotion. He has consulted with Advanta, Anheuser Busch, The Kroger Co., A.C. Nielsen, The Northern Trust, Sears, Whirlpool.

Bobby J. Calder is the Charles H. Kellstadt Distinguished Professor of Marketing and Professor of Psychology at the Kellogg School, Northwestern University. His work is primarily in the areas of marketing research, consumer behavior, and marketing planning. Previously he has taught at the Wharton School, University of Pennsylvania and the University of Illinois. He is a graduate of the University of North Carolina at Chapel Hill. Presently he serves as director of research for the Media Management Center at Northwestern and is co-director of the media major program at Kellogg. He is a consultant to organizations such as the United States Census, General Electric, Motorola, Aetna, Prudential, Baxter, Bristol Myers Squibb, the Army, the Executive Leadership Council, and the United Way of America.

Gregory S. Carpenter is the James Farley/Booz Allen Hamilton Professor of Marketing Strategy at the Kellogg School. He joined Kellogg in 1990. His teaching focuses on marketing planning and strategy. At Kellogg he teaches marketing policy and strategy to the MBA students as well as executive education programs at the James L. Allen Center. His research focuses on competitive brand strategy, including strategies for early market entry, and defensive marketing strategies. His work has been published in *Marketing Science, Management Science, Journal of Marketing Research,* and elsewhere in both the United States and Europe. He serves on the editorial boards of the *Journal of Marketing Research, Marketing Science* and *Marketing Letters.* In addition to teaching and research, Carpenter lectures and consults for a number of organizations on marketing planning and strategy issues, including General Electric, Citibank, Motorola and Unilever. He founded Political Market Research, a political research and consulting firm.

Anne T. Coughlan joined Kellogg in 1985 and is Associate Professor of Marketing. She teaches Channels and International Channels of Distribution and Quantitative Models in Marketing. She serves on the editorial boards of the *Journal of Marketing, Journal of Retailing, International*

Scientific Committee of CREER (Centre for Research and Education in European Retailing). Her research areas include distribution channel management and design, strategic alliances, network marketing, franchising, and competitive strategy. She has served on the boards of directors for Hendricksen—The Care of Trees and The Kent Funds. Coughlan was a visiting professor at INSEAD from 1997 to 1998.

Rashi Glazer is Professor at the Walter A. Haas School of Business, University of California, Berkeley, co-director of the Berkeley Center for Marketing and Technology and director of the Berkeley Portfolio of Marketing Management Executive Education Programs. He obtained an MBA in 1979 and a PhD in 1982 from Stanford University's Graduate School of Business and has been a member of the faculty at Columbia University. His teaching and research interests are in the areas of competitive marketing strategy, technology and information-technology strategy, interactive and database marketing, and consumer and managerial decision making. He is the co-editor of the new *Journal of Interactive Marketing* and an associate editor of *Management Science*. His articles have appeared in *Marketing Science,* the *Journal of Consumer Research,* the *Journal of Marketing* and other leading publications. He is the co-author of three books; *The Marketing Information Revolution, Readings on Market-Driving Strategies,* and *Cable TV Advertising*. His paper "Marketing in an Information-Intensive Environment: Strategic Implications of Knowledge as an Asset" won the 1992 Best Paper Award from the *Journal of Marketing*. He has been a consultant and conducted executive eduction programs for companies including Arbor Health Care; AT&T; BellSouth; CBIS/Matrixx; Deere & Co.; Equitable Life; Gemini Consulting; Genencorp; Hewlett Packard; IBM; Intel; Levi Strauss; MicroUnity Systems; MIPS; Mitsubishi; Motorola; Pacific Bell; Pacific Gas & Electric; SBC; Telegroup; Telekurs/Teknekron; Time, Inc.; Toshiba; Trans Union; Visa; and Wells Fargo. He is the developer of the INFOVALUE program for measuring the value of a firm's information and SUITS, an interactive computer simulation for teaching the strategic use of information and the integration of information technology strategy with business strategy. He has won several awards for teaching excellence at the MBA and Executive Education levels—twice receiving the Haas School's Best Teacher of the Year Award.

Dawn Iacobucci came to Kellogg in 1987 and is Professor of Marketing. She teaches service marketing, marketing research, and multivariate statistics. She has been the business manager of the Classification Society of

North America; she is editor of the *Journal of Consumer Psychology* and serves on the editorial boards of the *Journal of Consumer Psychology, Journal of Interactive Marketing, Journal of Marketing, Journal of Service Research*, and the *International Journal of Research in Marketing*. Her research areas include service marketing, models for dyadic and network interactions, relationship management, social marketing, and multivariate statistics. Her research has appeared in the *Journal of Marketing*, the *Journal of Marketing Research*, the *Journal of Consumer Psychology*, *Harvard Business Review*, the *Journal of Service Research*, the *International Journal of Research in Marketing*, the *Journal of Interactive Marketing*, the *Journal of Advertising Research*, *Sloan Management Review*, *Psychometrika*, *Psychological Bulletin*, the *Journal of Personality and Social Psychology*, *Social Networks*, and *Multivariate Behavioral Research*.

Dipak Jain joined Kellogg in 1986. He is Associate Dean for Academic Affairs, and the Sandy & Morton Goldman Professor of Entrepreneurial Studies and Marketing. He also teaches regularly at the Sasin Graduate Institute of Business Administration, Chulalongkorn University, Bangkok. He teaches marketing research, new products and services, and probabilistic and statistical models in marketing and has won the Sidney Levy Award for Excellence in Teaching, and the John D.C. Little Best Paper Award. He is marketing editor of *Management Science;* area editor of *Marketing Science;* associate editor of *Journal of Business and Economic Statistics* and a member of the editorial boards of the *Journal of Marketing*, and the *Journal of Marketing Research*. His research areas include the marketing of high-tech products, market segmentation and competitive market structure analysis, cross-cultural issues in global product diffusion, new product diffusion and forecasting models. He consults for IBM, Sears, US Robotics, U.S. Cellular, AT&T, Motorola, Harris Semi Conductor, Eli Lilly, Thomsen Electronics, Phillips, and Hyatt International.

Philip Kotler has been with Kellogg since 1962. He is the S.C. Johnson & Son Distinguished Professor of International Marketing. He teaches marketing management, international marketing, marketing for nonprofit organizations, and marketing of services. He has received honorary doctorate degrees from Athens University of Economics and Business, DePaul University, University of Stockholm, Cracow School of Economics, Groupe HEC. He has provided professional leadership to the Marketing Science Institute on its board of directors, the Institute of Management Sciences, the American Marketing Association, the Peter F. Drucker Foundation for Nonprofit Management. He has served on the editorial boards of the *Journal of Segmentation in Marketing, Journal of Nonprofit and Voluntary Sector Marketing, International Business Review, Journal of International Marketing.* Kotler's research areas include strategic marketing, marketing organization and planning, marketing for cultural organizations, hospitality, tourism and place marketing, international marketing, social marketing, marketing and economic development. His book, *Marketing Management: Analysis, Planning, Implementation and Control,* is in its tenth edition. He has also written *Marketing Models, Strategic Marketing for Nonprofit Organizations, Principles of Marketing, Social Marketing: Strategies for Changing Public Behavior, Marketing Places: Attracting Investment, Industry and Tourism to Cities, States and Nations, Marketing for Hospitality and Tourism, High Visibility, Standing Room Only: Strategies for Marketing the Performing Arts.* He has published over 100 articles in leading journals. He has consulted with IBM, Apple, General Electric, Ford, AT&T, Motorola, Honeywell, Bank of America, Merck, Ciba Geigy, JP Morgan, DuPont, Westinghouse, and Merrill Lynch.

Robert V. Kozinets joined Kellogg in 1997. He is Assistant Professor of Marketing and teaches international marketing and entertainment marketing. His professional experience includes: marketing director and consultant, Kozinets and Associates, Toronto, Canada; and marketing and research consultant, The Thaler Corporation, Alton, Canada. He consults for Honda, Mazda, Hyundai, Sandoz, Whitehall-Robbins, Novopharm, G.N. Johnston, NEBS, CN Hotels, Roger's Cable, Royal Insurance, and Easter Seals. His research areas include popular culture and global marketing, virtual communities and global consumption, internet consumer behavior, boycotts and consumer activism, cross-cultural and multicultural methods in marketing and consumer research.

Lakshman Krishnamurthi joined Kellogg in 1980. He is the A. Montgomery Ward Professor of Marketing. He teaches marketing research, marketing strategy, and regression methods. Recent professional awards include the 1988 John D.C. Little Best Paper Award for *Marketing Science;* 1991 Best Paper Award, AMA Summer Educators' Conference; Finalist, 1990 for the William O'Dell Award for his paper published in *Journal of Marketing Research,* 1985 to 1990. He has been the chair of the Department of Marketing since 1993. He is the academic director of the pricing strategies and tactics Executive Education program. His research areas are choice models, estimation of price and advertising elasticity, conjoint analysis, new product strategy, competitive advantage. He consults for Motorola and ZS Associates, and conducts executive education seminars for Motorola, Time Distribution Services, Colfax Communications.

Sidney Levy started with Kellogg in 1961. He was the A. Montgomery Ward Professor of Marketing and then the Charles H. Kellstadt Distinguished Professor of Marketing, and he is now Professor Emeritus and also head of the department of marketing at the University of Arizona. He teaches principles of marketing, marketing research, behavioral research methods in marketing, marketing behavior, psycho-social approaches to marketing, advertising policy and management, and systems marketing. His recent professional awards include: AMA/Irwin Distinguished Marketing Educator, 1988; ACR Fellow Award, 1982; *Journal of Marketing,* Maynard Award for best article, 1981; *Journal of Consumer Research,* invited lead article, 1996. He was chair of the Department of Marketing at Kellogg from 1980 to 1992 and president of the Association for Consumer Research in 1991. His research areas include consumer behavior, qualitative research, and communications.

Kent Nakamoto is Pamplin Professor of Marketing, Pamplin College of Business Administration, Virginia Polytechnic Institute & State University, Blacksburg, VA.

James A. Narus is Professor of Business Marketing at the Babcock Graduate School of Management, Wake Forest University in Charlotte, North Carolina. Professor Narus's teaching, research, and consulting interests include value-based marketing, the use of adaptive channels, the management of market offerings, and partnerships between firms in business markets. Professor Narus currently teaches graduate courses in business market management and marketing management in the Babcock School's full-time, evening, and Charlotte MBA programs. He has taught in executive development programs at Northwestern University, Pennsylvania State University, the University of Texas at Austin, Texas A&M University, Twente University (the Netherlands), and the Universidad Torcuato Di Tella (Argentina). Professor Narus has written articles and research papers on business market management topics that have appeared in the *Harvard Business Review, Sloan Management Review, California Management Review,* and the *Journal of Marketing,* among other journals. Professor Narus has co-authored with James C. Anderson of Kellogg a book entitled, *Business Market Management: Understanding, Creating, and Delivering Value,* published by Prentice Hall.

Steven J. Reagan is a founder and President of BHI Design, a marketing communications firm. He has completed numerous assignments in identity and brand development for major national and international companies. Reagan is a graduate of Illinois Institute of Technology's Institute of Design.

Mohanbir Sawhney is the Tribune Professor of Electronic Commerce and Technology. He has been with Kellogg from 1993 teaching strategic marketing for technology firms and marketing management. He was the Lavengood Professor of the Year in 1998 and runner-up for Professor of the Year in 1997 and 1996; he won the Sidney J. Levy Teaching Award 1994–1995; and was a finalist for the John D.C. Little Best Paper Award, 1996; winner of the MSI Research Proposal Competition on "Harmonizing Marketing-Manufacturing Relationships," 1995; finalist for the John D.C. Little Best Paper Award in 1994. He has been a reviewer for the *Journal of Consumer Research, Journal of Marketing Research, Management Science, Marketing Science,* and *Marketing Letters.* His research areas include marketing strategy for technology firms, entertainment marketing, cross-functional coordination in product development. He consults for AT&T, Dean Witter, Discover, Motorola, Texas Instruments, Thomson Consumer Electronics, Titan Industries Limited in India, Philips Electronics, Xerox, and Zenith Electronics.

John F. Sherry Jr. came to Kellogg in 1984. He is Professor of Marketing and teaches marketing behavior, international marketing, contextual inquiry and consumer experience, and postmodern consumer research. He won the Sigma Xi, Best Article Award, *Journal of Consumer Research,* 1989 to 1991. He was the president of the Association for Consumer Research in 1998; he is a fellow of the American Anthropological Association, and of the Society for Applied Anthropology. He was an associate editor for the *Journal of Consumer Research* from 1993 through 1996. He serves on the editorial review boards of the *Journal of International Consumer Marketing, Journal of Managerial Issues, Design Issues, CMC: Consumption,* and *Markets & Culture.* Research areas include consumer behavior, symbolic communication, ethnographic methods. He consults for The Coca-Cola Company; Glaxo; Eastman Kodak; Motorola, Inc.; Procter and Gamble; Ralston Purina; Tetra Pak Americas; and Turner Broadcasting.

Prabha K. Sinha is Managing Director of ZS Associates and was formerly Associate Professor of Marketing in the Kellogg Graduate School of Management at Northwestern University. Before joining the Kellogg faculty in 1983, he taught management science and management information systems at Rutgers University. Sinha's research has focused on marketing resource allocation, sales force sizing and deployment and marketing. He is published in journals such as *Management Science, Operations Research, Marketing Science,* and *Mathematical Programming.* In addition, he has contributed to books and special publications on marketing models. He is co-author of *The Fat Firm* (McGraw-Hill, 1997) with Andris A. Zoltners. Sinha has actively pursued the development of computer tools and implementation processes to apply his theoretical work. Over the past 16 years, Dr. Sinha has assisted over 100 firms in the United States, Europe, Latin America, Africa, and Asia with sales force issues such as organization, size, deployment, compensation, and sales information systems. Sinha also teaches business executives at Kellogg and at the Management Centre Europe.

Louis W. Stern has been at Kellogg since 1973. He is the John D. Gray Distinguished Professor of Marketing. He has taught marketing channels, marketing management, marketing, society, and public policy. He has held positions at the Marketing Science Institute, Cambridge, Massachusetts, 1983 to 1985 as Executive Director; National Commission on Food Marketing, Washington, D.C., 1965 to 1966. In 1994, Stern was named the American Marketing Association/Richard D. Irwin Distinguished Marketing Educator Award. He was listed as one of the twelve best teachers in U.S. business schools by *Business Week* magazine, October 24, 1994. He was elected the Kellogg Graduate School of Management Outstanding Professor of the Year Award, 1992; Outstanding Professor for Electives in the Executive Masters Program in 1990, 1991, 1993, and 1994; Sales and Marketing Executives-International (Chicago Chapter) Marketing Educator of the Year, 1990; Sales and Marketing Executives-International Marketing Educator of the Year, 1989; American Marketing Association Paul D. Converse Award, 1986; American Marketing Association Harold H. Maynard Award for best article on marketing theory, 1980. He served on the editorial boards of *Marketing Letters, Journal of Marketing,* and the *Journal of Marketing Research.* He has conducted research in the areas of design and management issues in marketing channels, antitrust issues in marketing, marketing strategies and policies. His text, *Marketing Channels,* published by Prentice Hall, is in its fifth edition. He has published over 40 articles in leading journals. Stern has consulted for Hewlett Packard, Motorola, Brunswick, Mobil Oil, Nynex, Boise Cascade, Ameritech, Roche Laboratories, Trinova, Johnson & Johnson, IBM, Ford, Xerox, Management Centre Europe (Brussels), and has affiliations with Chicago Strategy Associates, The Richmark Group, and Frank Lynn & Associates.

Brian Sternthal joined Kellogg in 1972 and is the Kraft Professor of Marketing. He teaches Advertising Strategy and won Kellogg Teacher of the Year in 1982. He was chair of the Department of Marketing, from 1992 through 1993; and served as editor of the *Journal of Consumer Research,* from 1993 through 1996. He conducts research in the area of information processing and persuasion.

Jacquelyn S. Thomas is a graduate of Northwestern University. She began her career at the Graduate School of Business at Stanford University. She is now a faculty member at Emory University.

Alice M. Tybout has been with Kellogg since 1975. She is the Harold T. Martin Professor of Marketing and she teaches advertising, consumer information processing, and marketing management to MBA students at the James L. Allen Executive Education Center. She has also taught at INSEAD, Fontainebleau, France, and Chulalongkorn University, Bangkok in Thailand. Her awards include: American Marketing Association Doctoral Consortium Faculty, 1981, 1983, 1984, 1985, 1986, 1990, 1995 to 1997; Buchanan Research Chair, 1983–1984; Association for Consumer Research, member 1972–present, treasurer, 1983; president, 1994; board of directors, 1995; Sidney J. Levy Teaching Award, 1995 to 1996; Trustee, Marketing Science Institute, 1988–present; and board of directors, American Marketing Association, 1997–present. Her research interests include consumer information processing, categorization processes, and philosophy and methods of theory testing. She has consulted for First National Bank of Chicago, Dow Chemical, Dow Elanco, Abbott Laboratories, Canada, Ernst & Young Ltd., Prudential Insurance, Xerox Corporation, Sunbeam.

Andris A. Zoltners is a founder and Managing Director of ZS Associates, a 300 person global consulting firm specializing on sales force issues. He has personally consulted over 100 companies in more than 20 countries. His areas of expertise are sales force strategy; sales force size, structure and deployment; sales force compensation; and sales force effectiveness. In addition to his consulting, he is a frequent speaker on the topic of sales force productivity. He is also Professor of Marketing at Kellogg where he has been a member of the faculty for over 20 years. Prior to this position, he received his PhD from Carnegie-Mellon University and was a member of the Business School Faculty at the University of Massachusetts. He has written over 40 academic articles, edited two books on marketing models, is an author of *The Fat Firm,* and has spoken at numerous conferences. He has taught sales force topics to Executive, MBA, and PhD students. He is the academic director of two Kellogg Executive Programs: Increasing Sales Force Productivity and Sales Force Incentive Planning: Compensating for Results.

Greg A. Zoltners has spent over five years consulting with and studying sales forces. His areas of expertise include new product forecasting, size and structure, and motivation. He obtained his bachelor's from Yale University in 1986, and his MBA from the J.L. Kellogg Graduate School of Management in 1990.

INDEX

ABB, 355, 356
Activity-based costing (ABC), 256, 346–347
Activity breadth/depth, 399
Advertising, 49, 63–65, 83, 87, 215–246
  branding by, 63–65
  brand linkage, 226–228, 245
  cognitive elaboration, 218
  color, 223–225
  comparative, 221–223
  convergent attributes (the big idea), 219
  creative strategies for prompting message elaboration, 228–231
  goal of awareness/familiarity, 49, 244
  hard sell, 218
  humorous appeals, 230–231
  Integrated Marketing Communications (IMC), 237–239
  measuring effectiveness of, 239–244
  media strategies to prompt message elaboration, 231–236, 245–246
  message discrepancy, 228–229
  spokespeople, 224–226
  story grammar, 219–221, 244
  threat appeals, 229–230
  using how consumers think, 218–231
  using what consumers think, 216–218
Age, targeting by, 14–16
AKZO Industrial Coatings, 348, 349, 354, 362
Allegiance Healthcare, 337
Amazon, 36, 56, 75, 76, 105, 140, 286
American Express, 38–39
Americatel, 3–4
Andersen Consulting, 93

Apple Computer, 29, 49–50, 86, 88, 359
Armani, 86
Arthur D. Little, Inc. (ADL), 347–348
Athletes, endorsements by, 86
AT&T, 118, 138
Attention economy, 179
Augmented product, 330
Avon, 264

Baxter Healthcare Corporation, 343, 344, 353, 354, 355
Benefits, 34, 37, 38, 40
BIC (disposable razors), 25–26, 29, 50, 53–54, 99
Black & Decker, 29
BMW, 113–114, 115
Body Shop, The, 27–28
Brand(s):
  creating/managing, 74–102
  defining, 76–78
  equity, 60
  essence (goal-based positioning), 39–42
  experiential, 90–96
  extensions, 84, 90, 198–202
  functional, 80–84
  image, 84–90
  intimacy levels of, 238
  marketers and, 59–60
  matrix of, 97
  personalities, 114
  strategy and brand types, 98–100
  synonymous with category, 106
  types of (three: image/experiential/functional), 80–98

Brand(s) *(Continued)*
  value, and market capitalization, 76
  value network, 116
Brand development index (BDI),
    11–13
Brand differentiation, 83, 125–127,
    332–340
Branding/brand design, 58–73, 98–100
Brand positioning, 31–57
  challenges to effective, 47–51
  competition-based, 32–39
  goal-based, 39–44
  information technology and, 55–57
  new product development
      (repositioning as extent of
      newness), 134 *(see also* Product
      development, new)
  repositioning (extent of newness of
      new product), 134
  statement of, 32, 51–54, 61
  value equation: integrating
      competition-based and goal-based
      positioning, 44–47
  writing a targeting/positioning
      statement, 51–54
British Airways, 24, 272–273
Bud Light, 32–33, 92
Burger King, 7–8, 41, 287
Busch Entertainment, 272
Business-to-business brands, 81–82,
    87–88, 100
Buyer(s). *See* Customer(s)/consumer(s)
Buyer learning, 72, 108–127
  brand choice, 119–121
  brand perceptions, 111–114
  brand value network/map, 116
  elements of (three), 110, 127
  perceptual distinctiveness, 113–114
  perceptual network, 112
  preference advantages, 117–119
  preference formation, 114–119
  valuation problem, 115, 120

Carrefour, 265, 266
Category build targeting, 9–11
Category development index (CDI),
    12–13

Category essence (goal-based
    positioning), 42–44
Category membership (competition-
    based positioning), 33–36
Caterpillar, 81–82, 87
Cendant, 75
Channel. *See* Marketing channel(s)
Chiat/Day advertising agency, 49
Cisco, 104, 105
Citicorp, 249–250
Cluster analysis, 206–207
Coca-Cola, 48, 55, 59, 67, 75–78, 87,
    89, 106, 113, 114, 117–118, 125,
    133, 135, 226, 272
Commodity offerings, 332–340
Commonsense Theory, 161
Compaq, 228, 247–248, 291, 302
Competition-based positioning, 32–39
Competitive advantage, 103–129,
    136–139
Competitive strategy:
  against brands that drive the market,
      117–119
  development of (creating sustainable
      competitive advantage), 136–139
  market-driving strategies (toward a
      new concept of competitive
      advantage), 103–129
  traditional concepts of (ill-equipped),
      104
Competitor analysis, and segmenting/
    targeting, 11–13
Computer-mediated communication
    (CMC), 175
Conjoint analysis, 139, 285
Core product, 330
Corporate branding strategy, 98
"Creative destruction," branding as, 73
Customer(s)/consumer(s):
  bill of rights for Information Age,
      405
  focus (brand design approach),
      65–67
  frame of reference, 336
  increasingly demanding, 261–263
  information safekeepers, 402
  learning *(see* Buyer learning)

new capabilities in Information Age, 388–389

understanding (see Marketing research)

using how consumers think, 218–231

using what consumers think, 216–218

Customer-centered mediators, 398–402

Customer equity principles, 302–319

acquisition (A), 305, 308–310

add-on-selling (A), 305–306, 314–316

components (three: A-R-A), 305

fundamental customer equity equation, 303–306

impact of marketing strategy on critical measures, 306–307

marketing mix and equation parameters, 308–316

retention (R), 305, 311–314

segmenting/targeting and equation parameters, 307–308

Customer intimacy position, 24–25, 56–57, 139, 140–141, 282, 283

Customer value, 136–137, 138–139, 279–287, 333, 339

analogous products, 284

assessment, 333, 339

benchmarking, 284

conjoint analysis, 285

determining value: managerial judgment, 283–284

dimensions (three) of, 137

economic dimension, 137, 284

experimentation, 284

functional/technical dimension, 137, 138

historical data analysis, 284

nature of (perceptual/multidimensional/contextual), 137

perceptions of, 136–137

pricing and, 279–287

psychological dimension, 137, 138–139

value-in-use analysis, 284–285

Customization, 57. See also Customer intimacy position

Cutty Sark, 226

Cyberspace: exporting qualitative techniques to, 174–180. See also Internet/information technology

Cyborg ecology, 176

Dell Computer, 34, 82, 247–248, 291–282, 302–303, 336

Differentiation. See Brand differentiation

DiGiorno pizza, 35–36, 222

Discipline-based segmenting/targeting, 25–26

Disney, 91, 92, 93, 95–96, 105

Doyle, Dane & Bernbach (DDB), 219, 220

Duracell, 48–49

eBay, 394, 402

Edmunds.com, 388

Elimination-by-aspects heuristic, 120

Evaluation facilitators, 400–401

Eveready, 48–49, 239

Executable idea, 61–62

Experiential branding, 90–96

Expertise, leveraging, 335–336

Explanation, 154–160

data and, 155–157

dimensions of (two):

levels of (four), 157–160

vs. predictions, 154

primary nature of, 155

Extensions, brand:

consumer perceptions of, 198–202

contradicting core associations, 84, 90

Family branding strategy, 98

Federal Express, 220, 306

Flexible market offerings, constructing, 332, 340–362. See also Market offerings

anticipating implementation problems with customers, 360–361

articulating present market offering for each market segment, 342–345

assessing customer value and supplier cost, 345–349

breaking away from the pack, 361

concepts, 340–342

Flexible market offerings, constructing
  (Continued)
  examples, 341, 343, 358
  existing standard services, 350–353
  formulating by market segment,
    350–357
  new services, 354–356
  optional services, 345, 353–354
  option menu *vs.* tailored-value
    package, 359–360
  practical consideration, 362
  preparation for, 357–362
  pricing implications, 345, 356–357
  strategy mix for services/programs/
    systems, 350
Focus groups, 158, 161, 171–172, 284
Functional brands, 80–84
Fundamental customer equity equation.
  See Customer equity principles

Gap analysis, 257
Garden Escape, 395
General Electric, 22, 99, 104–105,
    117
General Motors, 28, 99, 107, 273, 299
Gillette, 81, 83, 118–119, 221, 227
Global brands, building, 55, 57
GLS Inc., 335–336
Goal-based positioning, 39–44
  brand essence, 39–42
  category essence, 42–44
Goodyear's, 46–47
Green Mountain Energy Resources,
    93–94
Greif Brothers Corporation, 346, 361
Gross Rating Points (GRPs), 235–236,
    245–246

Häagen-Dazs, 114, 117
Hard sell, 218–219
Hewlett-Packard (HP), 24, 289–290
Home Depot, 264
Homeowners.com, 388–389
Horizontal mediation (metamediaries),
    399–400. *See also* Mediation/
    mediators
Hyperreality, 178

IBM, 81, 82, 86, 87, 99, 247, 286, 291,
    302, 396
Image brands, 84–90
Industrial Age marketing (assumptions/
    metaphors), 386–387
Information Age:
  customer bill of rights for, 405
  marketing (*see* Marketing in the
    Information Age)
  technology (*see* Internet/information
    technology)
Information asymmetry *vs.* information
  democracy, 386
Intel, 88, 101, 121, 398
Internet/information technology:
  attention economy, 179
  brand intimacy levels and, 238
  brand positioning and, 55–57
  computer-mediated communication
    (CMC), 175
  consumer research, 174–180
  cyber-interview, 177–178
  cyborg ecology, 176
  "deep hanging out," 182
  digital projectives, 178–179
  e-profiling, 177
  hyperreality, 178
  image branding opportunity,
    90
  information safekeepers, 402
  managing multiple marketing
    channels, 263–265
  marketing and (*see* Marketing in the
    Information Age)
  netnography, 176–177
  nuance and compromise, 179–180
  qualitative techniques, 174–180
  segmentation/targeting/positioning
    and, 55–57
  virtual communities, 176
  Web-based intrication strategy, 179
  Web Browser market, 273

Jello, 106, 113, 224

Key account management, 403–404
Knowledge banks, 335, 363